D1393591

COMPANION TO

SCENTED PLANTS

COMPANION TO

SCENTED PLANTS

STEPHEN LACEY
with photographs by Andrew Lawson

FRANCES LINCOLN LIMITED
PUBLISHERS

CONTENTS

TITLE PAGE *Lilium regale* 'Album' paired with annual *Ammi majus*.
LEFT A raised bed brings the aromas of thyme and lavender within easy reach of fingers.

AUTHOR'S NOTE

The first edition of *Scent in Your Garden* was published in 1991. It is here revised, updated and enlarged to become the *RHS Companion to Scented Plants*. Scent still seems to me the best reason to choose a plant for your garden.

In the intervening years, I have had wider experience of a great many more of the scented plants in this book, both hardy and tender, by growing them in my own garden in north Wales or in the garden I run for friends in Mallorca. As a result, many more of the book's plant entries are peppered with personal comment.

Indeed, this remains a very personal book, reflecting not just my preferences in plant selection (even within a single scented species, there are often dozens of varieties to choose among) but also my own take on scent generally (reactions to scents being somewhat subjective). It has been an interesting experience revisiting my text after such a time span and deciding how much I still agree with my earlier self, as well as a pleasure compiling information on the dozens of new scented species and varieties now available. I am grateful to the Royal Horticultural Society for the opportunity, and for its support.

Vibrant orange *Rosa* 'Rêve d'Or' on rose swag with yellow *R.* 'Goldbusch', butter yellow *R.* 'Molineux' and pink *R.* 'Wisley' in the Shrub Rose Garden at RHS Garden Rosemoor, Devon.

SCENT & THE GARDENER

Scent is the most potent and bewitching substance in the gardener's repertory and yet it is the most neglected and the least understood. The faintest waft is sometimes enough to induce feelings of hunger or anticipation, or to transport you back through time and space to a long-forgotten moment in your childhood. It can overwhelm you in an instant or simply tease you, creeping into your consciousness slowly and evaporating almost the moment it is detected. Each fragrance, whether sweet or spicy, light or heavy, comes upon you in its own way and evokes its own emotional response.

But although scent adds such a pleasurable layer to our enjoyment of a garden, few of us treat it at all seriously – it remains an optional extra in the composition, rather than an integral part to be managed and manipulated for maximum impact. We may have the odd scented plant here and there, but we rarely plan for specific effects or pursue deliberate themes. Often we do not even realize a plant is scented until we acquire it, for catalogues and reference books frequently make no mention of scent in their descriptions. And even if they do, it is generally as an aside which gives no clue of the precise flavour.

There are of course many good reasons why we fail to use scent effectively. First, although the nose can be highly sensitive, we seldom take the trouble to identify what we are smelling and to put our impressions into words. Consequently, we have not developed a means of comparing and classifying scents and our vocabulary for describing them is very primitive: the adjective 'sweet' encompasses everything from rose petals to five pound notes and dollar bills.

It has been suggested that this lazy attitude to scents has come about because the olfactory sense is no longer crucially important to us in our day-to-day life. For lower animals, scent is a means of navigating (salmon follow odour trails back to their spawning

Philadelphus and midsummer roses make excellent and often intoxicating partnerships of colour and scent.

grounds), locating food (most mammals smell food before they see it), sensing danger (all hunters have to approach their prey downwind), establishing territory (many animals spray their surroundings with urine or rub their scent glands), deterring (skunk), communicating (deer produce an alarm scent; bees inform each other of the location of nectar sources; and many animals read tribal and social status from each other's scent) and advertising sexual ripeness.

Although we no longer rely on our sense of smell for survival, we do make use of it constantly: the flavour of our food and drink comes from our sense of smell. If you hold your nose while you eat and drink, you only receive general impressions of sweetness,

Dark-flowered *Lavandula angustifolia* 'Hidcote' and yellow-flowered *Santolina* combine their scents with Hybrid Musk roses in this intimate, box-edged garden. Enclosed spaces increase the probability of scent lingering in still air rather than being dispersed and diluted in the breeze.

sourness, bitterness and saltiness through the taste buds in the mouth. It is because of this close relationship between taste and smell, and because most of our smelling is done through our mouth, that when we do attempt to describe a scent, it is so often in terms of foods: lemon, honey, mint, blackcurrant, raspberry, pineapple, curry, chocolate, vanilla, coconut, clove and almond. To make description and comparison even more difficult, each of us has different levels of sensitivity to scents and each of us reacts to them in different ways. Some people catch the most elusive flavours, while others have a relatively weak sense of smell and appreciate only the sledgehammer scents. Dark-haired people are said to be more sensitive than fair-haired people (because the olfactory mucous membrane is slightly pigmented), and smoking also impairs your sensitivity. Most of us have favourite scents and scents we detest. Sometimes our reactions are inexplicable; sometimes they are associated with places, people and events in our past.

Fragrances are themselves highly complex. They consist of a number of compounds that ebb and flow according to weather conditions and the life cycle of the plants. They can change and disappear from one moment to the next and can be quite different when savoured at close range than from a distance. So we can never exactly predict how they will taste or how we are going to react to them. But these uncertainties make the use of scent a more challenging and intriguing subject for the gardener. They should certainly not put us off trying to understand and manage it.

By being more aware of scents, nosing them carefully whenever you encounter them, trying to identify their predominant qualities and seeing whether you can pick up the same notes in other scents, you can slowly educate your palate, exactly as a wine connoisseur does. As well as helping you to build up your own internal library of scents, as it were, this will also increase the sensitivity of your nose.

To most gardeners, a capacity for memorizing things that they cannot see is, in any case, already a practised art. We invariably design and plant out of season, when plants are without flower and give no indication of their size and habit. And yet we manage to orchestrate colour schemes, to grade heights and to distribute shapes. The same artistry can surely be applied to the blending of scents.

SCENT AND EMOTION

Particular scents have been carefully selected by man for centuries: to be used as flavourings for food and drink, as religious offerings, to conceal body odours, to strew on floors to counter unpleasant smells, to keep laundry smelling fresh and to keep away bugs. More recently, there has been investigation into our emotional responses to different scents, with the result that fragrance is now used as a therapy to soothe patients; homely scents (such as of coffee and fresh bread) are often employed to influence potential purchasers into buying houses. The ultimate use of scents is, of course, perfumery, where fragrances are blended into sophisticated cocktails. I am lucky to have spent some time with perfumers, and been amazed at how they have developed their sense of smell to such an extent that they can deconstruct a scent into dozens of ingredients, likening the process to training your ear to listen to a piece of music and then breaking it down into chords and instruments. It seems extraordinary that gardeners, who are surrounded by and peculiarly susceptible to fragrances, have not attempted to absorb scent into their art too, and harnessed its power for their own ends.

The danger of gardening books which focus on one subject is that the reader soon loses a sense of perspective. After reading two hundred pages on flowering cherries, for example, you see the world entirely through a veil of pink and white blossom; you forget that cherries are just one kind of garden flora and one small highlight in the gardener's calendar. This is a book about the scented garden, but scent is not the most important consideration to the garden-maker. It is the visual impact of the composition, the interplay of colours, shapes, forms and textures, which is paramount. Gardens need an overall design, and planting schemes need structure, harmony and seasonal spectacle. If these are lacking, no amount of scented sorcery can compensate. I shall try to bear this in mind in this book and not allow myself to be so intoxicated by my theme that I forget the proper place of scent in the scheme of things; namely, as an undercurrent in the planting process, which can add another layer of pleasure to the composition and help to reinforce the chosen mood.

Laburnum drips its pea-scented flowers over *Allium hollandicum* and blue *Hosta*.

PLANNING FOR SCENT

When you are staring at a new plot and wondering how to tackle it, scent may be far from your thoughts. You will be planning paving and pathways, mapping out lawn and flower beds, and considering what character, atmosphere and style the garden will have – including whether it will be traditional or contemporary, whether it will have an emphatic design or follow nature. But whatever size or shape your garden, whatever type of garden you opt for and whatever features you introduce, you will have no difficulty injecting scent into it later on. Borders can be filled with roses and scented perennials, and pots with herbs and tender plants. Grass can be flooded with daffodils; trees hung with honeysuckles; shady pockets can be planted with winter shrubs and carpeted with bluebells. Whether with dry or damp soil, sun or shade, there is no habitat for which a scented plant cannot be found.

If you really want to make the most of scents, however, there are some points which you might bear in mind at this early stage and some features for which you may want to make room. First, to enjoy scent to the full, the air must be fairly still. Gentle breezes may waft scent to you but strong winds quickly disperse it, so shelter is vital. Windbreaks of evergreen and deciduous trees and shrubs will be needed on exposed sites. Research has shown that windbreaks which are 30 to 50 per cent porous, and which thus filter the wind, are the most effective; solid evergreen hedges and walls cause great turbulence by buffeting the wind and creating wind tunnels. As a general rule, on level ground a windbreak is capable of sheltering an area of up to ten times its height.

In larger gardens, the ideal combination is a natural windbreak on the boundary, together with internal walls. For as well as seeking to contain the scent, we need to encourage its free production. Most plants need warmth to reveal their scent, and walls help to trap and reflect the sun's heat. In cool regions, there is nothing like a sheltered, walled garden for providing an unforgettable experience for the nose, as anyone who has made a June visit to the English gardens of Sissinghurst Castle in Kent or Mottisfont Abbey in Hampshire will know; both have great collections of old-fashioned roses and on a warm, still day the air is heavy with the heady aromas of fruit and spice.

FRAGRANT FEATURES

Few of us have walled gardens or the means with which to construct them, but it may be possible to find a small, walled suntrap somewhere by the house. As the air cools, heat will continue to be radiated by the walls, ensuring prolonged warmth

Catmint, *Erysimum* 'Bowles' Mauve' and variegated sage spill around a painted obelisk with, in the foreground, foxy-scented *Phuopsis stylosa* growing in a paving crack.

A secluded sitting area in summer, swimming in the distinctive cherry pie fragrance of *Heliotropium arborescens* in both low-growing and standard forms.

and fragrance in the late afternoon and evening. A paved surface large enough to accommodate a seat would be an essential part of the suntrap. Seats are invitations to linger and rest, and in a relaxed state you are more receptive to a fragrant siege. Certainly, wherever you install a seat in your garden, you might think how you can entertain the nose – flanking it with *Daphne* or *Philadelphus*, perhaps, or with an ever-changing cast of pot plants such as narcissi, lilies, heliotrope and *Gladiolus murielae*. In London, I have a pair of drought-tolerant loquats (*Eriobotrya japonica*) in pots, which fill my small balcony with almond scent in early winter, before producing juicy (but fairly tasteless) fruits.

The seat itself may even be made out of scented plants: a small raised bed or trough can be turned into a fragrant seat by being given back and arm rests and planted with apple-scented camomile, creeping mints or spicy prostrate thymes (but beware of bees when you sit down). At Killerton in Devon, a slatted seat has low-growing *Sarcococca hookeriana* var. *humilis* planted under it, to give you a honeyed encounter in winter. Again using camomile, mint and thyme, and with the addition of perennial stock, *Matthiola incana*, *Dianthus*, and evening primrose *Oenothera stricta* self-seeding into the cracks, you can create a scented pathway (or stairway, bank or miniature lawn). As a lawn, flowering thymes make a handsome rug of pink, purple and white, but this is a labour-intensive feature, requiring much intricate hand-weeding and editing.

Clearly, you need most scented flowers to be near nose height, so to enjoy to the full the fragrance of scented small bulbs like crocuses and *Iris reticulata*, dwarf shrubs like *Daphne cneorum*, and alpines like *Phlox* and primulas, you will have to raise them above the ground. As an alternative to rock gardens, which are, in any case, not likely to be sympathetic additions to gardens in urban or lowland settings, raised beds or troughs usually slip into any design quite comfortably. Window boxes are another means of lifting plants off the ground, as are pots. I always plant a few pans of early bulbs to put out on the garden table through the winter months – some colour-coordinated partnerships of iris and crocus, and others clashing.

SCENT OVERHEAD

Arbours, arches and tunnels give you the opportunity of bringing climbing plants away from the boundaries and closer to the nose. Such plants can also be spun along trellises and up posts to make internal features. Jasmines and *Clematis*, as well as sweet peas, are handsome on tripods, and I once saw a long herbaceous border broken at intervals by short lengths of fence wrapped in honeysuckles and roses; this was a most effective means of introducing scent (the border perennials of high summer are not among the most fragrant groups of plants) and of providing architecture to counter the wispiness of the other ingredients. Climbing and rambling roses are also eminently suitable for stringing on ropes between upright posts.

Scent under windows is doubly welcome, with the fragrance of plants like roses, jasmine and tobacco flowers drifting indoors on warm days and evenings. Pots of fragrant plants beside doors, including those like lemon verbena and *Salvia discolor* with scented leaves to tweak as you pass, are similarly good value.

At Haseley Court in Oxfordshire, honeysuckles are presented as standards – supported by short posts and wire domes – on the corners of a knot garden. Wisterias can also look very stylish when grown as standards. And I have always rather fancied creating a bower out of the pliable branches of *Magnolia wilsonii* with its downturned creamy saucers scented of lemon. But, of course, trees and shrubs can also be left to create their own arbours. I remember seeing, in one garden in the south of England, a crossroads of grass paths in the middle of an open flower garden that had been turned into a bower of white blossom by the planting of a cherry tree on each corner.

Eucomis, Gladiolus murielae, and *Lilium regale* add a scented layer to a pot display featuring marguerites and silver *Plectranthus*.

Lines and avenues of plants can create living walls of scent. I am not thinking of grand entrance drives of lime trees, or broad walks of Loderi rhododendrons; even very small gardens can have room for a stream of lavender or an edging of clove-scented *Dianthus*. At home, I have a line of tender *maddenii* rhododendrons in pots to give a lily-scented ambush through May: I take the plants out of the cold greenhouse during a mild spell in March in readiness. Such concentrations of one sort of plant enable you to submerge yourself in a single scent, at full strength and with no distractions, and are always exciting.

When you come to select hedges, evergreens and trees for the garden's framework, your primary concern will usually be shape and form: you are looking for features that will hold the design together throughout the year. Hedges must be dense and robust, screening trees fast-growing, and specimen trees and evergreens have an emphatic outline or a particular character. Yet there will often be scented options. Hedge-trimming is far more enjoyable when each snip treats you to a whiff of fruit.

SCENTS FOR SUN AND SHADE

If you are a keen gardener, you will want a good number of planting areas. In the scented garden sunny beds are, on the whole, preferable to shady beds; this is partly because heat encourages the freer production of scent and partly because the largest proportion of scented plants are sun-lovers.

If your garden is sheltered and mild enough and your soil sufficiently well-drained to accommodate aromatic shrubs like thymes, lavenders, rosemaries, *Cistus* and suchlike, then the sunniest bed might be reserved for these plants. They all like to be roasted and on hot, still days will fill the air with the scents of the Mediterranean. They will set a theme for the bed and you can then add to this, using scented and non-scented ingredients – euphorbias and irises for striking contrasts in shape, perhaps; Spanish broom and tree lupin for yellow highlights. This sort of planting suits terraces and gravel gardens, and the peak flowering season will probably be early summer.

Sunny areas with a more fertile, moist soil are appreciated by roses and a large cast of perennials, annuals, bulbs and shrubs which are, in the main, summer-flowering. The larger shrubs and roses could furnish the back row of the border and create the promontories, while the low ingredients could fill the bays. Rather than attempting to keep a whole border pulsating with colour all summer, which is very hard, I suggest having different sections devoted to different parts of the season, with plants that bloom simultaneously grouped near each other. That way you get proper focal points: a midsummer medley of

lilies, roses, *Philadelphus* and pinks in one area, perhaps, with a late summer display of *Buddleja*, *Phlox*, *Verbena* and tobacco flowers in another. Good foliage plants and plants that bloom for a long season can be interwoven through the border to keep sections respectable outside their peak flowering period.

The cast for shady areas consists of all those shrubs, perennials and bulbs from woodland habitats. Since most are geared up to flower before the overhead canopy becomes too dense, spring is likely to be the season in which a shady border would reach its climax, with further good flushes of colour in autumn and winter. A single tree is often enough to establish the woodland mood.

Light shade gives you the greatest range of winter and spring shrub planting, encompassing deciduous magnolias, witch hazel, *Viburnum* and azaleas. Given heavy shade, I would veer towards evergreens such as *Mahonia*, *Skimmia* and rhododendrons. This is what I have done under the dense beech trees on the edge of my garden, where I have also added pools of early bulbs such as snowdrops, *Scilla* and daffodils. In the brighter spots, I can also get away with *Daphne*, and, in a good year, cardiocrinums will open their giant white trumpets in the shadows – perhaps the scent gardener's most exciting plant.

COLOUR AND SCENT

There is a vague relationship between colour and scent and, as a general rule, the less pigment there is in a flower, the more likely it is to be scented. White flowers are the most highly scented colour group, followed by pink, mauve and pale yellow flowers. Strong yellow and violet-blue flowers come next. The least scented colour groups are purple, true blue, orange and red flowers.

Colour has almost as great an impact on the senses and emotions as scent and in plant-packed gardens it usually becomes the dominant visual force; the eye notices shapes before colours only when the range of colours is very limited. Each colour gives a different reading and, by using it in isolation or in combination with

Azaleas are one of the few groups of scented plants which combine an intoxicating perfume with a range of hot, rich and gaudy colours. On warm, moist days their honeysuckle fragrance pervades the still, silent dells of woodland gardens. They give a second show of colour in the autumn, when their leaves ignite before falling.

other colours, you have the means of establishing a wide range of different moods. So, I like to decide at least which colours will be dominant in each planting area, even if the rest of the mix is to be random.

Various factors influence the choice of colours in a garden – existing features and background scenery, the quality of the light, personal preference and, most importantly, the availability of plants in each colour group. In temperate climates, yellow, white, pink and mauve flowers are fairly abundant all year; neither is there much of a shortage of purple or violet blue. Orange is a little more scarce; our main supply comes from berries, hips and turning leaves in the autumn. Pure red is always rare, as is true blue, though we get a good quantity of it in the spring from bulbs and woodland perennials. Shade-loving plants also tend to come in quieter and cooler colours than those that are sun-lovers.

The desire for scent will also affect your choice of colour. If you are planning a single-colour border or garden, white, yellow or pink/mauve are the best colours to select; there are plenty of flowers to choose from, and plenty of different scents. If you want a bed of hot reds and oranges and inky purples and blues, but also want the garden to be full of scent, then you will have more head-scratching. First, you can make use of those plants whose flowers do manage to combine strong colour with scent (often the results of man-made breeding): azaleas, wallflowers, sweet peas and roses, for example, have colourful, scented flowers; *Monarda*, hyssop, lavender and *Salvia* have colourful flowers and scented leaves; *Pieris* has colourful bracts and *Skimmia* colourful berries, and both have scented flowers.

But you might also think of arranging marriages between two plants, one chosen for its scent and the other for its intense colour. Trees and shrubs can host climbing plants (try a scented rambling rose up a purple-leaved plum, or a purple *Clematis* through a scented *Philadelphus*); two climbing plants will happily interweave (spicy-scented *Akebia* and ruby-red alpine *Clematis*); perennials and bulbs will thrive around the skirts of shrubs (lily of the valley under an exotic tree peony or brilliant scarlet tulips in front of sweet-scented osmanthus); and bulbs will happily grow through rock plants (honey-scented *Crocus chrysanthus* through alpine *Phlox*). So, a simultaneous reward for eye and nose is certainly achievable.

A dashing pairing of *Rubus cockburnianus* 'Goldenvale' and the richly honey-scented sweet pea, *Lathyrus odoratus* 'Matucana'.

There are scented plants for every season and no particular shortage at any one time. The many plants with scented leaves ensure there is never a dull moment for the nose, even when flowers are scarce. The goal should be to have a garden that entertains the nose at every turn on every day of the year. It is an absorbing challenge.

THE NATURE OF SCENT

As garden-makers, we already wear many hats. We play the part of draughtsman, architect, painter, sculptor, plantsman and even poet in the course of transforming our plot into a satisfying garden. But there is yet another hat waiting to be donned – that of perfumer. Like its colour, shape and texture, a plant's scent is a quality that deserves thoughtful treatment. Dropped into the composition at random, it is often submerged and lost; but sited with care and perhaps blended with complementary scents, it can deliver its flavour to maximum effect.

Success as a perfumer will always depend to some degree on chance. Who can say precisely how a scent will engage you at a particular moment or how others will react to it? But if we can identify the types of scent that we are using, and how and when they are released, we can at least try to anticipate their impact. There is no need to delve deeply into organic chemistry, but some understanding of the nature of scent and of the various scent groups will provide a useful basis from which to work. Not being a scientist, I have had to acquire botanical and chemical information on scents from various authoritative sources – in particular, *The Scent of Flowers and Leaves: Its Purpose and Relation to Man* by F. A. Hampton. Published in 1925 and alas long out of print, this is a delightful little book and an absorbing read, and it was my introduction and primary guide to the world of fragrant plants.

Scent, I learned from Mr Hampton, derives from volatile 'essential oil' stored by plants, and is released when the oil is oxidized. In flowers, the essential oil is known as attar and is usually stored in epidermal cells in the petal or petal substitute; double-flowered forms of scented plants, which have more petals, are therefore often noticeably more fragrant than their single-flowered counterparts. Unusually, in the musk rose *Rosa moschata* and the Synstylae rambler roses such as *R. filipes*, *R. mulliganii* (*R. longicuspis*) and 'Bobbie James', the scent is held in the stamens – double-flowered forms of these are therefore scentless. The

The lightly lily-scented *Rhododendron* 'Loderi King George', one of my favourite rhodos, blooms above bluebells and wild garlic.

Painted Lady butterflies drawn to *Buddleja davidii* 'Purple Emperor', one of many varieties of florally honey-scented butterfly bush.

scent is dispersed when the flowers open and varies greatly in strength and flavour from plant to plant; and even in an individual flower, it will appear, alter and vanish in response to temperature and the life cycle of the plant.

The flavour of a flower is usually complex as its essential oil is rarely pure; rather it consists of a number of different compounds that unite to present a scented bouquet. The different flavours are generally well-integrated but often you can separate the notes when sniffing. *Lilium regale*, for instance, gives a piercingly sweet top note but at the same time you can detect something rather nasty lurking underneath. The offending compound is called indole, responsible for the fetid and dung-like notes in many plants. A flower may also give you its top note at a distance and its bass note at close range. I remember bringing my first potful of ginger lily, *Hedychium gardnerianum*, indoors and enjoying the delicious viburnum-like scent that filled the room; but when I went to smell it more deeply, I was ambushed by a powerful blast of mothballs. And again, many scents are pleasant in dilution and nasty in concentration, while other scents have to be concentrated to be noticeable – a single bluebell gives off little perfume whereas a whole wood of them is ambrosial.

Highly scented lilies attract bees and hoverflies by day. In the evening, night-scented flowers lure in moths and beetles; to savour them yourself they should be placed near paths, doorways and open windows.

Flowers use their scents specifically to attract pollinators. Many insects, including butterflies, moths, bees and beetles, are highly sensitive to scent, and so this, usually in tandem with colour, shape and even texture, is an effective lure. Scents are blended to appeal to particular pollinators, and can even mimic the insects' own pheromones. For night-flying moths, scent is a particularly useful navigation medium, though the bright white petals, which many night-blooming flowers possess, also provide beacons. Many flies are also scent-lovers, but their preference tends to be for the more fetid and rotting scents, which certain plants such as *Stapelia*, *Dracunculus* and *Amorphophallus* obligingly provide.

CATEGORIES OF FLOWER FRAGRANCE

To select and blend flower scents effectively, we must know which flavours are available and which plants possess them. We also need an overview of the subject, so we can group related fragrances in our minds and contrast them with other scents. Because we

all react slightly differently to scents, and because plant scents are often composed of a cocktail of ingredients that ebb and flow, there can be no universal system of classification that would prove meaningful to every gardener. We must each follow our own nose. However, there are some generally accepted groupings that have been put forward by F. A. Hampton and other writers, and these can at least provide us with a framework. I have altered these groupings slightly to suit my own nose – and you may, of course, wish to alter my groupings to suit yours.

PLEASANT AND POPULAR SCENTS

The pleasant scents are extremely diverse and warrant detailed subdivision. The first recognizable group is the **exotic scents** – the heavy, tropically sweet perfumes possessed by such flowers as *Jasminum officinale*, tobacco flowers, *Clerodendrum trichotomum*, some narcissi and *Lilium regale*. The scent is not delicate and piercing but is thick and heady and often has a rather fetid bass note. This is most noticeable when you are smelling a plant at close range or when the flower is fading. The pot jasmine, *J. polyanthum*, is exquisite in thin wafts but can be overpowering in a warm sitting room or conservatory. One flower whose scent turns very quickly from sweetness to decay is *Hemerocallis lilioasphodelus* (*H. flava*), one of the most elegant of the yellow daylilies. As soon as the blooms fade, they begin emitting the most foul stench; I once brought a few indoors, but never again. Many scents in this category have a distinct character: *Trachelospermum*, *Stephanotis*, *Pittosporum tobira*, *Citrus* flowers and *Jasminum sambac* seem to me to have a definite smell of bubblegum; and most are free of any hint of decay. So are the tender *maddenii* rhododendrons – whose floral lily-like perfume is perhaps my favourite of all flower scents. There is a whiff of mothballs, not only in *Hedychium*, but also in *Carissa macrocarpa* and *Hosta plantaginea*. *Philadelphus coronarius*, the cottage-garden's mock orange, is deliciously fruity but its heady, cloying quality puts it into this group for me. The group comprises many white flowers and many that are night-scented.

Next, there are the **spicy scents**. At one end of the group are *Viburnum* like *V. carlesii* and *V.* x *juddii*; their scents verge on the exotic but their clove bass note nudges them into this group. I never find their scents unpleasant, even in quantity. A similar sweet clove scent is found in some stocks, *Phlox*, sweet rocket, wallflowers, *Daphne*, *Lonicera* x *americana* and, of course, pinks and carnations. The scents vary from plant to plant in the degree of sweetness and spiciness, and in some flowers, like those of *Rhododendron trichostomum*, the fragrance is almost pure clove. White and pink are the predominant colours.

Self-seeding *Hesperis matronalis* filters through the richly scented shrub rose 'Queen of Bourbons'.

Aniseed can be detected in nearly all primrose-scented flowers, such as *Corylopsis*, *Clematis rehderiana* and, of course, many primulas, and I think of these as belonging to the spice group. Yellow is the main colour here. Different spicy scents, some with nutty and peppery seasoning and with different degrees of sweetness, come from *Magnolia stellata*, witch hazels (where the spiciness is merged with a slightly stale fruity smell, reminiscent of the scent of parrots), *Cestrum parqui*, lime-flavoured *Hermodactylus tuberosus*, lemon-flavoured wintersweet and from many roses. These represent a mixed bag of colours.

Then there are the **vanilla and almond scents**. These are 'foody' and not too sweet, and are fortunately quite common in garden flowers, especially among woody plants. I include *Clematis armandii* and *C. montana*, *Abeliophyllum*, *Oemleria*, heliotrope, *Fabiana*, *Pieris* (sometimes), *Persicaria wallichii*, *Schizopetalon walkeri*, *Azara microphylla*, *Androsace*, *Choisya ternata* and cherries such as *Prunus* x *yedoensis*. White and pink are the principal colours.

Other related 'foody' scents are the coconut of gorse, *Heptacodium*, tuberose (*Polianthes*) and *Cardiocrinum*, and the chocolate of *Cosmos atrosanguineus* and *Lilium pumilum*.

Next come the **pea scents**. Many members of the pea family share a distinctive scent. Sometimes the pea scent is light, sweet and fruity, as in *Coronilla* and wisteria; sometimes it is slightly heavy and musty, as in laburnum and some brooms and lupins. Acacias, which are also members of the family, are in this category; they can also veer towards sweetness or mustiness. Yellow is the main colour and there is much similarity in flower shape.

I call the next group **French perfumes**, though one or two are more like cheap suntan lotion. Included here are all those scents that are piercingly sweet but floral, refined and without much spice or tropical heaviness: lily of the valley, *Mahonia japonica* and *Skimmia*; cyclamen and mignonette (*Reseda*); hyacinths (in spite of their fetid undertones) and *Clematis heracleifolia*; and the better scented lilacs. The violet scents also belong here; they are sharply sweet and very sophisticated. Apart from in sweet violets, the fragrance is found in *Iris reticulata*, *Leucojum vernum* and in some crab apples. A few of the French perfumes linger in the air but most require repeated sniffing; some, especially the violet scents, tire the senses quickly and you have to leave intervals between inhalations. There is a range of colours here, but white, pink and purple do perhaps dominate.

Rose scents are usually left in a category of their own, although they are varied and complex. Most roses have some hint of what we would recognize as a typical 'rose' perfume; it is also found in some crab apples and Japanese apricots. Perhaps the richest of the true rose scents is found among the old shrub roses, where the sweet French

Prunus 'Jo-nioi' is one of the best of the Japanese cherries for fragrance.

The white flowers of sweet rocket, *Hesperis matronalis*, glow especially brightly at dusk, when other colours are fading, and it is then that its cool scent is at its strongest. Although adapted for pollination by night-flying insects, during the daytime it is also popular with butterflies. It self-sows freely.

perfume is shaded with incense and spice, and among the modern shrub roses, climbers and Hybrid Teas, where it is blended with fruit and tea. The spicier scents seem to be the most pervasive in the air – the Rugosas, Hybrid Musks, Noisettes and Synstylae rambler roses; incense and fruit can also often be detected in these.

Often there is a dominant flavour in the rose scent and it is worth identifying this for use in scented schemes. Clove is clearly evident in the Rugosas, the climbing 'Noisette Carnée' and the modern shrub 'Fritz Nobis'. The tea scent is found in 'Lady Hillingdon', 'Gloire de Dijon' and the shrub rose 'Graham Thomas'. Fruity scents abound – raspberry in many Bourbon and Hybrid Perpetual roses, and in 'Cerise Bouquet'; apple in 'Max Graf', 'Nymphenburg' and the *R. wichurana* ramblers; lemon in *R. bracteata* and the shrub rose 'Agnes'; orange in 'The Garland'; banana in *R. mulliganii* (*R. longicuspis*) and 'Dupontii'.

There is a strange scent, pleasant but lacking sweetness, apparent in some roses which the experts call 'myrrh'. It smells like cold cream or calamine lotion. It is found in 'Belle Isis', 'Félicité Perpétue', 'Constance Spry' and 'Little White Pet'. But beware of the unpleasant scent that lurks in *R. foetida, R. fedtschenkoana*, and some yellow- or orange-flowered bushes and shrub roses with *R. foetida* in their parentage.

The **fruit scents** encompass a range of delicious flavours. The fragrance is more often warm and full than sharp; sometimes the scent of a particular fruit dominates, but usually it is shaded by other flavours into a fruit cocktail. Lemon seems to be the main flavour in evening primroses, *Magnolia grandiflora* and *M. sinensis*, boronias, *Primula florindae* and *P. kewensis* and *Clematis forsteri*; melon in *Magnolia obovata*; banana in *Magnolia* (*Michelia*) *figo* and *Muscari macrocarpum*; plum in freesias and *Iris graminea*; pineapple in *Cytisus battandieri* and *Philadelphus microphyllus*; raspberry in *Buddleja agathosma* and, some say, mignonette, though I cannot detect it; apricot in *Amaryllis belladonna, Osmanthus fragrans* and *Gardenia*. Other magnolias, honeysuckles and *Calycanthus floridus* deliver a well-balanced fruit cocktail. Appropriately, many of these flowers have colours in keeping with their scents – yellow for a lemon and banana scent, purple for a plum scent – but almost the whole spectrum is represented.

The **honey scents** are equally mouthwatering. The fragrance is rich and sticky-thick in *Crocus chrysanthus, Mahonia aquifolium, Crambe, Ozothamnus ledifolius, Euphorbia mellifera, Lobularia* and *Sarcococca*. It is a little more flowery in *Buddleja*; richly floral in sweet peas, *Mirabilis jalapa* and *Cestrum nocturnum*; and shades into 'musk' in *Centaurea moschata* and *Olearia moschata*.

Finally, I have a category for **rogue scents** that do not seem to fit into any of the main groups. In this category, I put scents that I find pleasant but that are not particularly sweet – the milk of magnesia of *Drimys winteri*, the mouse-and-sawdust of *Callistemon pallidus*, and the horse-and-elephant of *Rondeletia amoena*.

LESS PLEASANT SCENTS

There is no need to categorize the more unpleasant scents since we will not be wanting to include them deliberately in any scented scheme. But they do often find their way into the garden nonetheless.

Many gardeners grow members of the arum family. The most common is the bog arum, *Lysichiton americanus*, whose yellow spathes illuminate many a pondside in early spring. Its scent is not as bad as other arums and if only a few plants are grown, it may not be noticed. But grown in quantity in a confined ditch garden, the fetid scent is unappealing. The dragon arum, *Dracunculus vulgaris*, is much worse. It is one of those really foul-smelling, fly-pollinated flowers grown because of their curious appearance. Many also practise visual deception on their pollinators with blotched and bloody, flesh-like flowers to accompany the scent of putrid flesh. Dragon arum has a rich crimson spathe and maroon, rat's-tail spadix. When I first encountered it in a plantsman's garden I was nearly felled by the stink.

Ageratina ligustrina (*Eupatorium micranthum* or *E. ligustrinum*) also comes near the top of my list of unpleasant scents. A nursery catalogue sang the praises of this bushy evergreen shrub with its heads of tiny, rose-tinted white flowers and I succumbed; but the description omitted any reference to its scent. The overriding flavour was of urine, and on warm, late summer days the garden reeked.

Some unpleasant scents are tolerable. *Eucomis bicolor* is an extraordinary bulbous plant from southern Africa whose flowerheads look like greenish pineapples on sticks; they are not reliably hardy outside, except in warm regions, so I grow some in pots and overwinter them under cover. But I am careful not to site the pots near seats, for the meaty odour is nasty and relished by flies. Many other species of eucomis in cultivation have a more acceptable scent, flavoured of coconut.

The scents of shrubs like hawthorn, cotoneaster, mountain ash and privet come into my category of unpleasant odours, and they too are popular with flies. The rowan, *Sorbus vilmorinii*, in all other respects an ideal tree for the small garden, is particularly bad. These scents are heavy and claustrophobic, lacking in sweetness and often sickly, and many noses detect the flavour of fish in them. They do not always cause offence, and some people may even like them (especially hawthorn, for its nostalgic, pastoral associations), but they are not for blending into scented schemes. You may feel the same about flowers like those of common lilac and *Aesculus parviflora*, whose sweetness is overlaid with a rather stale smell; and candytuft (*Iberis sempervirens*) which to me smells of stale socks.

Dragon arum, *Dracunculus vulgaris*, is one of the foulest-smelling but most dramatic hardy perennials.

Narcissus poeticus var. *recurvus* and other pheasant eye daffodils have a light, clean scent and are also among the best for naturalizing: the simplest effects in gardening are often the most enchanting.

If you are going to grow flowers with very unpleasant scents, you have to try to find positions for them where they will give the least offence. If the scents carry, make sure they are far from house windows, main paths and sitting-out areas and that they are downwind.

CATEGORIES OF LEAF FRAGRANCE

Some of the flower scents are also found in leaves, but here they are generally less sugary. This is because in leaves scent has a different function: its purpose is to repel not to attract. Scent is used as a protection against disease and many of the compounds found in leaf scents are strongly antiseptic – oil of eucalyptus, thyme and clove are examples – and play an important part in the composition of medicines. Scent is also used to discourage insects and animals by presenting astringent tastes; some of the volatile oils act as natural herbicides.

Accordingly, leaf scents tend more towards the pungent, bitter and medicinal. How they are released depends on how they are stored. Where the essential oil is in capsules deep inside the leaf, it is released by rubbing or breaking. Where it is in cells close to the surface of the leaf, you need only to brush against it lightly. And where it is actually secreted on to the surface of the leaf, you can usually smell it without disturbing the leaf at all. Hot sunshine causes some scents to oxidize, while others seem to be most evident after rain.

Leaf scents are usually simpler in composition than flower scents, perhaps because subtleties of fragrance are not so important when you are producing a repellant rather than an attractant, but there are many more of them, and leaf scent groupings inevitably contain a diversity of flavours.

PLEASANT AND POPULAR SCENTS

There are no leaves with a fragrance comparable to the exotic scents of flowers, but many have warm **spice scents**. They are hugely diverse, ranging from the culinary herbs like bay, thyme, basil, marjoram, cardamom and rosemary to shrubs like sweet fern (*Comptonia*), spice bush (*Lindera*) and myrtle. Curry-scented *Helichrysum italicum* and *Escallonia illinita* belong here. Most of these scents are released into the air by heat.

I do not think there is primrose scent in any leaves but there is **aniseed**. It comes in a purer form than in flowers. Supreme examples are fennel, *Primula wilsonii* var. *anisodora* and

Agastache rugosa (*A. foeniculum*); there is also a touch in *Magnolia salicifolia*. The liquorice scent *of Myrrhis odorata* and *Acorus gramineus* 'Licorice' is quite close. These leaves generally need to be rubbed for the scent to emerge.

I do not know of any leaves with vanilla, almond or French perfume scents. But **rose scents** are found in the leaves of members of the geranium family. Here the scent has few of the perfumed top notes of rose flowers, but is made aromatic with fruit, mint and spice. Among *Pelargonium*, *P.* 'Attar of Roses' is especially good; and among the true *Geranium*, *G. macrorrhizum* and *G. endressii*. The musky, honey scent is found in olearias.

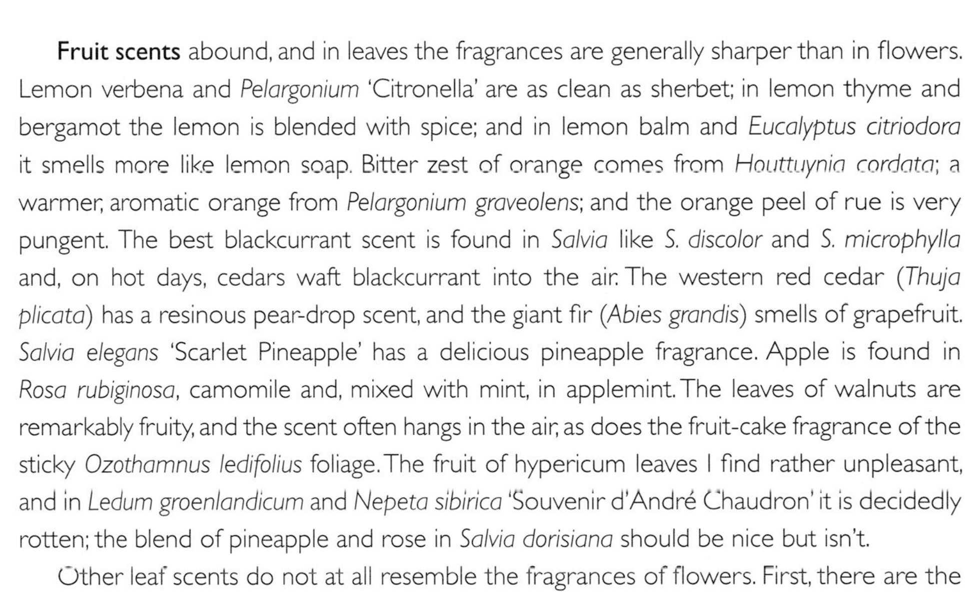

'Grace', one of a number of English roses with a strong and complex perfume, grows here with the catmint, *Nepeta sibirica* 'Souvenir d'André Chaudron', whose leaf scent is not particularly pleasant but it is a handsome, large-flowered perennial for the early summer garden.

Fruit scents abound, and in leaves the fragrances are generally sharper than in flowers. Lemon verbena and *Pelargonium* 'Citronella' are as clean as sherbet; in lemon thyme and bergamot the lemon is blended with spice; and in lemon balm and *Eucalyptus citriodora* it smells more like lemon soap. Bitter zest of orange comes from *Houttuynia cordata*; a warmer, aromatic orange from *Pelargonium graveolens*; and the orange peel of rue is very pungent. The best blackcurrant scent is found in *Salvia* like *S. discolor* and *S. microphylla* and, on hot days, cedars waft blackcurrant into the air. The western red cedar (*Thuja plicata*) has a resinous pear-drop scent, and the giant fir (*Abies grandis*) smells of grapefruit. *Salvia elegans* 'Scarlet Pineapple' has a delicious pineapple fragrance. Apple is found in *Rosa rubiginosa*, camomile and, mixed with mint, in applemint. The leaves of walnuts are remarkably fruity, and the scent often hangs in the air, as does the fruit-cake fragrance of the sticky *Ozothamnus ledifolius* foliage. The fruit of hypericum leaves I find rather unpleasant, and in *Ledum groenlandicum* and *Nepeta sibirica* 'Souvenir d'André Chaudron' it is decidedly rotten; the blend of pineapple and rose in *Salvia dorisiana* should be nice but isn't.

Other leaf scents do not at all resemble the fragrances of flowers. First, there are the **camphorous and pungent scents** of plants like achilleas, most *Artemisia*, tansy, and *Santolina*. I am not fond of these scents but I know other people find them less objectionable; the group includes some of the best grey-leaved plants so they are always well represented in gardens, even in mine. Most of these have to be rubbed for the scent to be released.

Resinous scents are common among leaves. They range from the turpentine of pines and other conifers, through the cedarwood of *Hebe cupressoides*, the incense of *Rosa primula*, the tobacco of *Calomeria amaranthoides* (*Humea elegans*), the gummy resin of *Cistus*, the fruity resin of thujas, abies and *Dictamnus albus*, and the pumpkin pie of *Nothofagus antarctica* to the cloyingly sweet resin of balsam poplar buds. Most of these infuse the air on warm days, especially in spring, and on a hot summer's evening the flower spikes of *Dictamnus* are so covered with inflammable oil that you can set fire to them; you get a whoosh of flame and the lemon scent is released.

Mint and eucalyptus scents are very similar. They share a piercing top note and shade into each other in many leaves. Mint is also present in some species of *Eucalyptus*, notably *E. coccifera*, which has a sharp peppermint fragrance. Most *Eucalyptus* species

A fine group of orange crown imperials (*Fritillaria imperialis*) whose fox-like scent floats across borders in spring.

have some sort of medicinal fragrance, and so do most lavenders, though sweetness and fruit often softens them. *E. glaucescens* is particularly fruity. Mint scents are also very often blended with some fruit or wintergreen, as in *Prostanthera*, catmints, *Calamintha* and *Elsholtzia*. They are at their coolest and most refreshing in the spearmints and peppermints of menthas and *Pelargonium tomentosum*.

Scents in the 'miscellaneous' category include the **fresh, green scents** of parsley and celery, the musty scent of ferns, the hay scent of *Dryopteris aemula* and the scent of wintergreen *Gaultheria procumbens*.

LESS PLEASANT SCENTS

There are few really nasty odours among leaves but *Salvia sclarea* var. *turkestanica*, the imposing biennial with white and pinkish mauve flowers, and *Phuopsis stylosa*, a prostrate perennial with bright pink flowers, both have a nasty sweaty aroma. I also find the foxy scent of *Fritillaria imperialis* unappealing. Many people dislike the smell of box leaves,

OTHER SOURCES OF SCENT

Scent can also be found in places less obvious than flowers and leaves. Many roots are fragrant. The best known are those of *Iris* 'Florentina', which are scented of violet; *Rhodiola rosea* (*Sedum rhodiola*), which are scented of rose; angelica; herb bennet, which are scented of clove; and magnolia. It is always a pleasant surprise to come across them, as you are digging in the border or taking root cuttings, but since they are not easily accessible, they can play little part in scented schemes. The same is usually true of the fragrant bark possessed by such plants as *Drimys*, *Calycanthus* and *Davidia*. The best way to enjoy scented wood is through fire: incense-laden bonfires in autumn and log fires in winter.

Scent can sometimes be detected in seeds. But, as with flowers and leaves, not all are pleasantly scented; the fleshy coat of ginkgo seeds smells disgusting. Fruits are better savoured in indoor warmth and many of the richest are, of course, tropical. The scents may carry freely when the fruits are assembled in quantity or are very ripe – pineapple, strawberry, apple, quince and chaenomeles (japonica), for example. Others have to be scratched or, when it is the flesh that is most fragrant, cut open to release their scent.

Apart from all the specific scents of flowers, leaves, roots, bark and fruits, the garden as a whole always has a general blend of wholesome earthy and vegetable fragrances. There is the scent of damp soil and foliage, of sun-dried grasses, and of freshly mown lawn. These set the background harmony.

likening it to cat's urine, but it is not nearly as bad as that of flowering currant, *Ribes sanguineum*; white and pale pink forms are often mintier and less offensive.

The meaty scent of clerodendrum foliage is awful and you notice it in the flowers sometimes too. The 'roast beef' in *Salvia gesneriiflora* is too fatty for me but I do not mind it in *Iris foetidissima*. Actually, I have discovered that you can condition people to respond to these meat scents in a certain way by describing the scent in advance. If I tell people that *Salvia confertiflora* leaves smell of roast lamb and mint sauce (which they do), then they invariably sniff them and say 'Delicious'. But if instead I tell them to prepare for an unpleasant smell, they will sniff them and say 'Yuck'.

SITES FOR SCENTED PLANTS

There are three points to bear in mind when choosing places for scented plants in the garden: how and when the scent is released and what sort of scent it is. All pleasantly scented flowers need to be within reach of the nose and most pleasantly scented leaves within reach of the fingers or the feet, since they generally have to be rubbed for the scent to be released. This really means that scented plants ought never to be far from paths – certainly not at the back of wide borders or separated from you by water or prickly undergrowth. The exceptions are those scented-leaved plants that float scent on the air but never seem to have much scent close to (such as *Cistus* and *Rosa primula*).

Flowers that are free with their scent, such as jasmine, honeysuckle and Rugosa roses, do not have to be close to paths but I would never put them so far away to deny yourself the chance of drinking deeper draughts. At the Oxford Botanic Garden, the scents of *Mahonia* and *Sarcococca* are used to guide the visitor to the secret winter garden, tucked behind the rockery. Scents come and go in tune with the life cycle of the plants and atmospheric conditions and if we are to use them effectively, we need to know exactly when they appear. Scented flowers, of course, have a flowering season and this may affect where you place them. Plants which open in the coldest months ought perhaps to be grown near the house and beside the paths in regular use; their scents can easily be wasted if they are growing at the bottom of the garden.

Leaf scents may also be seasonal. The majority of spice scents are at their best on a hot summer's day. Although the *Cistus* are evergreen, they also need the heat to reveal their gummy fragrance and it is their young leaves that are richest in flavour; accordingly, in the balmy days of early summer, their scent fills the air, while on a cold autumn, winter or spring day, there is not a whiff. *Nothofagus antarctica* smells strongly only in spring. And the Katsura tree (*Cercidiphyllum japonicum*) produces its sweet caramel scent only when its leaves are falling in the autumn.

We cannot do anything to control the weather, but it is worth noting that many fragrances are best after rain. The scent from the foliage of roses like *R. primula* and *R. rubiginosa* is unequalled at any other time. Some flowers reveal their scent as the temperature cools in the evening. These night-scented bloomers include jasmine, tobacco flowers, honeysuckles, night-scented stock, *Phlox*, sweet rocket, *Cestrum parqui* and

Pots of tobacco flowers (*Nicotiana*) inject scent into a softly harmonious summer display of *Diascia*, *Petunia* and *Verbena*.

Bluebells and fruitily scented yellow azaleas, *Rhododendron luteum*, are a frequently encountered duo in woodland gardens in early summer.

C. nocturnum, brugmansias, evening primroses, *Abronia*, *Verbena*, *Mirabilis jalapa*, petunias and *Daphne laureola*. The scents are mainly exotic or spicy, though there is a touch of fruit from honeysuckle and evening primrose, and honey from *Mirabilis* and *Cestrum*. Clearly, these must be assembled around windows, patios and wherever else you sit outside.

The nature of a plant's scent should also be taken into account. Just as in a well-planned garden you have a succession of visual encounters, each different and evoking its own mood, so you might orchestrate a succession of different scented encounters. As you move from one colour scheme to another, so you might move from one zone of fragrance to another.

Instead of choosing plants that perform simultaneously, we can also arrange a succession of similar scents. If we planted one area, for example, with *Mahonia aquifolium*, *Crambe*, *Lobularia* and *Sarcococca* we would give ourselves a honeyed zone lasting many months; this could contrast with another area given over to year-round vanilla and almond scents – *Azara microphylla*, *Oemleria*, *Clematis montana*, heliotrope and *Persicaria wallichii*.

Colour can point you towards an appropriate scent. If you decide on a yellow scheme somewhere, why not enhance it by injecting lemon fragrances; a bronze and white scheme

SCENT HARMONY AND CONTRAST

The complexity of scents, and the fact that many have elements in common, means that you never encounter serious clashes of flavour. The main worry is drowning one scent with another; if the air is full of jasmine, it is hard to catch the delicacy of mignonette (*Reseda*). None-theless, it can be entertaining to bring certain scents together, choosing those that you think might enhance each other. This involves dealing with them in terms of harmonies and contrasts, just as we do when match-ing colours. For close harmonies, select scents from the same group. We could choose a mix of fruit scents perhaps – *Cytisus battandieri*, an apple-scented rose, a blackcurrant-scented sage and lemon verbena – or a blend of clove-like scents – pinks, sweet rocket and *Lonicera* x *americana*.

could be flavoured with chocolate and peppermint. Many plants have exactly the scent that their appearance suggests – think of raspberry-scented, raspberry-ripple-coloured *Rosa* 'Ferdinand Pichard' or golden-brown, honey-scented *Euphorbia mellifera*. It is fun when the visual and olfactory impressions are as perfectly in tune as this.

Once we start mixing scents from different groups, we are really entering the realms of perfumery. I wish the great perfume houses could help us, but professional perfumers are concerned with extracted essential oils, which smell very different from scents as they occur in the garden. So it is a matter of feeling your own way. Certain scent groups seem naturally to harmonize – fruit and honey, almond and clove, for example. These are always good to stir together: *Primula florindae* and sweet alyssum; heliotrope and stocks.

Other scents seem to make happy contrasts quite naturally. Sweetness with spice or resin is the foundation for many a good scheme. We can generally look to flowers to provide the top note and leaves the bass note; and since most leaves have to be rubbed, we can control the release of the bass note to suit our mood. Thus the lemon scent of evening primroses might be enhanced by a drift of thyme; the apple scent of *Rosa wichurana* by a nearby pine. Roses teamed up with lavender is a well-loved association.

The combination of three compatible notes – rose, lavender, *Philadelphus* – strikes an even more sophisticated chord. And walled rose gardens which are packed with every shade of rose scent, from fruit and spice to tea and myrrh, give you a complete sensual immersion.

0
0·5
1
2m
1
1
4
5
6
7
2
3
BULBS
FILLERS
BULBS
8
11
9
10
12
8
13
1
15
14
16
17
BULBS
19
18
6
13
FILLERS
20
12
17
21
18
22
16
FILLERS
6
24
17
FILLERS
18
19
15
23
19
8
FILLERS
18
16
13
12
25
19
16
17
27
26
8
13
16
28
29
31
30
32
6
1
33
34
36
35
35

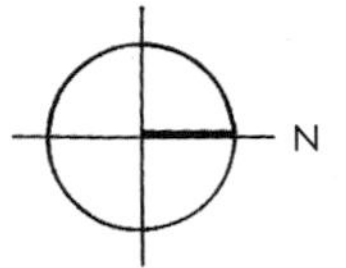
N

PLANNING YOUR GARDEN

The following four plans suggest some planting schemes for different settings in which scent is the dominant force, but in which associations of colour, form and texture are also considered. A moderate climate is assumed, with no excessive heat or cold; the only very tender plants being in the seasonal pot displays of the Terrace scheme.

PLANTING PLAN
A PAVED & GRAVEL GARDEN

This is a scheme for sunny and well-drained conditions. The bench is backed by a wall and flanked by shrubs and climbers with rich, mostly airborne scents, including *Azara* for winter, *Euphorbia* for spring, *Philadelphus* and *Trachelospermum* for summer, and *Buddleja* for autumn. Elsewhere across the garden are Japanese apricot (*Prunus mume*), *Abelia*, *Elaeagnus*, shrub roses and *Magnolia grandiflora*. In and around the gravel is an assortment of low, rounded, scented and aromatic shrubs and perennials. These include *Dianthus*, sage, *Santolina* and *Cistus*, speared by bronze fennel, night-scented lilies and evening primroses (*Oenothera*) and the more unusual incense of *Rosa primula*, the fruit-cake-scented *Ozothamnus ledifolius*, and lemony *Dictamnus*.

1 *Dictamnus albus* var. *purpureus*
2 *Daphne laureola* subsp. *philippi*
3 *Elaeagnus* 'Quicksilver'
4 *Daphne mezereum*
5 *Prunus mume* 'Beni-chidori'
6 *Cistus* × *cyprius*
7 *Abelia triflora*
8 *Lilium regale*
9 *Cytisus battandieri*
10 *Euphorbia mellifera*
11 *Rosa* 'Tuscany'
12 *Rosmarinus officinalis* 'Sissinghurst Blue'
13 *Helichrysum italicum*
14 *Philadelphus maculatus* 'Mexican Jewel'
15 *Myrtus communis* subsp. *tarentina*
16 *Iberis sempervirens*
17 *Origanum laevigatum* 'Herrenhausen'
18 *Santolina chamaecyparissus* subsp. *neapolitana*
19 *Salvia officinalis* 'Purpurascens'
20 *Rosa primula*
21 *Ozothamnus ledifolius*
22 *Ulex europaeus* 'Flore Pleno'
23 *Trachelospermum jasminoides*
24 *Buddleja crispa*
25 *Azara microphylla*
26 *Iris pallida*
27 *Daphne tangutica*
28 *Cistus laurifolius*
29 *Oenothera stricta* 'Sulphurea'
30 *Verbena bonariensis*
31 *Matthiola incana* 'Alba'
32 *Foeniculum vulgare* 'Purpureum'
33 *Rosa* 'William Lobb'
34 *Magnolia grandiflora*
35 *Iris unguicularis*
36 *Clematis armandii*

BULBS *Narcissus* 'Avalanche', *Cyclamen purpurascens*, *Crocus speciosus*, *Crocus* 'Snow Bunting', *Galanthus* 'S. Arnott'
FILLERS *Thymus pulegioides* 'Bertram Anderson', *Dianthus* vars

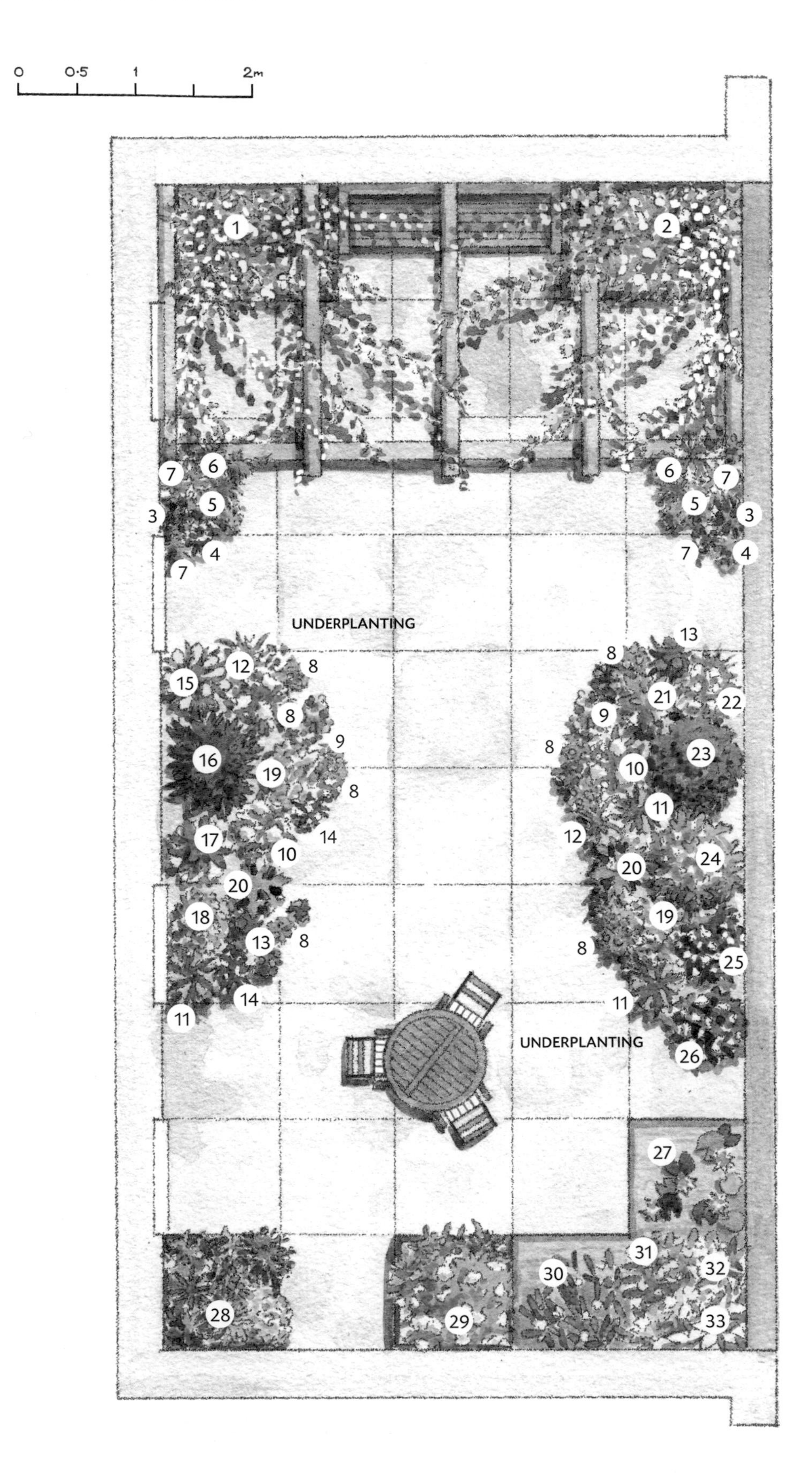
0
0·5
1
2m
1
2
6
7
5
3
4
7
6
7
5
3
7
4
UNDERPLANTING
13
8
12
8
15
21
22
8
9
9
8
23
16
19
10
8
11
14
12
17
10
24
20
20
18
19
13
8
8
25
14
11
11
UNDERPLANTING
26
27
31
30
32
28
29
33

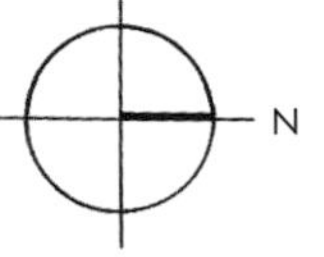
N

PLANTING PLAN
A TERRACE WITH POTS & PLANTERS

Everything in this scheme is growing in containers. The pergola is cloaked in jasmine, *Clematis* and honeysuckle for evening and daytime scent, with shade-tolerant ground-cover plants growing at their feet. Next to it are small pot assemblies of herbs and other scented-leaved plants to tweak such as pineapple sage and lemon verbena.

At the other end of the garden is a raised water garden with floating aquatics and bog plants behind, and adjacent to it are a pair of beds for alpines and rock plants, one filled with acid soil for rhododendrons. The central pot groups are built around hardier evergreen shrubs such as bay, winter-flowering loquat (*Eriobotrya*), *Choisya* and *Camellia*, and surrounded by seasonal bulbs, annuals and tender exotics – hyacinths, wallflowers and *Rhododendron* 'Fragrantissimum' for spring, and sweet peas, *Datura*, *Salvia* and *Hedychium* for summer and autumn. *Citrus* x *meyeri* 'Meyer' supplies slices of lemon for terrace drinks.

1 *Jasminum officinale* f. *alpina*, *Clematis cirrhosa* 'Wisley Cream' underplanted with *Sarcococca hookeriana* var. *humilis*, *Galium odoratum*
2 *Lonicera japonica* 'Halliana', *Clematis montana* underplanted with *Sarcococca hookeriana* var. *humilis*, *Galium odoratum*
3 *Aloysia citrodora*
4 *Salvia elegans*
5 *Lavandula dentata*
6 *Lilium regale*
7 Herbs – chives, marjoram, mint, basil
8 Scented *Pelargonium* – *P.* 'Attar of Roses', *P. tomentosum*, *P.* 'Chocolate Peppermint', *P.* 'Lady Plymouth', *P.* 'Prince of Orange', *P.* 'Citronella'
9 Wallflowers and *Tulipa* 'Orange Favourite', replaced later in the season by *Heliotrope*, *Verbena*, *Petunia*
10 White hyacinth, white *Cyclamen persicum*, replaced later in the season by *Cosmos atrosanguineus*, *Lobularia maritima*, *Nicotiana suaveolens*
11 *Lilium* 'African Queen'
12 *Gladiolus murielae*
13 *Hedychium*
14 *Mirabilis jalapa*
15 *Citrus* x *meyeri* 'Meyer'
16 *Eriobotrya japonica*
17 *Brugmansia*
18 *Coronilla valentina* subsp. *glauca* 'Citrina'
19 Sweet pea
20 *Salvia discolor*
21 *Datura inoxia*
22 *Choisya* x *dewitteana* 'Aztec Pearl'
23 *Laurus nobilis* (topiary standard)
24 *Cydonia oblonga*
25 *Camellia sasanqua* 'Narumigata'
26 *Rhododendron* 'Fragrantissimum'
27 Open water with waterlillies
28 Alpine/ rockery raised planter: *Daphne tangutica* Retusa Group, *Thymus vulgaris*, *Hyssopus officinalis*, *Stachys citrina*, *Primula auricula*, *Dianthus gratianopolitanus*, *Hermodactylus tuberosus*
29 Alpine/ rockery raised planter: *Rhododendron trichostomum*, x *Ledodendron* 'Arctic Tern', *Phlox divaricata*, *Corydalis flexuosa*
30 Open water with *Aponogeton distachyos*
31 *Primula florindae*
32 *Filipendula ulmaria*
33 *Lysichiton camtschatcensis*

UNDERPLANTING *Scilla sibirica*, *Galanthus elwesii*, *Muscari armeniacum* 'Valerie Finnis'

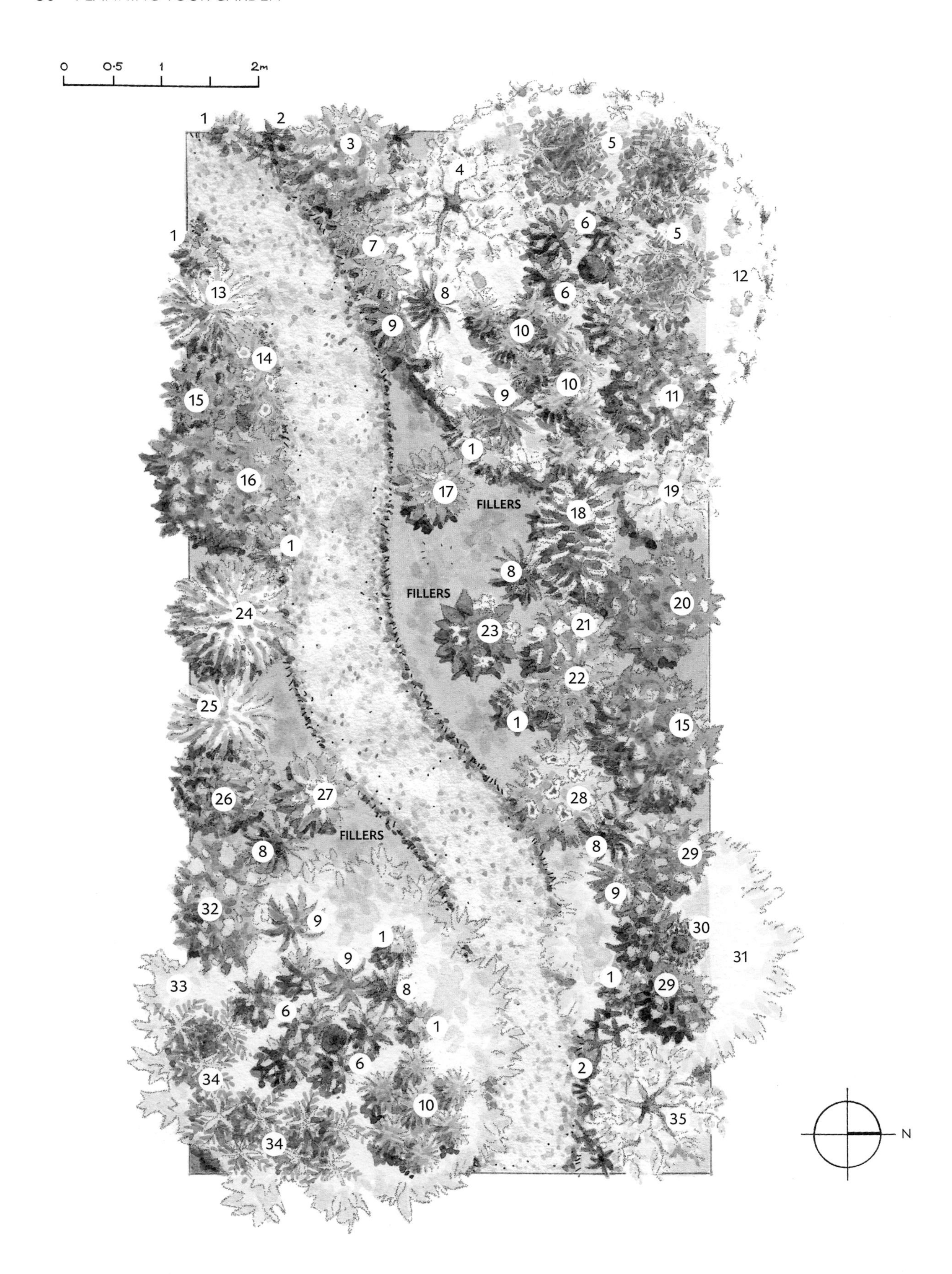

0
0·5
1
2m
1
2
3
4
5
5
6
6
7
8
9
10
10
9
11
12
1
13
14
15
16
1
17
FILLERS
18
19
1
8
FILLERS
20
24
23
21
22
25
1
15
26
27
28
FILLERS
8
8
29
9
32
9
1
9
30
31
33
8
1
29
6
1
6
2
34
10
35
34
N

PLANTING PLAN
A SHADY STROLL GARDEN

In this scheme a path meanders between lightly shaded beds of woodland planting, particularly colourful in winter and spring. The upper storey comprises small trees of *Magnolia*, *Cornus* and *Ptelea*, close to which are groups of scented evergreen shrubs – *Mahonia*, *Sarcococca*, *Skimmia* and *Camellia*. Witch hazels (*Hamamelis*) accompany them, and in the more open spots are *Osmanthus*, *Viburnum*, *Daphne*, fruitily scented azaleas and *Magnolia* (*Michelia*) *yunnanensis*, and the beautiful *Paeonia rockii*.

Under these woody plants is a tapestry of perennials – violets, scented-leaved geranium and *Myrrhis*, hostas, primroses and lily of the valley – together with bulbs – snowdrops, crocus, bluebells and pheasant eye narcissus – and, as a show-stopper, a fat clump of giant lily *Cardiocrinum giganteum*.

1 *Helleborus foetidus*
2 *Convallaria majalis*
3 *Magnolia yunnanensis*
4 *Hamamelis mollis* 'Wisley Supreme'
5 *Mahonia* x *media* 'Charity'
6 *Skimmia* x *confusa* 'Kew Green'
7 *Daphne odora* 'Aureomarginata'
8 *Iris foetidissima*
9 *Polygonatum* x *hybridum*
10 *Sarcococca confusa*
11 *Camellia* 'Cornish Snow'
12 *Magnolia* x *loebneri* 'Merrill'
13 *Osmanthus delavayi*
14 *Paeonia* 'Late Windflower'
15 *Daphne bholua* 'Jacqueline Postill'
16 *Rhododendron luteum*
17 *Hosta plantaginea*
18 *Actaea matsumurae* 'Elstead Variety'
19 *Corylopsis sinensis*
20 *Viburnum* x *juddii*
21 *Myrrhis odorata*
22 *Lunaria rediviva*
23 *Cardiocrinum giganteum*
24 *Osmanthus* x *burkwoodii*
25 *Lonicera fragrantissima*
26 *Rosa* 'Cornelia'
27 *Hosta* 'Honeybells'
28 *Paeonia rockii*
29 *Mahonia aquifolium* 'Apollo'
30 *Lonicera periclymenum* 'Serotina' (on *Cornus* trunk)
31 *Cornus mas*
32 *Angelica archangelica*
33 *Ptelea trifoliata* 'Aurea'
34 *Mahonia japonica*
35 *Hamamelis* x *intermedia* 'Pallida'

FILLERS *Viola odorata*, *Geranium macrorrhizum* 'Album', *Tellima grandiflora* Rubra Group, *Primula veris*, *Claytonia sibirica*, *Galium odoratum*

BULBS (scattered throughout randomly in generous drifts and groups) *Narcissus poeticus* var. *recurvus*, *Hyacinthoides hispanica*, *Crocus speciosus*, *Crocus biflorus* 'Blue Pearl', *Galanthus elwesii*

0 0·5 1 2m

N

PLANTING PLAN
A FORMAL SUMMER GARDEN

Although this scheme is geared to summer, there are shrubs on its four outer corners for other seasons and its borders wake with a surge of spring bulbs. Roses are a principal theme, with the emphasis on repeat-flowering varieties: the complex flavours of 'De Resht' and 'Gertrude Jekyll' complemented by the fruity scent of 'Felicia' and the myrrh of 'Little White Pet', which surrounds the central sundial lapped by thyme.

Other summer shrubs including *Philadelphus*, *Buddleja* and tree peonies add further backbone to the planting. *Phlox*, *Campanula*, *Saponaria* and scented-leaved *Agastache* and catmint are among the scented perennials, together with the unusual *Impatiens tinctoria*. And they are joined by annual sweet peas and tobacco flowers, self-seeding sweet rocket (*Hesperis*) and (with luck) *Verbena*, and the potent scents of *Lilium* 'Casa Blanca' and Pink Perfection Group.

1 *Cercidiphyllum japonicum*
2 *Nicotiana sylvestris*
3 *Rosa* 'Madame Knorr'
4 *Lilium* Pink Perfection Group
5 *Syringa microphylla* 'Superba'
6 *Buddleja davidii* 'Dartmoor'
7 *Hemerocallis lilioasphodelus*
8 *Verbena bonariensis*
9 *Rosa* 'Claire Austin'
10 *Lilium* 'Casa Blanca'
11 *Campanula lactiflora*
12 *Agastache* 'Blue Fortune'
13 *Galtonia candicans*
14 *Nicotiana alata*
15 *Phlox paniculata* 'Mount Fuji'
16 *Nepeta racemosa* 'Walker's Low'
17 *Iris pallida*
18 Sweet pea (on tripod)
19 *Saponaria officinalis* 'Alba Plena'
20 Box
21 *Rosa* 'Gertrude Jekyll'
22 *Philadelphus microphyllus*
23 *Viburnum* × *burkwoodii*
24 *Rosa* 'Felicia'
25 *Actaea simplex* Atropurpurea Group
26 *Paeonia delavayi*
27 *Phlox paniculata*
28 *Clerodendrum bungei*
29 *Rosa* 'Cornelia'
30 *Philadelphus* 'Sybille'
31 *Viburnum farreri*
32 *Rosa* 'De Resht'
33 *Impatiens tinctoria*
34 *Philadelphus maculatus* 'Mexican Jewel'
35 *Rosa* 'Constance Spry'
36 *Buddleja davidii* 'Nanho Blue'
37 *Rosa* 'Munstead Wood'
38 *Chimonanthus praecox*
39 *Rosa* 'Little White Pet'
40 *Thymus pulegioides* 'Bertram Anderson'

UNDERPLANTING

Herbaceous areas interplanted with *Narcissus* 'Actaea', *Hyacinthus orientalis* 'Delft Blue' and *Tulipa sylvestris*; rose and shrub areas with *Hesperis matronalis*, *Hyacinthoides non-scripta* and *Galanthus*

PLANTING WITH TREES & SHRUBS

CHOOSING SCENTED TREES

Trees offer a variety of fine scents and it is a pity that we cannot employ more of them in the garden. Only those with the largest gardens can indulge to the full. The rest of us must be content with one or two and savour the others elsewhere.

Protection from wind, ugliness and prying eyes is essential to the garden idyll, and trees are as much a part of the defences as walls and hedges. Among the scented candidates for screens and windbreaks are balsam poplars, *Laburnum*, limes and willows as well as a host of conifers; remember that a judicious mixture of evergreen and deciduous trees provides a better windbreak than a solid evergreen barrier. For strength of scent, balsam poplars and limes are hard to beat. The former are at their richest in the spring when the sticky buds are freely wafting their sugary, resinous fragrance; in summer, limes release their fruity scent through their flowers.

Eucalyptus are potentially the fastest-growing garden trees and might be considered where an instant vertical feature is required, though they will look exotic and alien in the skyline when they get big. Some are hardier than others. Some years ago I planted six different species to break the outline of a housing development built on the eastern boundary of my Welsh garden, and they were an entertaining temporary defence until the slower-growing limes and evergreens grew up. Their silvery-blue foliage conceals a variety of fruity, minty and medicinal fragrances and there is the bonus of honey-scented flowers. By far the hardiest of mine turned out to be *E. pauciflora* subsp. *niphophila*, and since it has not grown too big and developed a handsome trunk, it has been allowed to stay.

Because of their size, trees have a major impact on the character of the garden. It would therefore be eccentric to choose one entirely because of its scent. Its height,

Adding deciduous azaleas like *Rhododendron* 'Spek's Orange' to plantings of evergreen azaleas counterbalances the latter's woeful lack of scent.

Choisya, Ceanothus and *Cytisus* give a blend of strong and subtle scents to this shrub planting.

spread, density, shape and personality all have to be taken into account. Fastigiate trees, for example, are dynamic. They make dramatic focal points when used singly, and, when marshalled into lines or symmetrically placed, are strong formalizing influences. Many of the conifers, notably the cypresses, junipers and grapefruit-scented *Abies grandis*, form such columns and pyramids. A group of them, such as that famous phalanx of incense cedars (the fragrance, alas, is more like turpentine than incense) at Westonbirt Arboretum in Gloucestershire, England, can resemble a cluster of green rockets rising from a launch pad.

Equally sculptural are those trees that are emphatically horizontal, like the blue Atlas cedar and cedar of Lebanon, around which, on hot days, hangs the aroma of blackcurrant. In Britain, their presence usually betrays the whereabouts of a sizeable country house. Scots pine also has strong horizontal growth; with its fissured bark and craggy outline, it is one of my favourite trees.

The weepers are more graceful, represented, among scented trees, by weeping silver lime and weeping *Cercidiphyllum* as well as by a number of conifers, of which the most desirable is perhaps Brewer's weeping spruce. *Buddleja alternifolia*, with honey-scented flowers, is another candidate for the small garden. We tend to think of water as being the ideal backdrop for a weeping tree but they are always striking.

HOSTING SCENT

Where there is a scentless tree, you can inject fragrance by letting it play host to a scented climbing plant. Honeysuckles, *Clematis* and climbing roses are obvious contenders. Partners can be chosen so that they perform simultaneously or provide two seasons of scent. In a small garden in Oxford, I recall a pairing of a Chinese wisteria rambling through a scarlet crab, giving an encounter for the passing public that was both visually arresting and a treat for the nose.

Round-topped trees are generally more harmonious, their informal, curvaceous outlines blurring into the background. They give the garden a relaxed mood and many have great personality. The crabs and hawthorns lend a country air to the design, as do gnarled fruit trees (and there is a delicate fragrance in pear and apple blossom); there are no better ways of bringing a cottage character to a garden than by having a broken line of fruit trees down a path, or by positioning a crab or thorn on the corner of a small lawn. And how many centuries of garden history come with a quince?

Trees with striking leaves or bark really earn their place in smaller gardens since they entertain over such a long period. Large-leaved *Paulownia*, exotically scented *Catalpa* and, in sunny areas, glossy-leaved *Magnolia grandiflora* with lemon-scented flowers, make fine lawn specimens; as do *Stewartia* and, with their snow-white and python-patterned trunks, many sorts of *Eucalyptus*. Other scented round-topped trees, whose main visual contribution is a fleeting show of flowers or autumn colour include *Magnolia*, *Laburnum*, limes, *Halesia*, cherries and *Cercidiphyllum*. Some, like small-leaved lime and *Cercidiphyllum* (two of the best scented candidates for a garden), make lovely shapes and are worthy of being grown as specimens. Others can be kept as part of the garden's backdrop, making their presence felt when their scented moment comes. *Nothofagus antarctica*, for instance, can be tucked unobtrusively into a shrubbery, to ambush passers-by in spring with a mouthwatering pumpkin-pie fragrance.

Avenues of scented trees can also be memorable. Limes and walnuts are well suited to this role. The fruity scent from the leaves of the common walnut can be very strong on a still, damp day. A line of lilacs is a lovely feature, but definitely not for your own garden. The colourful frothing flowerheads (sweetly fragrant at their peak, sickly afterwards) are irresistible in early summer but the foliage is very dreary; the suckers are also a problem. An avenue of *Robinia* would be cheerful and, like limes, they do not object to regular pruning.

Other good tree choices for the small garden are crab apples, quince, *Stewartia*, *Ptelea* and the smaller *Magnolia* like *M.* x *loebneri* 'Merrill'. *Laburnum* is another option, though many people are wary of its poisonous seeds: its attractive, airy foliage casts little shade and, whether free-growing or trained into tunnels and arches, it is a brilliant feature when in bloom.

SCENTED HEDGES AND EVERGREEN FEATURES

We use hedges on the garden's boundary and as internal partitions. They can be formal, geometric and neatly clipped, imposing order on the groundplan and countering the casual shapes and patterns of shrubs and border plants; or they can be looser and more rustic, keeping the lines of the composition soft and helping the garden to blend with the countryside beyond.

For a tall, formal hedge the first plant that springs to mind is yew. It is neat, evergreen, dense and dark, and grows at a manageable speed. But where is its scent? Lawson's cypress and Leyland cypress are better endowed; though they are so fast-growing that

Honey-scented *Mahonia aquifolium* 'Moseri' combines its own fiery tints with those of orange tulips.

BOX

For a small formal hedge there is no competition: box. Some people think it smells of cats (or cats' urine), but others find it reminds them of nothing but other gardens, summer weather, and happy hours spent pottering. Borders edged in box always have an air of respectability, even if there is chaos within – as in a herb garden. The edging helps to contain floppy plants – box does not object to being buried in flowers and foliage all summer – and in winter, the outline is especially welcome. The most sophisticated use of box is, of course, the knot garden. For those who dislike the smell of box, or have a box blight problem, box honeysuckle (*Lonicera nitida*) could be substituted; it has fruitily sweet, cream flowers.

they must be pruned twice a year to keep them tight. But for a really pleasant scent the top prize goes to western red cedar, *Thuja plicata*. The leaves smell of pear-drops and ask to be tweaked every time you pass. It is fresh green in colour, dense and hardy. The dark form 'Atrovirens' is the best foil for flowers.

Seen beside a lawn, against rolling countryside, or behind a flower bed, flowering hedges can also look marvellous. There are many scented plants which can be used. For taller hedges, evergreen honey-scented *Berberis*, powerfully sweet *Osmanthus*, *Elaeagnus* and *Phillyrea* are worth considering, and, in milder areas, resinous *Escallonia*, musky *Olearia* and rosemary. For a deciduous hedge, shrub roses are excellent candidates, whether a wild species like *Rosa rubiginosa*, with apple-scented leaves (there are lovely dwarf hedges of this at Hatfield House in Hertfordshire), or a sophisticated hybrid like crimson, repeat-flowering 'Wild Edric' or 'De Resht'. The scent from a line of Rugosa roses is intense, and at Kiftsgate Court in Gloucestershire, England, there is a lively hedge of striped Rosa mundi (*Rosa gallica* 'Versicolor'). Other evergreen flowering plants for low hedges and edging include lavender, *Santolina* and germander.

Old shrub roses are at home in period box-edged parterres, and deliver some of the most sophisticated of flower fragrances.

Mixed hedges are still less formal, especially when casually clipped, with certain plants being allowed to grow tall out of them. They make wonderful wildlife habitats. Hawthorn, elder and privet can be used but their heavy scents do not win universal appeal. Weaving in honeysuckles (*Lonicera periclymenum* varieties and evergreen *L. japonica* 'Halliana'), dog rose and perhaps vanilla-scented *Clematis flammula* will add sweetness. *Oemleria* would fit well into a native-looking hedge: its almond scent is one of the most powerful of spring.

Evergreen shrubs grown singly or in groups will also add structure to the garden. Those of striking shape, like pencil-slim cypresses and junipers, spiky *Yucca*, pyramidal *Thuja* and topiary box, can act as lynchpins in the design. Diagonally ascending junipers are adept at disguising weak junctions in the design, such as where a grass bank meets a stone wall or a flight of steps. Other evergreens form mounds and hummocks, cushions and clouds, and give the garden a relaxed winter furnishing. Deciding how many you need is always difficult: plant too few and the winter garden looks cold and threadbare; plant too many and in summer the garden feels heavy. Some gardeners can live with sweeps of dead brown grasses and perennials, animated only by a few topiaries all winter, but I like a fuller, greener scene to look out upon.

CHOOSING SCENTED SHRUBS

In winter, when the majority of perennials are in hibernation, shrubs and trees have a special importance. Evergreens come to the fore; we are more aware of shapes and silhouettes; we notice the colours and textures of trunks and branches. And for the scent-conscious gardener, this is a rich season, with an array of good perfumes to enjoy.

Most of the winter-flowering shrubs are tolerant of shade, but flowers really do come to life in this gloomy season when they are caught by a shaft of sunshine. A witch hazel glowing in the afternoon sun is quite a different sight from one sitting in the shadows: a group of different coloured witch hazels planted together is even better. Perhaps you can find places for them where they are shaded in summer by a deciduous canopy or screen which drops in the autumn.

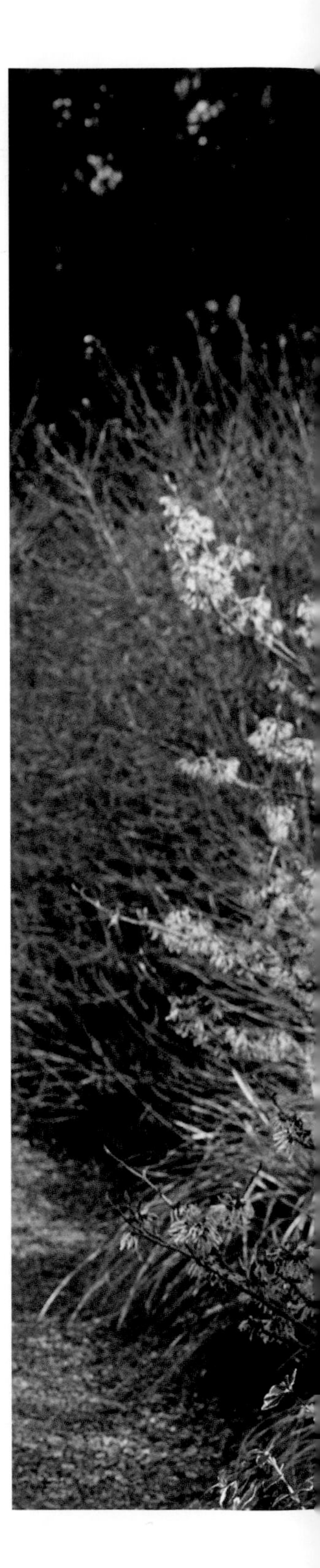

Backlit by dogwoods, witch hazels (*Hamamelis*) blend their fruity scents with the honey and almond of *Viburnum* x *bodnantense* 'Charles Lamont' in this winter scene.

SPICY SPRING SCENT

Pink and white schemes, infused with almond and spice, can be orchestrated using scented cherries like *Prunus* x *yedoensis* and 'Jo-nioi', *Magnolia* x *loebneri* 'Merrill', and, of course, *Viburnum*. The white-flowered *Viburnum* that carry us through the spring have a different scent from the earlier varieties. A rich, usually penetratingly sweet, clove fragrance replaces the honey and almond and at this time of year it is my favourite scent. You get the best value for money from *V.* x *burkwoodii* and its clones, because they are evergreen, bloom over a long period and even provide a splash of autumn colour. But *V. carlesii* and *V.* x *juddii* have a slightly superior, more refined scent.

Viburnum x *burkwoodii* flowers in early summer, and its sweet clove scent carries on the air.

The winter *Viburnum* are among the most valuable of this season's deciduous shrubs. They produce their honey and almond-scented, pink and white flowers on bare branches from autumn until early spring. An erect-stemmed clump is striking silhouetted against evergreens or lawn, or a clear sky. The winter cherry, *Prunus* x *subhirtella* 'Autumnalis', will pick up the pink colour in the distance; and underneath you might plant a pool of snow-drops and crocus.

A more sophisticated spicy scent comes from *Daphne bholua*, which I rate as one of the best new shrubs to come into general circulation in recent decades. The flowers are also white from pink buds, paler in the form 'Darjeeling', which with the white-flowered forms seems to be a little more tender than evergreen 'Jacqueline Postill' and deciduous 'Gurkha'. As with the *Viburnum*, the scent carries well on the air.

Sarcococca are very useful short evergreens for shady corners. Their honey scent is exhaled freely into the winter air, and they could be used in combination with different coloured – but scentless – hellebores, so that there is pleasure for the nose as well as the eye. *Mahonia japonica* could also be planted nearby. It delivers its lily-of-the valley-perfume over several months, and makes a pleasing specimen shrub; it was my mother's favourite scent. The various witch hazels provide a succession of warm colours from mid-winter onwards, blooming, like the *Viburnum*, on bare stems. The yellows tend to be sweeter-scented than the others; the reds and oranges have a mustier, fruit-spice scent that is exactly the smell of parrots. The yellows are lovely when underplanted with green *Helleborus foetidus* and clumps of orange-berried *Iris foetidissima*, whose leaves smell of roast beef.

In a rough corner of a larger garden there might be space for *Cornus mas* and willows such as *Salix aegyptiaca*, *S. triandra* and *S. pentandra*, which will provide a succession of spicy, honey and almond scents through the late winter and into the spring. Under trees, on lime-free soil, *Corylopsis* display their lemon and primrose scented tassels in early spring, and evergreen *Pieris* their panicles of cream, pitcher-shaped flowers, fragrant of lily of the valley and vanilla. I particularly love the warm coconut scent of gorse, which transports me in an instant back to my childhood walking the coastal paths of Anglesey in north Wales.

Spring is the climax of the shrub year and a wealth of colours and scents are on offer. The majority of spring-flowering shrubs are tolerant of some degree of shade, so the main display may still be under trees, in the shadow of walls and on the garden's fringes, the more open sites being left free for later plants that really need plenty of sunlight. *Mahonia aquifolium* has one of the most potent honey scents of early spring. You can put it into almost any unpromising site (it is tolerant of deep shade and dry soil) and it will still perform, wafting its scent over the garden. Honey and its related flavours are exhaled by many winter and spring flowers, and it is a scent which seems to enhance all others. For close association with *Mahonia* there are *Skimmia*, *Fothergilla* and orange and yellow *Berberis*, and, as underplanting, primroses and early daffodils.

Many clove-scented *Daphne* are in bloom now, including the excellent *D.* x *burkwoodii* 'Somerset'. You might use it to pick up the colour of a crab apple, whose pink, white and red blossom often surprises you with a violet or rose scent. The dwarf pink lilacs, like

Syringa microphylla 'Superba', might also contribute. And, if you have acid soil, so might sun-loving *Rhododendron trichostomum*. This small, dainty shrub looks very much like a *Daphne* and its pink flowers have a strong, but not sweet, resinous scent.

A different, fruity fragrance comes from the azaleas. In my view, *Rhododendron luteum* is unrivalled, both in appearance and in the potency of its fruit-cocktail scent. Its yellow flowers and lime-green young leaves create patches of sunlight in the woodland shadows and it has a natural charm that has been lost in many of the brilliantly coloured hybrids. It is a perfect partner for bluebells. In mild climates, tender white rhododendrons like 'Fragrantissimum' and 'Lady Alice Fitzwilliam' are among the woodland garden's spring delights; they are lily-scented with a dash of nutmeg. More of us can enjoy the hardier Loderi clones that bear heavy trusses of pink and white flowers. I have a couple of 'Loderi King George' in a north-facing bed hanging over the edge of my lawn, and love wandering over to drink in the light spicy fragrance. As spring ebbs into summer, the emphasis begins to shift from shade-tolerant to sun-loving shrubs such as brooms, lilacs and laburnums. Early roses like 'Frühlingsgold' and *R. spinosissima* (*R. pimpinellifolia*) are in flower, and filling the air is the fruity scent of the cottage-garden mock orange, *Philadelphus coronarius*. It is a fragrance that can drown all others, so it is perhaps best on the boundary where it can reach you in wafts.

Other mock oranges are more restrained. The pineapple scent of *P. microphyllus* combines deliciously with the sophisticated scents of shrub roses and the pure white and maroon-smudged flowers of 'Sybille' blend well with the roses' crimsons and pinks. *P. maculatus* 'Mexican Jewel' blooms a little later in my garden, and has perhaps the best scent of any *Philadelphus*. In sheltered, sun-baked borders, *Cistus* will be flowering. The gummy scents from their evergreen leaves can engage you on and off all year, but in the heat of summer, when many varieties are flush with sticky young growth, the fragrance is at its richest. The leaves of rosemaries and thymes will add spice to a group of them, *Umbellularia californica* a dash of fruit and New Zealand daisy bushes (*Olearia*) a touch of musk. And to add complementary top notes you could plant

There is no shortage of scented shrubs for shady borders and light woodland. On acid soil, the fragrant rhododendrons alone will provide a potent selection. The flowers of a number of the larger species and hybrids are fruitily lily-scented, shaded with spice and other flavourings.

honey-scented tree heathers (*Erica arborea* and its cousins) and *Ozothamnus ledifolius* (*Helichrysum ledifolium*), almond-scented *Colletia hystrix*, and vanilla-scented Spanish broom, *Spartium junceum*.

As a supplement to the largely scentless herbaceous plants of high summer there are some excellent scented shrubs. Mount Etna broom, *Genista aetnensis*, and tree lupin, *Lupinus arboreus*, are ideal in the perennial border. Though tall, the thinly clad broom casts little shade while the lupin is in flower continuously until the autumn. Their yellow flowers have sweet-pea scents that you often catch in the air. *Buddleja* can also be treated as honorary herbaceous plants, cut to the ground in spring. *B. davidii* and *B. fallowiana* provide a range of blue, purple and white blooms, while *B.* x *weyeriana* 'Golden Glow' is apricot-yellow. They have a flowery honey scent. And for prominent corners of the border there are the spectacular candelabras of yuccas.

The flowers of *Clerodendrum bungei* do carry a trace of the unpleasant meaty scent, so evident in the leaves. But their overriding sweetness, their size and the brightness of their pink make amends, and I have allowed my original single plant to colonize a 4.5m/ 15ft strip at the back of one of my borders. Bright pinks are very welcome at this time when the garden is becoming enveloped in tawny and misty shades. Its cousin, *C. trichotomum* var. *fargesii*, is more at home in light shade. The scent is a touch less sweet, resembling that of fading jasmine flowers, but is powerful and carries well. It is a valuable plant for bringing autumn interest to the woodland garden. The white flowers and turquoise fruits, set in crimson calyces, always catch the eye.

The sugary sweet scent of *Elaeagnus* x *ebbingei* ('Salcombe Seedling' is an especially good form) is strong on a warm autumn evening, and will stop people in their tracks as they search for the source: the flowers are almost invisible. This is often thought a dreary evergreen but, planted in the sun and pruned in spring, the silvery young growth contrasts strikingly with the gold of the dying old leaves, and the white flowers are generously borne. For more ornamental use, there are golden variegated forms of *E.* x *ebbingei* and *E. pungens*.

As autumn progresses, the early *Mahonia* reveal their erect racemes of yellow flowers; these varieties are not as pleasantly fragrant as the later species but outdoors they are not offensive and the colour is very cheery. *Osmanthus armatus* also offers a sweet bubblegum scent. But the fragrance I most look forward to, as the leaves turn, is the caramel of the Katsura tree (*Cercidiphyllum japonicum*) which, if conditions are right, is the accompaniment to a good display of yellow, and if you are lucky, pink autumn colour. There is a good shrubby form called 'Boyd's Dwarf'.

Hamamelis x *intermedia* 'Jelena' is one of the best witch hazels; it has a ripe fruity scent that reminds me of the scent of parrots.

TREES

ABIES
Pinaceae

Like most conifers, the firs release a resinous or fruity scent when the leaves are bruised. The bark is often resinous, too. Most make big evergreen trees, mainly conical in shape, but they are often slow-growing. For smaller gardens, the Korean fir, *A. koreana* (Z5), is a good choice; it achieves about 3m/10ft in its first 20 years, eventually reaching 12m/40ft, and bears remarkable purplish-blue cones from an early age. For large gardens, the Caucasian fir, *A. nordmanniana* (Z5), is one of the most desirable; it has bright green fruit-scented foliage and green cones, and grows more than three times as high and fast as the Korean fir. The following two species have the most distinctive strong scent.

A. balsamea, balsam fir or balm of Gilead, has dark green, glossy leaves with a powerful balsam fragrance; young foliage and the undersides of the leaves are a beautiful grey. The balsam fir makes a tall tree away from its cold homeland of North America, but is at its best when young, and I would be tempted to fell it on its 25th birthday; it would then be 6m/20ft high. The cones are purple. It has miniature (60cm/2ft) forms in the Hudsonia Group.
Lime-free or neutral soil. Z3

A. grandis, giant fir, also has dark leaves which are powerfully and sweetly resinous of grapefruit. But it is vigorous and makes a large tree. It has olive-green young shoots and bright green cones. It is more tolerant of shade and alkaline soils than many other fir trees.
Sun or light shade. Moist, well-drained soil. 15m/50ft in 20 years. Z6

AESCULUS
Sapindaceae

A. californica. Some of the horse chestnuts have scented flowers, including the common horse chestnut, *A. hippocastanum*. For garden use, the best species for scent is *A. californica*. This makes a wide-spreading, small tree or large shrub with small, fingered, metallic grey-green leaves and, throughout the summer, dense, erect heads of white, rose-tinged flowers. It makes an attractive and unusual low lawn specimen and is quite hardy away from the Sunshine State.
Sun or light shade. 3–9m/10–30ft. Z7

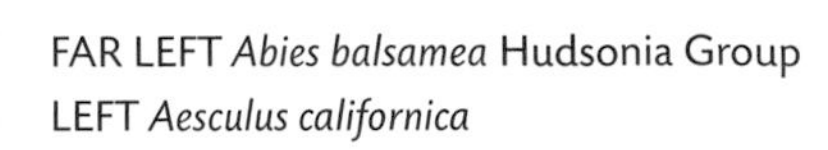

FAR LEFT *Abies balsamea* Hudsonia Group
LEFT *Aesculus californica*

LEFT *Betula lenta* RIGHT *Catalpa bignonioides*

BETULA

Betulaceae

B. lenta, sweet or black birch, native to the eastern United States, is not very common and less vigorous in Britain. It makes an upright tree with typical ovate, toothed leaves which turn bright, clear yellow in the autumn. The bark is smooth and black when young but becomes flaky with age. The shoots have a scent like wintergreen, or a medicinal rub, when bruised. It bears catkins in spring.
Sun. 9m/30ft in 20 years; ultimately 24m/80ft in the United States, but smaller in Europe. Z3

CARYA

Juglandaceae

C. tomentosa, mockernut or bigbud hickory, is, like most of the hickories, rare in cultivation. This is because the group will not tolerate root disturbance and can be difficult to transplant. But if seed is sown *in situ* or seedlings are transplanted when very young, they will prosper. The mockernut is a beautiful tree, and is the most fragrant of the hickories. The foliage has a sweet resinous scent; sometimes it carries in the air but at other times it must be coaxed by hand. The compound leaves are exotically long and composed of seven or more leaflets; they turn vibrant yellow in the autumn. The large buds are of interest in the winter.
Sun. Good loamy soil. 6m/20ft in 20 years; ultimately 24m/80ft. Z4

CATALPA

Bignoniaceae

C. bignonioides, Indian bean tree, is one of the most impressive specimen trees for the lawn of a large garden. It is rounded in shape and wide-spreading and the leaves are very large, heart-shaped and fresh light green in colour. Sweetly scented white flowers, marked in yellow and purple, are carried in showy, erect panicles in summer and are followed, in hot seasons, by slender seed-pods. Hybrids between this species and *C. ovata,* grouped under *C.* x *erubescens,* usually have a glorious lily scent.
Sun. Deep, moist soil. 15m/50ft. Z4

CEDRUS

Pinaceae

The cedars infuse the air with a warm, resinous, blackcurrant scent on hot days but the fragrance is generally not as strong in the foliage as in other conifers. There are three main species, all of which make very large, evergreen trees; they begin pyramidal in shape and later become wide-spreading. There are few finer and more stately lawn specimens for the largest gardens than cedars.
Sun. Moist, deep, well-drained soil.
C. atlantica, Atlas cedar, is almost identical to the cedar of Lebanon. It is fast-growing when young but takes a number of years for its branches to assume a horizontal poise. 'Glauca', its grey-blue form, is very popular and is known as the blue Atlas cedar.
12m/40ft in 20 years; ultimately 36m/120ft. Z6

C. deodara, the deodar, has a particularly graceful, pendent habit which distinguishes it from its cousins. A popular form, 'Aurea', is smaller, slower-growing and is golden-yellow in spring; for the rock garden, try a semi-prostrate golden form called 'Golden Horizon'. The species itself is often planted in small gardens because of its attractive appearance when young. 14m/45ft in 20 years; up to 60m/200ft. Z7

C. libani, the cedar of Lebanon, is the familiar, majestic tree of parks and stately homes with great horizontal, spreading branches. It is slower-growing than the Atlas cedar. 9m/30ft in 20 years; ultimately 36m/120ft. Z6

CHAMAECYPARIS
Cupressaceae

The false cypresses are among the most cultivated of conifers and have foliage which is pungently resinous-scented when bruised. As trees they are conical in shape, most becoming more spreading with age. Many make good screens and tall hedges, but they grow vigorously and many forms may need pruning twice a year. Moist, loamy soil.

C. lawsoniana, Lawson's false cypress, makes a large tree with leaves held in flat, ferny sprays. It is one of the best tall screens and hedges. It has given rise to many excellent clones, including: 'Columnaris', a narrow blue-grey column, 7.5m/25ft; 'Ellwoodii', a slow-growing, dark blue-green column, dense and compact, 7.5m/25ft; 'Erecta Viridis', a deep green, compact column, wonderfully neat and formal but best when comparatively young,

CERCIDIPHYLLUM
Cercidiphyllaceae

C. japonicum, the Katsura tree, from the Far East, is one of the loveliest garden trees. The leaves are heart-shaped, opening as a warm tan, becoming fresh green, and turning to yellow and sometimes pink in autumn. As they turn, a mouthwatering scent of caramel fills the air; you can also smell it in the fallen leaves. It is most frequently seen as a multi-stemmed tree, but with judicious pruning it can be trained to a single stem. The young leaves are susceptible to spring frosts so a sheltered position is needed in colder areas. There is a beautiful weeping form called *pendulum*, and I also grow the shrubby form 'Boyd's Dwarf'. Light shade. Rich, deep, moist soil. 9m/30ft in 20 years; 30m/100ft in the wild. Z5

Cercidiphyllum japonicum

9–27m/30–90ft; 'Fletcheri', a feathery, juniper-like, blue-grey, bushy cone, slow-growing, 6–12m/20–40ft; 'Green Pillar', a superb rich green column, 7.5m/25ft; 'Kilmacurragh', a pencil-slim, dark green column, 7.5–12m/25–40ft; 'Lanei Aurea', a golden pyramid, 7.5m/25ft; 'Pembury Blue', a glaucous blue-grey cone, slow-growing, 3.5–9m/12–30ft; and 'Pottenii', a grey-green cone, 9m/30ft. Z5

C. obtusa, Hinoki false cypress, has rich green foliage, horizontally borne in feathery sprays, and also makes a broad conical tree. ('Crippsii' is a good bright golden-yellow form, a third smaller in size.)
Moist, lime-free soil. 7.5m/25ft in 20 years; ultimately 23m/75ft. Z5

C. thyoides, white false cypress, has glaucous green foliage with a pungent spicy scent. It makes a pleasing compact cone.
Lime-free soil. 7.5m/25ft in 20 years; ultimately 6–15m/20–50ft, 24m/80ft in the wild. Z5

CLADRASTIS
Papilionaceae

C. kentukea (C. lutea), yellow wood, is a highly ornamental, round-topped, deciduous tree from the southeastern United States. It has beautiful and exotic, lettuce-green, pinnate leaves that turn a clear yellow colour in the autumn. But the sweet vanilla scent comes from the white pea-flowers that open in wisteria-like, dangling panicles in early summer; these seem to appear only on the more mature plants.
Sun. Acid soil. 9m/30ft in 20 years; ultimately 12m/40ft or more. Z3

CRATAEGUS
Rosaceae

The heavy scent of the hawthorns is a characteristic of the British countryside in late spring. At best it is a sweet musty fragrance, at worst the odour of decaying fish. This is from the common hawthorn or may, *C. monogyna*. The scent of *C. laevigata* (*C. oxyacantha*) (Z6) is similar but it is more or less absent from its heavily coloured forms such as 'Paul's Scarlet'.

CUPRESSUS
Cupressaceae

The cypresses release a fruity, resinous scent when bruised. In warmer areas, and near the sea, the Monterey cypress, *C. macrocarpa* (Z7), is a useful, fast-growing shelter and hedging tree; it has many good golden forms, and grows 14m/45ft or more in 20 years, ultimately 18–30m/60–100ft. The slim, dark green, Italian cypress, *C. sempervirens*, will also thrive in all but the coldest areas (its bright green variety 'Totem Pole' has proved totally hardy in my garden in Wales) and there is no better vertical column for a garden; 11m/35ft in 20 years, ultimately 24m/80ft.
Sun. All but waterlogged soils.

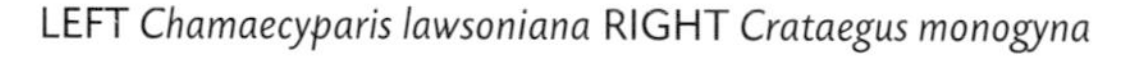
LEFT *Chamaecyparis lawsoniana* RIGHT *Crataegus monogyna*

LEFT *Eucalyptus gunnii* RIGHT *Eucalyptus pauciflora* subsp. *niphophila*

C. arizonica var. ***glabra***, smooth Arizona cypress, is one of the hardiest species. It is a beautiful, ghostly tree, feathery and conical with attractive peeling, reddish-brown bark. Its relative 'Pyramidalis' is outstandingly compact and blue. The scent is vaguely reminiscent of grapefruit. 7.5m/25ft in 20 years; ultimately 9m/30ft or more. Z6

CYDONIA
Rosaceae

C. oblonga, the common quince, has some of the most deliciously and distinctively scented fruit imaginable; in a bowl they will fill a room with fragrance. It is a small, round-topped, deciduous tree and makes a characterful, sometimes gawky, lawn specimen. The dark green leaves have woolly grey undersides, and blush-pink flowers – large and saucer-shaped – appear in spring. The fruits, which are in evidence in early autumn, are yellow and pear-shaped and are used for making quince jelly. 'Vranja' is a superior form. Like most fruit trees, it is rather a martyr to pest and disease.
Sun. Good, fertile soil. 7.5m/25ft. Z5

EUCALYPTUS
Myrtaceae

The gum trees always attract attention outside their Australian homeland. Many are not reliably hardy away from the milder and coastal areas, though there are more winter-hardy candidates. Apart from their obvious visual beauty, a main attraction is their incredible speed of growth. The evergreen foliage has a juvenile and adult phase; the leaves usually begin shorter and more rounded, and later become slender and pointed. Their scent is evident when the leaves are rubbed. They are easy to grow from seed, and are best established when very small. They generally form erect, narrow specimens, thinly clothed in foliage. The flowers are generally richly honey-scented.
Sun. Well-drained soil preferred.
The following are relatively hardy:

E. coccifera, Tasmanian snow gum, has greyish-green leaves which begin heart-shaped and turn into narrow sickles. When crushed, these release a scent of peppermint. The smooth trunk begins white and fades to grey. 17m/55ft in 20 years; ultimately 21m/70ft. Z9

E. dalrympleana is proving a most attractive and reliable species for gardens. It has larger leaves than *E. coccifera* and a beautiful smooth trunk which is a patchwork of cream, grey and light brown.
17m/55ft in 20 years; ultimately 24–36m/80–120ft. Z9

E. glaucescens, Tingiringi gum, has delicious fruity foliage. It has juvenile leaves of a very intense silver-blue and retains a fine glaucous colour in adulthood. It has creamy, peeling bark. 12m/40ft in 20 years. Z9

E. gunnii, cider gum, is the most popular species. Its round young leaves are a glaucous silver-blue, and its adult leaves green and sickle-shaped. The bark fades from light green and cream to brown and grey. A particular glory of this species is its juvenile foliage and it is very effective as a coppiced shrub.
23m/75ft in 20 years; ultimately 30m/100ft. Z9

E. pauciflora subsp. *niphophila*, snow gum, is perhaps the best garden eucalypt and is also, by happy chance, the hardiest. It has rounded green juvenile foliage and leathery, grey-green adult foliage. Its smooth trunk is truly one of the most handsome in the plant kingdom, a bloomy pure white, python-patterned in green and grey. It has a mild, fruity scent.
6m/20ft in the wild, in gardens achieves up to 15m/50ft in 20 years. Z8

FRAXINUS
Oleaceae

F. ornus, flowering or manna ash, is an interesting addition to the garden. It is not the best of the flowering ashes – that title goes to *F. sieboldiana* (*F. mariesii*) – but it wins the prize for scent which comes from its foamy heads of cream flowers in spring and is overpoweringly, though not always agreeably, of honey. It has pinnate leaves and makes a round-topped deciduous tree.
Sun. 12m/40ft in 20 years; ultimately 15m/50ft. Z5

HALESIA
Styracaceae

H. carolina, Carolina silverbell, is a pretty plant for the larger garden, particularly in a woodland clearing where it can be given a dark background. The branches drip with pure white bells during spring, and these are softly but sweetly scented. The leaves are more or less oval and turn yellow in the autumn, coinciding with small winged fruits. It is often seen as a multi-stemmed tree.
Sun or light shade. Moist, well-drained soil, preferably acidic. 4.5m/15ft in 20 years in Europe; a 9m/30ft-round-topped tree in the United States. Z5

H. monticola, mountain snowdrop tree, is altogether larger and even more impressive in flower and fruit than *H. carolina*. Again it is often seen as a multi-stemmed tree.
Sun or light shade. 9m/30ft in 20 years. Z5

JUGLANS
Juglandaceae

The large pinnate leaves of walnuts are fruitily resinous and this scent can often be enjoyed in the air, especially in the autumn; the scent is more pungent when the leaves are rubbed by hand. The two species commonly cultivated are susceptible to wind and to late frosts, so a sheltered site should be found. They also resent disturbance and should be established when very young, even from seed. Both the species described below are deciduous.
Sun or light shade. Good, loamy, acid or alkaline soil.

J. nigra, black walnut, is the more ornamental of the two species commonly grown but is less strongly scented. As a lawn specimen it is impressive and tropical in appearance, for its leaves are particularly long. Do not use it in mixed plantings, since it produces toxins which may kill other plants. It forms a round-topped, pyramidal shape, and is fast-growing. The nuts are tasty.
11m/35ft in 20 years; ultimately 24m/80ft or more. Z4

Juglans nigra

LEFT *Juglans regia* 'Buccaneer' RIGHT *Laburnam* x *watereri* 'Vossii', *Wisteria sinensis* and *Allium aflatunense*

J. regia, English or Persian walnut, is grown mainly for its nuts and soft fruits; particularly good clones can be bought from fruit tree specialists. It makes a smaller tree. The scent is strong and fruity and often hangs in the air.
7.5m/25ft in 20 years; ultimately 18m/60ft or more. Z6

JUNIPERUS
Cupressaceae

The junipers have feathery evergreen foliage that is pungently resinous. The majority of interesting varieties are too small for inclusion here and are listed under Shrubs.
Sun or light shade. All but water-logged soils.

LABURNUM
Papilionaceae

Among the most elegant garden trees, the laburnums produce their long, pendent racemes of golden-yellow flowers in early summer. The scent from the flowers is sweet but, as with many scented members of the pea family, also rather heavy and claustrophobic.
Sun or light shade. Any soil.

***L. alpinum* 'Pendulum'** makes an interesting lawn specimen. It is a particularly fine form of the Scotch laburnum, with a pronounced weeping habit. It is small, slim and slow-growing (unless grafted) and a much more sensible choice for suburban gardens than a giant weeping willow. The racemes are well over 30cm/1ft long and the trifoliate leaves are a shining deep green.
3m/10ft; 6m/20ft, if grafted. Z5

***L. x watereri* 'Vossii'** is the form most people choose for its immensely long racemes of flowers. It is spectacular when trained over a pergola. As a free-standing tree, it has a more conventional, rounded shape; though unremarkable when out of flower, it is by no means unattractive.
7.5m/25ft in 20 years. Z6

MAGNOLIA
Magnoliaceae

The majority of scented magnolias are treated in the chapter on Shrubs and, in the case of *M. grandiflora,* under Wall Shrubs. Some have notably fragrant leaves, but mostly the scent is from the flowers.

M. denudata, the yulan or lily tree, forms a large shrub or small tree of rounded shape and bears large, pure white, fleshy-petalled, lemon-scented blooms from early spring. Like all the spring-flowering magnolias, it is best planted where its frosted buds will not be caught by the early morning sun; an open or lightly shaded position facing west or southwest is ideal. It is one of the glories of the spring garden.
Neutral or lime-free soil. Usually up to 9m/30ft. Z6

M. kobus is a hardy deciduous Japanese magnolia, which forms a single or multi-stemmed medium-sized tree. It is notoriously slow to

LEFT *Magnolia* x *loebneri* 'Ballerina' RIGHT A hybrid crab apple

flower, but the loose white blooms are fragrant. They appear in spring, before the small dark leaves, and on a mature plant the display is spectacular. Sun (avoid shade). 9m/30ft or more. Z5

***M.* x *loebneri* 'Merrill'** always impresses me with its scent when I come across it in other people's gardens. It bears a mass of spidery white flowers in early spring. 'Leonard Messel' is a pink version. 'Ballerina' is a fine blush-white. They are superb shrubs.
Sun. Fairly lime-tolerant. 7m/25ft. Z5

***M. obovata* (*M. hypoleuca*)** produces huge, creamy, saucer-shaped flowers in early summer; these have a prominent central knob of crimson stamens and a strong fruity scent, in which the principal flavour is ripe melon. Scarlet fruits follow in autumn. It is deciduous, with very long and leathery leaves that are a beautiful shade of glaucous green. It is hardy and fast-growing, upright in habit, and makes a glorious feature for the woodland garden. The fragrance carries far.
Sun. Rich, moist, acid or neutral soil. 9m/30ft in 20 years; ultimately, 15m/50ft or more. Z5

M. salicifolia is a small tree distinguished by its willowy leaves. The scent comes not just from its white flowers, which are carried in spring, but from its leaves and bark, which release a sharp, spicy lemon and aniseed fragrance when bruised. It is a beautiful plant, and has a small, larger-flowered, broader-leaved clone called 'Jermyns'.
Sun or light shade. Neutral or lime-free soil. 6m/20ft or more. Z6

M. virginiana, the sweet bay, is one of the mainstays of gardens in the eastern United States. It likes heat and performs best in warm regions, where it produces its scented flowers for many weeks in late summer. Full sun. Retentive soil that is not strongly alkaline. 18m/60ft or more in the southeastern United States; up to 9m/30ft in Europe. Z5

MALUS
Rosaceae

Crab apples often have scented flowers and make very characterful trees, ideally suited to a cottage garden setting. Those with bicoloured blossom – white flowers from deep pink buds – are among the most beautiful of spring-flowering trees. They are deciduous and the leaves are fragrant when crushed. Many, however, are susceptible to the same diseases as apple trees.
Sun or light shade. Most well-drained soils.

***M. coronaria* 'Charlottae'** has large, semi-double, shell-pink flowers with an unusually strong violet scent; they open in early summer. It makes a wide-spreading tree and the oval leaves often take on pleasing colours in autumn.
7.5m/25ft in 20 years; ultimately 9m/28ft. Z4

***M.* 'Golden Hornet'** is a popular variety grown mainly for its golden

fruits which last well through the winter. But its white flowers, from pink buds, are also eyecatching and noticeably fragrant. It makes a stiff, upright tree. The red-fruited 'John Downie' also has scented white flowers.
7.5m/25ft in 20 years; ultimately 9m/30ft.

M. hupehensis also makes an upright tree and is second only to the Japanese crab, *M. floribunda,* in floral beauty. A cloud of white flowers appear in spring from pink buds. In scent it is superior to the Japanese crab.
7.5m/25ft in 20 years; ultimately 9m/30ft or more. Z4

NOTHOFAGUS
Nothofagaceae

N. antarctica. One of the hardiest of the southern beeches, this is a deciduous tree from Chile, whose small, rounded leaves are powerfully scented, especially in the spring. The fragrance is resinous, rather like pumpkin pie. The leaves turn yellow in the autumn. The flowers, borne in late spring, are also aromatic. It makes an attractive, rather quirky tree of open, usually spreading habit, but I pruned mine and kept it shrub-like for a number of years. It needs protection from wind.
Sun. Acid, well-drained soil. 11m/35ft in 20 years; ultimately 15m/50ft. Z8

PAULOWNIA
Paulowniaceae

P. fargesii is less common than *P. tomentosa*. It has large rounded leaves and tall, erect panicles of tubular flowers in early summer, which are pale lilac, stained with yellow, and scented of fruit and honey. It is a spreading, deciduous tree, ideal as a lawn specimen, though it needs a sheltered position.
Sun. Well-drained soil, not chalk. 12m/40ft in 20 years; ultimately 18m/60ft. Z7

P. tomentosa, the empress or foxglove tree, has darker flowers and lobed leaves; otherwise, it is similar to *P. fargesii*. It is an exotic feature wherever it is planted and is often grown simply for its tropical-sized leaves; several plants are grown in a group and cut back to within 5cm/2in of the old wood in spring. But this routine is of no interest to the scent-loving gardener! The tree is hardy, except when very young, but, unfortunately, the flowers are often caught by late frosts; so an annual fragrant feast of fruit and honey cannot be guaranteed.
Sun. Well-drained, slightly acidic soil. 12m/40ft in 20 years; ultimately 15m/50ft. Z6

LEFT *Nothofagus antarctica* RIGHT *Paulownia tomentosa*

LEFT *Pinus nigra* variety
BELOW *Populus balsamifera*

PICEA
Pinaceae

The spruces are similar to the firs in appearance, immediately distinguishable by the layman only when bearing cones: the cones of firs stand erect, those of spruces are pendent. They are evergreen and their foliage has the typical resinous scent associated with conifers. They are not suitable for shallow or alkaline soils, or hot, dry climates.
Sun. Moist, deep soil.

PINUS
Pinaceae

The pines have resinous-scented foliage and cones, and provide a further range of valuable garden evergreens. They are distinguished by their long, needle-like leaves which are borne in bundles of between two and five. Of the large, less ornamental species, the beach pine, *P. contorta,* and the maritime pine, *P. pinaster,* are useful on sandy soil, the latter for fixing sand dunes; the Austrian pine, *P. nigra,* is one of the best windbreaks, even on chalk and at high altitudes, as is, in maritime areas on acidic soil, the rapid-growing Monterey pine, *P. radiata.*
Many pines are tolerant of alkaline soil. Full sun. Well-drained soil.
P. ayacahuite, Mexican white pine, is a dreamy tree, of spreading habit, for warmer gardens. The leaves are long and glaucous green, and the cones pendulous and resinous.
9m/30ft in 20 years; ultimately 30m/100ft. Z7
P. bungeana, lace-bark pine, has one of the most beautiful barks of any tree, a peeling patchwork of colours like a python's skin; however, this only becomes evident after many years of growth. It makes a compact, upright, oval tree. Its scarcity in nurseries and slow growth have combined to keep it an uncommon tree.
7.5m/25ft in 20 years; ultimately 12m/40ft or more. Z5

POPULUS
Salicaceae

Few trees are as powerfully fragrant as the balsam poplars. In spring, and occasionally later, the air is filled with an extremely sweet, balsam scent, for the buds are sticky with fragrant resin. The scent, mouthwatering in moderation, is cloying in quantity, so a position on the garden's boundary should be sought.
Sun or shade. Any soil.
P. balsamifera, balsam poplar, makes a very tall, suckering tree in its native North America but does not perform as satisfactorily in Europe as *P. trichocarpa.* The oval leaves are green above and whitish below.
15m/50ft in 20 years; ultimately 30m/100ft. Z2
P. 'Balsam Spire' ('Tacatricho 32'). This hybrid is an excellent, fast-growing balsam poplar with a narrow habit and

LEFT *Prunus* 'Jo-nioi' RIGHT *Prunus padus*

a superb scent. It is not as prone to canker as its parents.
18m/60ft or more in 20 years; ultimately 60m/200ft.

***P.* x *jackii* 'Aurora'** is a form of balm of Gilead poplar whose young leaves are splashed with white and pink. It is immensely popular but in my view its freakish colouring makes it one of the most unsightly of all trees.
15m/50ft in 20 years; ultimately 30m/100ft. Z2

P. trichocarpa, black cottonwood. One of the finest of the balsam poplars, this makes a fast-growing, pyramidal tree. In scent, it is every bit as potent as *P. balsamifera* and it, or 'Balsam Spire', is an essential ingredient for the larger scented garden.
18m/60ft or more in 20 years; ultimately 60m/200ft. Z5

PRUNUS
Rosaceae

You can detect a honey or almond scent in the flowers of many members of this group, but it is usually extremely faint. I record here only the most potent varieties, though even they are always restrained in their outpourings. They are all flowering cherries and are small enough trees for most gardens. A dark evergreen backdrop shows off the white blossom perfectly, as does a clear blue sky.
Sun or light shade. All but waterlogged or very dry soils.

***P. hirtipes* 'Semiplena'** is difficult to find in nurseries and it is rather vulnerable to late frost and bud-stripping by birds. (A west-facing position, where there is much human traffic, may help solve these last problems.) I include it because it really is the loveliest early wild cherry; the white blossom is borne over a long period, usually beginning in winter, and there is a good almond scent. It makes an elegant, spreading tree.
7.5m/25ft in 20 years; ultimately 11m/35ft. Z6

P. padus, bird cherry, is a European native with striking flowers. The white, almond-scented blossom is borne on long, slender, drooping racemes rather than in a foaming mass. The bark has an acrid smell. The species itself is pretty in the wild garden or in woodland, but for gardens I would choose its clone 'Watereri', which has longer racemes. It makes an open, spreading tree.
9m/30ft in 20 years; ultimately 15m/50ft. Z4

P.* x *yedoensis, Yoshino cherry, is a beautiful, spreading cherry which produces its clusters of white, almond-scented blossom in early spring, just before its young green leaves expand.
9m/30ft in 20 years; ultimately 12m/40ft. Z6

Japanese flowering cherries. A number of these popular ornamental cherries are delicately almond-scented. Among the most fragrant are 'Amanogawa', a slim, columnar

PTELEA
Rutaceae

P. trifoliata, the hop tree, is an unusual and highly desirable ingredient for the scented garden. Its clusters of small, greenish flowers, borne in summer, have a powerfully sweet, spicy scent rather like *Viburnum*. According to one authority, they are probably the most fragrant flowers of any hardy tree. The light green leaflets are also covered in oil glands and release a fruitily pungent scent when bruised. Winged green fruits follow the flowers, and there is good yellow autumn colour from the foliage. It makes a low, spreading, rounded tree or large shrub. I grow the form 'Aurea' which brings an attractive lemon glow to a shady border.
Sun or shade. Any soil. Ultimately 6m/20ft. Z5

Ptelea trifoliata

variety with semi-double, pink blossom in spring, 7.5m/25ft; and 'Shirotae' ('Mount Fuji'), a spreading tree with large, semi-double, white flowers in early spring, 7.5m/25ft. But the prize for fragrance goes to 'Jo-nioi', a lovely cherry of spreading habit; it bears its single white flowers in spring, 11m/35ft. Z6

PSEUDOTSUGA
Pinaceae

P. menziesii, Oregon Douglas fir, is a fast-growing timber tree and too large for most gardens but it is powerfully and fruitily resinous. It is broadly conical in shape and has attractive corky, deeply fissured bark. It is unsatisfactory on alkaline soils.
Sun. Moist, well-drained soil. Ultimately up to 30m/100ft; 90m/300ft in the US. Z4-6

PTEROSTYRAX
Styracaceae

P. hispida, epaulette tree, is an unusual deciduous tree or large shrub that deserves to be grown more often. It has oval, toothed leaves, whitish underneath, and panicles of white, sweetly scented flowers in late spring or early summer; these are followed by spindle-shaped fruits. It is fast-growing and hardy.
Sun and heat. All but shallow and chalky soils. 4.5–9m/15–30ft. Z6

ROBINIA
Papilionaceae

R. pseudoacacia, false acacia or black locust, has some of the freshest green, most handsome foliage of any garden tree and I wish people

LEFT *Styrax japonicus* RIGHT *Stewartia sinensis*

would plant it instead of its golden form, 'Frisia'. A delicate, sweet, pea scent comes from the wisteria-like racemes of white flowers, borne in early summer. This deciduous tree can be difficult to establish, but once growing it is vigorous. A sheltered position should be sought as it is vulnerable to wind damage.
Sun or light shade. Most soils. 12m/40ft in 20 years; ultimately 24m/80ft. Z3

SALIX
Salicaceae
S. pentandra, bay willow, has broad, glossy leaves like a bay laurel; these are sweetly aromatic when bruised and in spring the scent hangs in the air. It is the last willow to produce its catkins; they appear in early summer, the male catkins being bright yellow. It is an attractive and useful tree, slow-growing for a willow.
Sun. All but dry soils. 14m/45ft in 20 years; ultimately 18m/60ft.

STEWARTIA
Theaceae
S. sinensis is the most scented member of a valuable group of trees and shrubs for acid, woodland conditions. The sweetly fragrant, white, cup-shaped flowers are borne singly among the oval, bright green leaves in late summer. It also has fiery autumn colours. Above all, it has spectacular bark, which changes from smooth orange-brown in the summer to purple in the autumn, and then peels in strips during the winter. It makes a pyramidal tree that does best in a sheltered position.
Sun. Deep, moist, acid soil. 9m/30ft in 20 years; ultimately 15m/50ft. Z6

STYRAX
Styracaceae
S. japonicus, Japanese snowbell, is among the most elegant flowering trees for small gardens. Its white, slightly scented flowers hang on long stalks along the slender branches in early summer; with the bright green, oval leaves the effect is crisp and refined. It is deciduous and makes a spreading tree. Being vulnerable to late frosts, it prefers a site protected from the morning sun.
Light shade. Light, moist, loamy, neutral or acid soil. 6m/20ft in 20 years; ultimately 7.5m/25ft.
S. obassia is a more fragrant but much less common species that makes a narrow, erect tree, with larger leaves; its white flowers are borne in drooping racemes. It is no less beautiful and desirable than *S. japonica*. It enjoys the same conditions.
9m/30ft in 20 years; ultimately 11m/35ft. Z5

TETRADIUM (EUODIA)
Rutaceae
T. daniellii is a deciduous tree with clusters of small, aromatic, cup-shaped white flowers in late summer, popular with bees, followed by attractive

fruits. The large leaves turn yellow in autumn. In the related *T. ruticarpum* the leaves are very spicily scented.
Sun or light shade. Well-drained soil.
9m/30ft or more. Z5

THUJA
Cupressaceae

T. koraiensis, Korean arborvitae, is variable in the wild, and can be seen in gardens either as a shrub or a small tree. It is identified by the silvery undersides to its leaves and its scent, which some compare to that of a rich fruit cake.
To 7.5m/25ft. Z5

T. plicata, western red cedar, is a superb evergreen tree for the largest gardens; it also makes a fine, feathery hedge. The dark green leaves have a deliciously fruity, pear-drop scent when crushed, which makes hedge-pruning a delight. Specimen trees are pyramidal in shape and their rusty orange-brown bark is spectacular.
Sun or shade. All but dry soils.
14m/45ft in 20 years; ultimately 30m/100ft or more. Z5

T. standishii, Japanese arborvitae, is uncommon but notable for having foliage sharply scented of lemon. It makes a spreading, conical tree with yellowish-green leaves and deep red-brown bark.
5.5m/18ft in 20 years; ultimately 18m/60ft or more. Z6

TILIA
Malvaceae

The limes have extremely powerfully scented flowers, and they would be planted more often if they did not drip honeydew (the result of aphid infestation) and their pollen did not contain a narcotic element that stupefies bees. Paths become sticky, plants become spotted with black mould and bees become a serious hazard. But the sugary sweet fruity scent in the air is delicious.
Limes are deciduous. Sun or light shade. Any soil.

T. cordata, small-leaved lime, has clusters of very scented, yellowish flowers in high summer. It makes a neat, pyramidal tree, and is a favourite of mine: I have planted several along my boundary.
9m/30ft in 20 years; ultimately 30m/100ft. Z4

T. x euchlora, Crimean lime, is one of the best of the limes for scent and it does not drip honeydew; bees remain a problem, however. It has attractive glossy green, heart-shaped leaves and makes a pleasing, rounded, rather pendulous specimen.
6m/20ft in 20 years; ultimately 15m/50ft or more. Z6

T. 'Petiolaris', weeping silver lime, is a popular and attractive weeping tree. It has white-felted undersides to its leaves and very scented flowers, but honeydew and bees pose problems.
11m/35ft in 20 years; ultimately 24m/80ft.

LEFT *Tilia cordata* RIGHT *Tetradium daniellii*

SHRUBS

AESCULUS
Sapindaceae

A. parviflora, bottlebrush buckeye, is a shrubby relative of the horse chestnut. It has typical fingered leaves and erect panicles of creamy white flowers. The scent is heavy and sweet, sometimes a little sickly, and can fill the air. It is particularly useful in woodland borders where, with hydrangeas, it ensures interest through late summer.
Sun or light shade. 2.5–4.5m/8–15ft. Z5

BERBERIS
Berberidaceae

Many of the barberries surprise you with a honey scent. They make dense neat shrubs and some can be marshalled into service as fragrant evergreen hedges. The flowers are borne in spring and the scent hangs in the air on warm days.
Sun or shade.

B. candidula is a low arching shrub, suitable for the front of the border or the rock garden. Its small, shiny evergreen leaves have white undersides and are protected by thorns. The bright yellow flowers are solitary and dangle on short stems.
1–1.2m/3–4ft. Z6

B. julianae, one of the hardiest of the evergreen barberries, makes an erect shrub with long slender leaves. The protective needles are conspicuous and extremely sharp. The flowers, which are pale yellow, are spaced in tight clusters along the branches. *B. sargentiana* is similar to *B. julianae* but slightly smaller and with reddish young shoots.
3m/10ft. Z6

B. verruculosa is closely related to *B. candidula* but is larger (2m/6ft) and has glaucous rather than white undersides to its leaves. It blooms in mid-spring and its golden-yellow flowers are honey-scented.
Z5

BUDDLEJA
Scrophulariaceae

Buddlejas provide the summer garden with some delicious honey scents. But the fragrance is not freely released into the air and you will want to position them where your nose can reach. They are deciduous but in milder areas not completely naked in winter.
Sun.

B. alternifolia is a graceful shrub whose narrow, grey-green leaves and arching growth look decidedly willow-like. But in early summer the pendent branches turn into colourful

FAR LEFT *Buddleja* 'Lochinch'
LEFT *Buddleja globosa*

LEFT *Berberis julianae* RIGHT Clipped box

streamers, so thickly studded are they with clusters of lilac flowers. It can be trained as a weeping tree or against a warm wall as a fan. It needs little pruning. There is a smaller form with silver leaves called 'Argentea'.
3–4.5m/10–15ft. Z6

B. davidii is the familiar butterfly bush of late summer. It grows vigorously and flowers on the current year's wood, so it should be hard pruned every spring. In the border it can be underplanted with daffodils and tulips, whose dying growth it will quickly conceal as it expands. 'Black Knight' is dark purple; 'Empire Blue' is violet-blue; 'Ile de France' is pure violet; and 'Royal Red' is reddish purple. 'Harlequin' has reddish-purple flowers and white-edged leaves. The 'Nanho' forms, in blue, purple and white, are only 1.5m/5ft high. 'Dartmoor' is unusual for its branching purple flowerheads, and useful for its slightly later flowering, and in my northern garden better coincides with the peak butterfly season.
3m/10ft. Z6

B. fallowiana* var. *alba is the *Buddleja* to choose if you want white flowers. They are set off to perfection by grey leaves and white stems. In appearance it resembles *B. davidii* but it is not quite as hardy and is often treated as a wall shrub. It grows to 2.5m/8ft. 'Lochinch', a *B. fallowiana* hybrid, is my favourite butterfly bush and combines hardiness with delicate colour. It has grey leaves and lilac plumes and is a vision of pastel beauty.
3m/10ft. Z9

B. globosa, the orange ball tree, is a distinctive *Buddleja* with panicles of orange drumsticks in summer. The proportion of flowers to coarse foliage is rather disappointing, and I would not recommend it for the small garden, but the scent is good. It grows relatively slowly and needs little pruning.
3m/10ft. Z8

***B.* x *weyeriana* 'Golden Glow'** is a much better golden-yellow *Buddleja* which is a later-flowering version of *B. globosa*. The balls of flower are looser and they are a softer colour. It begins blooming in high summer and goes on until the first frosts. It is a first-rate ingredient for late summer's hot colour schemes. *B.* x *weyeriana* itself, with gold and mauve flowers, is hideous.
3m/10ft. Z8

BUXUS SEMPERVIRENS

Buxaceae

Common box is a mainstay of formal gardens. Being evergreen and growing in a dense compact manner, it is a good structural ingredient and lends itself well to hedge, topiary, knot garden and edging work. It can also be left to form a natural shape as part of the shrub border. It thrives in any aspect, but is slow-growing. The scent of the leaves is pleasantly pungent to my nose but others find

Calycanthus floridus

it reminiscent of cats' urine. Queen Anne is said to have removed the box parterres at Hampton Court because she disliked the smell so much. The inconspicuous flowers that appear in spring are honey-scented. There are many cultivars with different attractions. 'Handsworthiensis' makes the best large specimen or hedging plant. 'Suffruticosa' is a dwarf box and the best for box-edging. And 'Elegantissima' is a fine cream-variegated box.
Sun or shade. Tolerates poor soil, grows faster in fertile ground. 1.2–2m/4–6ft. Z6

CALYCANTHUS
Calycanthaceae

C. floridus is the most desirable of the American allspices. It is a deciduous shrub, unremarkable in appearance but distinctively scented in all its parts. The oval leaves, which are rough and dark on top and pale and downy underneath, smell of camphor when rubbed, as do the roots and the wood. The tiny crimson flowers, resembling miniature waterlilies, smell deliciously of fruit cocktail and are produced in summer.
Sun or light shade. 2.5m/8ft. Z5

CAMPHOROSMA
Amaranthaceae

C. monspeliaca is a small evergreen shrub that looks like a grey heather with slender, woolly leaves and inconspicuous flowers. The scent, which is of camphor, is released by the young shoots when they are rubbed. It is a plant for the hot, dry border, and for coastal gardens.
Sun. 60cm/2ft. Z8

CARYOPTERIS
Lamiaceae

C. x clandonensis is a collective name for a group of hybrid caryopteris raised in Surrey, England. They are ideal for the late-summer border, providing a range of violet-blue flowers to set beside the yellows of that season. A turpentine scent comes from the grey leaves when they are rubbed. 'Arthur

RIGHT *Cistus* x *aguilarii*
FAR RIGHT *Cistus* x *purpureus* 'Alan Fradd'

Simmonds', the original clone, is pale violet-blue. 'Heavenly Blue' is similar but more compact. 'Ferndown' and 'Kew Blue' are richer in colour. Cut back each spring.
Sun. 90cm/3ft. Z8

CASSINIA
Asteraceae

C. leptophylla* subsp. *fulvida is an erect heather-like shrub, whose gold stems and undersides to its leaves give it a yellowish-green appearance. The small heads of off-white flowers open in summer and have a strong honey scent. It is hardy in warmer areas of the UK.
Sun. Well-drained soil. 1.2m/4ft. Z8

CHIONANTHUS
Oleaceae

C. virginicus, fringe tree, is a deciduous shrub or small tree from the eastern United States. It has narrow, oval leaves and panicles of pure white wispy flowers in summer; these are quite fragrant. It is a curious and entertaining shrub that deserves to be planted more often.
Sun. Moist, loamy soil. 3–9m/10–30ft. Z4

CISTUS
Cistaceae

No scent evokes the Mediterranean more surely than the aroma of rock roses. It is a resinous fragrance, called ladanum, that clings to the young shoots and leaves, and which, on hot days, fills the air. The best *Cistus* glisten with sticky gum and if they produced no flowers at all I would still grow them. As it is, their flowers are sumptuous, great white and pink saucers, often stained with yellow and blotched with crimson or chocolate. Individual flowers last no more than a day but they are borne in profusion in summer. *Cistus* are not the hardiest of shrubs, but they grow easily and quickly from cuttings. They are evergreen and need shelter from wind.
Full sun. Well-drained soil.

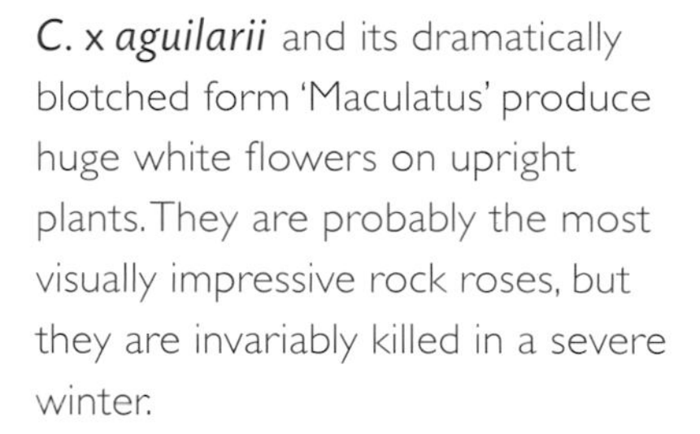

C. x aguilarii and its dramatically blotched form 'Maculatus' produce huge white flowers on upright plants. They are probably the most visually impressive rock roses, but they are invariably killed in a severe winter.
1.2m/4ft. Z8

***C. x argenteus* 'Peggy Sammons'** is a bushy evergreen shrub with pink flowers and grey-green foliage.
90cm/3ft. Z8

C. x cyprius is one of the hardier rock roses and will fill out into a sizeable shrub. It is extremely beautiful. Its white flowers have crimson blotches and its green leaves take on a pleasing leaden blue cast in winter.
1.2m/4ft or more. Z8

C. ladanifer is especially well coated in resin, and is known as the gum cistus. The rich green foliage is a fine backdrop for the blotched white flowers, which are slightly sharper in colour than in *C. x cyprius*.
1.2m/4ft or more. Z8

***C. ladanifer* var. *sulcatus* (*C. palhinhae*)** is a small compact shrub with exceptionally large pure white flowers that look stunning against the glistening dark foliage. But it is not very hardy.
60cm/2ft. Z8

C. laurifolius is a good garden *Cistus*, reliably hardy and producing white flowers all summer.
1.2m/4ft or more. Z8

Cistus x argenteus 'Peggy Sammons'

FAR LEFT *Clerodendrum bungei*
LEFT *Cornus mas*

***C.* x *lenis* 'Grayswood Pink' ('Silver Pink')** is a popular hardy hybrid with lilac-pink flowers and greyish foliage. 60cm/2ft. Z7

C.* x *purpureus is excellent for colour in the Mediterranean border. It is a hybrid of two very gummy species and does not disappoint in its scent. 'Alan Fradd' has white flowers. 1.2m/4ft or more. Z8

CLERODENDRUM
Lamiaceae

C. bungei is an invasive colonizer, sending up a forest of vertical stems, and needs to be sited with care. The large heart-shaped leaves, carried on purple stems, have a fetid odour and should be avoided. But the domes of sugary-pink flowers have a wonderfully sweet scent that carries in the air; they appear from rosy buds and make an invaluable splash of clear soft colour for late summer and autumn. It appreciates shelter from wind.
Sun. 1–2m/3–6ft. Z7

C. trichotomum is a deciduous species that makes a proper shrub or small tree, rather sparse in habit and clothed in soft ovate, purplish leaves. The foliage has a fetid odour when bruised. The white flowers smell like jasmine and are carried in loose heads in late summer; they have prominent crimson calyces and the bicoloured effect is pleasing. Later, turquoise blue (ultimately black) fruits appear, which are startling against the persistent crimson calyces. It is susceptible to cold winds and is slow-growing; but it is a splendid ingredient for the end of summer. The variety *fargesii* is hardier and more vigorous. Sun or light shade. 3.5m/12ft or more. Z6

CLETHRA
Clethraceae

C. alnifolia, the sweet pepper bush, is an interesting deciduous shrub for the woodland or bog garden. The sweet, *Viburnum*-like scent comes from the slender spikes of fluffy white flowers that open in high summer. It forms an erect suckering plant and is clothed in toothed leaves. It is useful for its late flowering and its tolerance of wet soil. 'Paniculata' is a superior form.
Sun or shade. Acid soil. 2.5m/8ft. Z4

C. barbinervis is a showier species, with longer white racemes in late summer rather like a *Pieris*, and a good strong scent. The dark leaves can take on good autumn tints. Sun or shade. Acid soil. 2.5m/8ft. Z4

COLLETIA
Rhamnaceae

***C. hystrix* (*C. armata*)** is a strange leafless, and, to all intents and purposes, evergreen, tangle of thorns for the hot, dry border. It looks rather like a gorse bush but the flowers are waxy and white. It billows with blossom all through the autumn and the scent is of almonds. But be careful when you are sniffing it.
Sun. 1.2–2.5m/4–8ft. Z8

***C. paradoxa* (*C. cruciata*)** is even more extraordinary than *C. hystrix*. The grey-green spines are broad, flat and triangular and give the plant a unique appearance. The tiny flowers are creamy-white and sweetly scented but unfortunately are not produced very freely outdoors.
Sun. 1.2–2.5m/4–8ft. Z8

COMPTONIA
Myricaceae

C. peregrina, the sweet fern, is a distinctive, small deciduous shrub for the woodland and bog garden. It has suckering growth and produces downy, fern-like leaves and, in spring, brown catkins. A spicy fragrance rises from the foliage on hot days, and can be captured if the leaves are dried. Sun. 60cm–1.2m/2–4ft. Z2

CORNUS
Cornaceae

C. mas, the cornelian cherry dogwood, emits a penetrating spicy fragrance that can fill a garden in late winter. The problem is that it is a very big shrub or small tree that looks dull for most of the year. The tufts of yellow flowers appear on bare stems and the effect is rather like that of a witch hazel. Sun or light shade. 6–12m/20–40ft. Z5

CORYLOPSIS
Hamamelidaceae

This group of shrubs has a delicate beauty that would probably pass unnoticed if they flowered in summer. But because they bloom in early spring, and look so well with that season's blue-flowered bulbs and perennials, they are worth a place in gardens. They produce short dangling racemes of pale yellow flowers on their bare, spreading branches, and these are delicately, often elusively, primrose-scented.
Light or medium shade. Acid soil.

C. pauciflora makes a low shrub and probably has the best flowers.
1.2–2m/4–6ft. Z6

C. sinensis var. *calvescens* *f. veitchiana* (*C. veitchiana*) is larger and has flowers with striking reddish anthers, and the best scent.
2m/6ft. Z7

C. sinensis var. *sinensis* (*C. willmottiae*) is even taller and makes a fine specimen. Its young leaves are tinged with purple, and there is a form with purple stems called 'Spring Purple'. Up to 3.5m/12ft. Z6

C. spicata is the species most commonly seen.
2m/6ft or more. Z6

CORDYLINE
Asparagaceae

C. australis, the New Zealand cabbage tree, is one of the more exotic-looking plants hardy in the British Isles – though hardy only in the milder counties. With maturity, the clusters of evergreen strap-like leaves are supported on stout limbs and accompanied in early summer with panicles of creamy flowers with a strong, vanilla-laced scent that carries well.
Sun. Well-drained soil. 3.5–7.5m/12–25ft. Z9

Cordyline australis

LEFT *Cytisus* x *praecox* 'Warminster' RIGHT *Daphne pontica*

CYTISUS

Papilionaceae

C. x ***praecox*** **'Warminster'**, the Warminster broom, is the most powerfully scented of the large hardy brooms. It has a heavy, suffocating odour, which many find disagreeable but which, to me, is very much a part of the late spring garden. Its cream pea-flowers are borne in such profusion that the spectacle will take your breath away if the scent does not. There is a good deep yellow form of *C.* x *praecox* called 'Allgold', and a white form called 'Albus'. They are deciduous shrubs, fast-growing but short-lived.

Sun. Acid or neutral soil. 1.2m/4ft. Z6

DAPHNE

Thymelaeaceae

Daphne give the garden some of its most sophisticated perfume. It is a gloriously sweet scent, often shaded with clove. They have a reputation for being difficult to grow and unpredictable, but this should not put you off, especially with the varieties listed here.

D. bholua is a superb shrub for the winter and spring garden. It can be deciduous or evergreen and produces flowers in shades of purplish pink and white. 'Gurkha' is a fine, tough deciduous selection with purple-stained white flowers, and 'Jacqueline Postill' is a splendid evergreen counterpart (liable to damage only in very cold winters) and probably the pick of the group. Since this *Daphne* blooms through the winter, the evergreen and deciduous forms produce quite different effects. 'Darjeeling' is paler in colour and a little less hardy in my experience, but has the advantage of flowering in early winter, well ahead of most other forms.

Light shade. Moist, well-drained soil. 2.5m/8ft or more. Z8

***D.* x *burkwoodii* 'Somerset'** is one of the easiest and most beautiful *Daphne* with a delicious clove scent. Its clusters of pink starry flowers are produced in spring, and have an excellent backdrop in its small bluish-green young leaves. It makes an upright, semi-evergreen shrub. There are gold and silver variegated forms. Sun or light shade. Moist, well-drained soil. 1.2m/4ft. Z6

D. laureola, spurge laurel, is a useful small British native evergreen with tiny yellow flowers that are buried in the shiny foliage and make no visual impact. They open in late winter and early spring and play tricks with their perfume; sometimes they fill the cool evening air with fragrance, but more often than not they are scentless.

Shade. Moist, well-drained soil. 90cm/3ft.

The subspecies *philippi* is 30cm/1ft smaller. Z7

D. mezereum, mezereon, is also native to Britain and does well on chalk soils. In late winter its naked vertical stems are studded with

reddish-purple stars. 'Alba' is a good white form; 'Bowles' White' is even better.
Light shade. Moist, well-drained soil. 1–1.2m/3–4ft. Z5

***D. odora* 'Aureomarginata'** is a hardy form of *D. odora,* and has golden-edged evergreen leaves. It is one of the more popular and reliable *Daphne*, and the scent is rich and fruity. It makes a neat bush and the tight clusters of pinky-purple stars are borne in late spring.
Sun or light shade. Moist, well-drained soil. 1.2m/4ft. Z7

D. pontica flowers a month or so later than *D. laureola* and has narrower leaves, but is otherwise similar.
Shade. 1–1.5m/3–5ft. Z7

DEUTZIA
Hydrangeaceae

The deutzias are a colourful group of deciduous shrubs that flower in early summer. They are dreary after flowering, but a plant in bloom is a fine sight. They are attractive either in the border, with shrub roses and hardy geraniums, or in the less formal parts of the garden.
Sun or light shade. Moist, fertile soil.

D. compacta has billowing heads of small white stars that emerge from pink buds in high summer. The scent is of honey and almonds.
1.5m/5ft. Z6

D. x elegantissima bears its panicles of sweet, rose-pink flowers in early summer. There is a form in deeper pink called 'Rosealind' and one in pale pink called 'Fasciculata'.
1.5m/5ft. Z6

DIPELTA
Caprifoliaceae

D. floribunda is a deciduous shrub that resembles weigela in its foliage and funnel-shaped flowers, though it is more upright in growth. The sweet-scented flowers are white, tinged with pale pink and yellow,

and are carried in generous heads during spring. It thrives in woodland conditions. Light shade. 3–4.5m/10–15ft. Z6

ELAEAGNUS
Elaeagnaceae

E. x ebbingei gives one of the best late season scents. It is evergreen and fast-growing; it can also be

LEFT *Deutzia* x *elegantissima* 'Fasciculata' RIGHT *Elaeagnus* x *ebbingei* ABOVE *Dipelta floribunda*

used for hedging. It is tolerant of shade, though there is a much freer production of flowers in the sun. On warm evenings in autumn, the fruity sweetness from the tiny, concealed, white funnels will fill the air. The leathery green leaves have metallic silver undersides, and are an extraordinary sandy grey when young. Its parent, *E. macrophylla* (Z8), is a more elegant shrub and also deliciously fragrant. The yellow-variegated forms of *E.* x *ebbingei*, 'Gilt Edge' and 'Limelight', are very showy. 3m/10ft. Z7

E. pungens is another quick evergreen. It is less stiff in growth than *E.* x *ebbingei* and its leaves are smaller, with wavy margins and duller undersides. The sweet-scented flowers are also white and produced in autumn. The species itself is seldom grown, for its variegated forms – including the best-selling 'Maculata' – always steal the show.
Sun or shade. 3.5m/12ft. Z7

***E.* 'Quicksilver'** is a superior form of the oleaster or Russian olive. In fact, it is arguably the best silver-leaved shrub in cultivation. The slender leaves are a sparkling silver and the plant develops an extremely graceful shape. The scent, which is piercingly sweet, comes from the minute yellowish flowers which hide under the foliage in early summer. As the centrepiece of a grey border or as a bright contrast to purple-leaved shrubs, it has no equal. In colder climates, it makes a good olive substitute to create a Mediterranean effect. *E. commutata* (*E. argentea*) is a suckering shrub very similar in appearance to 'Quicksilver' but about 1m/3ft shorter (Z2).
Sun. Well-drained soil. 4.5m/15ft. Z4

ELSHOLTZIA
Lamiaceae

E. stauntonii is eyecatching in autumn, when it opens its mauve-pink bottlebrushes. It is not grown much but makes an interesting latecomer for the wilder garden, where its unrefined appearance is not out of place. The leaves release a minty scent when crushed. It is usually killed to ground level each winter, but it should in any case be cut hard back in spring to the lowest pair of buds on each stem. Full sun. Good soil. 1–1.5m/3–5ft. Z5

ERICA
Ericaceae

E. arborea, the tree heath, brings stature to the heather garden and a welcome contrast in shape to Mediterranean schemes of *Cistus* and lavender; it balances a specimen of rosemary rather well. In spring it is a mass of white flowers whose honey fragrance carries far. It is fairly hardy. *Alpina* is a shorter, hardier variety (Z7). Sun. Acid soil. 2m/6ft in cold areas, over 6m/ 20ft in mild areas. Z9

E. erigena (E. mediterranea) is another excellent spring-flowering

LEFT *Erica arborea* var. *alpina* RIGHT *Escallonia rubra* 'Crimson Spire'

Eucryphia x *nymansensis* 'Nymansay'

heather, scented of honey. It is tolerant of lime. There is a lovely pink-flowered form called 'Superba'. And there are many dwarf, compact varieties for the rock garden, among which rose-coloured 'Brightness' and white 'W.T. Rackliff' are exceptional.
Sun. 60cm–2m/2–6ft. Z8

***E.* x *veitchii* 'Exeter'** is a superb, vigorous heather for gardens in milder areas. In spring it produces huge plumes of white flowers with a delicious honey scent.
Sun. Acid soil. 2–3m/6–10ft. Z9

ESCALLONIA
Escalloniaceae

This is a useful group of shrubs that carry heads of white, pink or red blossom at intervals throughout the summer. They are evergreen and have glossy leaves and young shoots that are sticky to the touch and sweetly, if not altogether pleasantly, rosily resinous. They are susceptible to cold and in inland gardens must be given sheltered locations. But they are tolerant of salt-laden wind and are familiar coastal hedging plants. 'C. F. Ball' is an impressive variety bearing masses of large crimson-red flowers all summer. It is vigorous, forms a slightly arching shrub, and is well endowed with fragrance. 'Donard Beauty' has rather large leaves and quantities of rose-red flowers. Sun or light shade. Well-drained soil. 3m/10ft. Z8

E. illinita has a pungent aroma that has been compared to that of a pigsty, but for many people is pure curry. It has white flowers.
Sun or light shade. Well-drained soil. 3m/10ft. Z8

***E. rubra* var. *macrantha* (*E. macrantha*)** has still not been superseded as a coastal hedging plant. It has rosy-red flowers and attractive, fragrant foliage. Its varieties 'Crimson Spire' and rose-pink 'Ingramii' are also good.
Sun or light shade. Well-drained soil. 3m/10ft. Z8

EUCRYPHIA
Cunoniaceae

The eucryphias are among the most exciting large shrubs or small trees for the late summer garden. They are popular with owners of rhododendron woodland, who are looking for shrubs to extend the season. The large, single, pure white flowers, which have a shimmering boss of stamens, exhale a honey scent. But plants may take a few years before starting to bloom. They are columnar or pyramidal in shape and need a position sheltered from the wind. They are not suitable for very cold gardens.
Light shade. Cool, moist, acid soil.

E. glutinosa is the hardiest species, but although it is visually spectacular, its scent is less strong than in other eucryphias. It is deciduous and takes on fiery tints in the autumn. It flowers in high summer.
6m/20ft or more. Z8

***E.* x *intermedia* 'Rostrevor'** is a vigorous, fairly hardy hybrid that blooms in late summer. Its yellow-centred flowers are smaller than in *E. glutinosa* but a shrub smothered in bloom is a glorious sight and has a fine scent. It is evergreen.
6m/20ft or more. Z9

E. lucida is trustworthy only in milder regions but is one of the prettiest evergreen eucryphias. Its white flowers are pendulous and are especially heavily scented.
Ultimately 12m/40ft. Z9

***E.* x *nymansensis* 'Nymansay'** is the most popular eucryphia in England

LEFT *Fothergilla major* Monticola Group RIGHT Broom

and would always be my first choice. Fast-growing, fairly hardy and evergreen, it has an advantage over 'Rostrevor' in its tolerance of limy soil. The white flowers and honey scent are superb and are enjoyed in high summer.
Ultimately 12m/40ft. Z8

FOTHERGILLA
Hamamelidaceae

Fothergilla are deciduous shrubs that help awaken the woodland garden in spring. They produce little cream bottlebrushes as their leaves are expanding. These give off a sweet scent flavoured with hops. Their oval leaves are unremarkable until the autumn when they assume a variety of magnificent, rich colours.
Light shade. Acid soil.

F. gardenii is a dwarf spring-flowering *Fothergilla* for the front of the shady border. 'Blue Mist' is a superb variety with striking blue leaves.
90cm/3ft. Z5

F. major, a slow-growing shrub, is the best species and makes a plump erect subject for squeezing between colourful rhododendrons. It has good glossy foliage, which turns yellow in the autumn, and plenty of scented flower spikes in spring. The Monticola Group are generally more spreading than the usual form of the species. In autumn, the foliage becomes a bonfire of scarlet, orange and gold.
2–3m/6–10ft. Z5

GAULTHERIA
Ericaceae

The gaultherias provide a number of evergreen ground-cover plants for the desperate gardener. At best they are quietly interesting, at worst (*G. shallon*), monstrous invaders.
Sun or shade. Acid soil.

G. forrestii has dark, leathery, oblong leaves and spreads by suckers. Its attraction lies in its fragrant white waxy flowers, which are carried on white-stalked racemes in spring.
30cm–1.5m/1–5ft. Z6

G. procumbens, the wintergreen or partridge berry, is a carpeting plant to grow under rhododendrons and azaleas. It is neat and dwarf, with tiny blush-white lampshades in high summer that are followed by red fruits. It is a little dull for the small garden but particularly useful in large areas of woodland. The aromatic 'wintergreen' scent is evident in all its parts.
15cm/6in. Z3

GENISTA
Papilionaceae

G. aetnensis, the Mount Etna broom, develops into a tree-like specimen and makes a fine arching focal point for a summer herbaceous border, a waterfall of clear brassy yellow for a hot colour scheme. The flowers have a sweet scent and this wafts gently. It is fast-growing but, unlike the cytisus brooms, long-lived. It is perfectly hardy.

LEFT *Hamamelis japonica* 'Zuccariniana' RIGHT *Hamamelis* x *intermedia* 'Pallida'

Sun. All but waterlogged soils.
4.5m/15ft or more. Z8

G. cinerea is a broom that provides a mass of golden-yellow flowers at midsummer, which have the typical fragrance of the pea family. Its specific name refers to the greyish cast of its foliage.

Sun. Well-drained soil. 2–3m/6–10ft.
Z7

HAMAMELIS
Hamamelidaceae

The witch hazels produce their sea-anemone flowers on bare twigs in winter, and are perhaps the most interesting shrubs of that season. The flower scent in the yellow varieties is fruitily or spicily sweet, and becomes more pungent and less sweet in the hotter colours. They develop long outstretched branches, and one of these can be trained vertically to establish early height. The leaves are oval and hazel-like, and have a yellow and flame autumnal colouring.

Sun or light shade. Acid or neutral soil. Ultimately 4.5m/15ft.

H.* x *intermedia varieties provide some lovely red and orange flowers (notably 'Diane' and 'Jelena') but generally lack strong scent – orange 'Aphrodite' is an exception. The yellows are usually richer. Pale yellow 'Moonlight' is a good choice, as is the excellent, very fragrant golden-yellow 'Vesna'. 'Pallida' remains my favourite witch hazel. It makes a spreading shrub with large sulphur-yellow flowers and is wonderfully luminous when silhouetted against sombre evergreens.
Z6

***H. japonica* 'Zuccariniana'** is a splendid late-flowering witch hazel, with small pale lemon-yellow flowers and a powerful scent. It is distinctly erect when young and has good yellow autumn colour.
Z6

H. mollis, the Chinese witch hazel, is the commonest and most popular species. It is very beautiful and floriferous, bearing its clusters of large, golden-yellow flowers through winter and early spring. It has a strong scent which it passes on to its clones. 'Brevipetala' is a vigorous, upright form with orange-yellow flowers; 'Coombe Wood' has rich yellow flowers, slightly larger than in the species, and a more spreading habit; 'Goldcrest' has yellow flowers suffused with red; and 'Wisley Supreme' is an excellent, highly scented rich yellow.
Z6

H. vernalis gives us some small-flowered witch hazels in copper, orange and orange-yellow. 'Sandra' has cadmium-yellow flowers which, like those of its parent, have a particularly pungent scent. Its foliage is more entertaining than most, being purple-tinged in spring and fiery orange and scarlet in autumn.
Z5

LEFT *Hebe cupressoides* CENTRE *Hydrangea anomala* subsp. *petiolaris* RIGHT *Illicium anisatum*

HEBE

Plantaginaceae

Like chrysanthemums and dahlias, the large *Hebe* do have a smell, and yet I would not really classify them as scented plants. It is a smell which will be especially familiar to owners of coastal gardens where these evergreen shrubs are much used as informal hedges, but it is hard to describe beyond saying it is warm, green and wholesome and can also be found in the flowers of *Skimmia*. In fact, one or two large *Hebe* do have scented flowers, too, but this is a different and sweeter fragrance.

H. cupressoides is one of a number of *Hebe* that look decidedly un*Hebe*-like and in its grey-green branches, this species resembles a miniature cypress. The foliage even gives off the resinous scent of cedar to complete the mimicry. It is a neat, small evergreen for combining with heathers and conifers at the front of the border or in the rock garden. The heads of tiny pale blue flowers, produced at high summer, are not very exciting.
Full sun. Fertile, well-drained soil. 60cm–1.2m/2–4ft. Z8

***H.* 'Midsummer Beauty'** is a popular *Hebe* with long racemes of sweetly scented mauve flowers all summer and autumn. It makes a mound of long slender evergreen leaves and is hardy except in the coldest inland gardens.
Full sun. Well-drained soil. 1.2m/4ft. Z8

***H. stenophylla* ('Spender's Seedling')**. This hardy *Hebe* carries racemes of white, sweetly scented flowers during the summer.
Sun. 1.2m/4ft. Z8

HYDRANGEA

Hydrangeaceae

A light scent can be found in many hydrangeas, including varieties of *H. aspera* and *H. paniculata*, and climbing *H. anomala* subsp. *petiolaris*. They are a hugely valuable group of flowering plants for late summer, especially in shady areas.

H. scandens* subsp. *chinensis* f. *macrosepala is a lacecap hydrangea with notably scented white flowers. It has thin leaves and long arching branches. Sun or light shade. Moist, well-drained soil. 3m/10ft.

ILLICIUM

Schisandraceae

I. anisatum is a fleshy-leaved evergreen whose foliage releases the spicy scent of aniseed when crushed. It is not a plant for cold climates but in a sheltered spot in a mild area, in woodland conditions, it does well. The curious spidery flowers are greenish-yellow and are produced in spring. It is slow-growing.
Light shade. 2–6m/6–20ft, depending on locality. Z8

HEPTACODIUM
Caprifoliaceae

H. miconioides is a fairly recent introduction to gardens. A large deciduous shrub, it is valuable for its shapely growth and foliage, and for flowering in the autumn, when it produces clusters of white starry flowers, lightly coconut-scented. It is said to be popular with butterflies, but mine never seems to attract them.
Sun or light shade. 3m/10ft or more. Z5

Heptacodium miconioides

I. floridanum has a fruitier, spicy fragrance and is smaller and more compact. The flowers are maroon-purple and appear in early summer. This American species is even less hardy than its cousin, but it is most definitely worth trying against a warm wall in mild areas.
Sun. Acid soil. 2–2.5m/6–8ft. Z9

I. simonsii is the showiest and most fragrant species, with pale yellow, spicily-scented flowers held among the leathery leaves in spring.
Light shade. Well-drained, acid soil. 2–2.5m/6–8ft.

JUNIPERUS
Cupressaceae

The junipers have a distinctive, pungently fruity scent. Their value lies in their contribution to the garden's evergreen backbone. Not only are they more versatile and tolerant than other conifers but they also come in all shapes and sizes, and a variety of colours. Sun or light shade. Acid or alkaline soil.

J. chinensis, the Chinese juniper, has forms with good columnar and conical habits. 'Pyramidalis' is a fine glaucous blue form over 2m/6ft high. Z4

J. communis, the common juniper, provides a range of evergreens with very different habits: 'Compressa' makes a compact miniature cone for the rock garden or alpine trough; var. *depressa* and 'Depressa Aurea' make prostrate groundcover in green or gold respectively; 'Hibernica', the Irish juniper, used to be the garden designer's favourite when conifers were more in fashion, forms a dense dark column which gradually attains

3m/10ft or more; and 'Hornibrookii' is an excellent carpeter. Z3

J. **'Grey Owl'** is an excellent semi-prostrate juniper with smoky grey-green spreading branches.

J. horizontalis provides more creeping junipers in various colours. Z3

J. x pfitzeriana gives us those interesting spreading junipers with ascending branches, so useful for growing on awkward corners and concealing weak junctions in the garden's groundplan. 'Wilhelm Pfitzer' is a good green form; 'Old Gold' is one of the best yellows.
90cm/3ft or more. Z3

J. procumbens **'Nana'** is a fresh green, prostrate juniper for covering banks.

J. sabina, the savin, is the most pungently scented of all the junipers. The species itself is an attractive, short spreading shrub, up to 1.2m/4ft high; 'Tamariscifolia' is a good prostrate blue-green form. Z3

J. scopulorum **'Skyrocket'** is a superb, slim, vertical juniper, like a blue-grey pencil stroke in the landscape. It grows to 3m/10ft. Z6

J. squamata **'Meyeri'** is a popular, semi-erect, blue juniper.
4.5m/15ft or more. Z5

x LEDODENDRON

Ericaceae

x *L.* 'Arctic Tern' (*Rhododendron* 'Arctic Tern') is a beautiful, *Daphne*-like small shrub, exactly like a white-flowered counterpart to *Rhododendron trichostomum*, which is one of its parents. It has the same resinous scent.
Light shade. Well-drained, acid soil.
90cm/3ft. Z7

LEDUM

Ericaceae

***L. groenlandicum* (*Rhododendron groenlandicum*)**, the Labrador tea, is a useful dwarf evergreen for damp sites. Its dark oval leaves, rust-felted underneath, have the potent scent of rotten fruit. But it is an attractive-looking shrub, and bears clusters of white flowers in late spring.
Sun. Lime-free soil. 60–90cm/2–3ft. Z2

Ledum groenlandicum

LIGUSTRUM

Oleaceae

The heavy, musty-sweet scent of their flowers is not one of the main attractions of the privets. Luckily, when they are grown as hedges, they are prevented from flowering by summer pruning. Those that are given their freedom can always be sited away from paths and from positions where the wind is likely to carry the scent towards you – variegated and golden forms of *L. ovalifolium*, *L. lucidum* and *L. sinense* are highly ornamental as foliage shrubs; green-leaved *L. quihoui* is a valuable late-flowering shrub, with impressive feathery white plumes in autumn.

LINDERA

Lauraceae

L. benzoin, the spice bush, is remarkable mainly for the powerful spicy scent released when the foliage is crushed. It does have other ornamental qualities – its large, rounded leaves turn yellow in the autumn, and, on female plants, the undistinguished greenish flowers are followed by red fruits in the autumn. It grows best in the woodland underdry.
Sun or shade. Lime-free soil. Up to 3.5m/12ft. Z5

LONICERA

Caprifoliaceae

The shrubby honeysuckles are rarely as generous with their scent as the climbers, nor are they so visually

RIGHT *Lonicera fragrantissima*
FAR RIGHT *Lonicera standishii*
BELOW *Lupinus arboreus*

spectacular. But many do have fragrant flowers; even the evergreen hedging honeysuckle, *L. nitida* (especially good in the clone 'Fertilis'), and the ground-covering species *L. pileata*, can surprise you with their fruity sweetness. For garden ornament, the most interesting are the winter-flowering sorts, and those with unusual foliage.

L. fragrantissima, *L. standishii* and their hybrid *L.* x *purpusii* ('Winter Beauty' is a good form) are all very similar and it is hard to decide which is the best. They produce tiny clusters of small cream flowers all through the winter on more or less deciduous stems; bare branches are clearly an advantage in displaying the flowers, and *L. fragrantissima* usually loses out on this score, although it seems to be the most floriferous. They are all ungainly in summer, being inelegant of habit and clothed in large coarse leaves, and only detract from their companions in the border. Nevertheless they are intensely sweet at close range, and I always grow one to cut for indoors and usually choose *L.* x *purpusii*.
Sun or shade. 2m/6ft.

L. syringantha is the prettiest of the fragrant summer-flowering shrubby honeysuckles. Its blue-green leaves, reddish-purple stems and arching habit make it a lovely foil for pink flowers in the sunny border, and in early summer it bears its own clusters of small lilac funnels; they seldom make much of a show but they have a delicious hyacinth scent. To encourage fine foliage, prune it hard.
Full sun. Up to 2m/6ft. Z5

LUPINUS
Papilionaceae

L. arboreus, the tree lupin, is a much-neglected shrub. Easily raised from seed and fast-growing, it provides a wonderful contrast in form for the summer garden, making a mound of fingered, evergreen leaves and producing its erect racemes of yellow, pea-scented flowers for a full four months; their fragrance carries on the air. It looks as well in the shrub border as it does on a bank silhouetted against grass. Unfortunately, it is short-lived.
Sun. Well-drained, fertile soil. 2m/6ft. Z8

MAGNOLIA
Magnoliaceae

The scent of magnolia flowers is as exotic as their appearance. Many have the fragrance of tropical fruit with a subtle shading of eastern spice, but it varies from one variety to another. The commonly grown star magnolia, *M. stellata* (Z4), which produces spidery white flowers on bare branches in early spring, is relatively poorly endowed, as are many of the popular tulip- and lily-flowered forms of *M.* x *soulangeana* (Z5) and *M. liliiflora* (Z6). But there are also some notable scented hybrids:

M. 'Apollo' has large open flowers in a rich lilac-pink and a fine scent.
4.5m/15ft. Z6

Magnolia x wieseneri

M. 'Charles Coates' is a superb hybrid whose flowers resemble those of *M. sieboldii*, but they are held erect instead of nodding. They have a fruity fragrance.
9m/30ft or more. Z6

M. 'Heaven Scent' has very fragrant goblet-shaped flowers in gradations of deep lilac-pink and blush.
6m/20ft. Z5

M. 'Jane'. This upright hybrid bears reddish-purple starry flowers, white inside, in late spring and has a rich scent. Sun. Retentive, acid soil preferred. 4.5m/15ft. Z5

M. sieboldii is an attractive spreading magnolia whose white lemon-scented cups appear on and off throughout the summer. These have prominent dark rose stamens and nod on long stalks. The crimson fruits are also eyecatching.
Sun or light shade. Neutral or lime-free soil. 3.5–4.5m/12–15ft. Z6

M. sieboldii* subsp. *sinensis is my favourite summer-flowering magnolia. Its laundry-white cups, with their boss of crimson stamens, are downturned, and looking up through their branches is an experience to be savoured. The flowers have a deliciously rich fruity scent in which lemon is the dominant note. *M. wilsonii* is similar but has narrower leaves and smaller flowers.
Sun or light shade. All but very alkaline soils. 6m/20ft. Z6

***M. x soulangeana* 'Picture'** is a vigorous soulangeana hybrid with a good scent. The white goblets are flushed with purplish-pink. 'Sundew' is a seedling from 'Picture' with fragrant creamy-white flowers.
Sun. 6m/20ft. Z5

M. 'Susan' bears fragrant, purplish-pink, starry flowers on its bare branches in mid-spring.
Sun. Retentive, acid soil preferred.
3.5m/12ft. Z5

***M. x wieseneri* (*M. x watsonii*)**, another magnolia for warmer regions, has one of the most powerful scents of all – a glorious tropical fruit cocktail. The large, upward-facing flowers are creamy-white with rose-crimson stamens, and appear at midsummer among the sizeable leathery leaves.
Sun or light shade. All but strongly alkaline soils. 6m/20ft. Z6

***M. yunnanensis* (*Michelia yunnanensis*)**. This and ***M. maudiae* (*Michelia maudiae*)** have only recently become available to gardeners and are exciting new scented additions. Flowering in early summer, they look like small-flowered magnolias, and have the same deliciously rich fruity scent as *Magnolia grandiflora*. *M. yunnanensis* opens cream flowers from soft suede-brown buds, and has glossy green foliage. It can be clipped to shape. I have found it very hardy in my garden, coming unscathed through a winter that killed other evergreens. 3m/10ft. Z8

M. maudiae has long grey-green leaves and white flowers. Moist, well-drained soil. Sun or light shade.
4.5m/15ft. Z8

MAHONIA
Berberidaceae

M. aquifolium, the Oregon grape, provides useful evergreen groundcover for shade, though for ornament I always choose its bronzy form 'Atropurpurea', 'Apollo', or the hybrid *M. x wagneri* 'Undulata' in preference. Its polished, holly-like leaflets are burnished with purple in winter, and in spring the dense heads of yellow bells make a bright

FAR LEFT *Magnolia* 'Heaven Scent'
LEFT *Mahonia aquifolium*
BELOW *Mitchella repens*

of yellow flowers, scented of lily of the valley. It makes a vertical, architectural shrub and, although it is not as elegant in leaf as *M. lomariifolia, M.* x *media* 'Lionel Fortescue' and *M.* x *media* 'Buckland', it is a useful evergreen feature.
Sun or shade.
3m/10ft or more. Z8

contrast. The scent is of honey and it fills the air. Blue-black berries succeed the flowers.
Sun or shade. Any soil. 1–2m/3–6ft; 'Undulata' is taller. Z5
M. japonica has a lily-of-the-valley scent. This comes from lax racemes of yellow flowers, borne from late autumn until early spring. It is one of the best winter performers with evergreen holly-like foliage. It differs from 'Charity' in shape as well as flower: it is dense and spreading, rather than gaunt and upright.
M. japonica Bealei Group is similar to *M. japonica* but its racemes of flowers are shorter and more or less erect (Z4).
Sun or shade. 3m/10ft. Z7
M. lomariifolia is, without doubt, the aristocrat among *Mahonia*, though its scent is weak. It is erect in growth and bears erect racemes densely packed with flowers in early winter. But its main attraction lies in its evergreen foliage which is finer, with smaller leaflets, than in other species. It is not completely hardy, alas, and outside mild areas is often grown as a wall shrub – in this location mine has hardly suffered in even the coldest winters. *M.* x *media* 'Lionel Fortescue' and 'Buckland' are only slightly coarser and are good substitutes for colder gardens.
Sun or shade. Up to 3.5m/12ft. Z9
***M.* x *media* 'Charity'** is the most popular of those early winter-flowering *Mahonia* in Britain that give more or less erect racemes

MITCHELLA
Rubiaceae

M. repens, partridge berry, is a prostrate evergreen ground-cover shrub with fragrant white jasmine-like flowers at midsummer, followed by red berries. Shade. Z6

MYRICA
Myricaceae

M. cerifera, the wax myrtle, is a large, more or less evergreen shrub

with narrow, glossy, aromatic leaves. Its white winter fruits have a covering of wax which is used to make fragrant candles.
Sun. Damp, acid soil. 9m/30ft or more. Z6

M. gale, the sweet gale or bog myrtle, is the best known of its genus, and is useful for damp spots on acid, preferably peaty, soil. The whole plant releases a sweetly resinous aroma when bruised. It is a deciduous shrub, with narrow tapering leaves. Tiny golden-brown catkins, males and females on separate plants, are borne on the bare stems in early spring.
Sun. 1–1.2m/3–4ft. Z4

M. pensylvanica, the bayberry, is useful for a very different problem site: arid soil, especially in coastal areas. It is a bigger plant than sweet gale, with oblong aromatic foliage and grey fruits in winter, but is also deciduous.
Sun. Acid soil. 2m/6ft. Z3

NEOLITSEA
Lauraceae

N. sericea is a large and handsome shrub with glossy and aromatic evergreen leaves, which are grey-brown when young. Clusters of greenish flowers appear in autumn. It succeeds outside in sheltered spots in the milder areas.
Sun or light shade. Moist, well-drained soil. 6m/20ft. Z9

OEMLERIA
Rosaceae

O. cerasiformis produces pendent clusters of powerfully vanilla-scented white flowers in late winter just as its fresh green leaves are appearing. I grow it beside the drive, in spite of its dull summer appearance, because it is such a delicious encounter on a cold day. It is easily grown, and could be incorporated into a wild-style hedge.
Sun or shade. 3m/10ft. Z3

OLEARIA
Asteraceae

Most of the Australasian daisy bushes are too tender to be grown outdoors except in the mildest areas. Those listed here are the hardier sorts, ideal for sheltered sunny borders or, in coastal regions, for hedges. The evergreen foliage is usually scented of musk, but the flowers often have a sweet hawthorn fragrance.

O. x haastii is the hardiest and thus the most commonly seen daisy bush in Britain. It is a bushy evergreen with small, dark, leathery leaves that are white-felted underneath. It produces its scented white flowerheads in high summer. This is a useful hedging plant on the coast.
Sun. Well-drained soil. 1.2–2.7m/4–9ft. Z8

O. ilicifolia is an attractive species with grey-green, toothed leaves, white-felted underneath, which bears heads of scented white flowers at

LEFT *Oemleria cerasiformis* RIGHT *Olearia macrodonta*

midsummer. Its foliage has a strong musk scent. It is reliably hardy in many areas and is more impressive than the commoner *O.* x *haastii*.
Sun. Well-drained soil. 3m/10ft. Z9

O. macrodonta, the New Zealand holly, is a vigorous shrub with glossy, silvery-green, holly-like leaves scented of musk and generous heads of fragrant white flowers in summer. It is an excellent screening plant for maritime areas.
Sun. Well-drained soil. 2.7m/9ft. Z9

O. nummulariifolia is a distinctive species with small, stubby, yellow-green leaves. Its white flowers, borne in midsummer, although not as eyecatching as in other species, have the delicate scent of heliotrope.
Sun. Well-drained soil. 2.7m/9ft. Z9

ORIXA
Rutaceae

O. japonica, Japanese orixa, is an unusual deciduous shrub of spreading habit, whose bright green leaves have a spicy orange scent when crushed. It is at its most lovely in the autumn when the foliage turns the palest shade of yellow; the flowers, green and borne in spring, are less impressive.
Sun or light shade. Any well-drained soil. 2.5m/8ft. Z6

OSMANTHUS
Oleaceae

This is an invaluable genus of scented evergreen shrubs. The small-leaved species can be clipped into quite formal shapes and can also be used as hedging. They thrive in nearly all soils and all positions and some are reliably hardy to Zone 6. The scent comes from their clusters of white jasmine-like flowers and is normally piercingly sweet.

O. armatus has long, slender, dark, leathery leaves with prominently toothed edges and is quite distinct from its cousins. Funnily enough, this autumn-flowering species is seldom grown, offered or discussed; but it is a most attractive shrub. The scent is of bubblegum.
Sun or shade. 2.5–4.5m/8–15ft. Z7

***O.* x *burkwoodii* (x *Osmarea burkwoodii*)**, a popular hybrid osmanthus, has a dense habit and small, dark leaves. The flowers appear in spring and their scent of honey and vanilla fills the air on a warm still day. It is an easy, slowish-growing plant, reliable even on thin chalk.
Sun or shade. To 3m/10ft. Z7

***O. decorus* (*Phillyrea decora*)**, an excellent spring-flowering shrub, is distinguished by its large untoothed leaves.
Sun or shade. 3m/10ft. Z7

O. delavayi is a parent of *O.* x *burkwoodii* and is very similar though very slow-growing and usually a much smaller shrub. It produces a mass of white blossom in spring, with the unmistakable scent of suntan lotion.
Sun or shade. 3m/10ft. Z8

O. heterophyllus has holly-like leaves. There are a number of coloured versions of this species, which flowers in autumn. Its dense, slow-growing habit lends it to hedge work.
Sun or shade. 3m/10ft. Z7

O. yunnanensis produces flowers in late winter but its main attraction is its superb foliage; the leaves are long, exotic and toothed. It is faster growing than many of its cousins but is less hardy, and is suitable only for warmer areas.
Sun or shade. Often 9m/30ft or more. Z9

Osmanthus x *burkwoodii*

LEFT *Paeonia rockii* RIGHT *Philadelphus* 'Manteau d'Hermine'

OZOTHAMNUS
Asteraceae

O. ledifolius (Helichrysum ledifolium) is an interesting small dense evergreen for the sheltered sunny border. The young shoots and the undersides of the small leathery leaves have a sticky yellow covering which smells strongly of fruit cake. It is also inflammable and gives the shrub the name of 'kerosene bush' in its native Tasmania. The heads of murky white flowers are powerfully honey-scented at midsummer.
Sun. Well-drained soil. 90cm/3ft. Z9

PACHYSANDRA
Buxaceae

P. axillaris is a low colonizing ground-cover shrub with serrated edges to its broad evergreen leaves and inconspicuous pale pink, scented flowers, resembling those of *Sarcococca*, in early spring.
Shade. Moist, well-drained soil. 15cm/6in. Z7

PAEONIA
Paeoniaceae

P. delavayi is one of the richest endowed of the tree peonies for scent – a fruit cocktail fragrance. It is a suckering shrub with handsome, finely-cut leaves and large flowers of a sumptuous deep red filled with a boss of yellow stamens. In some forms, including the one I grow, the leaves unfurl in lovely tints of crimson and grey and retain this through the early summer flowering period; in other forms the leaves turn green just before flowering: the effect is quite different.
1.5m/5ft. Sun or light shade. Most soils. Z5.

P. rockii is famed for its large semi-double flowers in early summer, which in its best forms are white with prominent damson-black blotches. Many of these have a strong, cleanly sweet fragrance. The elegantly cut leaves often open a beautiful glaucous grey-green flushed with purple. It is one of the most coveted of all garden shrubs.
2m/6ft. Sun or light shade. Most soils. Z5

PEROVSKIA
Lamiaceae

P. atriplicifolia, Russian sage, is treated much like a herbaceous perennial in that it is cut to the ground in early spring. You then get erect, fresh white shoots, clad in grey, finely-cut leaves which are scented of turpentine. In late summer they are topped with tall, thin plumes of violet flowers. You need a group to make any real impression and may have to stake gently, but it is worth treating this plant seriously because it can give an excellent late show. It is a good companion for red and purple fuchsias, such as the hardy 'Mrs Popple'. 'Blue Spire' is a superior form.
Full sun. Good soil. 90cm/3ft. Z6

PHILADELPHUS
Hydrangeaceae

The fruity scents of *Philadelphus*, ranging from heady mock-orange to pure pineapple, are among the fragrant highlights of the year. There are so many desirable species and varieties available that it is hard to make a choice, but in your deliberations about relative heights and flower size, you might also consider strength of scent. Some are overpowering; others are much more subtle. They all flower around midsummer. For the rest of the year they are somewhat dull, having a relaxed habit and unremarkable foliage (except in the golden and variegated forms of *P. coronarius*). Old flowering shoots should be pruned to within 2.5cm/1in of the old wood immediately after flowering. Sun or medium shade. All soils, even chalk.

P. 'Avalanche' has pure white, single flowers, profusely borne and richly scented. It makes a semi-erect shrub and has small leaves.
1.5m/5ft. Z5

P. 'Beauclerk' has large, single, broad-petalled flowers that are white with a central flush of pink. They have a delicious scent that is not too strong. It makes a spreading shrub.
2.5m/8ft. Z5

P. 'Belle Etoile' is one of the best varieties. It has a measured fragrance and is very free with its white, crimson-flushed flowers.
1.5m/5ft. Z5

P. coronarius, the familiar mock-orange of cottage gardens, has an overwhelming fragrance. Plant it on the garden's boundary so that it reaches you in moderation. It makes a large, upright shrub (to 3.5m/12ft) with single, creamy-white flowers. The golden ('Aureus') and white-variegated ('Variegatus') forms are among the best coloured foliage shrubs; they are smaller, easier on the nose, and best in light shade.
Z5

***P. maculatus* 'Mexican Jewel'** is a recent addition to gardens and I rate it the best scented of all *Philadelphus* – a refined fruity, sweet shop perfume, well laced with pineapple. The purple-blotched white flowers are quite angular and appear above the haze of tiny leaves. It is not as hardy as the others but in my garden has not been troubled by cold winters.
2m/6ft. Z8

P. 'Manteau d'Hermine' is a superb, short, compact *Philadelphus* for the front of the border. It has small leaves and pure white, double flowers and is deservedly one of the most popular varieties.
1–1.2m/3–4ft. Z5

P. microphyllus is an attractive species with small leaves and richly pineapple-scented, single white flowers in early summer. It makes a compact, bushy shrub.
Full sun. 2m/6ft. Z6

P. 'Sybille' has almost-square flowers, arching branches and white, crimson-stained flowers. Its fragrance is delicious.
1.5m/5ft. Z5

P. 'Virginal' bears pure, double white flowers and has a magnificent scent. It is large and erect.
2.7m/9ft. Z5

PHILLYREA
Oleaceae

The most valuable species for scent, *P. decora,* is now listed under *Osmanthus,* but the two other species are also worthy. Both are interesting, more or less hardy, large evergreens.
Sun or shade. All soils.

Philadelphus 'Beauclerk'

PONCIRUS
Rutaceae

***P. trifoliata* (*Citrus trifoliata*)**, the Japanese bitter orange, is a thorny deciduous shrub at its peak in spring when it carries its large, white starry flowers on bare green branches. The scent from the flowers is the sweet bubblegum scent of the *Citrus* family. In mild areas these are followed by small downy oranges. It is perfectly hardy and makes a very interesting feature, or it can be clipped and used as an impenetrable hedge.
Full sun. Fertile, well-drained soil. 2.5m/8ft shrub to 6m/20ft tree. Z8

Poncirus trifoliata

P. angustifolia makes a compact dome of narrow, dark leaves and bears clusters of sweetly scented flowers in early summer.
3m/10ft. Z8
P. latifolia has dull white, less fragrant flowers. But it bears small glossy leaves on arching branches, and is an excellent foliage feature, resembling a dwarf holm oak.
4.5m/15ft or more. Z8

PIERIS
Ericaceae

This is a genus of attractive, lime-hating evergreens for the shady border. They are very useful in rhododendron woodland, contributing panicles of pitcher-shaped flowers in spring that look like those of lily of the valley. The scent shades from lily of the valley to vanilla. The foliage is slender, dark and leathery and in many varieties is brilliant red when young. They need a location that is well protected from the cold winds of spring.
Light shade. Acid soil.
***P.* 'Forest Flame'** is one of the hardiest and more vigorous varieties with striking new red growth in spring. It produces large drooping panicles of scented flowers.
3m/10ft or more. Z7
P. formosa* var. *forrestii is probably the best *Pieris*, with brilliant young foliage and long panicles of flowers. It is not for cold gardens, however. There are two excellent selections in 'Jermyns', with particularly rich colouring of new growth and inflorescence, and 'Wakehurst', which has broader foliage.
3m/10ft or more. Z8

LEFT *Pieris japonica* 'Christmas Cheer' RIGHT *Pieris japonica* 'Firecrest'

P. japonica is a beautiful foliage shrub, glossy-leaved with its young growth tinged with copper. Its flowers hang in elegant panicles. But its young shoots are quite susceptible to frost damage, and gardeners in cold areas should plump for its variety 'Christmas Cheer' with rose-flushed flowers. 'Firecrest' is also good.
1.5–3m/5–10ft. Z6

RHODODENDRON
Ericaceae

This important genus provides the garden with some wonderful scents, sweet, spicy and aromatic. For spring colour and diversity of size and form, it has no rivals. However, the large hybrids, with their huge, exotic heads of flowers, and the richly coloured species are seldom scented. Scent is concentrated mainly among the deciduous azaleas and a range of white-flowered species. Many of the latter are tender, and have been listed under Tender Plants.
Light shade. Retentive but well-drained, lime-free soil.

R. arborescens is a large deciduous azalea which blooms usefully late, in early to midsummer. The funnel-shaped flowers are white, tinged with pink and with protruding red stamens, and are fruitily sweet-scented. The foliage is glossy and often has good autumn colour. It is not grown very much but it is extremely attractive. Up to 6m/20ft. Z5

R. atlanticum is an attractive deciduous azalea from the eastern United States with small white, often pink-tinged flowers borne in spring which have a rich, spicy, rose scent. It is stoloniferous and makes a large clump under ideal conditions.
Sun or light shade. Deep, damp soil. Up to 1.5m/5ft. Z6

R. auriculatum flowers in high summer. It is an evergreen rhododendron with very large, dark, leathery leaves and huge trusses of large white flowers that are spicily sweet. It needs shade from strong sunshine, and grows best in mild climates, where a long growing season ensures that the young shoots ripen properly before the early frosts. Its white-flowered hybrid 'Polar Bear' is more showy; 'Argosy', white with a crimson basal stain, is also good.
4.5m/15ft or more. Z6

R. ciliatum is a pretty rhododendron with hairy, oval leaves and clusters of bell-shaped flowers in spring. The flowers open pink from rose-red buds and are spicily sweet. It makes a neat evergreen dome for the front of the shady border, but needs protection from cold winds and early frosts.
1–1.2m/3–4ft. Z8

R. decorum, a splendid large evergreen rhododendron with leathery leaves, produces impressive

LEFT *Rhododendron luteum* RIGHT *Rhododendron occidentale*

lax trusses of white or pale pink, fruitily scented flowers in early summer. It is a variable species and some of the best forms are rather tender.
Up to 7.5m/25ft. Z7
R. fortunei bears clusters of pale lilac-pink, scented, bell-shaped flowers in spring. It is an attractive rhododendron, well worth growing, but for southern gardens its subspecies *discolor* is even better; this has huge trusses of blush-pink flowers from early summer. Both have given rise to some truly splendid hybrids that have inherited their parents' scent, among which 'Albatross', a magnificent large shrub with lax trusses of richly scented white trumpets, and the Loderi clones, listed below, stand supreme.
3m/10ft or more. Z7
R. glaucophyllum is interesting for its resinous scented foliage, reminiscent of saddle soap, but it is not in the front rank of rhododendrons. It makes a bushy evergreen shrub with slender dark leaves, white beneath, and produces heads of rosy flowers in springtime.
1–2m/3–6ft. Z8
R. griffithianum has very large white flowers, well scented, in spring. It requires shelter.
4.5m/15ft. Z8
R. heliolepis has strongly aromatic, evergreen, glossy leaves but its rosy-purple, crimson-marked flowers, borne in small clusters in early summer, are unscented. Its subspecies *brevistylum* is similar but blooms slightly later.
3m/10ft. Z8
R. Loderi Group provides some of the most exciting of the large scented rhododendrons. The finest is probably 'Loderi King George'. This makes a substantial, vigorous, evergreen shrub clad in large, mid-green leaves and in spring bears huge trusses of funnel-shaped flowers. These are white, blush-pink in bud, and have a light but marvellous spicy, fruity fragrance. 'Loderi Pink Diamond' is an excellent pale pink version. The Loderi hybrids are best planted alongside a path and encouraged to arch over, so that you can reach up to the flowers. The bare stems are beautifully coloured and flaked.
Light shade, sheltered from cold winds.
Up to 7.5m/25ft. Z8
R. luteum is the yellow deciduous azalea commonly encountered in woodland gardens. Its fruity honeysuckle fragrance fills the spring air and comes from beautiful heads of tubular, bright yellow flowers. It is a deciduous shrub and in autumn its slender leaves assume crimson and orange tints. In spite of a deluge of rival hybrid azaleas, this remains one of the glories of the spring garden, stunning among bluebells.
Sun or light shade. 2.5m/8ft. Z5
R. moupinense, an attractive short

evergreen rhododendron, is ideal for the front of the border or the rock garden. It bears its large white or pink, sweetly scented flowers singly or in small clusters in late winter and although they are frequently spoiled by frost, they are lovely in a mild spell. The leaves are leathery and oval.
Up to 1.2m/4ft. Z7

R.* x *mucronatum makes a small spreading evergreen rhododendron and produces pure white, sweetly scented, funnel-shaped flowers in spring.
Up to 1.2m/4ft. Z6

R. occidentale is a deciduous shrub valuable for extending the azalea season well into early summer. It has cream or pale pink flowers, stained in yellow, and a delicious honeysuckle fragrance. It gives good autumn colour. In its best forms this is a lovely species, which has been much used for hybridizing.
2.5m/8ft. Z6

***R. prinophyllum* (*R. roseum*)**, the roseshell azalea, is another desirable species of deciduous azalea, but this time with clear deep pink flowers in spring and a scent of clove.
2.5m/8ft. Z3

R. rubiginosum, a large, upright rhododendron, has aromatic, lance-shaped leaves and pink or rosy-lilac flowers in late spring.
6m/20ft. Z6

R. saluenense is a small aromatic evergreen rhododendron with small, dark, glossy leaves. It produces clusters of rosy-purple flowers in the spring.
Up to 1.2m/4ft. Z6

R. serotinum is one of the last rhododendrons to flower, in late summer. It is a lax-growing evergreen with large, sweetly scented, bell-shaped flowers, tinged and spotted with pink.
3m/10ft or more. Z8

R. trichostomum is a favourite of mine. Often mistaken for a *Daphne*, it has small narrow leaves and tight heads of tubular flowers in spring. These can be white, pale pink or rose and are strongly scented of clove. This evergreen enjoys a more sunny spot and is so dainty and so unlike a rhododendron that it can easily be accommodated in mixed plantings.
Up to 1.2m/4ft. Z7

R. 'Turnstone' is a short, compact hybrid which inherits rich lily fragrance from tender *R. edgeworthii* but hardiness from its other parent, *R. moupinense*. I am finding it a very reliable plant outside in my garden. The flowers are soft pink.
Up to 90cm/3ft. Z8

R. viscosum, the swamp honeysuckle, is a bushy deciduous azalea with a magnificent spicy sweet fragrance. It performs late – in early summer – and produces clusters of white, pink-flushed, funnel-shaped flowers. It usually colours well in the autumn. It tolerates but does not need damp ground.
2.5m/8ft. Z3

R. yedoense* var. *poukhanense, the Korean azalea, is a spreading deciduous shrub bearing small clusters of sweetly scented, rosy-purple flowers in spring. It also gives good autumn colour.
1.2m/4ft. Z5

Azalea hybrids

There are a huge number of colourful deciduous azalea hybrids and many have that delicious sweet honeysuckle scent. The Ghent group usually have elegant, long funnelled flowers, good autumn foliage and strong scent: 'Daviesii' is

Rhododendron trichostomum

white with a yellow centre; 'Nancy Waterer' is a rich golden-yellow; and 'Narcissiflorum' is a double, clear yellow and a first-rate, compact plant. They are reliable, hardy shrubs.
1.5m/5ft.

The Knap Hill group have impressive trumpet-shaped flowers and good autumn foliage. The flower colours are generally much more vivid than the Ghents but the scent is usually weak or absent: 'Lapwing', in creamy yellow, flushed pink, and 'Whitethroat', a fine double white with compact growth, are notable exceptions.
1.5m/5ft. Z5

The Mollis group bear striking large trumpet flowers in late spring. But they invariably disappoint the nose and they are also susceptible to late frosts.
1.2m/4ft.

The Occidentale group have round full trusses of flowers which are especially well scented though not usually of brilliant hue. They have a long flowering period in early summer and good autumn foliage: 'Exquisitum' is flesh-pink with an orange flash; 'Irene Koster', the best variety, is smaller-flowered, pink-flushed white.
1.5m/5ft. Z7

Azaleodendrons are hybrids between deciduous azaleas and evergreen rhododendrons. They have the habit of azaleas but are semi-evergreen. Some have a good fragrance, notably 'Govenianum', an erect, compact shrub with lilac-purple flowers, and 'Odoratum', a small bushy shrub with pale lilac flowers, both of which are now rare. They flower in summer.
1.2–1.5m/4–5ft.

A new race of late-flowering azalea hybrids has been bred by Mr Denny Pratt of Cheshire, England. Some inherit strong scent from *R. viscosum* and *R. occidentale,* while colour is furnished by *R. bakeri* and the Knap Hill hybrids. 'Anneke', in gold and yellow, and 'Summer Fragrance', in cream and yellow, both of which are richly and fruitily fragrant, are among the better known. They bloom around midsummer.
2–2.5m/6–8ft.

RHUS
Anacardiaceae

R. aromatica is sometimes grown in gardens in its native eastern United States but is uncommon in Britain. Its chief attraction is its handsome, three-fingered leaves, which release an appealing resinous aroma when bruised, but the dense clusters of yellowish flowers in spring are also of merit. It makes a spreading, deciduous shrub.
Sun. 1–1.5m/3–5ft. Z3

RIBES
Grossulariaceae

R. odoratum, the clove currant, is quite unlike the common flowering currant, described below. It makes a lax, erect shrub clothed in shiny, fresh green, lobed leaves which take on fiery autumn tints. Its scent comes

LEFT *Rhus aromatica* RIGHT *Ribes odoratum*

from the golden-yellow flowers, which appear on short racemes in spring, and is of clove. It makes an attractive and unusual addition to the border. Sun or light shade. 2–2.5m/6–8ft. Z5

R. sanguineum, the flowering currant, haunts every old shrub border and I find its minty-sweet, sweaty leaf scent, which hangs in the air, extremely unpleasant. I cannot imagine anyone choosing this shrub specifically for its fragrance, but the dangling racemes, which appear in spring, are highly ornamental and come in pink, red, crimson and white. The leaf scent is less offensive in the pale and white-flowered forms such as the excellent 'White Icicle'; the flowers are scentless. It is deciduous and shade tolerant.
2–2.5m/6–8ft. Z6

RUBUS
Rosaceae

R. odoratus, flowering raspberry, suffers from having an excess quantity of large, vine-like leaves in proportion to its heads of flower; it is also a vigorous colonizer. But for the wild garden, this deciduous shrub is a desirable ingredient. The single, bright pink flowers, which are carried in clusters atop the stems for a long period during the summer, are mildly fragrant, while the young shoots have a scent of resin.
Sun or shade. 2.5m/8ft. Z4

SALIX
Salicaceae

***S. aegyptiaca* (*S. medemii*)**. You may not think of willows as being a likely source of garden scent, but some have aromatic foliage (the bay willow, *S. pentandra* – described under Trees – and the rare balsam willow, *S. pyrifolia*, for example) and some have scented catkins (including the almond-leaved willow, *S. triandra*, used for basket-making). Of the latter, the musk willow, *S. aegyptiaca*, is the most potently sweet. Perfumed drinks were made from its male catkins and they were even eaten as sweetmeats. The catkins are conspicuously large and bright yellow and are produced on the bare greyish twigs in late winter. It is a large, vigorous shrub, with lanceolate leaves.
Sun or light shade. All but dry soils.
4.5m/15ft. Z6

Sambucus nigra

SAMBUCUS
Adoxaceae

Elder flowers have a heavy musky scent that will not appeal to all noses. Elders are very useful, fast-growing, deciduous shrubs which thrive anywhere. In the wildlife garden the common elder is an important specimen or hedgerow plant, popular with insects when in flower and with birds when in berry. Elsewhere, it is the coloured and cut-leaved varieties that are most valuable, as background foliage to fleeting border flowers.
Sun or shade. All soils.

S. nigra, the common elder, has large flat heads of cream flowers in early summer, followed by generous bunches of black berries. It comes in many leaf colours, including a bewitching sombre purple and a striking golden-variegated form, and is also available in a good ferny form called 'Laciniata'. Subspecies *canadensis* 'Maxima' produces massive flowerheads.
From 3m/10ft to small tree size. Z6

***S. racemosa* 'Plumosa Aurea'** is the finest of the golden-leaved elders and arguably the best golden shrub in cultivation. It has beautiful cut foliage, tan when young, and puffs of yellow flowers in early summer; these are occasionally followed by a splendid show of scarlet berries. The foliage scorches in strong sunlight so a lightly shaded position is best.
2.5m/8ft. Z5

SARCOCOCCA
Buxaceae

The sweet or Christmas boxes should be in every garden. They are unassuming dwarf or small evergreens that produce tufts of flowers in late winter. The flowers are inconspicuous but release a powerful rich honey scent into the air. They are good companions for hellebores and *Mahonia*, which flower simultaneously,

FAR LEFT *Sarcococca hookeriana* var. *humilis*
LEFT *Skimmia japonica* 'Rubella'

and are handy for tucking into narrow beds.
Shade. All but very dry soils.

S. confusa makes a bushy spreading shrub. It has long, slender, pointed leaves, fresh green and glossy, and creamy flowers followed by small black fruits.
1.5m/5ft. Z6

S. hookeriana* var. *digyna is one of the more commonly offered forms. It has slender, purplish-green leaves borne on upright branches. The flowers are pink-tinged and are followed by black fruits.
Up to 1.2m/4ft. Z6

S. hookeriana* var. *humilis, another popular form, is a dwarf suckering shrub with beautiful dark shiny foliage that makes cushions of greenery for the front of the shady border. The creamy flowers are followed by black berries.
Up to 60cm/2ft. Z6

S. ruscifolia. The variety *chinensis* is preferable to the species itself, being more vigorous. It is similar in appearance to *S. confusa* but the berries are red.
1.5m/5ft. Z8

SKIMMIA
Rutaceae

This group of small evergreens make good plants for shady borders and tubs, but they dislike strongly alkaline soils. Gardeners on chalk or lime can grow them in ericaceous compost and water them with rainwater. *Skimmia* have narrowly oval, leathery leaves and make neat, dense, dome-shaped shrubs. The panicles of flowers carried in spring are scented – the fragrance shades from lily of the valley to one reminiscent of *Hebe*. On female plants the flowers are followed by prominent clusters of scarlet fruits in the autumn. You need a male plant in the group for berries to be borne.

S. anquetilia is not common, but highly desirable for the scented garden because of its foliage which has a fruitily aromatic fragrance when crushed. I have found it an easy plant in my garden, making a small compact evergreen shrub, and producing good red fruits.
90cm/3ft. Z8

***S. x confusa* 'Kew Green'** is one of the best *Skimmia* for flowers, with its panicles turning from green to creamy yellow. It is male but a poor pollinator.
90cm/3ft. Z8

S. japonica has produced an array of excellent plants. *S. japonica* 'Veitchii' (usually sold as *S.* 'Foremanii') is a vigorous female with fine fruits; 'Nymans' is also good. The males bear the best flowers and, for sweet scent, 'Fragrans' is the clone to choose; 'Rubella' is an interesting colour variant, with red-budded flowers. Subspecies *reevesiana* is hermaphrodite so the crimson-red berries always appear after the cream flowers: it is smaller, (about 60cm/2ft high. Z9).
90cm/3ft. Z8

S. laureola, in a male form, has good greenish-cream fragrant flowers. The leaves are very pungent when crushed.
Usually under 90cm/3ft. Z8

SPARTIUM
Papilionaceae

S. junceum, Spanish broom, is popular for its long summer flowering and its tolerance of hot, dry conditions. It does particularly well by the sea. It makes an erect, often leggy shrub but can be kept

LEFT *Spartium junceum* RIGHT *Staphylea colchica*

neat and bushy by spring pruning. The blast of bright yellow, pea flowers begins in summer and continues until autumn; the flowers are scented of vanilla.
Sun. 2.5m/8ft or more. Z8

STAPHYLEA
Staphyleaceae

S. colchica, bladdernut, is an erect deciduous shrub that bears panicles of white flowers in spring; the famous plantsman and author E. A. Bowles likened their scent to that of rice pudding. Conspicuous inflated seed capsules follow.
Sun or light shade. Loamy soil.
3m/10ft or more. Z6

SYRINGA
Oleaceae

The lilacs are the heralds of summer and a mainstay of the late spring garden. The larger forms, the size of small trees and bearing great plumes of flowers, are deciduous background plants for the sunnier parts of the shrub border and for the wild garden – while the smaller forms, which are less obtrusive in leaf and often longer-flowering, can be slipped into the mixed herbaceous border to provide early flowers. The flower scent is distinctive enough to be described as 'lilac' but varies within the group from very sweet to unpleasantly heavy. Beautiful as the bigger lilacs are, they are large and dreary lumps after flowering; the smaller lilacs are easier to live with.
Sun or light shade. All but very alkaline soils.

S. x *chinensis*, the Chinese or Rouen lilac, is a pretty but uncommon shrub with arching panicles of pale lilac-coloured flowers with a good scent. It makes a bushy but often rather lax plant.
3m/10ft. Z3

S. x *hyacinthiflora* is a variable hybrid from which many attractive clones have been selected. It is similar to the common lilac but makes a more spreading shrub and has looser heads of flower; it also blooms earlier in the spring. 'Clarke's Giant' is a fine lilac-blue with large heads; 'Esther Staley' is a splendid pink, red in bud.
3.5m/12ft. Z3

S. x *josiflexa* **'Bellicent'**, an exceptionally beautiful large lilac, produces long plumes hung with drooping flowers. These are a pale, clear pink and sweetly scented. It is quite stunning when at its peak – if you only have room for one sizeable lilac, this is the one to choose.
3m/10ft or more. Z5

S. meyeri **'Palibin'** is a commonly grown short lilac with small leaves. Loose panicles of sweetly scented, lilac-pink flowers are produced in early summer.
Up to 1.5m/5ft. Z5

S. microphylla **'Superba'** is the best of the small lilacs and one of the most desirable small scented shrubs. It blooms over a very long period – after its spring burst, intermittently until autumn. The flowers, which appear from rosy buds, are clear pink and are carried in rounded heads. I would not be without it.
1.2m/4ft. Z4

S. x *persica*, the Persian lilac, is more delicate in appearance, with graceful sprays of flowers and slender leaves. The flowers are nicely scented and pale lilac; there is an even lovelier white form called 'Alba'.
2m/6ft. Z5

S. x *prestoniae*, another variable hybrid, gives a range of large lilacs in different colours. They extend the lilac season well into summer. Many have fine heads of drooping flowers and all are scented. 'Elinor' in lilac-pink is the most freely available, but 'Audrey' in deep pink and 'Isabella' in lilac-purple are also good.
4.5m/15ft. Z2

S. sweginzowii is definitely the connoisseur's choice, with its elegant, arching branches and long panicles dripping with sweetly scented, pale pink flowers.
3.5m/12ft. Z6

S. vulgaris, the common lilac, is available in such a quantity of single and double-flowered cultivars, in all colours, that it is hard to make a choice. Here is a selection: 'Charles Joly', a double dark reddish-purple; 'Firmament', a single clear lilac-blue; 'Katherine Havemeyer', a double lavender-purple; 'Madame Lemoine', a double white; and 'Andenken an Ludwig Späth' ('Souvenir de Louis Spaeth'), a single wine-red.
4.5m/15ft. Z4

THUJA
Cupressaceae

The fruity scent of their foliage makes thujas appealing conifers for the fragrant garden. Their role is as specimen evergreens, of various sizes, or as backdrops, screens and hedges; *T. plicata*, the western red cedar (described under Trees), makes one of the best evergreen hedges, and the best-scented one.

T. occidentalis, the American arborvitae or white cedar, gives a range of conifers of all shapes and sizes, though mainly dense and conical. The most popular are 'Danica', a dwarf, dark green globe which turns bronze in winter; 'Ericoides', a dwarf, grey-green cone, also bronze in winter; 'Holmstrup', a pleasing, dark green pyramid which grows slowly to 2–3m/6–10ft; 'Rheingold', a 1.2m/4ft dome which changes its shade of gold each season; 'Smaragd' ('Emerald'), a bright green pyramid, 3m/10ft high, and a fine hedging plant; and 'Sunkist', a golden pyramid, slowly reaching 1.2m/4ft.
Sun. Z3

T. plicata, the western red cedar, passes its scent on to its clones, of which these coloured forms are the most popular: 'Rogersii', a dwarf golden globe, which in winter assumes good bronze tones; 'Stoneham Gold', a broad, bright golden cone, slowly growing to 90cm/3ft; and 'Zebrina', a broad, golden-variegated pyramid, ultimately tree size.
Sun. Z5

ULEX
Papilionaceae

U. europaeus **'Flore Pleno'** is the double-flowered form of British

FAR LEFT *Syringa microphylla* 'Superba'
LEFT *Syringa* x *persica* 'Alba'

LEFT *Thuja occidentalis* 'Holmstrup'
BELOW *Ulex europaeus*

gorse. The warm coconut scent of gorse is the scent of my childhood on the island of Anglesey, and while one wouldn't want the coarse wild plant in the garden, this form is compact, does not set seed, and is a lovely plant for the sunny border. The brash yellow flowers appear in a flush in spring – terrific with blue-flowered bulbs – and sporadically thereafter.
2m/6ft. Sun. Well-drained soil. Z7

UMBELLULARIA
Lauraceae

U. californica, California laurel, is a large, aromatic, evergreen shrub or small tree, whose oval, leathery leaves are pungently fruity when crushed. It is said that prolonged sniffing causes headaches and sneezing and can even render a person unconscious! Small umbels of yellowish flowers are produced in spring, and are occasionally followed by fruits. It needs a warm situation, sheltered from early frosts.
Sun. Well-drained soil. Z9

VIBURNUM
Adoxaceae

This group of shrubs gives the garden some of its most fabulous scent. The fragrant varieties (by no means all *Viburnum* are scented) fall into two categories: those which flower on bare stems during the late autumn, winter and early spring; and those which flower during spring. All need to be within reach of the nose. Plant them in the shrub border in front of deciduous trees.
Sun or light shade. Most soils.

***V. awabuki* (*V. odoratissimum* hort.)** is included here for convenience, but it is really only successful in milder regions. It would make an interesting plant for a large conservatory, or possibly a wall that receives full sun. It is an evergreen, with large leathery leaves; these sometimes turn bronze during the winter. The conical panicles of pure white flowers are produced at an unusual time, in late summer: having said that, I have cultivated it in Mallorca for a number of years and have yet to see any flowers.
3–7.5m/10–25ft. Z8

V. x bodnantense is a fine winter-flowering *Viburnum*, producing its rose-pink clusters of flowers, which are fairly frost-resistant, on and off from autumn until spring. The scent is honey-sweet, suffused with almond, and on warm days carries in the air. 'Charles Lamont' is a good form. 'Dawn' is a superb vigorous selection, with large pink flowers and large foliage; 'Deben' is white from pink buds, lovely but damaged by bad weather. They are deciduous and have an upright habit.
3m/10ft. Z7

V. x burkwoodii is a semi-evergreen with wonderfully glossy leaves, some of which take on lively autumn tints. The dense, rounded clusters of pure white flowers appear mainly in

FAR LEFT *Viburnum carlesii* 'Diana'
LEFT *Viburnum* x *juddii*

spring; the sweet scent, like a clove carnation, carries well. It is a lovely backbone plant for the flower border. Several excellent forms and hybrids are available, notably 'Anne Russell', with pale pink flowers; 'Fulbrook', with larger white flowers, distinctive foliage, and a graceful habit; and 'Park Farm', a magnificent, vigorous plant with larger leaves and larger white flowers.
2.5m/8ft. Z5

V.* x *carlcephalum, fragrant snowball viburnum, is a popular, spring-flowering, deciduous *Viburnum*, but rather coarser than *V. carlesii* and, in my view, less desirable; the leaves are larger and the heads less elegant, bigger and more compact. But the scent is sweet and potent.
2.5m/8ft. Z5

V. carlesii has the best scent of the spring-flowering deciduous *Viburnum*: a sweet clove fragrance and far-reaching. It is a rounded shrub with dull greyish-green foliage and white flowers. Its three clones are even better than the species: 'Aurora' has red flower buds which open pale pink; 'Charis' is particularly vigorous, also red-budded but with white flowers; and 'Diana' has red buds and more reddish flowers than 'Aurora'.
1.2–2.5m/4–8ft. Z5

***V. farreri* (*V. fragrans*)**, a much-loved constituent of the English cottage garden, blooms on and off on bare branches all winter. The flowers are white, tinged with pink, and are scented of honey and almond. In old age it is usually more spreading than its less elegant offspring *V.* x *bodnantense* but in youth it is equally upright. It is deciduous.
3m/10ft. Z6

V.* x *juddii is another outstanding spring-flowering deciduous shrub. It is similar to *V. carlesii* but bushier, neater and more robust. The heads of white flowers are also usually a touch bigger. The scent is sweet but with an extra dash of spicy clove.
1.2m/4ft. Z5

V. tinus, laurustinus, is a commonly grown evergreen shrub and one with which I have a love-hate relationship. Its attractions are that it makes a neat, bushy background plant (or informal hedge), is tolerant of quite deep shade, and is winter-flowering. Its drawback is that at no moment in the year does it really give you a thrill. Unless, of course, you catch a waft of honey scent; but this is very unpredictable. Frequently there is not a trace, or it is only very faint. It is also a martyr to viburnum beetle, which damages leaves and eradicates flowers. The white flowers appear from pink buds on and off from autumn to early spring. In some years they are succeeded by blue fruits. 'Eve Price' is a compact, smaller form with bright pink buds and pink-tinged flowers.
Shade. 2–3.5m/6–12ft. Z8

WEIGELA
Caprifoliaceae

A few weigelas take you by surprise with a honey scent, though most of the genus are scentless or very faintly scented. Weigelas are popular deciduous shrubs for early summer, producing masses of tubular flowers along the previous year's shoots; flowering shoots should be pruned hard after the blossoms fade. They have rather uninteresting foliage, except for the coloured-leaved forms, so they need to be given positions where they can be unobtrusive after flowering.
Sun or light shade. Any soil.

W. **'Mont Blanc'** is one of the best white weigelas; it is vigorous, with large flowers, and has a good scent. But it is not commonly offered.
2.3m/7ft. Z5

W. **'Praecox Variegata'** is a cream-variegated hybrid of strongly scented *W. praecox*. It has rose-pink flowers.
2.3m/7ft. Z5

YUCCA
Asparagaceae

Most of us think of yuccas as border perennials but since they are strictly shrubs I include them here. The spiky clumps of sword-shaped, evergreen leaves strike a tropical note in the planting, and the tall stems hung with cream bells combine wonderfully with yellow *Kniphofia* (red-hot pokers) and blue *Agapanthus*. As architectural specimens on corners of borders or growing in paving cracks, they have few equals. But bear in mind their dangerous, dagger-sharp leaf tips, which are at eye level for children and dogs. The flowers have a sweet scent.
Sun. Well-drained soil.

Y. filamentosa, Adam's needle, has more or less stiffly erect, grey-green leaves with curly threads at the margins. The loose, broad panicles of flowers are borne in high summer.
Up to 2m/6ft. Z5

Y. flaccida has narrower, greyer leaves which are more lax and generally bent downwards from the middle. The flowers are borne on shorter panicles. 'Ivory' is a superb free-flowering selection.
1–1.2m/3–4ft. Z5

Y. gloriosa, Spanish dagger, flowers less freely, often not at all. But when the bells do appear they are on massive narrow panicles. The foliage is stiff and dangerous.
Up to 2.5m/8ft. Z7

ZANTHOXYLUM
Rutaceae

Z. piperitum, Japanese pepper, is a spiny, medium-sized shrub with very attractive and highly aromatic pinnate leaves, which turn a good yellow in autumn. Small yellow flowers, produced in early summer, are followed on female plants by red fruits: the black seeds inside are used as a pepper in Japan.
2m/6ft. Sun or part shade. Z6

ZENOBIA
Ericaceae

Z. pulverulenta is an attractive, small deciduous shrub for association with rhododendrons. Clusters of bell-shaped, white flowers appear in summer and these have a scent of aniseed. The ovate leaves are glaucous when young and in autumn assume fine red tints. It is a very desirable plant.
Sun or shade. Moist, acidic soil.
1.2–2m/4–6ft. Z6

XANTHORHIZA
Ranunculaceae

X. simplicissima, yellowroot, is a curiosity I enjoy growing to catch out the experts. It is a low, gently suckering shrub with finely-cut leaves and drooping sprays of unusual chocolate-coloured starry flowers in spring. These have the unmistakable salty smell of seaweed. The stems are bright yellow inside, and the foliage takes on good yellow and brown autumn tints.
Sun or shade. 90cm/3ft. Z3

Xanthorhiza simplicissima

PLANTING WITH PERENNIALS, BULBS & ANNUALS

There are scented perennials and bulbs for every season; annuals in the warmer months. In the depths of winter, the scents of perennials and bulbs are usually best savoured indoors. Assaulted by wind, frost and rain, flowers are spoiled, while their fragrances are lost in the cold air; and some plants are too diminutive to be properly appreciated.

Bulbs are well worth growing in pots to be kept outside, or in a cold frame or plunge bed (a bed of sand in which the pots are sunk to their rim), and brought into the warmth of the house as the flower buds become visible. In the autumn I always plant up potfuls of crocuses, narcissi, violet-scented *Iris reticulata* (with me, this iris is not reliably perennial anyway) and forced hyacinths, to enjoy indoors from Christmas onwards. Other potfuls I leave out on the garden table to smell as I pass by.

Flowers can also be cut as they come into bud. Snowdrops, especially the large 'S. Arnott', bunched in jars, surprise you with the potency of their honey scents. And Algerian irises, forms of *I. unguicularis,* deliver some sophisticated sweet perfumes; pale lavender-blue 'Walter Butt' has a particularly good primrose scent. The Edwardian plantsman and garden writer E. A. Bowles gives detailed advice on the picking of Algerian irises in his book *My Garden in Spring* (1914). In frosty weather he suggests pulling the buds as soon as the coloured parts of the flower are visible above the spathes, and placing them immediately in water up to their necks. This prevents them drooping, and as they lengthen and burst open they are transferred to a display vase.

Wallflowers bring a warm aniseed scent to spring bedding.

WALLFLOWERS

Wallflowers are a luxury I would not want to be without. I say luxury because I buy my plants each autumn. My local garden centre has such good plants that there does not seem much point in raising them myself. Their warm spicy scent echoes the eastern image conjured up by their sumptuous colours, and I wish I had room to plant carpets of them. In my congested borders they have to be arranged in small groups. I have mixed-colours here and there, and single colours teamed with foliage like bluish catmint and, more particularly, fennel. There is more than a trace of aniseed in wallflower scent, and the green and bronze fennels, also aniseed-scented, are happy bedfellows.

By mid-February, snowdrops and spring snowflakes, with *Crocus tommasinianus* for colour (the best crocus for colonizing), should be revealing themselves under bare-stemmed shrubs like witch hazel, *Daphne bholua* 'Gurkha', Japanese apricot (*Prunus mume*), spicy *Cornus mas* and sweetly scented willows. The stinking hellebore, *H. foetidus,* is also in bloom. It does not stink unless you bruise it, and even then not much; but in some forms, notably 'Miss Jekyll's Form', a lily-of-the-valley fragrance can be detected in the flowers. *H. foetidus,* with its evergreen fingered leaves, is an ideal foil for snowdrops and will seed itself among them, and on shady banks is a natural companion for primroses. The purplish winter leaves of *Tellima grandiflora* Rubra Group are also excellent with snowdrops and primroses, but its sweetly scented flowers do not appear until early summer.

As spring advances, the shrub season builds up to its climax, for which the bulbs and early perennials provide a multicoloured understorey. Sweet violets, primroses, grape hyacinths and daffodils are among the scented candidates that require or tolerate a degree of shade, and can be grouped under magnolias, cherries, and acid-loving woodlanders like *Corylopsis* and *Fothergilla*. But the more scented daffodils, the jonquils and tazettas, perform better when they are nurtured in sunny, sheltered sites (or in pots). The sinister snake's head, *Hermodactylus tuberosus,* is an interesting companion bulb for them; its velvet-black and lime-green harmonizes well with the different shades of yellow, orange and white and it has a delicate clove scent. There are also honey-scented tulips around to fuel the scheme.

In late spring, the bulbs start to give way to perennials and biennials. In shady, and often sunny borders too, lily of the valley is now displaying its tiny white bells. It has a habit of thriving just where you are sure it won't and of not thriving just where you are sure it will;

Bergamot-scented *Monarda* and spicily scented *Phlox* are among the best perennials for summer fragrance.

Cardiocrinum giganteum has a coconut-laced scent, and is one of the most arresting plants that can be grown in gardens.

so the answer is to try a few roots everywhere. The scent can be elusive outdoors so it is worthwhile picking a few stems for the house.

Sunny borders that are predominantly herbaceous are probably a little short of colour at this time of year, so wallflowers, and tulips, will give them a fillip. Other scented plants that can help are *Iris* 'Florentina', stocks, perennial honesty (*Lunaria rediviva*) and false Solomon's seal (*Maianthemum racemosum*). The latter's creamy plumes are an eyecatching feature – they look well behind lime-green euphorbias and tulips; you expect a heavy meadowsweet scent from them but in fact they have a refreshing lemon fragrance.

By midsummer, the garden is likely to be awash with pastel colours. This is the season for all those favourite perennials of the cottage garden – peonies, irises, lupins and pinks among them – and the air is infused with the scent of roses, honeysuckles and mock orange. Pinks (*Dianthus*) have the most potent scent of these early perennials and if your soil is dry and limy enough, you can use them on path edges, to spill from raised beds, and to bulge out of paving cracks, perhaps in the company of *Matthiola incana* 'White Perennial' whose warm clove scent will hang in the air. All sorts of fruity and vanilla scents may be detected in bearded irises; lavender-blue *I. pallida* subsp. *pallida* (var. *dalmatica*) is one of the best. Another iris worth having is *I. graminea*. The slender flowers are violet-blue and rosy-purple, and smell of stewed plums.

Peonies and roses were made for each other; they share a rounded, petal-packed shape and a pinky colour range. I also let myrrh-scented *Valeriana officinalis* seed around my shrub roses. Lupins can provide a rocket-shaped note of contrast, and lily-scented daylilies like yellow *Hemerocallis lilioasphodelus* (*H. flava*) a further splash of contrasting colour and leaf texture.

EVENING SCENTS

Strolling in the garden on warm early summer evenings, you can take in the fragrances of night-scented plants. I am very fond of that of the sweet rocket, *Hesperis matronalis*. The white and pale lilac heads of this tall, self-sowing biennial glow in the half-light and waft a clove fragrance for yards around; I let it seed itself right through my main border.

Lilium regale is also powerful at night and is one of the best of the midsummer lilies. In the border *L. regale* looks well in silvery schemes of white roses and *Artemisia*, and beneath crimson and yellow roses that pick up the shading on its reflexed trumpets. If your soil is not too acidic, you should also try the Madonna lily, *L. candidum*, though it can be tricky to establish. *L.* 'African Queen' and Pink Perfection Group are among the most reliable border lilies. It is worth having bulbs in pots as well as growing in the border; I always have some of *L. regale*, 'African Queen' and 'Casa Blanca', which gives me a good succession of scent.

A fruity, evening-scented summer scheme can be orchestrated using honey-scented annual *Mirabilis jalapa* and biennial evening primroses – lemon-scented, pale yellow *Oenothera stricta* (*O. odorata*) is a favourite of mine – with petunias contributing a touch of vanilla. Annual tobacco flowers are essential in the scented garden, especially the night-scented whites, with their powerful fragrance, exotic enough to transport you to tropical climes. *Nicotiana alata* 'Grandiflora' is the most potent, but for visual drama, choose giant *N. sylvestris* with its drooping funnels. One year I recall much enjoying the evening scent of white *Verbena*, which I planted in pots with deep-purple scented heliotrope and *Argyranthemum frutescens*, a scentless tender perennial that creates a haze of glaucous blue leaves and is always studded with white daisies. I could not get over the strength and sweetness of the *Verbena* scent and kept popping out of the back door just to drink it in. Night-scented stocks and almond-scented *Schizopetalon walkeri* will contribute further layers of fragrance.

The most entertaining midsummer perennial is burning bush, *Dictamnus albus*. You can ignite the fragrant volatile oil on the flowerheads with a match, and an orange flame flickers up each stem, releasing the resinous scent of lemon into the air. No damage is done to the plant. Success can never be guaranteed – it never works when you have an audience – for conditions have to be exactly right: the latter part of a hot dry day. I usually succeed in one garden or another during the course of its flowering period.

Crambe cordifolia is another characterful plant. Like a giant *Gypsophila*, *Crambe* releases a large cloud of tiny white, honey-scented flowers from stems 2m/6ft high. It is good with roses and strongly coloured perennials like scarlet Maltese cross, *Lychnis chalcedonica;* but

I have it all alone on a shrubbery corner, leaning over grass. Seen from the lawn it glows against the shadows of an old copper beech tree. Elsewhere, in a paved corner of my garden, its relative the sea kale will also be in bloom. The honey scent is probably stronger but you have to bend down to savour it.

The giant lily, *Cardiocrinum giganteum*, is at home in woodland clearings and between rhododendrons. I cannot look at it without thinking of that bizarre photograph in Gertrude Jekyll's *Wood & Garden* that shows a clump of these plants towering over a cowled monk. The monk turns out to be her head gardener in disguise. 'The scent seems to pour out of the great white trumpets, and is almost overpowering', she writes, 'but gains a delicate quality by passing through the air, and at fifty yards is like a faint waft of incense.' Sadly, I never have big enough groups to notice this. To my nose, there is a good dose of coconut in the scent.

Compared to shrubs, perennials are as a group poorly endowed with scent, so areas entirely devoted to them, such as summer herbaceous borders and especially new wave, naturalistic perennial schemes (clogged with all those scentless grasses!) in the Dutch and German style tend to be lacking in fragrance. There are, however, some stalwarts. Early in the season – and later if you chop some of them down in late May to delay flowering – come the violet-blue flowers of *Campanula lactiflora*, with their honeyed, alyssum-like scent. You need to put your nose to them to drink it in. I like them in association with scarlet *Crocosmia* 'Lucifer'.

Hyacinths and grape hyacinths inject scent among pots of spring tulips. Pale blue *Muscari armeniacum* 'Valerie Finnis' is particularly well endowed, with a sweet shop fragrance: it is also well worth growing in small pots to put on outdoor tables or bring into the house.

Phlox are generously scented. They can contribute great swathes of colour and, with monkshoods and Japanese anemones, provide a backdrop for dashing individuals like tiger lilies and *Fuchsia*. The fragrance is sweet and peppery, and in the cool of the evening becomes quite strong on the air. An attractive companion for it is the herbaceous,

Aniseed-scented *Agastache* grows with *Lythrum* and *Persicaria* in this contemporary planting.

non-climbing *Clematis*, *C. tubulosa* (*C. heracleifolia* var. *davidiana*). 'Wyevale', with violet-blue flowers and a good sweet scent, is one of the best varieties.

Persicaria are often honey-scented, from the slender white *P. amplexicaulis* 'Alba' to the late-flowering, beefy ones like *P. wallichii*. *Agastache* and *Monarda* contribute aniseed and bergamot leaf scents, and do not overlook *Verbena bonariensis* whose lightly scented lilac heads are around for months on end. In sunny, open areas, they will seed about, their skeletal shapes popping up in unexpected places in borders and between paving cracks.

I am very fond of the sweet shop scent of the double white soapwort (*Saponaria*). It is not invasive like its parent, and is a lovely partner for blue *Agapanthus*. So are galtonias. These bulbous plants flower in late summer and their fragrant white bells are also perfect with orange and yellow *Kniphofia*. Later in the season, the best perennial scent comes from *Actaea* (*Cimicifuga*): the purple-leaved forms are among those with delicious bubblegum fragrance.

The honeyed floral perfumes of sweet peas are the essence of summer.

SCENTED ANNUALS FOR CUTTING

Doyen of the scented annuals is the sweet pea. It is a moderately labour-intensive plant but provides so much cutting material for the house that it remains a favourite. In the best varieties its perfume is both honeyed and sophisticatedly floral. The trellises and wigwams erected for it can be useful design features and focal points, not only in the vegetable garden but in the border too.

Adding annuals and tender perennials is a good way of bolstering the scented content of herbaceous schemes. The multicoloured strains of sweet sultan and snapdragon and the extraordinary poached eggs of *Limnanthes douglasii* bring a carnival spirit to the garden and always remind me of seaside holidays and promenades planted with riotous bedding. Snapdragons and limnanthes are good at self-sowing, as is that other favourite, sweet alyssum. It does not have to be grown in a straight line, alternating with blue lobelia; it can be allowed to appear where it likes, taking you by surprise with its thick honey fragrance.

Tender perennials, either bought in annually or lifted or propagated from cuttings and overwintered in a frost-free greenhouse, are also valuable in extending the season of the summer border. *Cosmos atrosanguineus*, with its blood-black, chocolate-scented flowers, is a sumptuous perennial that one would not want to be without. It will often survive outdoors under a bark mulch, but I find it prefers a nomadic existence; it is lifted in the late autumn and spends the winter in the border of my unheated greenhouse. Salvias are one of my favourite groups of plants. Useful for late colour, and possessing fragrant leaves, are lamb and mint sauce-scented *S. confertiflora,* with wonderful rusty-red flower spikes, shrubby, blackcurrant-scented *S. microphylla,* and minty *S. uliginosa* in kingfisher blue. Again, with protection, they will survive winters in the milder areas but it is sensible to take cuttings in early autumn as a precaution. Other *Salvia* and plants to use in pots and for bedding out are listed in the chapter on Tender Plants (see pages 280–301).

To round off the year, there is a flush of scented pink and white-flowered bulbs. In sunny borders there are the great trumpets of crinums followed, a little later, by the pink stars of *Amaryllis belladonna* that have a pleasant peachy scent. Late-flowering hostas are also a feature now, displaying their white funnels, sweetly scented but with a hint of moth-balls, over fresh green foliage; they associate well with pink and white colchicums.

CYCLAMEN FROM AUTUMN TO SPRING

In the shade, tucked around the boles of deciduous trees, cyclamen are in flower. To have a patch of these in the autumn garden should be the goal of every gardener. Not only are they in bloom for a long time but their patterned leaves remain in evidence throughout winter and spring, making another lovely foil for snowdrops. To encourage a wider colonization you can transplant seedlings in the early spring; one gardener I know scatters the seed by going over the seedheads with a strimmer as they are opening, and this has proved highly successful. There are scented strains of *C. hederifolium*, but a richer scent comes from *C. purpurascens* – and also *C. persicum*, but this needs to be grown in pots and brought under cover when the weather turns really cold.

Tree lupin, *Lupinus arboreus*, is an attractive scented sub-shrub for sunny borders, associating well with perennials.

PERENNIALS

ACORUS
Acoraceae
A. gramineus 'Licorice' is a short, grassy-leaved evergreen with leaves that are strongly liquorice-scented when bruised. It is not a showy plant, but one to tuck into a corner somewhere as a curiosity.
Sun or light shade. 30cm/1ft.

ACTAEA (CIMICIFUGA)
Ranunculaceae
The bugbanes are an invaluable group of late-flowering perennials with ferny, cut leaves and wiry stems bearing white or cream bottlebrush flowers. Some are unpleasantly scented, but these here have a delectable bubblegum fragrance.
A. matsumurae 'Elstead Variety' has brown-tinged green leaves, and in autumn a showy flush of white flowers open on the brown stems above them.
Light shade. Moist soil. 1.5m/5ft.
A. simplex Atropurpurea Group comprises a selection of brown, purple and near-black leaved varieties, of which 'Brunette' is the best known. The white flowers appear on the tall dark stems in early autumn.
Light shade. Moist soil. 2m/6ft.

ADENOPHORA
Campanulaceae
A. liliifolia, common ladybell, is a close relative of the *Campanula*, and an unusual perennial for the border. It bears loose panicles of pale blue, delicately scented bells in high summer. It should be propagated from seed, as it has fleshy roots which resent disturbance.
Sun or light shade. All but very dry soils. 46cm/18in.

AGASTACHE
Lamiaceae
A. mexicana is unreliable in cold areas, but is another interesting perennial with aromatic leaves. Its sage-like flowers, borne in high summer, vary in colour from rose-pink to crimson. Sun. 60cm/2ft.
A. rugosa (*A. foeniculum*) has leaves strongly scented of aniseed when rubbed. The young foliage also has an attractive purplish cast, which makes a good foil for early summer flowers, especially pale yellows. Its own flowers – chunky violet spikes that appear in late summer – are rather disappointing. The hybrids, such as violet 'Black Adder' and 'Blue

Agastache rugosa

RIGHT *Anthemis punctata* subsp. *cupaniana*
FAR RIGHT *Berlandiera lyrata*

Fortune', are more attractive.
Sun. Any fertile soil. 90cm/3ft.
A. rugosa f. *albiflora* 'Liquorice White' is a good white-flowered *Agastache* with leaves scented of liquorice. There is also a blue version.
Sun. 90cm/3ft.

ANTHEMIS
Asteraceae
A. punctata subsp. *cupaniana* makes a fine silvery mat for the front of the border, and its foliage has a camomile scent. White daisies appear in early summer. It is at its best when young and should really be divided and replanted each spring.
Sun. Well-drained soil. 30cm/1ft.

ARTEMISIA
Asteraceae
Artemisia give the garden some of its laciest and most shimmering silver foliage but the flowers of these species are worthless. They are superb in front of pink shrub roses, with blue irises, and among white flowers. The leaves are pungently – to my nose usually unpleasantly – scented when rubbed.
Full sun. Well-drained soil.

ASPHODELINE
Asphodelaceae
A. lutea, asphodel, is an ancient garden plant and a characterful perennial. The straw-yellow stars open on the erect flower spikes in early summer, are delicately scented and have the perfect foil in their grassy, bluish foliage.
Full sun. Well-drained soil. 90cm/3ft.

ASTER
Asteraceae
A. sedifolius has starry lavender flowers with a honeyed scent. It is not perhaps in the first rank of asters but in its short form 'Nanus' (46cm/18in) is worth a place in the scented garden. It flowers in late summer.
Light shade. 90cm/3ft.

ASTILBE
Saxifragaceae
A. rivularis is a large perennial making a handsome foliage effect with its deeply cut leaves, bronze when young. The frothy, scented greenish-white flowers are borne in summer.
Light shade. Moist soil. 2m/6ft.

BERLANDIERA
Asteraceae
B. lyrata is not commonly encountered in the UK but grown in the United States for its small, chocolate-scented yellow daisies, striped red on their reverse and with a central boss of maroon stamens. They open in the evening, and are borne in summer above the grey-green leaves. Sun. Well-drained soil. 30cm/1ft.

CALANTHE
Orchidaceae
C. discolor is a terrestrial orchid from the Far East that is hardy outside in a sheltered spot except in very cold areas. It has large, oblong leaves and its tall stems carry up to 20 chocolate-brown flowers with pale pink lips; these are sweetly scented and appear in early summer. Plant shallowly under a leaf-mould mulch in an acid bed. Light shade.

CAMPANULA
Campanulaceae
C. lactiflora is one of the most valuable midsummer perennials bearing clouds of soft violet bell-shaped flowers, deeper coloured in 'Prichard's Variety'. Plants may be cut

LEFT *Clematis tubulosa* 'Wyevale' CENTRE *Corydalis flexuosa* RIGHT *Crambe cordifolia*

down in late May to delay flowering, create sturdier growth, and extend the season. The flowers have a refined honeyed scent.
Sun or light shade. Any soil. 1.5m/5ft.

CHLORANTHUS
Chloranthaceae

C. oldhamii is an interesting woodland perennial with serrated leaves and pendulous stems of tiny but strongly fragrant white flowers in spring. It is best in milder areas.
Light shade. Moist, well-drained soil. 30cm/1ft.

CLAYTONIA
Portulacaceae

C. sibirica, Siberian purslane, is a useful ground-cover perennial for shade with striped mauve-pink, starry flowers in late spring, which have a honey scent. It is short-lived but renews itself by seeding about. *C. virginica* with slender leaves is also scented.
Shade. Moist, well-drained soil. 20cm/8in.

CLEMATIS
Ranunculaceae

C.* x *aromatica is a short, non-clinging *Clematis* with starry purple flowers through late summer. It has a strong spicy scent. It is good in a pot. 2m/6ft.
***C. recta* 'Purpurea'** is a floppy herbaceous *Clematis* for training through a shrub; mine disguises the bare base of the gawky shrub rose 'Agnes'. Its main attraction is its purplish foliage, but this varies in intensity among seed-raised plants. Cream blossom, often with a heavy scent, is borne at midsummer and is followed by silver seedheads.
Sun or light shade. 1.2m/4ft. Z7
C. stans has recurved flowers in late summer like *C. heracleifolia* in shades of white and violet, and an equally refined perfume. 90cm/3ft.
***C. tubulosa* (*C. heracleifolia* var. *davidiana*)** is a herbaceous *Clematis* whose pale violet-blue flowers have a delicious and sophisticated sweet scent. The flowers resemble those of a hyacinth and appear in whorls up the stems in late summer. It has broad, dark foliage and makes a good clump. 'Wyevale' is a superior selection with stronger colour and an equally strong scent; the hybrid 'Côte d'Azur' is a wonderful mid-blue.
Sun or light shade. Well-drained, fertile soil. 1.2m/4ft. Z3

CORYDALIS
Papaveraceae

C. flexuosa is one of the most desirable spring perennials for shady areas, bearing tubular flowers of an often intense blue over ferny, often purple-flushed leaves. The flowers have a light but sophisticated scent, laced with coconut. 'China Blue' is a dashing pale gentian-blue variety. *C. elata* is also scented. Light shade. Moist, leafy soil, acid to neutral. 15cm/6in.

CRAMBE
Brassicaceae

C. cordifolia produces a cloud of tiny white flowers, like a giant *Gypsophila*, in early summer and these have a strong honey scent. It is a large plant but the real bulk – the huge, green, heart-shaped leaves – is low down, while the top is airy and transparent. It can be grown happily at the back of the herbaceous border, but to enjoy the scent, you will have to grow it where the nose can reach, such as on a shrubbery corner.
Sun. 2m/6ft, and as much across.

C. maritima, sea kale, is grown outside the kitchen garden mainly for its broad, glaucous blue, cabbage-like leaves. These are a splendid foil for flowers of all colours and have good purplish tints when young. But its stiff, tight heads of white blossom are also richly honey-scented. Unless you keep cutting the leaves, it needs plenty of room to luxuriate. It comes readily from root cuttings.
Sun. 60cm/2ft.

DELPHINIUM
Ranunculaceae

D. brunonianum has comparatively large flowers for its diminutive stature; they are pale purplish-blue and borne on branching racemes in early summer. The scent, which is of musk, comes from the kidney-shaped, hairy leaves. It is not common, but a good plant for the front of the border or in the rock garden. (*D. leroyi* and *D. wellbyi* are two other scented species that used to be grown but are now extremely rare.)
Sun. 46cm/18in.

CONVALLARIA
Asparagaceae

C. majalis, lily of the valley, is an indispensable member of the scented garden. Its small, white bells hang on a short raceme above the broad leaves in late spring and can fill the air with their piercingly sweet scent; more often, though, the scent is elusive outdoors. It resents disturbance and can be a difficult plant to establish; once settled, it will colonize readily, even along the base of a hedge. 'Fortin's Giant' is a fine, large-flowered form; I find 'Hardwick Hall', with yellow edges to its leaves, the easiest and most vigorous form; 'Variegata' has cream stripes; and the mauve-pink variety *rosea* has reputedly the sweetest scent of all. Sun or shade. All soils. 23cm/9in.

Convallaria majalis

LEFT *Dictamnus albus* CENTRE *Geranium* x *oxonianum* RIGHT *Geranium endressii* 'Wargrave Pink'

DICTAMNUS

Rutaceae

D. albus, burning bush, is a curious perennial whose flowerheads can be ignited with a match on a warm, still summer evening; they are covered in a volatile oil, fragrant of lemon, like the foliage. The pinnate leaves and wispy flowers are very attractive; they are white in this species and purplish in var. *purpureus*. They are sometimes difficult to establish and should not be disturbed when happy.
Full sun. Well-drained or dry soil. 60cm/2ft. Z3

DISPOROPSIS

Asparagaceae

D. pernyi is a gently colonizing woodland perennial resembling Solomon's seal but with polished evergreen leaves, and white bells. These have a light lemon scent.
Light shade. Moist, well-drained soil. 46cm/18in.

DISPORUM

Colchicaceae

D. megalanthum is a woodland perennial of Solomon's seal-like appearance, with clusters of scented white bells in late spring, presented above deep green, ribbed leaves and followed in autumn by red berries.
Light shade. Moist, well-drained soil. 30cm/1ft.

D. nantouense has creamy bells, flushed with maroon-brown, more lightly scented. It is easier to grow than *D. megalanthum*. Related species such as *D. leucanthum* and *D. viridescens* are also scented.
Light shade. Moist, well-drained soil. 60cm/2ft.

DRYOPTERIS

Dryopteridaceae

D. aemula, a British native hay-scented fern, is seldom grown but is worth hunting down for the sake of its evocative hay scent that is particularly marked when the fronds are dying. It is an attractive, evergreen fern.
Light shade. Moist, well-drained soil. 60cm/2ft.

ECHINACEA

Asteraceae

E. 'Art's Pride' is one of a number of daisy-flowered coneflowers to have a thick honey perfume, though purple-flowered *E. purpurea* often disappoints – one of the most reliable is its white form 'Fragrant Angel'. 'Art's Pride' has slender rays of coral-orange; 'Sundown' is a richer coppery tone with broader rays. They have a long summer flowering period and are a magnet for bees and butterflies, but plants can be short-lived.
Sun. Fertile soil. 60cm/2ft.

GERANIUM

Geraniaceae

G. endressii is a pretty ground-covering plant that smothers itself

in cheerful, bright pink flowers all through the summer and autumn. Its foliage has a pronounced rose scent when brushed against, pleasing in small doses but cloying in quantity. There are a number of variants in different shades of pink, among which salmon 'Wargrave Pink' is perhaps the best; *G.* x *oxonianum* and its forms provide more pink flowers and fragrant leaves on bigger, more vigorous plants. These geraniums make a fine underplanting for shrub roses.
Sun or shade. All soils.
46–76cm/18–30in. Z3

G. macrorrhizum is a lovely edging and ground-cover plant that is blessed by gardeners for its tolerance of dry, shady conditions. It flowers only in late spring but its comparatively brief performance is made up for by a display of fiery leaf colour in the autumn. The species itself has magenta-pink flowers and is surpassed in beauty by the pale pink 'Ingwersen's Variety' and, even better, 'Album', whose white flowers are set off perfectly by the red calyces. The foliage has a heavy rose scent when brushed against, and is a source of oil of geranium.
Shade. 30cm/1ft. Z3

HELLEBORUS
Ranunculaceae

H. foetidus has a very elusive flower scent, of lily of the valley, which is most pronounced in the rare, taller 'Miss Jekyll's Form'; it is also evident in the rather tender *H. lividus*.
H. foetidus is an excellent perennial for the shady border with its elegant, fingered leaves, dark and evergreen, and its contrasting clusters of lime-green bells. These are produced in late winter and are edged in maroon. It seeds itself freely and is lovely with snowdrops.
Sun or shade. All soils. 46cm/18in. Z6

H. odorus is easily grown, with greenish-yellow flowers produced often in mid-winter ahead of most hellebore hybrids. The scent is elusive but can be sweet on a warm day.
Light shade. Any good soil. 46cm/18in.

HEMEROCALLIS
Hemerocallidaceae

Numerous daylilies have scented flowers. The sweet lily scent is generally too heavily laced with fetid undertones for my liking; indoors it quickly becomes revolting. Strong scent is confined mainly to the species, especially those with yellow flowers, and some hybrids. The species do not flower for as long as the hybrids and usually have smaller blooms, but they have a poise and simple charm that the hybrids often lack. They are attractive companions for early roses and violet geraniums.
Sun or light shade. All but dry soils.

H. citrina is a night-blooming daylily with slim, citron-yellow trumpets over dark leaves in midsummer.
90cm/3ft.

H. dumortieri is a good early daylily, producing its rich apricot-yellow funnels from brown buds in early summer.
60cm/2ft.

***H. lilioasphodelus* (*H. flava*)** is the pick of the species, with clear lemon-yellow flowers in early summer.
60cm/2ft.

H. middendorfii has orange-yellow flowers from brown buds in early summer.
60cm/2ft.

H. minor has clear yellow flowers, flushed brown on the outside, in early summer.
46cm/18in.

RIGHT *Helleborus foetidus*
FAR RIGHT *Hemerocallis lilioasphodelus*

LEFT *Hosta plantaginea* RIGHT Bearded iris and white lilac

HOSTA

Asparagaceae

This group of perennials is grown almost entirely for its broad, chunky foliage, especially beloved by flower arrangers and, of course, slugs; there are dozens of varieties available showing variations of leaf colour, size and shape, and since they are all so eyecatching for so long, it is tempting to fill every border with them. Their flowers are a much neglected quality. They are elegant trumpets, borne on erect stems, and some breathe a sweet lily scent.

Sun or shade. Fertile, retentive soil.

***H.* 'Honeybells'** is a hybrid with a notable fragrance. It has pale lilac flowers in late summer and fresh green leaves. 'Royal Standard', with white flowers and good, light green leaves, is slightly scented. And of the newer varieties 'Summer Fragrance', with lilac flowers and cream-edged leaves, and 'Sugar and Cream', with white flowers and cream-edged leaves, have a sweet smell.

60cm/2ft. Z3

H. plantaginea is a late-summer flowering hosta that enjoys sunnier conditions than other hostas; it makes a good tub plant. It has wonderful lettuce-green leaves and pure white flowers. The Japanese variety, *japonica* (*grandiflora*), is every bit as desirable. If you can keep your plants free of slug holes, they are one of the glories of the late border.

60cm/2ft. Z3

IRIS

Iridaceae

***I.* 'Florentina'** has sweetly scented, greyish-white flowers in May; its dried rhizomes are also scented, of violets, and are the source of orris root. This is an attractive iris, its floral beauty enhanced by the grey-green fans of foliage.

Sun. Well-drained soil. 60cm/2ft.

I. foetidissima, the native British gladwin iris, is valued by gardeners for its evergreen, sword-shaped foliage and its tolerance of dry, shady positions. The wishy-washy lilac flowers are not very striking, but the seed-pods are sensational in the autumn when they crack open to reveal the brilliant orange seeds within. The scent interest comes from the leaves that have a slightly fetid odour when broken, reminiscent, to the imaginative, of roast beef. The flowers are a more attractive pale yellow in the variety *citrina*, and there is a robust variegated version. Unfortunately, all these forms are now prone to rust attack: once stalwarts in my garden, I can no longer grow them becaue of this.

Sun or shade. Any soil. 60cm/2ft. Z5

I. germanica, the common purple bearded iris. In spite of the great influx of more flamboyant hybrids, this iris with its sweetly scented flowers is still worth growing. It is reliable, early and does not require

LEFT *Iris graminea* CENTRE *Iris unguicularis* RIGHT *Lunaria rediviva*

staking, which many of the newer forms do. A variety of fruity and vanilla scents can be detected in a number of the tall, intermediate and dwarf hybrids but it is difficult to compile a list; named varieties seem to come and go faster than Hybrid Tea roses. Plants should be split and replanted every few years, during high summer.
Full sun. Well-drained soil. 60–90cm/ 2–3ft. Z3

I. graminea is called the plum-tart iris because of the fruity scent of its flowers; they are small, reddish-purple and produced in early summer. This is a beautiful iris, with distinctively grassy leaves. For years I grew its broad-leaved variety, *pseudocyperus,* thinking it was the species, and wondered what all the fuss was about; the scent of this variety is elusive, usually absent. Now I have the species itself and have realized what I was missing.
Sun. 46cm/18in.

I. hoogiana is exceptionally handsome in flower and has a good rose scent. The blooms are lavender-blue, with a yellow flash, and appear in early summer; the foliage is bluish-green. It is an easily grown iris for the front of the border.
Sun. Well-drained soil. 60cm/2ft.

***I. pallida* subsp. *pallida* (*I.p.* var. *dalmatica*)** is a pastel beauty, valuable as much for its fans of greyish foliage, which remain respectable throughout the summer, as for its pale lavender-blue flowers; these appear in early summer and are very sweetly scented. It is an old garden plant of the first order.
Sun. Well-drained soil. 90cm/3ft.

***I. unguicularis* (*I. stylosa*)**, Algerian iris, is an essential plant for the fragrant garden. It blooms cheerfully on and off throughout the winter months, and it can be brought indoors to sniff in a vase. It has rich violet flowers, marked in golden-yellow, and these appear in quantity among the narrow, evergreen leaves. There are a number of colour variants; 'Mary Barnard' is a good strong violet and 'Walter Butt', in pale lavender, has an outstanding cowslip scent. It makes a good clump and wants roasting hot sunshine and dry soil to flower well; the base of a sunny wall is ideal. It resents disturbance.
Full sun. Poor, dry soil. 60cm/2ft.

LUNARIA
Brassicaceae

L. rediviva, perennial honesty or money plant, has white or pale lilac flowers, delicately scented of stocks, which appear in spring. Like the more common biennial honesty (which, incidentally, has a faint musty scent of its own), it has rice paper seedheads in the autumn and is an attractive plant for the spring border.
Sun or light shade. Any soil. 60cm/2ft.

MORINA
Caprifoliaceae

M. longifolia is a distinctive, evergreen, thistle-like plant that bears whorls of tubular, rose-pink and white flowers up stout stems in summer. But it is the prickly leaves that have a fragrance, of orange peel. It contributes an eyecatching silhouette to the border and its flowerheads are popular for dried flower arrangements.
Sun. 90cm/3ft.

Morina longifolia

LUPINUS
Papilionaceae

Lupins are plants that no cottage garden can be without. The tall spires of flowers, standing erect above the fingered foliage, are one of the delights of early summer. They come in almost every colour of the spectrum. There are some good seed strains available but for the most outstanding you need to purchase from a specialist breeder. The flowers have the typical, heavy, peppery, pea-family scent. Cut away the spikes after flowering and disguise the presence of the plants – which become sad and mildewy – by growing something slightly taller in front, such as *Phlox*.
Sun or light shade. 1.2m/4ft.

MAIANTHEMUM
Asparagaceae

M. formosanum has clusters of heavily scented starry white flowers borne on red stems. Light shade. Moist, well-drained soil. 90cm/3ft.
M. henryi is a woodland perennial with clusters of white or yellow tubular flowers in early summer, held on stems above the elliptic leaves and possessing a rich lily-of-the-valley fragrance; they are followed by red berries. Light shade. Moist, well-drained soil. 60cm/2ft.
M. racemosum (Smilacina racemosa) looks very like Solomon's seal until it reveals its flowerheads which are frothy cream plumes instead of pendent bells. It is one of the taller spring perennials and is valuable for this reason; the blooms, which have a surprisingly sweet lemony scent, appear in spring on 90cm/3ft stems. It is good with early oriental poppies

and tulips. I have also grown the shorter, colonizing *M. stellatum;* it is rather too weedy for the border. Light shade. Fertile, retentive, lime-free soil. Z3

MEEHANIA
Lamiaceae
M. urticifolia is a colonizing ground-cover plant with nettle-like leaves and spikes of large lavender-blue flowers in late spring, which have a deliciously fruity scent. I have it trailing over a low wall.
Sun or light shade. Moist, well-drained soil. 30cm/1ft.

MELITTIS
Lamiaceae
M. melissophyllum, bastard balm, is an interesting relative of dead nettle for the front of the shady border or woodland garden. The hairy leaves are markedly sweet-scented when dry. The tubular flowers are white with pinkish lower lips, and are borne in whorls in early summer.
Fertile, retentive soil. 46cm/18in.

MEUM
Apiaceae
M. athamanticum, baldmoney or spignel, with its spicily fragrant foliage and umbels of white or purplish flowers in summer, is a curiosity for the sunny border. Sun. 46cm/18in.

MONARDA see under Herbs

NEPETA
Lamiaceae
***N. cataria* 'Citriodora'** is a catmint with lemon-scented, grey-green leaves. The flowers are pale pink and appear in summer.
Sun. Well-drained soil. 90cm/3ft.
N.* x *faassenii, catmint, is one of the best edging plants, especially good lining a path under roses or running beneath a low retaining wall. The haze of greyish, aromatic foliage and lavender-blue flowers can be enjoyed for many weeks; if plants are cut back hard after their first early summer flush, they will provide a display on and off until the autumn. The young blue foliage is a striking complement to daffodils in the spring. 'Six Hills Giant' (90cm/3ft) is a more commonly offered form. It is larger, tougher, and generally considered preferable, especially in cold, damp areas. *N. racemosa* 'Walker's Low' is slightly shorter in height and a good selection. Sun. Well-drained soil. 46cm/18in. Z3
***N. sibirica* 'Souvenir d'André Chaudron'** is shorter than its parent and more beautiful in flower but beware: the leaf scent is fruitily fetid and quite nauseating. 46cm/18in.

LEFT Pink lupins CENTRE *Maianthemum racemosum* RIGHT *Nepeta* x *faassenii* 'Kit Cat'

FAR LEFT *Paeonia lactiflora* 'Sarah Bernhardt'
LEFT *Paeonia emodi*

PAEONIA
Paeoniaceae

Peonies are among the showiest perennials in the early summer border and are an integral part of the cottage garden. Most people grow the Chinese hybrids, forms of *P. lactiflora*, which produce those great globes or dishes of pink, crimson or white petals; most of these have a sweet scent, sometimes spicy, fruity and rosy, sometimes a bit soapy. The species peonies, though harder to find in nurseries, are also of great beauty, in leaf as well as flower, and bloom a month or so earlier; some of these are scented too. The common peony, *P. officinalis*, has a rather unpleasant smell. All peonies resent disturbance. Deep, rich soil.

P. emodi is rarely offered but is a real gem. It has pure white, scented flowers, single and filled with golden stamens, in May, and bright green foliage. Its excellent white-flowered hybrid 'Late Windflower' is also scented.
Light shade. 90cm/3ft.

P. lactiflora is seldom grown, in spite of its great beauty. It has large, white, scented flowers, single and filled with golden stamens, and excellent reddish foliage. It is hard to make a choice among the more commonly offered hybrids, but among the doubles I would suggest, for scent, 'Duchesse de Nemours' in creamy white, 'Baroness Schroeder' in blush white, 'Sarah Bernhardt' and 'Claire Dubois' in pale pink, 'Laura Dessert' in palest lemon, 'Président Poincaré' in deep carmine, and 'Philippe Rivoire' in crimson. Among the singles, 'White Wings' is good. The huge, single dishes of the Imperial or Japanese peonies, which are filled inside with smaller petals, have their own appeal; 'Calypso' in carmine and gold, and 'Crimson Glory' in ruby-red have a good scent.
Sun or shade. 90cm/3ft.

PERSICARIA
Polygonaceae

***P. alpina* (*P. polymorpha*)** is useful for producing a tall feature early in the season and giving a long-lasting performance with plumes of creamy flowers that gradually mature to pink. Unfortunately, the scent is strong and horsey. 2m/6ft.

***P. amplexicaulis* 'Alba'** is the white version of the commonly encountered red knotweed of summer borders, which produces bottlebrush flowers on wiry stems for months on end. It has a delicate honey scent, and is lovely with dark dahlias. Sun or part shade. All but dry soils. 90cm/3ft.

***P. wallichii* (*P. polystachya*)** is a tall invasive perennial for the wild garden or pondside. It is valuable for its autumn display of white, vanilla-scented plumes, though its pointed foliage, with its red veins and stems, is attractive all summer. Good groundcover, but only where its vigour will not be embarrassing.
2m/6ft.

PETASITES
Asteraceae

P. fragrans, winter heliotrope, is only for very brave or reckless gardeners. It is an extremely vigorous colonizer but fun to grow in a self-contained bed in a wild garden, ideally bounded by water. It has large, rounded foliage – smaller than the familiar *P. japonicus*, though – but its heads of white flowers, which have a strong sweet vanilla scent, appear in late winter just before the leaves start to expand. Retentive soil. 30cm/1ft.

PHLOX
Polemoniaceae

P. maculata is a little shorter than the more common *P. paniculata* and has cylindrical rather than pyramidal heads. It is usually seen in its lilac-pink 'Alpha' and white, lilac-eyed 'Omega' forms, which have the sweet, peppery *Phlox* scent. They make a change from other *Phlox* and are very pretty.
Sun or light shade. Fertile, retentive soil. 90cm/3ft.

P. paniculata is a mainstay of the border in high summer and provides great blocks of colour in shades of pink, violet, crimson-purple, salmon and white. The peppery sweet scent carries well in the evening. I am very fond of the ordinary, lavender-blue, wild species and grow it in a big group next to red *Persicaria*. 'White Admiral' and 'Mount Fuji' are fine whites; 'Sandringham' and 'Balmoral' are good pinks; these tend to have better scents than the stronger colours. They can be prone to eelworm and mildew, and should be divided regularly.
Sun or light shade. Fertile, moisture-retentive soil. Up to 1.2m/4ft. Z4

PINELLIA
Araceae

P. cordata is an interesting member of the arum family with handsomely veined arrowhead leaves and greenish mousetail flowers which have a strong fruity scent.
Light shade. Moist, well-drained soil. 20cm/8in.

POLYGONATUM
Asparagaceae

P. x hybridum, Solomon's seal, I mention because it is a favourite spring perennial of mine, but its scent is very slight. It drips its white, green-tipped bells from arching stems, and is a characterful subject for the shady border or wild garden. Shade. Retentive soil. 90cm/3ft. Z4

PRIMULA
Primulaceae

P. veris, cowslip, is a plant that looks its best in the wildflower meadow; seedlings can be planted in the grass in autumn and thereafter annual mowing is delayed until midsummer. The rich yellow bells have a distinctive sweet scent of their own.
Retentive, limy soil. 15cm/6in. Z5

P. vialii is a startling little primula that produces erect scarlet pokers from which hang violet bells; these sometimes have a good scent. Its foliage appears rather late in the year and although easily raised from seed, plants are neither long-lived nor easy to establish; but always a talking point when in flower.
Light shade. Retentive soil. 30cm/1ft.

P. vulgaris, primrose, is lovely on shady banks, again in grass if possible and with bluebells. It is too well known to need description but a surprising number of people have never sniffed the pale yellow flowers.

LEFT *Phlox maculata* 'Alpha' RIGHT *Primula vulgaris*

The scent is passed to many of the double kinds and is evident in many polyanthus. It is sensational in some Cornish gardens colonizing on grass banks with intense pink *Cyclamen repandum*.
Light shade. Retentive soil. 5cm/2in. Z5

SALVIA
Lamiaceae

Salvia are a fascinating group of plants for the scent-conscious gardener. The scent comes from the leaves, and the range of flavours among the different species is staggering. Pineapple, blackcurrant, sage, rose, roast lamb and even old socks are present. I am not covering them all here: I have listed sage under Herbs and the tender species are included under Tender Plants.
Sun. Well-drained soil.

S. glutinosa, Jupiter's distaff, a hardy *Salvia* with pale yellow, hooded flowers, blooms during late summer. The coarse, heart-shaped leaves have a fruity but rather clammy aroma. It is interesting rather than spectacular. 90cm/3ft.

S. uliginosa is a striking autumn perennial with branching spikes of flowers in kingfisher blue. The foliage is sufficiently minty to disguise the fetid undertones. It is moderately hardy in cold areas if given a mulch.
Sun. Retentive soil. 1.5m/5ft.

SAPONARIA
Caryophyllaceae

***S. officinalis* 'Alba Plena'** is a white, double-flowered form of pink soapwort and has a delicate and delicious sweet-shop perfume. It is a lovely addition to the front of a late summer border, especially good with purple *Salvia* and blue *Agapanthus*. It does not have the invasive instinct of its parent. There is also a mauve-pink form. Sun. Any soil. 60cm/2ft.

SILENE
Caryophyllaceae

S. nutans, Nottingham catchfly, is a British native with white, night-opening and night-scented flowers from purple-striped pouched buds. Annual *S. noctiflora* is also well-scented.
Sun. Well-drained soil. 60cm/2ft.

SMILACINA see ***Maianthemum***

TELLIMA
Saxifragaceae

***T. grandiflora* Rubra Group** is a favourite of mine for the front of a shady border. It makes neat clumps of scalloped leaves that turn an attractive crimson in winter; they are an ideal foil for snowdrops. Wispy racemes of tiny greenish bells appear in early summer and their scent is piercingly sweet. I could not do without it.
Sun or shade. Any soil. 60cm/2ft.

THALICTRUM
Ranunculaceae

***T. actaeifolium* 'Perfume Star'** is a beautiful meadow rue which produces a cloud of rose-scented, lavender flowers above its ferny leaves in early summer. Two other more unusual scented thalictrums are white-flowered *T. omeiense* and mauve *T. punctatum*.
Light shade. Moist, well-drained soil. 90cm/3ft.

VALERIANA
Caprifoliaceae

V. officinalis, common valerian, bears pale pink flowers above its toothed leaves in early summer. They have a

Saponaria officinalis

LEFT *Tellima grandiflora* RIGHT *Viola odorata*

myrrh or calamine lotion scent; some people find it a little heavy, even unpleasant. It gently seeds itself about between shrub roses in my garden. Sun or light shade. Any soil. 90cm/3ft.

VERBENA

Verbenaceae

V. bonariensis is a distinctive and popular perennial for the summer border. The flat heads of mauve flowers, loved by butterflies, have a light *Phlox*-like scent and are presented at nose height on wiry branching stems. It seeds itself freely in open ground, and is a striking feature when grown in a large group. Sun. Well-drained soil. 1.5m/5ft. Z10

VIOLA

Violaceae

A honeyed scent is evident in many of the cultivars of viola, those smaller, more perennial counterparts to the pansy. They come in all colours, plain and with faces, and perform for months on end. 'Aspasia' in yellow and cream, 'Little David' in cream, 'Inverurie Beauty' in violet, 'Maggie Mott', a cream-centred mauve, and 'Mrs Lancaster' in white, are notably well endowed with fragrance.

V. cornuta is honey-scented and comes in shades of violet and white. It is a charming, thoroughly perennial viola, which gently infiltrates neighbouring plants through the growing season. It is good with shrub roses. Sun or light shade. Any soil. 30cm/1ft.

V. odorata, the British native sweet violet, is an easy plant that seeds itself about. It comes in all colours from purple and pink to yellow and white, and some of these are named; 'Coeur d'Alsace' is usually a particularly fine deep pink. The main flowering is in spring, but many perform in the autumn and, during mild spells, right through the winter. The violet scent is refined but can be elusive. Shade or, on retentive soil, sun. Fertile soil. 15cm/6in.

Florist's sweet violets are derived from *V. odorata* and the North American species *V. obliqua*. They are hardy but because the flowers, particularly of the double varieties, are easily spoiled by wet and frosty weather, they are best suited to cold frame culture. When you lift the glass roof, the blast of refined perfume is a real treat. They are superb in a Mediterranean climate. Fertile, retentive soil. 15cm/6in.

YPSILANDRA

Melanthiaceae

Y. thibetica is an evergreen grassy-leaved perennial with spikes of white or pale lilac, starry flowers, with prominently protruding stamens, in early spring. They have a strong lily-of-the-valley scent. Light shade. Moist, well-drained soil. 60cm/2ft.

BULBS

AMARYLLIS
Amaryllidaceae
A. belladonna flowers usefully late, in the autumn. Its clusters of large rose-pink stars, which have a fruity apricot scent, are supported on dark purple stems. The leaves appear afterwards and persist through the winter. It likes a well-drained position, though not too dry. Pink and white forms are available.
Sun. 60cm/2ft.

ARISAEMA
Araceae
A. candidissimum is a curious and hardy Chinese plant that is well worth growing. Its flowers take the form of spathes. These are pure white, striped inside with pink and outside with green; the spadix is greenish-yellow. The flowers have a slight scent and appear in early summer. Large, three-lobed leaves follow the flowers.
Sun or light shade. Retentive, acid soil. 30cm/1ft.

CARDIOCRINUM
Liliaceae
C. giganteum, the giant Himalayan lily, is among the most imposing of garden plants. Its tall stems are topped with pure white trumpet flowers, splashed inside with crimson-red. They have a cool, sweet scent, laced with coconut. This is a plant for the woodland garden and is wonderful in an open clearing between rhododendrons. Bulbs flower in high summer and die afterwards, leaving offsets which can be lifted the following spring and replanted with their noses just above the surface. I leave mine in the ground to regenerate naturally. Offsets take 4 years to flower, and seed takes 12 months to germinate and up to 8 years to produce flowering-sized bulbs. But it is most definitely worth the wait. The variety *yunnanense* is usually shorter in stature, and has chocolate stems and less pendent flowers. It is only marginally less impressive.
Light shade. Deep, rich, retentive soil. 2.3–3m/7–10ft.

CRINUM
Amaryllidaceae
C. x powellii produces its rose-pink trumpets on stout stems in late summer and these have a light fragrance of lilies. The flowers are very impressive but are rather let down by the coarse, often battered and yellowish, strap-like leaves. Plant them with the necks protruding above the soil. It needs protection from the wind and in

RIGHT *Arisaema candidissimum*
FAR RIGHT *Cardiocrinum giganteum* var. *yunnanense*

LEFT *Crocus biflorus* 'Blue Pearl' RIGHT *Cyclamen hederifolium*

very cold areas, a winter mulch will be necessary. There is a good white form, 'Album'.
Full sun. Fertile soil, not too dry. 90cm/3ft.

CROCUS
Iridaceae

Crocuses can flood autumn, winter and early spring borders with colour, but to enjoy their scent you really need to grow some at nose level, on banks, in pots and in raised beds. The winter crocuses are often ruined by bad weather and it is a wise precaution to put a pane of glass over them as they come into flower. Growing some in pots in a cold frame, to bring indoors at flowering time is also well worthwhile. Outdoors they like ample moisture while in leaf.
Sun. Well-drained soil.

***C. biflorus* 'Blue Pearl'** is a lovely fragrant lavender-blue. They bloom in late winter.

C. chrysanthus is the most important scented species and gives us a range of named varieties in shades of lavender, violet, purple, yellow and white; 'Cream Beauty', buttery 'E. A. Bowles', maroon-striped yellow *C. chrysanthus* var. *fusco-tinctus*, and white 'Snow Bunting' are beautiful and especially rich in the thick, golden honey scent.

C. laevigatus blooms in mid-winter and its lilac, feathered cups have a powerfully sweet scent. Its variety *fontenayi* has a buff exterior.

C. longiflorus has bluish-violet flowers – paler on the outside – in autumn and a good, sweet scent.

C. speciosus is the easiest of autumn-flowering crocuses, often naturalizing in borders, under trees and in thin grass. The scented flowers come in various shades of lilac-blue and white, and there are a number of named varieties. No garden should be without it.
Sun or light shade. 10cm/4in.

C. versicolor has purple-veined lilac flowers in winter. They have a fine scent, as have those of its white, purple-striped version 'Picturatus'.

CYCLAMEN
Primulaceae

There are two species of hardy cyclamen with a pronounced scent, *C. hederifolium* (in its scented strains) and *C. purpurascens; C. coum* and its cousins, which make such a splash of carmine, pink and white in the late winter garden, are scentless. Other cyclamen worth growing for their lily-of-the-valley or honey fragrance, but requiring cold frame cultivation, include autumn-flowering *C. cilicium* and spring-flowering *C. balearicum* and *C. pseudibericum*. The frost-tender *C. cyprium* and *C. persicum* benefit from a little heat; both are deliciously fragrant but the latter, described under Tender Plants, has not passed its scent to the

large-flowered florist's strains.
Shade. Well-drained soil.
***C. hederifolium* (*C. neapolitanum*)** produces its flowers in late summer, the first appearing just before the leaves. It comes in all shades of pink and white. The musky sweet fragrance is often absent or very faint, but there is a strongly scented strain in circulation. The foliage displays great variety in shape and silver marbling and remains in beauty from autumn until spring. It will colonize dry, shady areas around the boles of deciduous trees and enjoys a dressing of leaf-mould during the summer.
***C. purpurascens* (*C. europaeum*)** is a lime-loving, strongly scented species that blooms through the summer and autumn. It is usually evergreen, its leaves being circular with some patterning. It is reliable in all but the coldest areas.
Well-drained soil.

EUCOMIS
Asparagaceae

E. autumnalis is one of a number of eucomis with a pleasant coconut scent – in contrast to the foul meaty smell of the commonly grown *E. bicolor*. The flowers look like pineapples and are produced in late summer. In this species they are short and greenish-white.
***E. zambesiaca* 'White Dwarf'** is similar but whiter, with a good coconut scent. It is excellent in pots.
Sun. Good, well-drained soil. 30cm/1ft.

GALANTHUS
Amaryllidaceae

Many snowdrops have a pronounced scent, most noticeable when you bring them indoors. The common snowdrop, *G. nivalis*, is not well endowed; the double form is a little better. But among the best varieties to choose for a strong honey fragrance are 'S. Arnott', a superb and vigorous snowdrop with perfect flowers, and 'Straffan', a splendid late-blooming variety, with large flowers. They can be divided, like all snowdrops, immediately after flowering, or in autumn.
Light shade. Fertile, retentive soil.

GALTONIA
Asparagaceae

G. candicans, the Cape hyacinth of southern Africa. The flower spikes drip with white, green-tipped bells during high summer; and these have a delicate scent. This is an invaluable border plant and superb in combination with *Agapanthus* and *Kniphofia*.
Sun. Well-drained, fertile but not dry soil. 90cm–1.2m/3–4ft.

HERMODACTYLUS
Iridaceae

***H. tuberosus* (*Iris tuberosa*)**, snake's head, is a desirable spring bulb with a distinctive and rather sinister colour scheme: the iris-like flowers have

LEFT *Galanthus* 'S. Arnott' CENTRE *Hyacinthus orientalis* RIGHT *Iris reticulata*

greenish-yellow standards and velvet black falls. These appear in spring and have a delicate spicily sweet scent. It needs a sheltered position.
Sun. Well-drained, limy soil. 30cm/1ft.

HYACINTHUS
Asparagaceae

H. orientalis The florist's hyacinths can be grown outside or in bowls to be enjoyed indoors: for Christmas blooms, plant prepared bulbs in fibre in late summer and keep them somewhere cool until the emergent flowerheads are 5cm/2in high; then introduce them by stages into the warmth. All colours are available. Unfortunately, as the flowers of new varieties get bigger, the scent becomes weaker; the old Roman hyacinths, taller and more elegant, were very sweet, but where are they now?
Sun. Well-drained soil.
10–20cm/4–8in.

IRIS
Iridaceae

I. reticulata enjoys the same conditions outside as the variety *bakeriana* and also needs a raised bed if you are to savour the violet scent; but there are few more rewarding bulbs to grow in pots to bring indoors at flowering time. The flowers are a rich imperial purple with a prominent orange-yellow flash on the falls. They are produced in mid-winter. To my nose, none of the named colour variants is as scented as its parent.
15cm/6in.

I. reticulata* var. *bakeriana is rare and lacking in vigour, but it is a beautiful dwarf iris with a violet

HYACINTHOIDES
Asparagaceae

H. non-scripta, English bluebell, fills whole woods with its sweetly honeyed balsam scent in late spring, and is lovely to introduce through shady areas of the garden, especially in association with yellows like double-flowered gorse and lemon azaleas. The Spanish bluebell, *H. hispanica*, is more substantial, equally invasive, but less scented; I have the blue and white forms colonizing among lime-green *Smyrnium perfoliatum* by a beech hedge.
20–40cm/8–16in.

Hyacinthoides non-scripta

LEFT *Leucojum vernum*
BELOW *Lilium candidum*

scent and colour, and purple and white markings on the falls. Outside, it should be planted in a raised bed, but it may be grown satisfactorily in pots in a cold frame.
Sun. Well-drained soil. 15cm/6in.

LEUCOJUM
Amaryllidaceae

L. vernum, spring snowflake, looks much like a snowdrop but has green strap-like leaves and inner and outer segments (petals) of uniform length; the flowers resemble lampshades. This winter-flowering species is small with violet-scented flowers; the larger, more imposing, summer snowflake, *L. aestivum,* which flowers in spring, is unscented.
Sun or shade. Retentive or damp soil. 15cm/6in.

LILIUM
Liliaceae

L. auratum, the golden-rayed lily of Japan, bears large, open flowers during late summer. They are waxy white, streaked in golden-yellow and speckled with crimson, and sometimes as many as 30 are carried on a stem. The scent is spicily sweet. It is not an easy lily to cultivate, being prone to virus, but is certainly one of the most stunning of the lilies. It enjoys shelter and is suitable for growing in pots. The variety *platyphyllum* is stockier, larger in flower, and perhaps more amenable.
Dappled sunlight. Well-drained, lime-free, humus-rich soil. 1.5–2.5m/5–8ft.

L. candidum, Madonna lily, has been in cultivation for centuries. The tall stems carry numerous pure white, honey-scented open trumpets during high summer. It is a traditional feature of the cottage garden and thrives in the sunny border among perennials, which shade its basal foliage. It sends up new leaves in late summer so is best transplanted soon after flowering. Plant shallowly, with the nose at soil level. It is not always easy to establish, and hates acid soils like mine.
Sun. Limy or neutral soil. 90cm/3ft.

L. cernuum is a dainty lily with small turk's cap flowers, that are rosy-lilac in colour and spotted. It has a sweet scent. It is not especially easy to grow nor is it long-lived, but it is an interesting plant for open positions. It blooms at midsummer.
Sun. Well-drained, humus-rich soil. 60–90cm/2–3ft.

L. duchartrei, Farrer's marble martagon. This beautiful lily bears umbels of small white fragrant turk's cap flowers, which are spotted with purple and become reddish-purple as they mature. It is stoloniferous and stem-rooting and can form large colonies under ideal conditions, though it has not yet done that for me in my raised bed.
Shade. Moist, well-drained, neutral to acid soil. 30–90cm/1–3ft.

L. formosanum* var. *pricei is the hardy, dwarf form of the tender *L. formosanum,* and can be safely

RIGHT *Lilium hansonii*
FAR RIGHT *Lilium regale* 'Album'

grown outside in all but the coldest regions. It produces long, pure white, sweetly scented trumpets in late summer. It does well planted deeply among dwarf shrubs. Though short-lived, it comes readily from seed and flowers in its first year.
Sun or light shade. Well-drained, humus-rich soil. 30–60cm/1–2ft.

L. hansonii bears orange-yellow, lightly scented turk's caps in early summer and is among the easiest to grow. The flowers are speckled in brown and are not as recurved as other turk's cap species. In the right conditions it will persist for many years. Light shade. Deep, fertile soil. 1.2–1.5m/4–5ft.

L. kelloggii is an interesting rare lily from northwest California with pendulous pale mauve-pink turk's caps, spotted maroon, which are honey-scented and appear in high summer. Light shade. Retentive soil. 30cm–1.2m/1–4ft.

L. leucanthum* var. *centifolium has trumpets that are white inside and a wonderful blend of green and rose-purple outside. They have a sweet fruity scent. It is an uncommon lily but well worth seeking out, as it is stunning when in flower.
Sun. Well-drained soil. 2–2.7m/6–9ft.

L. monadelphum produces its drooping reflexed trumpets at midsummer. They are creamy yellow in colour, tinged and sometimes spotted with wine purple, and have a strong scent, sweet but slightly fetid at close range. It is an adaptable plant.
Light shade. Most soils. 90cm–1.5m/3–5ft.

L. nepalense is one of the most exotic-looking lilies, and from tiny bulbs you get huge recurved trumpet flowers in greenish-cream flushed maroon inside. They have a refreshing lime perfume. They need space as the stems wander underground, and I have found they are best in a raised bed. The similar but taller *L. majoense* is also well-scented.
Light shade. Moist, well-drained acid soil. 60–90cm/2–3ft.

L. parryi is an exceptionally lovely lily from the West Coast of America. The slightly reflexed trumpets are a clear lemon-yellow and are borne in high summer. The scent is powerful and sweet. It is not an easy lily to grow, however, requiring dry conditions above ground and moist below; open woodland sites can be acceptable.
60cm–2m/2–6ft.

L. pumilum is one of my favourite lilies, with often short stems bearing small orange-scarlet turk's cap flowers of lacquered, oriental appearance. They have a delicious chocolate scent. Unfortunately, I do not find them long-lived in my garden.
Sun or light shade. Moist, well-drained soil. 30–60cm/1–2ft.

L. regale is, with *L. candidum*, the most familiar of fragrant garden lilies. Its white, yellow-throated trumpets are slightly reflexed and are shaded rose-purple outside. They open in high summer, sometimes 30 to a stem, and have a delicious fruity scent that carries well. A position between low shrubs suits it admirably, for its young shoots are susceptible to early frosts. It comes readily from seed and flowers in its second or third year. A fine pure white form, 'Album', is available.
Full sun. Most soils. 90cm–2m/3–6ft.

L. x testaceum, the Nankeen lily, has scented turk's caps in a delicate shade of creamy apricot. It flowers in high summer. It is an easy lily to grow but is now becoming rare.

Full sun. Deep, fertile, acid or alkaline soil. 1.2–2m/4–6ft.

Hardy hybrid lilies

Numerous hybrid lilies have been bred from scented lily species. The Oriental hybrids (O), which include strains and clones derived from *L. x parkmanii,* generally thrive in open, woodland conditions, on acid, gritty, humus-rich soil, with their heads in the sun and their roots in the shade; the Trumpet and so-called Aurelian hybrids (T) usually prefer full sun and a drier soil: most make good pot plants. There are also dwarf and double-flowered scented Oriental hybrids, and giant Goliath lilies which are Oriental/Trumpet hybrids. The following are among the best fragrant varieties.

'African Queen' (T) is one of my favourite lilies, and makes a good garden perennial. The flowers are soft orange, flushed crimson in bud. 1.2–1.5m/4–5ft.

'Black Dragon' (T) is a strong, vigorous lily with large white, recurved trumpets, stained reddish-brown outside. It flowers in high summer. 1.2–2m/4–6ft.

'Brasilia' (O) has white flowers edged and dotted in rose-pink. 1.2m/4ft.

'Casa Blanca' (O) is a superb scented lily, with large, pure white flowers in high summer. 1.2m/4ft.

Golden Splendour Group (T) is a rich yellow, flushed orange-red in bud. 1.2–1.5m/4–5ft.

'Green Dragon' (T) is similar to 'Black Dragon' but has a green reverse. They are both highly desirable lilies.

Imperial Groups (O) – **Crimson** is a strain of flamboyant lilies with open, white flowers, suffused and speckled with bright rose-red. **Imperial Gold** have open, glistening white flowers, striped in gold and peppered with crimson spots. **Imperial Silver** is similar to Imperial Gold but lacks the rich stripe. They bloom in high summer. 1.2–1.5m/4–5ft.

'Limelight' (T) bears unusual greenish-yellow funnels in high summer. It is a reliable and impressive variety which tolerates some shade. 1.2–2m/4–6ft.

Olympic Group (T) provide a range of splendid scented trumpet lilies, from cream to pink and yellow. 1.2–1.5m/4–5ft.

Pink Perfection Group (T) is a strain of bright pink trumpet lilies which flower in July. 1.5–2m/5–6ft.

'Stargazer' (O) is a well-known crimson-red, white-edged lily with a powerful scent. 90cm/3ft.

MUSCARI

Asparagaceae

M. armeniacum is one of the most common of the grape hyacinths. Its bright azure blue pokers appear in spring and are delicately honey-scented. It is a vigorous colonizer for the front of the border. The grassy

LEFT *Lilium* Pink Perfection Group RIGHT *Muscari armeniacum* 'Valerie Finnis'

foliage is evident throughout the winter. It is lovely with primroses. 'Valerie Finnis' is a pale blue form with an intense sweet-shop scent.
Sun or light shade. Most soils. 20cm/8in.

M. botryoides is less vigorous than *M. armeniacum* and trustworthy among choice plants, even in the rock garden. Its china-blue flowers have a good honey scent. The white form, 'Album', is more commonly available.
Sun. 15cm/6in.

M. macrocarpum has bright yellow flowers and an astonishingly strong and intoxicating fruity-spicy perfume. It is hardy in milder areas, but most often grown in pots – it is one of the most desirable of all pot bulbs for scent.
Sun. Well-drained soil. 20cm/8in.

M. muscarimi **(*M. moschatum*)** is a curiosity with flowers that change from purple to yellowish-green as they age. Together with *M. macrocarpum*, it has the best scent of all muscari, a sweet musky fragrance which carries in the air on warm days.
Sun. 20cm/8in.

NARCISSUS
Amaryllidaceae

This great tribe contributes colour throughout spring. The larger daffodils are at their best at the back of the border, where their dying leaves are concealed by the growth of other plants, or in grass, where they can be left to naturalize; their foliage must not be cut down until 6 weeks after flowering. The smaller daffodils are for the front of the border, the rock garden, raised beds or for pots (those grouped under *N. jonquilla* and *N. tazetta* are especially suited to pot culture); some may also be grown in grass. There is scent in most of them. Often it is pleasantly mossy and often it is nastily fetid; but in some it is powerfully sweet and these are the varieties I describe here.

N. assoanus **(*N. juncifolius*)** is a miniature jonquil with narrow leaves and small, deep yellow flowers in early spring. These have a good scent. It can be grown outside in sheltered spots but is perhaps best as a pot bulb.
Sun. Well-drained soil. 15cm/6in.

N. jonquilla, jonquil, has perhaps the sweetest scent of all daffodils. It has narrow rushy leaves and small, very shallow-cupped, bright yellow flowers. 'Flore Pleno' and 'Pencrebar' are double forms with outstanding scents. There are many excellent, powerfully scented, single jonquils, derived from this and other jonquil species, including: 'Baby Moon', dwarf yellow; 'Bobbysoxer', yellow with orange cup; 'Lintie', clear yellow with orange cup; 'Orange Queen', deep orange-yellow; 'Sugarbush', white with pinkish cup; 'Sundial', pale yellow with orange cup; 'Suzy', bright

LEFT *Muscari macrocarpum* RIGHT *Narcissus jonquilla*

LEFT *Narcissus poeticus* var. *recurvus* RIGHT *Tulipa tarda*

yellow with bright orange cup; and 'Trevithian' in lemon-yellow. Outside, they need a sheltered position. They are superb pot bulbs.
Sun. 30cm/1ft.

N.* x *odorus is the Campernelle jonquil, and has bright yellow flowers. There is a good double form.
30cm/1ft.

N. poeticus var. ***recurvus***, old pheasant's eye narcissus, is a lovely, unsophisticated daffodil for naturalizing in grass. It blooms at the end of the daffodil season and has white flowers with a tiny, yellow, orange-rimmed cup. 'Actaea' is a similar variety but with larger flowers, a finer shape, and more vigour; and 'Cantabile' gives single flowers of perfect, exhibition quality. All have an outstanding sweet scent.
Sun or light shade. Retentive soil.
38cm/15in.

N. rupicola is similar to *N. assoanus* but it has larger flowers, singly borne, and glaucous greyish leaves. It is also a better garden plant with a stronger scent.
Sun. Well-drained soil. 15cm/6in.

N. tazetta is a very sweetly scented, bunch-flowered daffodil that needs a hot, dry, sheltered site to perform satisfactorily outside, but is excellent in pots. The closely related *N. canaliculatus* is more commonly offered; this has white flowers with golden cups. Fine named hybrids of *N. tazetta* include white 'Avalanche', 'Minnow', a lemon-yellow dwarf; 'Cragford' and 'Geranium', both white with orange cup; 'Silver Chimes' in creamy white; and white 'Cheerfulness' and 'Yellow Cheerfulness', both doubles. These are reliable outside, if given sun and shelter, and also make good pot bulbs; the popular Christmas pot tazetta 'Paper White' is unreliable outside except in mild areas – the scent is a bit horsey for me.
46cm/18in.

NOTHOLIRION
Liliaceae

N. thomsonianum is a rare plant for the connoisseur. It bears pale rose-lilac flowers that are funnel-shaped with recurving tips, like a lily. These are carried on tall stems in spring and are sweetly scented; the leaves are long and narrow. It requires a sheltered position and cool greenhouse treatment is usually necessary in colder regions.
Full sun. Well-drained soil.
90cm/3ft.

TULIPA
Liliaceae

Scent is not a quality you expect to find in tulips but a few species, and even a few tall hybrids, possess a warm sweet scent. They are all good in pots as well as in the border.

T. aucheriana is, in its most scented form, a dwarf pale pink tulip, striped in greenish-yellow with a deep golden-yellow base. But it is very

SCILLA
Asparagaceae

S. autumnalis produces racemes of scented violet-blue flowers in early autumn. It is good in a pot.
Sun or light shade. Well-drained soil. 5–10cm/2–4in.
S. mischtschenkoana is a miniature plant that produces its pale, cup-shaped flowers with its strap-like leaves in early spring. They have a lovely sweet-shop scent.
Sun or light shade. Well-drained soil. 5–10cm/2–4in.
S. sibirica is the commonly grown *Scilla*, with intense blue starry flowers. They have a light but delightful sugary scent.
Sun or light shade. Well-drained soil. 10cm/4in.

Scilla sibirica

variable. It is excellent as a pot plant, but short-lived outside.
Sun. Well-drained soil. 15cm/6in.
T. clusiana, lady tulip, is a striking species with scented white flowers, striped in crimson-pink in spring. It appreciates heat and shelter.
Sun. Well-drained soil. 30cm/1ft.
T. saxatilis has lilac-pink flowers with a prominent yellow centre. It is a good perennial only in a hot sunny spot. Sun. Well-drained soil. 30cm/1ft.
T. sylvestris is easily cultivated and one of the few tulips which can be satisfactorily naturalized in grass. It is often shy to flower though. The blooms are bright yellow with pointed segments and open in mid-spring.
Sun or light shade. Moist soil. 30cm/1ft.
T. tarda is a dwarf tulip for sunny rock gardens and raised beds. It produces bunches of white, starry flowers, tinged greenish-yellow on the outside and filled with yellow within. These appear in mid-spring and have a noticeable scent. It is easily grown and reliable. Sun. Well-drained soil. 15cm/6in.

Hybrid tulips

It is always worth smelling a tulip to test its scent. The best known scented hybrids are 'General de Wet' ('De Wet'), in bright golden-orange, 'Bellona' in golden-yellow, and 'Prince of Austria' in bright orange-red. They are good, tall-stemmed plants but 'Prince of Austria' seems to have vanished from bulb lists. 'Lighting Sun' is a new introduction with a sweet scent. 'Apricot Beauty', orange 'Ballerina', brown 'Brazil' and the parrot tulip 'Orange Favourite' are also spicily fruit-scented.
Sun. 38cm/15in.

Tulipa sylvestris

RHS GARDEN HARLOW CARR

'RHS Garden Harlow Carr has had a Scented Garden within it for many years, and because of its popularity it was refurbished by the RHS after 2002 with the help of local funding. An intimate, hedged and paved enclosure, it has a succession of seasonal scents, encompassing winter *Viburnum*, spring hyacinths, *Hesperis matronalis* and *Valeriana officinalis*, and summer roses, *Philadelphus* and tobacco flowers. Scent is a feature in many other parts of the garden, too, notably in the woods where azaleas and Loderi rhododendrons thrive, and along the stream where meadowsweet and lemon-scented Himalayan cowslip, *Primula florindae*, have naturalized. Container displays at Harlow Carr include scented lilies and sweet peas, which are also grown in the Productive Garden. In the Alpine House, the scents can be as potent in autumn as in spring, thanks to bulbs like autumn crocus and *Scilla autumnalis* – this last accompanied by a sign encouraging visitors to smell it.'

Paul Cook, Curator at RHS Garden Harlow Carr

The Scented Garden in spring with borders of daffodils, tulips and hyacinths at RHS Garden Harlow Carr

ANNUALS & BIENNIALS

ABRONIA
Nyctaginaceae
A. fragrans, sand verbena, is a half-hardy annual or perennial of trailing habit. Its domed heads of white or pink flowers appear from high summer until early autumn. They have a sweet scent which carries freely in the late afternoon and evening.
Sun. Well-drained soil. 15cm/6in or more.

ANTIRRHINUM
Plantaginaceae
A. majus, snapdragon, sometimes has a light scent. This half-hardy annual comes in a kaleidoscope of brilliant colours, as singles or doubles, and in a range of heights. It often self-sows. Rust can be a problem, and resistant varieties are available. A summer bedding favourite. Sun. Well-drained soil. 23–90cm/9in–3ft.

ASPERULA
Rubiaceae
A. orientalis, blue woodruff, is a charming, old-fashioned hardy annual for the front of the border. Its slender leaves are borne in whorls and create a hazy effect; they are topped from high summer until autumn with clusters of tubular, violet-blue flowers, which have a sweet scent.
Sun. 30cm/1ft.

CALENDULA
Asteraceae
C. officinalis, pot marigold, has a distinctive tangy scent in flowers and foliage. It is a medicinal and culinary plant and is as much at home in the herb garden as the flower border. The flowers are brilliant orange. Many garden varieties are available, including creams and yellows, and forms with extra large, fully double flowers. It is fully hardy, can be sown *in situ* in autumn or spring, and will seed itself thereafter. The flowers are good for cutting.
Sun or light shade. 46cm/18in.

CENTAUREA
Asteraceae
C. moschata, sweet sultan, is a hardy annual now most commonly seen in its Giant or Imperialis strain. The large, fluffy flowers are borne on tall stems from high summer until early autumn and are excellent for cutting. They come in shades of rose-pink, white, purple, and lemon-yellow and all have a powerful, musk-sweet fragrance. Another cottage garden favourite.
Sun. 60cm/2ft.

RIGHT *Antirrhinum majus*
FAR RIGHT *Calendula officinalis*

RIGHT *Dianthus barbatus*
FAR RIGHT *Exacum affine*

DIANTHUS
Caryophyllaceae

D. barbatus, sweet William, is usually grown as a biennial; seed is best sown early, under glass, in mid- to late spring. The flowers are borne in generous heads during early summer and contribute much to the cottage garden mood. Single and double flowers are available, in single or mixed colour collections. Some flowers have pronounced eyes, and the colour range encompasses lilac, mauve, rose and magenta-pink, white and blood red. At their best, they have a superb clove fragrance, but highly selected strains often have little or no scent. The flowers are good for cutting. The 'Magic Charms' series, grown as annuals, also give a range of pink, red and white coloured flowers with a good scent.
Sun. 15–60cm/6in–2ft.

D. caryophyllus, carnation, can make an excellent and easy half-hardy annual. The Chabaud Giant is one of the best strains with large, double, fringed blooms usually in crimson, salmon and rose-pink. The 'Knight' series of F1 hybrids also gives fine bedding plants in a superb range of colours including yellows and whites and many with flecks. Dwarf and pendulous carnations are also available. The clove scent is invariably powerful.
Sun. Well-drained soil. 30–46cm/12–18in.

DRACOCEPHALUM
Lamiaceae

D. moldavica, dragon's head, is an unusual hardy annual, popular with bees. It has hooded, wide-lipped, violet-blue flowers, which are carried in whorls throughout the summer. But the scent comes from the leaves, whose fragrance is like that of lemon-scented balm. It makes an erect bushy plant.
Sun or light shade. 46cm/18in.

ERYSIMUM
Brassicaceae

E. cheiri (*Cheiranthus cheiri*), wallflower, with its Persian carpet colours and warm, aniseed scent, is an almost indispensable feature of the late spring garden, and the traditional partner for tulips. It is treated as a biennial and seed is sown outdoors in late spring. The seedlings are thinned during the summer and plants are transferred into their final positions in autumn. Wallflower seeds are available in single or mixed colours.
Sun. Well-drained soil. 46cm/18in.

E. x *marshallii* (*E. allionii* hort.) is a true annual with heads of rich orange flowers during the summer. Other species appear in catalogues from time to time, some under the name of 'alpine wallflowers'. All can be treated as biennials, and the majority have some degree of clove scent.
Sun. Well-drained soil. 46cm/18in.

EXACUM
Gentianaceae

E. affine, Persian violet, is a tender annual that must be grown in the greenhouse or as a house plant. Seed can be sown in early spring for summer flowering or, if a minimum temperature of 60°F/16°C can be maintained, in late summer for spring flowering. It is a compact and attractive plant whose lavender flowers have a strong and exotic scent.
15cm/6in.

GILIA
Polemoniaceae

G. tricolor, birds' eyes, is an easy-to-grow, unusual hardy annual, that has small lavender and white flowers. These have a throat beautifully

LEFT *Hesperis matronalis* RIGHT *Limnanthes douglasii*

marked in maroon and yellow, and have a powerful honeyed scent laced with chocolate.
Sun. Well-drained soil. 46cm/18in.

HELIOTROPIUM
Boraginaceae

H. arborescens (*H. peruvianum*), cherry pie, a half-hardy annual, is usually offered in the strain called 'Marine', which has very dark leaves topped with large heads of deep violet flowers. Although visually seductive, its vanilla-like, heliotrope scent, though noticeable, is not as strong as that possessed by the perennial varieties propagated by cuttings; these are described under Tender Plants.
Sun. 46cm/18in.

HESPERIS
Brassicaceae

H. matronalis, sweet rocket, is an essential plant for the early summer border. The tall heads of white or lilac flowers really come into their own in the evening when they become luminous and fill the air with a light, sweet scent. Although a perennial, younger plants are preferable and sweet rocket is usually treated as a biennial; it will self-sow freely. Its double-flowered forms, which have to be propagated by cuttings, or, more slowly by division, have long been rare, coveted and virus-ridden, but thanks to micro-propagation, clean stock is in circulation.
Sun or light shade. 1.2m/4ft.

IBERIS
Brassicaceae

I. amara, rocket candytuft, is, for the scent-conscious gardener, a preferable species to the common candytuft, *I. umbellata*. There are different strains available; plants can be dwarf, with rounded heads, or have tall, erect heads like the Giant Hyacinth Flowered strain. Flowers are white or pink with a sweet scent and are treated as hardy annuals.
Sun. 15–38cm/6–15in.

IONOPSIDIUM
Brassicaceae

I. acaule, violet cress, is a tiny lilac-flowered plant that has to be grown in a raised bed for its delicate honey scent to be appreciated. It is hardy, can be sown *in situ* and enjoys moisture. It will often seed itself. Light shade. 7.5cm/3in.

IPOMOEA
Convolvulaceae

I. alba (*Calonyction aculeatum*), moonflower (*fleur de lune*), is a half-hardy climber, related to morning glory, that can be grown as an annual against a sheltered wall outside or in the greenhouse. At its best in the evening and early morning when the huge white saucers breathe their heady, exotic scent, it flowers continually in summer.
Sun. 6m/20ft.

LATHYRUS
Papilionaceae
L. odoratus, sweet pea. The piercing honeyed scent of sweet peas epitomizes summer in the cottage garden. Unfortunately, the modern Spencer varieties have obtained their size, colour and perfection of form largely at the expense of fragrance. But there are still many fragrant strains and selections available to give the nose a real feast. As well as the Old-fashioned or Grandiflora mixes, you can also acquire individual colour forms such as lavender 'Chatsworth', 'White Supreme', 'Painted Lady', the oldest sweet pea variety and a carmine and white bicolour, and – my favourite – 'Matucana' ('Cupani'), a luxurious maroon and mauve bicolour. These are all powerfully sweet. To obtain the best plants, sow singly in 7.5cm/3in pots under glass in late winter. Plant out when large enough, in early spring. Support the seedlings with bushy twigs and then train them onto wigwams or trellises of canes and string. Feed, water and deadhead regularly.
Sun. Deep, rich soil. 2–2.5m/6–8ft.

LIMNANTHES
Limnanthaceae
L. douglasii, poached egg flower or meadow foam, is a popular hardy annual which self-sows freely and is much visited by bees. The white, golden-centred saucers are delicately scented and appear all summer above the hazy foliage.
Sun and light shade. Any soil. 15cm/6in.

LOBULARIA
Brassicaceae
L. maritima (Alyssum maritimum), sweet alyssum, is one of the most popular hardy annuals, not least for the rich golden honey scent released by the lacy flowers. It blooms from early summer until autumn and the colour range encompasses white, lilac, pink, carmine and purple. Its dwarf habit makes it ideal for edging, rock gardens and raised beds. It often self-sows, but plants become less compacted and revert to white.
Sun or light shade. Well-drained soil. 10cm/4in.

LUPINUS
Papilionaceae
L. elegans, in its Fairy strains, gives spikes of white lupin flowers, tinged rose-pink, above the fingered foliage. Their honeyed scent is particularly marked in the evening,
Sun or light shade. 60cm/2ft.
L. luteus, yellow lupin, is the plant the scent-conscious gardener should grow as a soil improver. The tall, dense spikes of yellow flowers have a sweet, beanfield fragrance; and plants 'fix' nitrogen and can be dug back into the soil at the end of the season. Treat as a hardy annual.
Sun or light shade. 60cm/2ft.

MATTHIOLA
Brassicaceae
M. incana. From this species are derived the annual and biennial stocks, without which no scented garden would be complete. The clove fragrance is delicious both by day and by night. The half-hardy annual stocks are available in Ten Week and Seven Week strains, comprising rather dumpy, double and single flowers; and in Giant Imperial, Excelsior and Beauty of Nice strains with erect, columnar heads. The colour range comprises crimson, rose, lilac, white, apricot and yellow.
Sun. 38–76cm/15–30in.

Matthiola incana Brompton strain

MIRABILIS
Nyctaginaceae

M. jalapa, marvel of Peru, was a favourite plant of the Victorians. Its trumpet-shaped flowers, produced all summer, can be pink, rose-red, yellow or white and have a rich and complex, fruity and honey scent. They do not open until late afternoon, hence the alternative common name of 'four o'clock'. It is usually grown as a half-hardy annual.
Sun and heat. Well-drained soil. 60–90cm/2–3ft.

Mirabilis jalapa

The hardy biennial stocks are available in the East Lothian and Brompton strains. The East Lothian stocks are sown in high summer to produce dwarf plants for flowering under glass the following spring (Beauty of Nice stocks also perform well as winter pot plants if sown in high summer); they can also be treated as late-flowering annual stocks. The Brompton stocks are sown in high summer for flowering outdoors the following spring. Both have medium-sized spikes of flowers in the same colour range as the annual stocks.
Sun. 46cm/18in.

M. incana 'White Perennial' persists for a couple of years before looking tatty. The powerfully fragrant white flowers are set against a mound of grey leaves. The lilac version is equally desirable. It will seed itself, and is one of my favourite terrace and paving-crack plants.
Sun. 46cm/18in.

M. longipetala subsp. *bicornis*, night-scented stock, never looks much by day, but the wispy lilac flowers open in the evening to pour out their clove scent. It is hard to believe that so insignificant a thing is so potent that it can fill the air with sweetness. Sow the seed *in situ* under windows and beside paths in order to enjoy the scent. Sun. 30cm/1ft.

NEMESIA
Scrophulariaceae

N. caerulea (*N. fruticans* hort.). There are various strains of nemesia in shades of white, lilac, violet and pink with a potent vanilla or chocolate scent, such as 'Fragrant Lady' (mixed colours) and 'Wisley Vanilla'

LEFT *Nicotiana mutabilis* CENTRE *Nicotiana sylvestris* RIGHT *Nemesia caerulea*

(blush white), and they make excellent, showy half-hardy annuals for summer containers.
Sun or light shade. 23cm/9in.
N. cheiranthus, in its 'Shooting Stars' and 'Masquerade' strains, has extraordinary-looking flowers with yellow lips, purple markings and a crown of elongated white petals behind. They have a lovely coconut scent. They are grown as a half-hardy annual, germinated in light, warm conditions in spring.
Sun. Well-drained soil. 30cm/1ft.

NICOTIANA
Solanaceae
N. alata is a half-hardy annual that has given rise to the various strains of coloured tobacco flowers, those popular bedding plants which have starry blooms in carmine-pink and red, white and lime-green. Many of them have a good scent and have the advantage over the more potent 'Grandiflora', described below, in keeping their flowers open during the day. Sun or light shade. Fertile soil. 25–90cm/10in–3ft.
***N. alata* 'Grandiflora'** is the familiar white tobacco flower, whose large starry flowers fill the evening air with an exotic scent. By day it is rather weedy-looking but at dusk it glows with an ethereal beauty. It is treated as a half-hardy annual.
Sun or light shade. Fertile soil. 90cm/3ft.
N. mutabilis is an attractive, newly introduced species with a haze of small flowers that open white and fade to a deep pink.
Sun or light shade. Fertile soil. 1.2mcm/4ft.
N.* x *sanderae strains include 'Fragrant Cloud' (white) and 'Sensation Mixed' (ranging from white to deep pink) and grow into excellent, free-flowering sturdy plants. Sun or light shade. Fertile soil. 90cm/3ft.
N. suaveolens is an unusual annual with white, tubular flowers, shaded greenish-purple on the outside, which are powerfully scented at night.
Sun or light shade. 60cm/2ft.
N. sylvestris is visually the most impressive tobacco flower and is among the most architectural of annuals. It forms a bulky, leafy, bright green plant with stout stems topped with panicles of drooping, tubular, white flowers. In the evening, the exotic scent is released. This half-hardy annual is excellent as a specimen or in a group.
Sun or light shade. 1.5m/5ft.

OENOTHERA
Onagraceae
O. biennis, common evening primrose, releases a sweet, lemon scent in the evening, when it opens its bright yellow saucers. It is a popular annual or biennial which self-sows freely; indeed, it can prove too energetic, and may need to be

LEFT *Oenothera biennis* CENTRE *Verbena* RIGHT *Phacelia campanularia* 'Blue Wonder'

confined to the wilder parts of the garden.
Sun. Well-drained soil. 90cm/3ft.
O. caespitosa is a very lovely, dwarf species with a superb sweet scent, slender, hairy leaves and particularly large, white flowers which by morning have faded to pink. It is usually treated as a hardy biennial, but is often perennial, and is grown ideally in a raised bed.
Sun. Well-drained soil. 15cm/6in.
O. pallida* subsp. *trichocalyx is an evening primrose of bewitching beauty and neat habit. Its large, sweetly scented flowers are pure white, and have the advantage of remaining open during the day. Although a biennial or perennial plant, it is often treated as an annual.
Sun. Well-drained soil. 46cm/18in.
***O. stricta* (*O. odorata*)** is a great favourite of mine in its variety 'Sulphurea' and usually behaves as a biennial with me, self-sowing into paving cracks. The large saucers open a creamy yellow in the evening, when they exhale their lemon scent; by the next morning they have faded to peach. Sun. Well-drained soil. 60cm/2ft.

PAPAVER
Papaveraceae

P. nudicaule, Iceland poppy, produces silky-textured, sweet-scented poppies in a range of white and sunset colours. 'Party Fun' ('Meadow Pastels') is a good strain. It can be grown as a biennial for early flowering.
Sun. Well-drained soil. 46cm/18in.

PETUNIA
Solanaceae

Petunias are among the most popular summer bedding plants, and it comes as a surprise to many people to discover they sometimes have a honey or vanilla scent, most evident in the evening. But colour rather than scent has been the quality pursued by the plant breeders, and I cannot recommend any particularly fragrant strains; however, white, violet-blue and purple petunias seem to be better endowed than others. They are treated as half-hardy annuals.
Sun. Well-drained soil. 23cm/9in.

PHACELIA
Boraginaceae

P. campanularia. The best known of this group of Californian hardy annuals, it does have fragrance but it is commonly grown for the dazzling, gentian-blue flowers which it produces all summer. It is beloved by bees. Its relative, *P. ciliata*, with lavender-blue flowers is also scented.
Sun. 15cm/6in.

PROBOSCIDEA
Pedaliaceae

***P. louisianica* (*Martynia louisianica*)**, unicorn plant, is a rare, half-hardy annual with downy, heart-shaped leaves, sticky to the touch, and large, gloxinia-like flowers. These come in shades of cream, rose and purple, are marked in yellow and purple, and have a strong scent not found pleasant by some. The flowers are followed by strange fruits shaped like curved horns. It can be grown outside in a sheltered spot but is more reliable under glass. Sun. 60–90cm/2–3ft.

RESEDA
Resedaceae

R. odorata, mignonette, is one of the best known fragrant hardy annuals. Alas, the scent is often elusive, but at its best is piercingly honey-sweet, tinged with raspberry, and can be powerful by day and night. It has rather weedy-looking flowers of greenish-white, but modern strains have better colouring and bigger heads. It succeeds well as a pot plant indoors – seed can be sown in late summer for spring flowering. Outside, seed can be sown from early spring onwards to ensure a succession of bloom; it makes a long-lasting cut flower. Sun. 30cm/1ft.

Reseda odorata

SCABIOSA
Caprifoliaceae

S. atropurpurea, sweet scabious. This upright, bushy species bears dark purple, pink or white, flat pincushion flowers on tall stems and is beautifully scented. The newer garden varieties have larger, fully double flowers with raised centres. 'Ace of Spades' is a good strain. They are treated as hardy annuals and bloom in late summer and autumn. They last well in water.
Sun. 46–90cm/18in–3ft.

SCHIZOPETALON
Brassicaceae

S. walkeri is an interesting half-hardy annual whose white, fringed flowers release an almond scent in the evening. Seed must be sown either in small potfuls, to be planted out in the late spring, or directly into the ground earlier in the season.
Sun. 30cm/1ft.

TAGETES
Asteraceae

I cannot believe anyone would choose to grow French or African marigolds because they like the scent. Even whitefly evacuate the greenhouse at the first whiff of it and indeed, many growers use marigolds to keep pests at bay. But it you like your scents good and pungent, the seed catalogues offer a tempting array of sunshine strains.

TROPAEOLUM
Tropaeolaceae

T. majus, nasturtium. The nasturtium offers honey-scented flowers notably in its 'Gleam' varieties. These are semi-double, and come in shades of yellow, orange and scarlet. They are bushy and semi-trailing in habit. Nasturtiums are hardy annuals and are useful for cheering up neglected parts of the garden. They look particularly well on gravel paths and drives, where they will often self-sow, and when hoisting themselves up shrubs like *Cotoneaster horizontalis*. The flowers can be used in salads. Sun or shade. 30cm/1ft.

VERBENA
Verbenaceae

V. x hybrida, common garden *Verbena*, is available in many strains and is grown as a half-hardy annual. The sweet, exotic scent, which is released in the evening, is more pronounced in the white, pink and violet shades than in the brilliant reds. It is a cheerful plant, producing its tight heads of flower all summer, and looks well in pots and in the border. 'Showtime' is a strain giving bright, compact plants. Mauve-blue 'La France', grown as a half-hardy perennial, is deliciously fragrant.
Sun. 23–30cm/9–12in.

ZALUZIANSKYA
Scrophulariaceae

Z. capensis is an unusual half-hardy annual that is powerfully fragrant at night. It bears white, starry flowers which remain closed during the daytime. *Z. villosa* has white flowers with an orange centre, and has an equally potent scent. *Z. ovata*, grown as a tender perennial, is also superb.
Sun. Well-drained soil. 30cm/1ft.

WALLS & VERTICAL PLANTING

Walls are prized by all keen gardeners. They offer support for a range of climbing plants and protection for a number of shrubs not hardy enough to withstand life in the open. Scent-conscious gardeners value them above all for their help in creating a warm, still, microclimate in which fragrances are richly diffused and held captive.

While few people have gardens girdled by stone and brick, most of us have house walls that can be cloaked in greenery. The most precious aspects are those that enjoy warmth and shelter from cold winds, and those gardeners who rise to the challenge can be rewarded with flourishing shrubs and climbers of a very exotic character.

Terraces and sitting-out areas benefit from being backed by sunny walls so that the air is warm and still as you sit, and the aromas intense. Night-scented plants ought to be present to take over from the daytime fragrances; and you will want to make sure that no unpleasant scents can disturb you in this, the fragrant garden's inner sanctum. You are unlikely to be sitting outdoors much in the coldest months of the year, so the sun-loving scented wall shrubs and climbers that perform in winter and early spring are not prime candidates for such areas. Reserve these for summer-bloomers. Having said that, I have given a prime spot to autumn-flowering *Buddleja auriculata*, since it needs the warmth and I love having its lemon-scented flowers to pick on Christmas Day.

Wintersweet, *Chimonanthus praecox*, is one of the pleasures of mid-winter and, brought into the warmth of a room, its cut stems will fill the air with a spicy lemon scent. The inner segments of the flowers are purplish but the outer segments are disappointingly translucent and you may like to partner it with the more cheerful yellow of winter jasmine; and perhaps underplant with violet winter irises. It can be grown in the open, and the flowers are fairly frost-proof but its wood enjoys a good summer ripening, which is why in colder areas a wall that receives full sun is advisable.

A bower of honeysuckle, *Lonicera* x *americana*, deliciously scented by day and night.

Rose-scented Japanese apricot, *Prunus mume* 'Omoi-no-mama'.

JAPANESE APRICOTS

It took me a long time to discover Japanese apricots. They bloom on bare stems in late winter and, although they can also be grown in the open, appreciate the shelter and warmth of a sunny wall. The perfume is wonderfully sophisticated and seems to vary greatly from variety to variety. Rose-scented 'Beni-chidori', in rich rose-pink, is my favourite apricot and would be sensational against a whitewashed wall, with white 'Omoi-no-mama' ('Omoi-no-wac') for brick or grey stone. Unfortunately, like many fruit trees, they are prone to attack by pests and disease so their foliage does not tend to look very attractive in summer.

In cold areas, *Daphne bholua* might be offered a sheltered, part-shaded nook near a wall. This is a plant worth cosseting since it can be in bloom throughout the winter season, and some forms, such as 'Darjeeling', are not very hardy. A bush of evergreen *D. odora* 'Aureomarginata' could provide some accompanying foliage and would take over the scent production from its cousin in late spring.

Azara microphylla flowers in late winter. Its scent is of vanilla, and it is a tonic to catch a cloud of it as you hurry to the house door. A number of other vanilla and almond-scented plants are in flower at the same time or are poised to enter the stage, and it could be entertaining to devote a corner to them. The colour scheme would be green, pink and white and you would have flowers over many months. *Viburnum farreri* opens in autumn, *Abeliophyllum distichum* in mid-winter, *Clematis armandii* in late winter and *Choisya ternata*

Ceanothus, here blended with *Clematis orientalis* 'Bill MacKenzie', often have a light scent.

and *Clematis montana* in spring. The large evergreen leaves of *Clematis armandii* would counter the skimpy appearance of both azara and abeliophyllum, and *Choisya ternata* would offer a mound of glossy foliage to clothe the ground.

Space is always short on sunny walls and choosing just a few plants among the many exciting summer performers is exceedingly difficult. For me, ceanothus is the sovereign of the late spring season. To have a cloud of blue – a rare colour among shrubs – drifting across your wall or fence is a treat. But, though some ceanothus often have a good dose of honey scent, I have to admit that there are plants with a more enticing fragrance.

Moroccan broom, *Cytisus battandieri*, with its pineapple scent, is a candidate, and the rich yellow cones are set strikingly against silvery leaves. But it does need a high wall. Mine was against a wall 2.5m/8ft tall, and I was constantly having to cut it back to prevent the wind catching its top growth and ripping the whole plant from its wire supports. I should have done better to plant it as a free-standing specimen; except in very cold areas, it will thrive happily in the open in a sheltered position, though it takes up a lot of room. Honey scents go well with pineapple and you could partner the broom with *Olearia macrodonta* and *Ozothamnus ledifolius*; the colour scheme would be yellow and white. The white flowers of *Abelia triflora* would also make a deliciously sweet accompaniment.

Roses are always tempting; their colour, scent and romantic associations enhance every planting scheme. But since you do not actually need a wall to grow roses, they do not usually top my list of candidates for the most prized wall positions. The same applies to wisteria, though I love the Japanese variety dangling over my sitting-room window. An assortment of other shrubs and climbers are more deserving. First, there is *Carpenteria californica,* a fine evergreen shrub with large, delicately scented white saucers. It performs at the same time as the Moroccan broom and on a high wall they make excellent companions. Then there are the myrtles. You get a double dose of spicy scent from these evergreens, for both the leaves and flowers are aromatic. Some species bloom in late spring but others, including the common myrtle that is the best choice for most gardeners, perform in late summer; near a seat you can enjoy the fragrance of the flowers in the air and tweak the leaves as you sit. Honey-scented itea is a good alternative to myrtle for flower scent.

I would want *Cestrum parqui* somewhere but nowhere too prominent. Late at night the fragrance from the tiny greenish flowers is potently and spicily sweet, but in the daytime and early evening, the scent is unpleasantly meaty (though, thankfully, it is not noticeable in the air). *Buddleja crispa* is certainly a candidate for a good position, and you could grow something taller above it such as a passionflower. Its lilac flowers and sweet scent appear through late summer and autumn. Purple heliotropes are attractive in front of it. For a higher wall, you might consider *Buddleja agathosma*, which has been growing in my garden for a great many years, unscathed by the coldest winters; the scent is not quite raspberry – raspberry ripple ice-cream is the nearest I can come to describe it.

Among summer-flowering climbers, star jasmine, *Trachelospermum jasminoides* is one of my favourites. Its exotic scent has the flavour of orange blossom and none of the headiness of real jasmine. It survived at –4°F/–20°C in one garden I know, so once established, it is hardier than generally supposed. In colder areas, you will also have to provide a warm wall for *Jasminum officinale*; I grow it in its 'Clotted Cream' form. In London and the warmer areas, the pot jasmine *J. polyanthum* is also reliable outside. Honeysuckles are essential somewhere in the vicinity of your sitting-out area, but you need not waste a sunny wall on them. If there is no fence or pergola close by, then you could grow them as standards, trained up a post. They fill the air with scent in the cool of the evening. It is usually a fruity fragrance – all forms of *Lonicera periclymenum* are delicious – but *Lonicera* x *americana* and *L. japonica* 'Halliana' are distinctly clove-like.

Towering trees of *Magnolia grandiflora* are a feature of many gardens in the eastern United States, but in Britain this magnolia is usually encountered on a sunny wall, for it benefits from having every ray of sunshine to ripen its wood. The great cream goblets open into lemon-scented waterlilies and you have to bury your face in them to enjoy a deep draught of fragrance. A few flowers are usually within your reach from the ground

A spring pairing of vanilla-scented *Clematis montana* and *Wisteria sinensis.*

In mild regions, many shrubs and climbers which I have listed under Tender Plants (see pages 280–301) can also be considered for a protected wall. *Acacia*, tender *Buddleja*, *Callistemon*, *Coronilla*, lemon verbena and *Prostanthera* are among them. Such supposedly tender plants are forever surprising you with their resilience and powers of rejuvenation.

but your chief goal should be to be able to stretch lazily out of your bedroom window and drink from there. All wispy companions look inadequate next to this magnolia's substance and architectural presence, so I should choose something like spiky yuccas, whose creamy candelabras shine crisply against the magnolia's glossy foliage; or *Pittosporum tenuifolium*, whose tiny chocolate flowers deliver their honey scent in spring, before the magnolia has begun. There are some good small compact forms of magnolia available now – you could also consider one of the michelias, now also classed under *Magnolia*.

Walls that are shaded and cold offer less scope for adventurous planting. But you do not have to resort entirely to ivies and pyracanthas. Many honeysuckles are happy here, as are *Holboellia*, *Schisandra* and *Pileostegia* and many *Clematis*, including the vanilla-scented montanas; and many climbing roses will tolerate shade, including white 'Madame Alfred Carrière' and pink 'New Dawn'. The semi-evergreen honeysuckle, *Lonicera japonica* 'Halliana', which has an exceptionally strong *Gardenia*-like fragrance, can also be expected to thrive. Winter-flowering shrubby honeysuckles – *Lonicera fragrantissima*, *L. standishii* and *L.* x *purpusii* – may be trained against a shaded wall and their creamy, lemon-scented flowers often show up better here than in the open. *Daphne laureola* and *D. pontica* are low evergreen companions for them; their greenish-yellow flowers are carried in spring, and late evening is the best time to catch their elusive scent. You might also include honey-scented *Mahonia aquifolium* – which responds well to vertical training and climbs surprisingly high – and berberis; these will inject some strong colour.

I think my favourite scented shrub for a shady wall is *Osmanthus* x *burkwoodii*. Its white flowers, borne in spring, are vanilla-sweet and the fragrance carries well. The small, dark, evergreen leaves are a fine foil for other plants and the whole shrub is very compact and can be clipped to shape. *Pieris*, *Skimmia* and *Viburnum* x *burkwoodii* produce their scented white flowers at the same time and are also shade-tolerant and evergreen. The autumn-flowering varieties of osmanthus help to bring late interest to shady walls, as do *Mahonia* such as *M. lomariifolia* and the hardier *M. japonica* Bealei Group. They have bold, dramatic foliage and the racemes of flowers stand erect.

You do not need walls in order to grow hardy climbing plants. These can be spun around pergolas, along fences and trelliswork, over outbuildings, up poles and trees, and

Training honeysuckles at nose height on posts and wire hoops, like standards, is an effective way of adding scent to borders – especially perennial borders, for which there are comparatively few candidates with strong airborne scent.

across ropes and wires; they can even be used as groundcover, under trees, down banks and over tree stumps.

If you are planning a tunnel or arch for walking under or an arbour or bower for sitting in, be sure to choose plants whose flowers you can enjoy from below. Most would display their flowers on the outside so you would find yourself under a canopy dripping only with rain. Lilac-blue and white wisterias and yellow laburnum hang downwards and are the most exciting plants for such features; with their pliable branches, magnolias like *M. wilsonii* are also contenders. In the United States, I encountered a long pergola planted with *Akebia*; their vanilla-scented flowers do not dangle but their sausage-shaped fruits do. The pendent seed-pods of wisterias are also a bonus in hotter climates than Britain.

Roses, honeysuckles, jasmines and *Clematis* are the main candidates for covering other areas. Primrose-scented *Clematis rehderiana* and meadowsweet-scented *C. flammula* extend the season into late summer and autumn (also *C. terniflora* in the United States); *Lonicera periclymenum* 'Serotina' and many roses also last well. *Clematis cirrhosa* var. *balearica* performs through the winter.

WALL SHRUBS

ABELIA
Caprifoliaceae
The abelias are deciduous or evergreen shrubs valuable for their long, and late, flowering season. They are not stunning visually, but make attractive companions for plants with strong colour. Even the hardiest varieties appreciate the warmth and protection of a wall that receives sun, unless grown in the milder regions.
Sun or light shade. Moist, loamy soil.
A. chinensis releases a fine, sweet, honeysuckle scent from its clusters of white, tubular flowers, which appear from rose-tinted buds during summer and autumn. It is not commonly offered but is one of the best abelias for fragrance. It makes a spreading deciduous shrub. 1–1.5m/3–5ft. Z7
A.* x *grandiflora is the most popular abelia and one of the hardiest, being virtually evergreen, but its scent is very faint. Its clusters of white, tubular flowers come from pink buds, and are borne in summer and autumn. The small, pointed leaves are a good, bright green and it makes a loose, arching mound. 1–2m/3–6ft. Z6
A. triflora has a very good, sweet scent, resembling that of *Osmanthus delavayi*. The flowers are white and come from pink buds in early summer. It is deciduous and vigorous and erect in habit. I grow it as a wall shrub in part shade, but I have seen it in the open as a small tree in Ireland. 3m/10ft or more. Z7

ABELIOPHYLLUM
Oleaceae
A. distichum wants a sunny wall in order to ripen its wood. The white flowers, vanilla-scented, are borne on the bare twigs in winter. It is well worth planting as it takes up little space and performs at a useful time. The effect is of a small, white-flowered forsythia. Sun. 1.2m/4ft. Z4

AZARA
Salicaceae
The azaras are an extremely valuable group of evergreen shrubs or small trees from Chile which can be tried on a sunny wall. They are not entirely hardy but some are proving tougher than previously thought.
Sun. Moist, loamy soil.
A. lanceolata has slender, bright green, toothed leaves and produces its puffs of dull yellow flowers in quantity in early spring. It grows best in cool, mild, damp climates. This interesting and unusual evergreen is half-hardy.
Up to 6m/20ft. Z9
A. microphylla, the most common azara, is reliably hardy in all but

RIGHT *Abelia triflora*
FAR RIGHT *Abeliophyllum distichum*

FAR LEFT *Azara serrata*
LEFT *Camellia* 'Quintessence'
BELOW *Buddleja crispa*

the coldest areas. It has small, dark, rounded leaves and produces its clusters of insignificant yellow flowers in late winter; the air around the plant can be thick with vanilla essence at this time. It makes an attractive, erect shrub for a small garden.
Up to 6m/20ft. Z8

A. petiolaris has comparatively large, holly-like leaves and small racemes of pale yellow flowers in spring. It is the most beautiful azara in flower and the scent is strong and sweet. It seems to be quite reliable on a warm wall.
Up to 3.5m/12ft. Z8

A. serrata is a good glossy evergreen with puffs of mustard-yellow flowers, fruitily scented, which appear in late spring.
3m/10ft. Z8

BUDDLEJA
Scrophulariaceae

B. agathosma is an uncommon but attractive shrub of lax habit, bearing mauve, raspberry-scented flowers on bare branches in spring, followed by large, grey, jagged-edged leaves. Over many years in my garden it has never been affected by cold winters.
Sun. 3.5m/12ft. Z8

B. auriculata is listed under Tender Plants but has proved hardy in my garden in all but the coldest winters, after which it has regenerated from the base. Z9

B. crispa is one of the most desirable candidates for a sunny wall. A pastel beauty, it has woolly grey leaves and short, rounded panicles of lilac flowers, borne over a long period from summer until the first frosts. The scent is the light, honey fragrance characteristic of *Buddleja*. It makes a bushy, wide shrub, and a proportion of the old wood should be pruned hard back every spring to encourage new flowering growth.
Sun. 2–3.5m/6–12ft. Z8

CAMELLIA
Theaceae

Scent in camellias is usually light but it becomes more noticeable under glass; outdoors, a warm wall is helpful in drawing it out. It is more likely to be found in single and semi-double flowered varieties. Most of the popular showy camellias including, I understand,

all the cultivars of *C. reticulata*, are scentless. But in certain cultivars of *C. japonica* the scent is more pronounced; reddish-pink 'Kramer's Supreme', 'Scented Red', white 'Emmett Barnes', pink and white 'Nuccio's Jewel', and silvery-pink 'Scentsation' are good examples. Among cultivars of *C.* x *williamsii*, single pink 'Mary Jobson' is notable. There is also a light scent in the two very handsome white camellias 'Cornish Snow' and *C. transnokoensis*. The most scented camellia species, *C. lutchuensis*, from the Ryukyu Islands between Japan and Taiwan, has been used by hybridists to breed more scent into camellias; a number of scented hybrids are available including 'Fragrant Pink', 'Scentuous' (semi-double white, blushed pink), blush-pink 'Quintessence', and 'High Fragrance' (semi-double light pink).

***C. sasanqua* 'Narumigata'** is the best known scented camellia with a refreshing, rose-like fragrance. It has single, cup-shaped, white flowers, pink-tinged at the edges, in the autumn, and typically dark, glossy leaves. Outside, it can be trusted against a sunny wall – the sasanquas need more sun than other camellias – but it makes a very good evergreen cool glasshouse shrub and may be stood outside for the summer. It may be pruned in spring. Blush-pink 'Rainbow', and single white 'Fukuzutsumi' and 'Setsugekka' are also well scented.
Sun or shade. Acid or neutral soil. 3m/10ft. Z8

CEANOTHUS
Rhamnaceae

These magnificent shrubs, comprising the only really sizeable, truly blue-flowered plants that we can grow in gardens, are not normally praised for scent. But some do surprise you with a faint honey fragrance; some also have distinctly aromatic foliage. Evergreen 'Puget Blue' (Z8), which has intense mid-blue flowers in late spring and early summer, has both these qualities.
Sun. Well-drained soil. 2.5m/8ft or more.

***C. arboreus* 'Trewithen Blue'** has the honey scent in some measure and is also evergreen, but unlike 'Puget Blue' its mid-blue flowers are produced in quite long panicles; it grows taller and lives longer. (The evergreen ceanothus are usually very vigorous but have a short life.) Z9

CESTRUM
Solanaceae

C. parqui begins to pour out a magnificent and exotic spicy-sweet

CARPENTERIA
Hydrangeaceae

C. californica is an evergreen, with slender, leathery leaves, for a sunny wall. The large, single white flowers, lit by a boss of golden anthers, are produced at midsummer and are delicately, but sweetly, fragrant. A proportion of the old wood may be removed in spring to keep the plant youthful. 'Ladham's Variety' has larger flowers.
Sun. Well-drained soil. 1.5m/5ft. Z7

Carpenteria californica

LEFT *Cestrum parqui* RIGHT *Chimonanthus praecox* 'Luteus' BELOW *Choisya ternata*

perfume from its small, greenish-yellow, tubular flowers in the late evening. It blooms for many weeks during the summer, though, unfortunately, in the daytime the flowers smell rather fetid. The shrub has long, narrow leaves, and is usually deciduous.
Sun. Well-drained, fertile soil. 2.5m/8ft or more, unless continually cut back by hard winters. Z8

CHAENOMELES
Rosaceae

The japonicas or ornamental quinces merit inclusion for their deliciously scented fruits which have a powerful, aromatic fragrance. Plants will grow happily in the open border, but they are popular subjects for a sunny or slightly shaded wall; a properly espaliered specimen is very decorative, even when out of flower. Prune back the previous season's growth after flowering. The cup-shaped flowers, produced in spring, come in a range of red, pink, salmon, white and even yellow colours.
Sun or shade. 1–3m/3–10ft depending on variety. Z5

CHIMONANTHUS
Calycanthaceae

C. praecox, wintersweet, is a plant for the patient gardener, as it may take five years or more to begin flowering. But it is worth the wait. The waxy, translucent yellow bells, purple-stained inside, have a spicy lemon fragrance which is among the finest of the season; a few twigs indoors will scent a whole room. The flowers are produced on the bare branches throughout the second half of the winter. It is a dreary-looking plant in summer, though. 'Grandiflorus' and 'Luteus' are forms with better flowers, but the scent is not as good. Cut out weak shoots immediately after flowering, otherwise little pruning is required. In sunnier areas it succeeds as a free-standing shrub in an open position. Sun. 2.5m/8ft. Z6

CHOISYA
Rutaceae

C. ternata, Mexican orange blossom, is a beautiful evergreen shrub with glossy, trifoliate leaves and heads of white, starry flowers in spring. The foliage is aromatic when crushed, and the blossom has a heavy almond scent. It is hardy enough to thrive in the open but resents cold winds and

LEFT *Cytisus battandieri* CENTRE *Drimys winteri* RIGHT *Edgeworthia chrysantha* 'Red Dragon'

needs a sheltered position, so it is often grown as a wall shrub. It makes a neat, dome-shaped specimen but is at its best in youth and it is a sound policy to prune the whole shrub back to 46cm/18in every few years. There is a popular golden-leaved form called 'Sundance'. *C.* × *dewitteana* 'Aztec Pearl' has green, finely fingered foliage.
Sun or shade. 2m/6ft. Z8

CYTISUS
Papilionaceae

C. battandieri, Moroccan broom, is a handsome deciduous shrub. The fragrance from its erect, golden-yellow racemes is of pineapple. It flowers at midsummer. Its foliage is quite untypical of brooms, being rounded, trifoliate and silvery. It is usually trained against a sunny wall, but it is big and if no suitable wall is available, it may be tried as a free-standing specimen in a sheltered spot.
Sun. 4.5m/15ft. Z8

DRIMYS
Winteraceae

D. winteri, winter's bark, is a tall evergreen shrub that needs wall protection outside milder regions. Its bark and large, grey-green leaves are attractive and aromatic when crushed, but beware: if the oil is accidentally transferred from fingers to mouth or eyes it can cause a burning sensation and even temporary blindness! The jasmine-like, white flowers are also scented; the fragrance is of milk of magnesia.
Sun or light shade. Acid soil. 4.5m/15ft or more. Z9

EDGEWORTHIA
Thymelaeaceae

E. chrysantha, paper bush, is a striking deciduous shrub in late winter, when its clusters of golden-yellow tubular flowers appear on the bare, pliable branches. They open from silky white buds and have a fruitily spicy scent. The leaves are long and slender. Although quite frost hardy, it needs warmth and shelter to do well in the UK, and outside the milder counties is best against a house wall. It does well in a pot under glass. There is a deep orange form called 'Red Dragon'.
Sun or light shade. Well-drained fertile soil. 2m/6ft. Z7

ESCALLONIA
Escalloniaceae

***E.* 'Iveyi'** is one of the more tender *Escallonia*, requiring the protection and heat of a sunny wall outside mild areas. It is also the most beautiful. Its glossy, dark, evergreen leaves have the fruity resinous aroma typical of *Escallonia* but its flowers are sweetly scented too. These are pure white and are borne in panicles during late summer and autumn.
Sun. Well-drained soil. 3m/10ft. Z8

EUPHORBIA
Euphorbiaceae

E. mellifera. I have seen this splendid euphorbia growing luxuriantly in its

Escallonia 'Iveyi'

native Madeira. In milder gardens in Britain, it can also attain an impressive size. In colder areas it should be given a warm wall – mine is killed to the ground in very cold winters but always regenerates. It produces almost spherical heads of tan flowers in early spring which look and smell like golden honey; they are even sticky to the touch. They are popular with ants. The leaves are long, slender and bright grass-green, with a central white vein, and it makes a striking evergreen foliage plant.
Sun. Well-drained soil. 2m/6ft. Z8

HOHERIA
Malvaceae

H. lyallii is an unusual deciduous shrub for a sunny wall. It has heart-shaped, grey-green leaves, toothed and downy, and in high summer bears quantities of white, saucer-shaped flowers, that have a honey scent. This is a fine plant for a white garden.
Sun. Well-drained soil. 4.5m/15ft. Z9

ERIOBOTRYA
Rosaceae

E. japonica, loquat, has enormous, coarse, dark evergreen leaves, which are ribbed and toothed, and it is a very popular foliage shrub with garden designers. On drier soils (it is very drought-tolerant), the foliage is not quite so impressive. The white flowers, produced in panicles in winter, are strongly scented of almonds; yellow, pear-shaped fruits follow but are seldom ripened outside of the mildest climates. They do ripen on my London balcony. It makes an excellent pot plant.
Sun. Up to 9m/30ft. Z8

Eriobotrya japonica

H. sexstylosa is an evergreen hoheria of narrow, upright shape and with slender, glossy, toothed leaves. Its white flowers, which appear in high summer, are slightly smaller than those of *H. lyallii* but have the same honey scent. It is another desirable plant. 'Stardust' is a good selection. Sun. 4.5m/15ft. Z9

ITEA
Iteaceae

I. ilicifolia never fails to raise eyebrows when, in high summer, it turns from an unassuming holly-like shrub into a flowering waterfall. The pendent racemes of greenish-white flowers, which look like sprays of millet, can be 30cm/1ft in length. They are scented of honey. The dark, glossy leaves are a good foil for other plants right through the year. It grows best against a sunny wall. *I. virginica* (Z5), with shorter, fragrant, creamy racemes, is hardier and suitable for open positions on moist soil. Sun. 3m/10ft. Z9

JASMINUM
Oleaceae

J. humile 'Revolutum', Italian yellow jasmine, does not have the powerful sweet scent of its climbing relatives but has some fragrance. The flowers are bright yellow and are carried in clusters among the airy foliage during high summer. It is reliably hardy against a sunny wall and is more or less evergreen; it can be tried as a free-standing shrub in all but the coldest areas. Sun. 1.5m/5ft or more. Z8

LAURELIA
Atherospermataceae

L. sempervirens, Chilean laurel, is a handsome evergreen worth searching out for its spicy scent, similar to bay, released by the foliage when crushed. The long leathery leaves are bright green and serrated and clusters of yellowish-green flowers appear in early spring. It grows best in a mild climate but can be tried against a sunny wall

Hoheria sexstylosa

elsewhere, except in the coldest areas. Over 15m/50ft in mild areas. Z9

LOMATIA
Proteaceae

L. myricoides is one of the hardier members of a lovely group of scented southern hemisphere evergreens. It makes an airy

LEFT *Itea ilicifolia* RIGHT *Jasminum humile* 'Revolutum'

LEFT *Luma apiculata* CENTRE *Luma apiculata* RIGHT *Magnolia grandiflora*

spreading shrub, sparsely clothed in long narrow leaves, and in midsummer it bears clusters of cream, jasmine-like flowers which are wonderfully sweetly scented. It needs a sheltered spot, and is not suitable for cold areas. It is very distinctive in habit and a fine contrast to leathery-leaved evergreens, but it is seldom grown.
Sun. Acid soil. 2m/6ft or more. Z9
L. tinctoria is a dwarf suckering shrub with pinnate leaves that bears its creamy, heliotrope-scented flowers towards the end of summer. But it likes similar conditions to *L. myricoides* and is almost as hardy.
60–90cm/2–3ft. Z9

LUMA
Myrtaceae
L. apiculata (*Myrtus luma*) is a relative of myrtle and has superb peeling, cinnamon and cream bark. It is at its best as a free-standing tree in mild areas, but against a wall it is also very beautiful. It produces its blossom over a long period in late summer and autumn. It is less hardy than common myrtle.
2–6m/6–20ft; 18m/60ft as a tree. Z9

MAGNOLIA
Magnoliaceae
M. grandiflora is the queen of wall shrubs. Its huge, glossy, evergreen leaves, rust-felted underneath, bring grandeur to their setting, while the great saucer-shaped flowers, creamy yellow and spicily lemon-scented, are as exotic as waterlilies. The flowers are borne intermittently through the late summer and autumn. They can be grown as free-standing shrubs in sunny climes and in the southeastern United States they make great trees. But elsewhere they need the heat of a sunny wall to perform well; they can be pruned in spring. The species takes a while to settle down to flowering, and its precocious clones are preferable: 'Exmouth' has narrower leaves and is the hardiest; 'Goliath' is the best selection of all but not for very cold gardens. 'Kay Parris' and 'Little Gem' are superb compact forms.
Sun. Fertile soil. 7.5m/25ft or more. Z7
***M.* 'Maryland'**, an evergreen hybrid between *M. grandiflora* and *M. virginiana*, with lemon-scented creamy flowers in late summer.
Sun. 9m/30ft. Z6

MYRTUS
Myrtaceae
The myrtles have recently been savaged by the botanists and broken up into half a dozen genera – see also *Luma* and *Ugni*, but to keep things simple, I group others here. The larger species are usually treated as slow-growing evergreens for a sunny wall and well-drained loamy soil, but they are not reliably hardy in cold areas. The leaves are aromatic

LEFT *Myrtus communis* CENTRE *Prunus mume* 'Beni-chidori' RIGHT *Rhaphiolepis umbellata*

and the white blossom is spicily sweet. Both these scents fill the air on warm days.
Sun. Well-drained, loamy soil.
M. communis, common myrtle, produces its flowers in late summer and in both foliage and blossom is a real feast for the nose. It does well against a wall, although it may sometimes be cut to the ground by frost. Its variegated and narrow-leaved forms, including the subspecies *tarentina*, are slightly less reliable outside. This is an interesting plant with historical associations.
2–3m/6–10ft. Z8
Myrtus lechleriana (Amomyrtus luma) produces good coppery-coloured young leaves and blooms early, in spring, but is not very hardy. 2–7.5m/6–25ft. Z9. *Myrteola nummularia* is the only really hardy myrtle. It is a prostrate plant for a sunny spot in the rock garden and flowers in early summer.
2–7.5m/6–25ft. Z9

PITTOSPORUM
Pittosporaceae

P. daphniphylloides forms a large shrub with long, leathery evergreen leaves and produces clusters of pale yellow, sweetly scented flowers in early summer followed by red fruit. It is proving hardier than previously thought. 3m/10ft. Sun or light shade. Moist, well-drained soil. Z8
P. tenuifolium, kohuhu, is the most common *Pittosporum*. Its dark purple flowers, borne in spring, are small and unobtrusive but they waft a thick honey scent. The fragrance is at its strongest in the evening. The evergreen foliage, popular with flower arrangers, is shiny, wavy-edged and fresh green, and the leaves are complemented beautifully by the black twigs. It may be pruned after flowering. There are many forms available with variegated, purple, silver and golden foliage.
Sun. Well-drained soil. Up to 12m/40ft. Z8

PRUNUS
Rosaceae

P. mume, Japanese apricot, has a powerful rose scent that carries well on the air. Its blossom, which comes in white and all shades of pink, single and double, appears on the bare stems in late winter. In the open it will grow into a large shrub or small tree, but looks well on or near a wall where its scent can be captured. Single-flowered, intense pink 'Beni-chidori' (a cheery sight outside my kitchen window) and semi-double white 'Omoi-no-mama' are fine forms but prone to pests and disease.
Sun or light shade. Fertile, well-drained soil. 9m/30ft.

RHAPHIOLEPIS
Rosaceae

R. umbellata is a slow-growing evergreen for a sunny wall.
It has thick, leathery, oval leaves and makes an attractive, rounded shrub. Its white flowers, borne in

Romneya coulteri 'White Cloud'

panicles during summer, have a sweet, bubblegum scent. It makes a nice conservatory plant in cold areas. *R. indica*, with pink flowers, is also scented. Sun. Well-drained soil. 3m/10ft. Z8

ROMNEYA
Papaveraceae
R. coulteri, California tree poppy, is surprisingly sweetly scented for a member of the poppy family. It is a suckering sub-shrub, whose erect growths should be cut back to ground level in early spring if the winter has not done the job for you. The large white saucers, with their prominent central boss of golden stamens, appear from high summer until autumn and are set off perfectly by the deeply-cut, glaucous grey foliage. It can be difficult to establish but afterwards the problem is its colonizing vigour. Its variety 'White Cloud' has bigger flowers. Sun. Well-drained soil. 1.2–2.5m/4–8ft. Z8

UGNI
Myrtaceae
***U. molinae* (*Myrtus ugni*)**, Chilean guava, is an erect shrub related to myrtle whose white flowers are tinged with pink. It flowers in spring and is hardy enough to be worth trying in all but very cold areas. Its red fruits are supposed to taste of strawberries but I cannot confirm this; Queen Victoria's favourite jam was reputedly made from them. 1–2m/3–6ft. Z9

VITEX
Lamiaceae
V. agnus-castus, chaste tree, is a valuable, but in the UK seldom grown, autumn-flowering shrub which benefits from the heat of a sunny wall. The lance-shaped leaves, grey on their undersides, are pungently aromatic and the violet flowers, borne on erect racemes, are sweetly scented. It is spreading, slow-growing and deciduous. Sun. Well-drained soil. 2.5m/8ft. Z6

SALVIA
Lamiaceae

S. microphylla is a shrubby *Salvia* with small, fruitily scented leaves and small, lipped flowers. It comes in an array of colours from crimson and red to yellow and peach. In protected sites on well-drained soil, it is reliably hardy, but can succumb in very cold winters. It blooms all summer and autumn. Sun. Well-drained soil. 60cm–2m/2–6ft. Z8

Salvia microphylla

CLIMBERS

ACTINIDIA
Actinidiaceae
A. deliciosa (*A. chinensis* hort.), Chinese gooseberry, is a deciduous climber grown principally for its kiwi fruits. Its sweetly scented flowers are an unexpected bonus; they open in clusters at midsummer, beginning white and fading to biscuit. The large, hairy, heart-shaped leaves are impressive, as is the plant's vigour. For fruits you need a female and a male plant; 'Hayward' is a popular female clone and 'Tomuri' a popular male. But this plant needs a great deal of space, and you may not think it is worth it. It dislikes strong midday sun, so a partly shaded wall or pergola that receives some sun is ideal. All but very dry soils. 9m/30ft. Z7

A. kolomikta is a startling deciduous plant whose leaves look as if they have been dipped first in whitewash and then in raspberry juice. I cannot stand the sight of it but others swoon in admiration. The clusters of white, slightly scented flowers appear in early summer. It is less vigorous than other actinidias and may take a few years for its leaves to colour. It wants a wall that receives full sun.
6m/20ft. Z4

A. polygama is similar to *A. kolomikta* but its leaves are white-dipped without any pink, and the scent is stronger – so altogether a more desirable climber. Sun. 6m/20ft. Z4

AKEBIA
Lardizabalaceae
A. quinata is a fascinating climber for a sheltered, sunny pergola. It has elegant leaves, composed of five rounded leaflets, and in mild winters is evergreen. In spring, curious three-sepalled, chocolate-purple flowers appear, which release a spicy scent on warm days. Even more curious purplish, sausage-shaped fruits sometimes follow. It is a vigorous climber. Often recommended for shady walls, but all the best plants I have seen have been in full sun.
9m/30ft. Z4

BILLARDIERA
Pittosporaceae
B. longiflora is an unusual evergreen climber for a sunny wall in warmer areas. It is a dainty thing, with slender leaves and small, scented, greenish-yellow funnels in high summer. But it is at its best in the autumn when it is hung with rich violet-blue, oblong fruits. A novelty, not a show-stopper. It makes a good conservatory plant. Sun. 2m/6ft. Z9

FAR LEFT *Actinidia kolomikta*
LEFT *Akebia quinata*

LEFT *Clematis flammula* RIGHT *Clematis* 'Apple Blossom'

CLEMATIS

Ranunculaceae

Scent among the climbing *Clematis* is found chiefly in the small-flowered species, not the large-flowered hybrids. These may not provide the same splashes of colour, but they have a natural charm that more and more gardeners are coming to appreciate. They look as well growing up trees and shrubs as on walls and pergolas. *Clematis* do particularly well on limestone and they need a cool, shady root run. Container-bought plants should have their rootballs planted 5cm/2in below soil level. Most need little or no pruning. Deep, fertile, moist soil.

C. afoliata is an unusual *Clematis* that is suitable for planting against a sunny, sheltered wall in warmer areas. It has tendrils instead of leaves, and bears clusters of pointed, straw-green flowers in spring, which have a *Daphne* fragrance; the scent is elusive outdoors but pronounced when the plant is grown in a conservatory. 2.5m/8ft. Z9

C. armandii is a handsome and vigorous evergreen with long, dark, leathery leaves. The creamy flowers, sometimes flushed with pink, appear in spring and are scented of almonds. It should be trimmed lightly after flowering. 'Snowdrift', with pure white flowers, is a superior selection, together with the hybrid 'Apple Blossom', with bronze young foliage and pinky flowers. This popular and desirable plant needs shelter from cold winds and a sunny aspect. 6m/20ft. Z8

C. cirrhosa* var. *balearica, fern-leaved *Clematis*, has finely cut, evergreen leaves which turn bronze in the autumn and carries its bell-shaped, creamy flowers, usually speckled with crimson inside, through the winter. The flower scent is elusive outdoors, but if the plant is grown in a conservatory its lemon fragrance can be properly savoured. 'Wisley Cream' is a good variant. Sun or shade. 3m/10ft. Z8

***C.* 'Edward Prichard'** is a low *Clematis* with slender starry flowers. These are white shading to lilac at the tips, and have a pronounced scent. It is good in containers. 1.2m/4ft.

***C.* 'Fair Rosamond'** is, as far as I am aware, the only large-flowered hybrid with a pronounced scent; it has been described as a blend of cowslip and violet. The flowers are white, flushed pink, and have prominent purple stamens. It blooms in early summer and can be grown in a tub. Sun or shade. 2m/6ft.

C. flammula is a deciduous plant similar to traveller's joy or old man's beard, *C. vitalba*, but, for garden purposes, altogether superior. It is vigorous, while still being manageable, has good polished leaves, and its white flowers, produced in late summer and autumn, are powerfully scented of

LEFT *Clematis forsteri* CENTRE *Clematis rehderiana* RIGHT *Clematis* x *triternata* 'Rubromarginata'

meadowsweet; the scent is enjoyable in the air, but overpowering at close range. Being from southern Europe, it appreciates sun and shelter from cold winds. It is excellent when trained up an outbuilding or tree.
Up to 4.5m/15ft. Z6

C. forsteri is a New Zealand evergreen species that has yellow-green starry flowers with a fair degree of lemon scent. The related species *C. petriei* is especially well endowed and is more hardy and vigorous. It has green flowers in spring; they are larger on male plants, but the females carry attractive seedheads. A sheltered, sunny position is needed; in cold areas, these make excellent plants for the cool conservatory.
Z9

***C.* 'Lemon Dream'** is a newly introduced spring-flowering *Clematis* with double, lemon-white bell-shaped flowers. These have a delicious grapefruit scent. 2m/6ft.

C. montana is one of the glories of the spring garden. It bears its four-sepalled flowers, rather open and square-looking, in magnificent quantity. The species itself is white and has a strong vanilla scent; 'Grandiflora', which has larger white flowers, is unscented. *C. montana* var. *rubens* is a bright mauve-pink, and 'Elizabeth' is a large-flowered pale pink; both are vanilla-scented. *C. montana* var. *wilsonii* blooms later in the year; it is white and strongly scented. The montanas thrive in sun or shade and because of their vigour are much used for covering unsightly buildings. They are deciduous.
6m/20ft. Z5

C. rehderiana flowers from high summer until autumn and releases a delicious primrose fragrance from its small, pale yellow bells. I think this is one of the most desirable of all *Clematis*. This deciduous climber is lovely up a wall or tree.
Sun or light shade. 7.5m/25ft, but can be hard pruned in early spring.
Z6

C. serratifolia is worth growing for its lemon scent. It is an unusual *Clematis*, similar in appearance to *C. tangutica* and *C. orientalis*, but with smaller, paler bells, filled with brown filaments. It blooms profusely in late summer. It is deciduous.
Sun or light shade. 3m/10ft. Z5

***C. terniflora* (*C. paniculata* hort.)** is related to *C. flammula* and its white flowers release the same hawthorn fragrance. It is a popular *Clematis* in the United States, but needs more sun than the British climate can provide. It is a vigorous grower and flowers in autumn.
9m/30ft. Z9

***C.* x *triternata* 'Rubromarginata'**, an unusual and vigorous hybrid, between *C. flammula* and *C. viticella*, bears a mass of purple-edged white flowers in late summer and autumn. These have the flammula scent.
Sun or light shade. 3.5m/12ft. Z6

C. viticella 'Betty Corning' is a lightly scented, very attractive member of this useful *viticella* tribe, with lavender-blue bells in summer.
3m/10ft. Z5

DECUMARIA
Hydrangeaceae
D. barbara is a self-clinging, semi-evergreen climber. It is similar and related to the climbing hydrangeas and schizophragmas, but its white flowers are all fertile; they are borne in small, erect corymbs during summer and are honey-scented. It can be grown up a wall or tree.
Sun or light shade. Moist, well-drained soil. 7.5m/25ft or more. Z7
D. sinensis is an evergreen species that enjoys the same conditions as *D. barbara*. It bears pyramidal panicles of creamy flowers – also honey-scented but much less strongly – in early summer.
3m/10ft. Z6

ERCILLA
Phytolaccaceae
E. volubilis is a curious self-clinging evergreen climber which has dense spikes of pinkish bottlebrush flowers in spring. These have a scent like meadowsweet.
Sun or light shade. 3m/10ft. Z7

HOLBOELLIA
Lardizabalaceae
H. coriacea is a handsome, vigorous, evergreen climber with sweetly scented purple-tinged and greenish-white bells in spring, followed by purple fruits.
Sun. 6m/20ft. Z7
H. latifolia is a little less hardy, but another desirable twining evergreen. It bears very sweetly scented, greenish-white and purplish flowers in early spring, and these may be followed by purple, sausage-shaped fruits. The leaves are long, glossy and luxuriant. A sheltered wall is necessary in areas subject to frost. The flowers of the rarer *H. brachyandra* have a rich melon scent.
Sun. 6m/20ft. Z9

JASMINUM
Oleaceae
The common jasmine gives us one of our most potent evening scents. Its heavily sweet, exotic fragrance is always delightful on the air, but can be overpowering, even unpleasant, in quantity. Plant this away from the house, where its scent will reach you diluted and in wafts; the other jasmines can be planted beside windows and doors.
Sun. Fertile soil.
J. beesianum has small, deep rose-red flowers in early summer, followed by shiny black berries. It is an interesting plant, but perhaps not among the most distinguished jasmines. It is evergreen in mild areas.
3.5m/12ft. Z6
J. officinale, common jasmine, is a vigorous, usually deciduous, climber

LEFT *Holboellia coriacea* RIGHT *Jasminum officinale*

FAR LEFT *Jasminum* x *stephanense*
LEFT *Lonicera* x *americana*

that is beautiful when scrambling up an outbuilding, a pergola or even over a tree stump; in cold areas, though, it needs a sheltered wall that receives full sun. The pure white flowers open from pink-tinged buds throughout the summer. It is best left unpruned. Spanish or royal jasmine, *J. affine*, is a superior form with slightly larger flowers; 'Aureum' has yellow-blotched leaves; 'Clotted Cream' is a cream variety with a piercingly sweet perfume.
6m/20ft or more. Z7

J.* x *stephanense is a hybrid between the previous two species. It is a lovely plant that bears sweetly scented pale pink flowers in summer. It is evergreen in mild areas, and its young leaves often display creamy variegation.
6m/20ft. Z7

LONICERA
Caprifoliaceae

Honeysuckles are a mainstay of the scented garden. In the cool of the evening or early morning, the air will be filled with fruity or spicy sweetness; in the heat of the day, they have to be sniffed. They are usually at their best scrambling freely over fences and pergolas or up trees, rather than pinned vertically to walls; little pruning is then necessary. They are not fussy about soil but, like *Clematis*, enjoy a cool root run. They are prone to aphid attack and regular spraying may be necessary.

L.* x *americana is a superb deciduous hybrid honeysuckle with a powerful clove scent. Its flowers are yellow, suffused with reddish-purple, and make an impressive display in summer.
Sun or part shade. 6m/20ft. Z6

L. caprifolium, early cream honeysuckle, flowers at midsummer but its blooms are a blend of white and yellow, with little or no red present, and have the typical fruity honeysuckle fragrance. This splendid plant is deciduous.
Shade. 6m/20ft. Z6

L. etrusca is an unusual and beautiful semi-evergreen honeysuckle for a wall that receives full sun, though it is not hardy in very cold areas; it

Lonicera periclymenum

makes a good conservatory plant. The flowers begin cream, suffused with red, and mature to a rich yellow colour; they appear throughout late summer and have a fruity scent. 3.5m/12ft. Z8

***L.* x *heckrottii* 'Gold Flame' hort.** is a weak-stemmed shrub rather than a climber and needs to have the support of a wall. It bears rich orange-yellow flowers, suffused with reddish-purple, during late summer, and these have a spicy sweet scent. It is slow-growing. Shade. Z5

***L. japonica* 'Halliana'** is the finest form of the Japanese honeysuckle and a desirable plant for all but very cold gardens. In warmer climates, including parts of the USA, it is an invasive weed. It is more or less evergreen, and it is in bloom from early summer; the flowers open white and mature to yellow, and have a powerful tropical fragrance, reminiscent of *Gardenia*. It is very vigorous and may need hard pruning in spring. Sun or light shade. 9m/30ft. Z5

L. periclymenum, common honeysuckle, is a familiar hedgerow and cottage-garden plant, but has really been superseded by its two famous cultivars: 'Belgica', the early Dutch honeysuckle, produces its pale yellow and reddish-purple flowers mainly at midsummer; 'Serotina', even better, produces its darker flowers through the summer and autumn; 'Graham Thomas' has no pink in the white and yellow flowers. All are deciduous and have a rich fruit scent. 6m/20ft. Z5

L. splendida is an evergreen worth

PASSIFLORA
Passifloraceae

P. caerulea, passionflower, bears the most intricate and intriguing of garden flowers; each displays a circular pattern of purple, blue and greenish-white filaments surmounted by a central column bearing stamens, stigmas and ovary of chunky proportions, and is more like a product of the Industrial Revolution than of Mother Nature. The flowers appear throughout the summer and have a delicate, sweet scent; they are followed by orange, egg-shaped fruits. It will thrive on a sunny wall in all but the coldest regions, but needs protection for its first couple of winters. It is evergreen and relatively pest-free. 'Constance Elliott' is a beautiful white form. 4.5m/15ft. Z7

Passiflora caerulea

trying in all but very cold areas. It has lovely bluish-green foliage and bears its scented flowers, yellowish inside and reddish outside, throughout the summer. It needs shelter from cold winds.
Full sun. Z9

PILEOSTEGIA
Hydrangeaceae
P. viburnoides produces panicles of cream, honey-scented flowers in late summer and autumn, and is an attractive self-clinging evergreen alternative to climbing hydrangea or schizophragma for a shady wall. Like these, it is slow to get started.
6m/20ft. Z8

SCHISANDRA
Schisandraceae
S. chinensis is an unusual deciduous climber with scented flowers and aromatic leaves. The flowers, borne in spring, are pale rose-pink, and hang on long stalks; they are followed by attractive scarlet fruits on female plants. It is a novelty for a wall or pergola.
Sun or light shade. 6m/20ft. Z5
S. grandiflora is a handsome species with well-scented, ivory flowers in early summer, followed by red fruits on female plants. Sun or light shade. 6m/20ft. Z8
S. rubriflora is a more common species, bearing pendulous dark red bells in spring; it also has attractive fruits. Again, the flowers are fragrant and the leaves aromatic. It is an eyecatching plant in flower and fruit for walls or pergolas.
Shade. 6m/20ft. Z8

SCHIZOPHRAGMA
Hydrangeaceae
S. integrifolium produces heads of bracts in the manner of climbing hydrangea, *H. petiolaris* (itself lightly scented), but altogether larger and more impressive. They are cream and honey-scented, stronger than in *S. hydrangeoides*, and appear in high summer. It is self-clinging but grows slowly until established. Flowering is better if the wall is not too shady.
Sun or shade. 9m/30ft. Z7

STAUNTONIA
Lardizabalaceae
S. hexaphylla succeeds on a sheltered, sunny wall in all but very cold areas. It is a leathery-leaved evergreen which bears small racemes of white, violet-tinged flowers in spring; these have a sweet scent. Edible, purple fruits follow after a hot summer. It is a handsome foliage plant, worth a place in the conservatory if it cannot be grown outside.
12m/40ft. Z8

TRACHELOSPERMUM
Apocynaceae
T. asiaticum is reliable on a sunny wall in all but the coldest areas. Its creamy-yellow, jasmine-like flowers

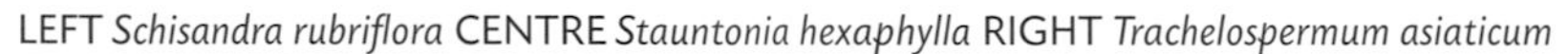
LEFT *Schisandra rubriflora* CENTRE *Stauntonia hexaphylla* RIGHT *Trachelospermum asiaticum*

LEFT *Trachelospermum jasminoides* 'Variegatum' RIGHT *Wisteria sinensis*

have a refined heliotrope scent that is irresistible; they appear in high summer. It is evergreen, with small, dark leaves and a dense, compact habit. 5.5m/18ft. Z8

T. jasminoides, star or confederate jasmine, is powerfully orange-blossom scented, with larger flowers and leaves. It is in the very first league of fragrant plants. Once established, this evergreen can be trusted outside on a sunny wall but it is slightly less hardy than *T. asiaticum*; in cold areas, it should head the list of conservatory plants. It does well in London. The flowers are pure white and borne in high summer. *Trachelospermum* flower on old wood, so little pruning should be done; they like good soil. 'Variegatum' is a white and pink-splashed, evergreen version – not to my taste. 9m/30ft. Z9

WISTERIA
Papilionaceae

The long violet racemes of wisterias drip down many a house front in early summer, but familiarity has not bred contempt. They are sensational trained over pergolas and across bridges, and can also be grown as standards. They are vigorous growers but generally take a few years to start flowering. Pruning established plants consists of shortening the new, long, lateral growths to 15cm/6in after flowering, and shortening them again to two or three buds in winter. They are deciduous.

Sun. Deep soil.

W. brachybotrys* 'Shiro-kapitan'** (W. venusta* 'Alba'**) is one of the loveliest white wisterias, its racemes unfurling at the same time as its silky young leaves. The flowers have a richly honeyed floral scent that carries well.
7.5m/25ft. Z5

W. floribunda, Japanese wisteria, produces its long racemes in early summer after its young foliage has expanded. In my view, this gives it the edge over the Chinese species. The flowers have a delicate pea scent. The species has been superseded in gardens by its many varieties, including 'Multijuga' ('Macrobotrys'), with immensely long racemes, and by the superb white 'Alba'.
7.5m/25ft. Z4

W. sinensis, Chinese wisteria, has a much stronger and sweeter pea scent than *W. floribunda* and it carries in the air. It flowers in spring on bare stems, and the flowers show up very well on a pale wall. But it is also worth trying up trees. (Wisterias up trees need not be pruned.) 'Alba' is a good white; 'Prolific' a floriferous violet-blue. 15m/50ft or more, if unpruned. Z5

Wisteria brachybotrys 'Shiro-kapitan' on a pergola at RHS Garden Hyde Hall

RHS GARDEN HYDE HALL

"At RHS Hyde Hall, shrubs such as *Elaeagnus*, *Lonicera* and *Sarcococca* are used at key locations and strategic junctions as fragrant lures to attract people along the garden circuit. *Cassinia leptophylla* subsp. *fulvida*, a honey-scented, heather-like shrub from New Zealand which proves hardy here, is among the best scented plants in the garden, together with the summer-flowering clematis *C.* x *triternata* 'Rubromarginata' and, growing over the oak pergola leading to the Hilltop Garden, *Wisteria brachybotrys* 'Shiro-Kapitan' whose white flowers give off a scent of vanilla and honey for four weeks.

Hyde Hall's low rainfall suits plants from the drier climates, and in the informal, rolling design of the Dry Garden, the assembly of *Cistus*, rosemary, cotton lavender, juniper and *Salvia* contributes a warm gummy aroma. This is evident also in the adjacent formal Herb Garden, and will be in the new Mediterranean Garden now being planned, which will include lines of lavender such as you see in the fields of Provence. In summer, the collection of English Roses is another notable scented feature."

Ian Legros, Curator at RHS Garden Hyde Hall

ALPINE, TROUGH & WATER GARDENS

When you meet a rose, the first thing you do (at least, I do) is to draw it to your nose. We may also try our luck with a large flowering shrub or tree. But when presented with a lowly alpine, few of us think to smell it. It is true that scented plants are not abundant among alpine flora, and that the great majority of the most commonly grown rock garden plants – *Aubrieta*, *Campanula*, saxifrages, *Veronica*, *Sedum*, *Lewisia*, gentians, *Geranium*, *Sempervivum* and so on – lack fragrance. But there is enough scent among alpines to warrant keeping your sense of smell alert.

If we are to enjoy a flower's scent, it usually needs to be within reach of the nose. The smaller the plant, the higher it needs to be raised off the ground. So these fragrant rock plants should be at a comfortable height for sniffing. Troughs and raised beds will be ideal homes for many, and some may be grown vertically, nearer nose level, in retaining walls.

You can open the year with dwarf bulbs such as violet-scented *Iris reticulata* (whose purple flowers look so good against a tiny blue conifer like *Juniperus squamata* 'Blue Star') and crocuses like *C. versicolor* and *C. chrysanthus*. The latter comes in many colour forms and each has its own degree and quality of honey scent. I was once given, as a Christmas present, a box containing an assortment of different honeys from around the world and had an entertaining time matching their scents to those of the crocuses opening in pots in the house. Some of the matches were close, but the real lessons learned were that the flavours even within one species of plant can be very diverse, and that labels such as 'honey-scented' cover endless nuances.

Scilla mischtschenkoana is another excellent bulb for the alpine garden. It colonizes freely and its pale flowers, which appear over a long period from early spring, have a very sweet scent and make an attractive foreground for yellow, fruitily fragrant,

Rock gardens do not need to be mountainous constructions – low beds, mounded gently with a few large stones, fit more happily into the average garden, with sinks and troughs for the choicer alpines. Here, an assortment of pinks drench the garden in summer scent, while creeping thyme in the paving cracks awaits brushing by feet. *Campanula*, *Diascia* and white *Lychnis* add further colour.

This stone square brings old-fashioned rock gardening into a modern design context. It is filled with camomile and an assortment of thymes, providing leaf aromas: *Dianthus* could also be added for airborne flower scent, though would be less forgiving when trodden on.

small-flowered narcissi. Grape hyacinths such as *Muscari armeniacum* 'Valerie Finnis' and dwarf tulips should also be offered a home here.

As spring advances alpine gardens become flooded with flowers. The most sophisticated scents are provided by the *Daphne*. The prostrate garland flower, *D. cneorum,* will cover a large area if its stems are encouraged to root as they creep overground; this is done by placing stones over them. An established plant, mounding itself over rocks and trailing down walls, is quite a spectacle when in flower as well as a feast for the nose, and this species – in its best form, 'Eximia' – would be on my shortlist for any alpine garden. Other *Daphne* are equally rich in perfume. *D. sericea* Collina Group is neat and easy to accommodate, and *D. tangutica* Retusa Group is small enough for a trough; both of these are good in pots in the cold greenhouse. Recently, there has been a flurry of excellent new hybrids introduced, many by Robin White of Hampshire, England, including the superb *D.* x *transatlantica* 'Eternal Fragrance' which flowers almost continuously.

Another important group of scented alpine plants are the pinks (*Dianthus*). The warm fragrance is exhaled by a number of species and hybrids, and since it will hang on the air on still days, plants can happily be used at ground level, edging paths and sprouting from paving cracks. My favourite hybrids are those with intricate maroon, plum and crimson lacing, which look especially good in partnership with striped and splashed roses like Rosa mundi (*Rosa gallica* 'Versicolor') and 'Ferdinand Pichard'. A similar heady scent, though not as strong, is evident in many of the alpine *Phlox*, and in perennial wallflowers (*Erysimum*) where it is blended to a greater or lesser degree with aniseed. The scent of *Onosma alborosea* also has an aniseed flavour. The onosmas make striking occupants of rock garden crevices and walls; their clusters of drooping flowers contrast with all around them and are a substantial size. The scent of *Primula reidii* var. *williamsii* is also too good to miss. And for long-lasting colour, the more scented varieties of viola, such as 'Mrs Lancaster' and 'Little David', ought to be found a place in the garden.

To supplement the flower scents, a range of plants with aromatic leaves can be added – origanums and thymes for spice and *Stachys citrina* for a dash of mint chocolate. Various dwarf rhododendrons will add further hot aromas.

Scent is not commonly found among the high alpines. These are the plants which are kept dry through the winter months by a heavy covering of snow and in cultivation must usually be grown under glass to protect them from rain. But enter an alpine house during spring and early summer and you will soon find the exceptions. *Dionysia aretioides* has flowers with a rich cowslip scent and those of *Androsace cylindrica* have a strong almond scent; while the connoisseur's favourites *Petrocallis pyrenaica* and *Thlaspi cepaeifolium* subsp. *rotundifolium* are also delicious. The scent from these is often so powerful that it wafts through the vents and you can savour it even in the garden outside.

A miniature rock garden of aromatic leaves and scented flowers in a stone 'table' trough.

Sun and good drainage are basic requirements of most alpines: equal parts, by volume, of loam, moss peat/peat substitute and coarse grit is the standard medium. But the alpine garden will inevitably have shady parts, and you may also have paved shady corners behind the house just begging for a trough.

Here you can make special beds for those shade-loving species of gentian, primula, lily and ericaceous shrub. These need a moist, humus-rich soil though drainage should be good. They are largely lime-hating plants so the soil used should be neutral or acid and the rocks surrounding it granite or sandstone – railway sleepers are excellent alternatives. In limy areas, the beds must be raised about a metre or a couple of feet above the ground to prevent leaching from the surrounding land, and they should be watered with rainwater, not from the tap. In my own shady raised beds I have used a mixture of loam-based ericaceous compost, shredded pine bark and lime-free grit. Shade may be from walls, buildings or trees, but there should be no overhanging branches or eaves likely to cause dripping. The scented plants for such beds include shrubs such as *Daphne blagayana*

ALPINE HOUSES

An alpine house is little more than an unheated greenhouse with extra ventilation. For the scent-lover, it provides a splendid opportunity to enjoy a range of early-blooming plants, their flowers protected from the elements and seen to perfection, and to accommodate a range of plants that are not quite hardy or damp-tolerant and that can be kept on the dry side during the winter and protected under insulating material during very cold spells. In the first category come winter and spring bulbs like crocuses and narcissi, irises and even florist's hyacinths. The smaller *Daphne* are usually well suited to pots and make excellent companions. In the second category come Mediterranean lavenders and rosemaries. You might consider training lemon-scented *Clematis forsteri,* or some of the other New Zealand *Clematis*, over a narrow strip of roof. And if the greenhouse is big enough, and the climate not too hostile, a scented camellia such as *Camellia japonica* 'Scentsation' or rhododendron such as 'Lady Alice Fitzwilliam' might also be tried; these would be plunged outside in a shady place for the summer, in their pots. Of all the plants you can grow in an alpine house, I think the show auriculas would be my first choice. They are such bizarre characters, especially those with green, white and grey-edged leaves, and you can spend ages marvelling at their intricate patterning and their unfolding buds, heavily dusted in meal. Add to this a piercing scent – primrose-lemony with an undertone of chocolate – and you have a nonpareil.

and *Mitchella repens;* bulbs such as *Arisaema candidissimum, Lilium cernuum, L. duchartrei, L. nepalense* and snowdrops; and perennials such as *Anemone sylvestris, Linnaea borealis, Aquilegia viridiflora, Corydalis flexuosa, Phlox divaricata* and *Trillium luteum.* In mine I also grow short rhododendrons like *R. trichostomum* and x *Ledodendron* 'Arctic Tern'.

PONDS AND WATER GARDENS

A pond makes one of the best of garden features. Everyone is attracted to water, and its plant and animal life are a source of interest throughout the year. Mine is outside the kitchen window for its bird watching opportunities.

Surrounding the pond with an area of boggy ground enables you to grow moisture-loving perennials in addition to those in the water itself. The ground is made boggy by having the soil slope down over the edge of the pond into a mud shelf and allowing the water to rise by capillary action; a second ledge underwater prevents the soil from spilling into the pond's depths. The mud shelf should be thickly planted with marginal plants to prevent erosion. Ponds may be formal affairs, of geometrical shape, and used as centrepieces for mown lawns or paved terraces. Or they may be natural, edged in rushes and shaded by willows.

There is not an abundance of scented candidates for water gardens. But, as with alpine gardens, it is by no means impossible to pursue a fragrant theme. Firstly, floating on the water itself, there can be scented waterlilies. There are numerous hybrids available, in colours ranging from rose-pink to sulphur-yellow, which exhale a fruity fragrance. Early in the season, the water hawthorn, *Aponogeton distachyos,* offers a contrasting note of vanilla and its white spikes and slender leaves emphasize the waterlilies' buxom, rounded form.

Among marginal plants, which will stand in a moderate depth of water, are plants with fragrant leaves such as the sweet flag, whose valuable strap-like foliage is scented of cinnamon; brass buttons (*Cotula coronopifolia*); and galingale (*Cyperus longus*). For the damp ground near the water there are also plants with scented flowers. The white version of bog arum (*Lysichiton camtschatcensis*) can kick the season off in early spring with its huge spathes, but you need to be able to reach them with your nose to catch the sweet scent. Larger gardens with natural ponds may also be able to accommodate some of the willows with scented catkins such as *Salix aegyptiaca* and *S. triandra;* and the scented-leaved bay willow, *S. pentandra.*

My favourite pondside fragrances come from the primulas. In early summer *P. alpicola, P. sikkimensis* and *P. prolifera* (better known by its former name, *P. helodoxa*) waft their lemon scent, perfectly complemented by the aniseed of *P. wilsonii* var. *anisodora*, if you can grow it within the reach of your fingers. But the richest fragrance comes from the later-blooming giant Himalayan cowslip, *P. florindae.* A self-sown colony of these sulphur beauties looks stunning and the scent is intoxicating.

Of the shrubs you can grow at the waterside, the sweet pepper bush, *Clethra alnifolia,* would always be high on my list. The spikes of white flowers, which appear in high summer, are as heavily and sweetly scented as *Viburnum*. And for aromatic foliage, the sweet fern, *Comptonia peregrina,* and the bog myrtle, *Myrica gale*, are indispensable. Rhododendrons such as *R. viscosum* and *R. atlanticum* can also be relied upon for strong fruity flower scents.

Lysichiton camtschatcensis **has a clean scent unlike its foul-smelling yellow cousin, the skunk cabbage.**

ALPINE & TROUGH PLANTS

ALYSSUM
Brassicaceae
A. montanum. This ground-hugging *Alyssum* bears loose heads of soft yellow, very fragrant flowers in early summer. It has small grey evergreen leaves.
Sun. Well-drained soil. Up to 15cm/6in.

ANDROSACE
Primulaceae
A. ciliata forms a tiny mound of rosetted leaves, and in early summer produces rose-pink flowers that are strongly scented of almonds.
Gritty soil in the alpine house.
A. cylindrica has rosettes of downy, grey-green leaves and white flowers, with a strong almond scent.
Gritty soil in the alpine house.
A. pubescens makes a small hummock of tightly packed, grey rosettes. The short-stemmed, white flowers are scented of honey. It resents wet weather and will need the protection of a sheet of glass through the winter. It is suited to tufa cultivation and does well in the alpine house.
Sun. Gritty soil.
A. villosa is easier to grow than *A. pubescens*, and makes mats of hairy, grey-green leaves which, in spring, are surmounted by white or pink honey-scented flowers, some with a reddish eye.
Sun. Gritty soil.

ANEMONE
Ranunculaceae
A. sylvestris, snowdrop windflower, is a beautiful anemone that has white drooping flowers in spring that are lit by golden stamens and have a delicate scent. It has deeply cut leaves and a running rootstock, and thrives in cool corners or in woodland borders.
Light shade. Humus-rich soil. 30cm/1ft.

AQUILEGIA
Ranunculaceae
A. fragrans. This lovely plant is a little taller than others in this section, but is deserving of a special spot in the garden. It has bluish-green leaves and long-spurred, white flowers which have an apple-like scent.

FAR LEFT *Anemone sylvestris*
LEFT *Androsace villosa* var. *arachnoidea* 'Superba'

LEFT *Aquilegia fragrans* RIGHT *Daphne cneorum* 'Eximia'

Sun or light shade. Moist, well-drained soil. 60cm/2ft.

A. viridiflora is a fascinating columbine with dainty foliage and small flowers coloured green and chocolate that have a sweet, fruity scent. It is a plant that is lost in the border, and I grow mine in a raised bed.

Sun or light shade. Moist, well-drained soil. 30cm/1ft.

CAMPANULA
Campanulaceae

C. thyrsoides is a most unusual and impressive *Campanula* with flowers that are not only sweetly scented but also yellow. They are carried on a flower spike 30cm/1ft high. The leaves are narrow and hairy. It dies after flowering but is otherwise easy to grow and readily raised from seed.

Sun. Well-drained soil.

DAPHNE
Thymelaeaceae

The low-growing *Daphne* are essential for scented rock gardens, raised beds and troughs. Their refined, clove-shaded fragrance is superb. The flowers are often followed by shiny, highly poisonous fruits. *Daphne* are woody plants, and the taller species are described under Shrubs.

D. blagayana is an evergreen, rather straggly species for a raised bed which bears scented, cream flowers in spring and has broad leaves. It is not difficult to grow, provided it has a cool, moist root run. Leaf-mould and fibrous soil should be incorporated, and each spring, the previous year's stems should be pegged down and covered with stones. This encourages the plant to layer, and it will gradually cover a wide area.

Light or medium shade. Well-drained soil. Up to 60cm/2ft. Z6

D. cneorum, garland flower, is perhaps one of the supreme rock garden *Daphne*. The richly scented, rose-pink flowers emerge from red buds and a large plant in bloom in late spring is an exceptionally beautiful sight. It can make a dense mound of foliage, if its shoots are clipped back during its youth and it is layered as it advances. Its roots should be kept cool with peat and leaf-mould. 'Eximia' is a superior, vigorous variety; 'Variegata' has cream-edged leaves and is more compact. Sun or light shade. Well-drained soil. 30cm/1ft. Z5

D.* x *napolitana has clusters of rosy-pink flowers on a compact plant in spring and summer. 'Bramdean' has a dwarf, spreading habit.

Sun or light shade. Well-drained alkaline or neutral soil. 60cm/2ft. Z6.

***D.* x *rollsdorfii* 'Wilhelm Schacht'** produces a mass of deep lilac-pink flowers in early summer and again later in the season on a compact plant. Sun. Well-drained soil. 46cm/18in. Z6

***D. sericea* Collina Group (*D. collina*)** is a pretty dwarf

FAR LEFT *Daphne tangutica*
LEFT *Daphne* x *transatlantica* 'Eternal Fragrance'

shrub with evergreen leaves which produces clusters of highly scented, rosy flowers in spring. Its roots should be allowed to reach cool, peaty conditions below the soil. Sun or light shade. Well-drained, acid or alkaline soil. 60cm/2ft. Z7

***D.* x *susannae* 'Tichborne'** is a very good newcomer, with a mass of rich lilac-purple flowers in spring. Sun. well-drained soil. 25cm/10in. Z6

D. tangutica is an evergreen shrub which in late spring bears white flowers suffused with rose. Its fragrance is particularly good at night. It is a lovely plant. Sun or light shade. Humus-rich, acid or alkaline soil. 1.2–1.5m/4–5ft Z7

***D. tangutica* Retusa Group (*D. retusa*)** is a short version of *D. tangutica* and is one of the easier – although painfully slow – species to grow. It makes a neat mound of evergreen leaves. Sun or light shade. Humus-rich, acid or alkaline soil. 60cm/2ft. Z7

***D.* x *transatlantica* 'Eternal Fragrance'** is an excellent new hybrid that produces its white flowers in flushes from spring to autumn. There are also forms with pink flowers and variegated foliage. Sun or light shade. Well-drained soil. 60cm/2ft. Z6

DIANTHUS
Caryophyllaceae

The clove scent of pinks and carnations is one of the most evocative of fragrances and on warm, early summer days and evenings it will infuse the air. The alpine pinks are at home nestling among stones in the rock garden, while the larger pinks and carnations are just as happy lining cottage-garden paths or fronting rose borders. All benefit from a mulch of pea gravel. Sun. Well-drained, limy soil.

D. arenarius is a very fragrant pink for the rock garden. Similar to *D. squarrosus*, it forms mats of green foliage above which white, cut-petalled flowers appear all summer. 46cm/18in.

D. gratianopolitanus, Cheddar pink, is a British native that varies in colour from deep rose to flesh-pink and even white. The flowers are fringed and strongly scented, appearing in early summer. It forms mats of narrow, blue-green leaves and revels in cracks between rocks. 10–20cm/4–8in.

***D. hyssopifolius* (*D. monspessulanus* subsp. *sternbergii*)** is an unusual, fragrant pink that has large, fringed, rose–red flowers over a glaucous mat of foliage. 30cm/1ft.

D. petraeus has narrow leaves and tiny white flowers which are very sweetly scented. The form with double white flowers and its subspecies *noeanus,* also white, are equally desirable. 25cm/10in.

Dianthus squarrosus

D. squarrosus is an easy alpine with narrow green leaves and white flowers. It is very sweetly scented. 30cm/1ft.

D. superbus makes a lax plant with broad green leaves and lilac-pink flowers all summer; these are green-eyed, deeply cut and very fragrant. 30–60cm/1–2ft.

Hybrid Dianthus

There are a huge number of named varieties of pink. They come in a range of heights and colours and can be double or single, blotched, laced and fringed; most are highly scented. They root easily from cuttings (known as pipings).

Among the smaller pinks, I recommend 'Little Jock', a semi-double rose-pink with a darker eye; 'Nyewood's Cream', a compact, cream white; and 'Waithman Beauty', a single crimson, marked in white. 15cm/6in or less.

The larger pinks can be divided into two groups. The old–fashioned and laced pinks generally bloom only at midsummer but include some wonderful old world characters. Among these I recommend 'Bridal Veil', a double fringed white with a crimson centre; 'Brympton Red', a crimson with deeper marbling; 'Musgrave's Pink' ('Charles Musgrave'), a single white with a green eye; 'Dad's Favourite', a semi-double white, laced and centred with crimson; 'Hope', a pink with maroon lacing; 'Inchmery', a pale pink; 'Laced Romeo', a rose-pink with crimson lacing; 'London Delight', a mauve-laced pink; and 'White Ladies', a double, fringed white and an improvement on the popular 'Mrs Sinkins'. 23–30cm/9–12in.

Among the modern hybrids, which flower on and off all summer, I recommend: 'Doris', a double shrimp-pink; 'Gran's Favourite', a white, laced with mauve; and 'Haytor', a double white. 23–30cm/9–12in.

And among the newer pinks, I especially like 'Mendlesham Minx' and 'Mystic Star', both crimson splashed in white.

Spicy-scented border or clove carnations have become scarce. This is a pity because they are a handy size and flower in late summer, when pinks are over or are tiring. 'Old Crimson Clove' and 'Fenbow Nutmeg Clove' are the most likely to be offered by nurseries.

DIONYSIA
Primulaceae

D. aretioides is one of the easier dionysias but needs to be grown in the alpine house; it succeeds well in tufa. It forms tight cushions of hairy rosettes which are studded in spring with almost stemless, yellow flowers; they exhale the scent of cowslips. It should be watered sparingly and with great care.

Sun. Well-drained soil.

LEFT *Dianthus* 'Doris' RIGHT *Dianthus* 'Brympton Red'

LINNAEA
Caprifoliaceae

L. borealis, twin-flower, is an attractive prostrate, creeping, evergreen sub-shrub found in the colder parts of the northern hemisphere. The flesh-coloured bells appear in pairs during early summer and are almond-scented. The American subspecies *americana* has larger, crimson-pink flowers.
Shade. Lime-free soil.

Linnaea borealis subsp. *americana*

ERYSIMUM (CHEIRANTHUS)
Brassicaceae

***E. cheiri* 'Harpur Crewe'**. This bushy perennial wallflower has double, golden-yellow flowers with a strong aniseed scent. It is an old favourite for the rock garden and makes a good splash of colour in early summer. The double, red and yellow wallflower 'Bloody Warrior' makes a curious companion for it, and is also scented. Both are readily propagated by summer cuttings and plants are best renewed every couple of years, as old plants are inclined to die suddenly.
Sun. Poor, well-drained soil. 30cm/1ft.

***E. helveticum* (*E. pumilum*)**. This tiny, semi-evergreen wallflower has heads of fragrant, bright yellow flowers in early summer.
Sun. Well-drained soil. 10cm/4in.

***E.* 'Moonlight'**, with pale yellow flowers from red buds, is a perennial wallflower with a sweet clove scent. It makes a low mound of foliage and blooms in spring. Other scented hybrid erysimums are also available. They are useful plants for the front of the border, as well as the rock garden, since they provide cheerful colour in the gap between spring and summer.
Sun. 15–30cm/6–12in.

LEONTOPODIUM
Asteraceae

***L. haplophylloides* (*L. aloysiodorum*)** is rare in the UK. It is strongly lemon-scented in leaf and flower. It is a Himalayan relative of edelweiss and has white hairy leaves and heads of grey-white flowers in early summer. It dislikes winter damp.
Sun. Well-drained soil. 23cm/9in.

LEFT *Origanum dictamnus* RIGHT *Origanum laevigatum* 'Herrenhausen'

OLSYNIUM

Iridaceae

***O. filifolium* (*Sisyrinchium filifolium*)** comes from the Falkland Islands and produces pendent bell-shaped flowers above its tuft of rushy leaves in late spring. These are white, veined in reddish-purple, and are sweetly scented. Sun. Well-drained soil. 15cm/6in.

ONOSMA

Boraginaceae

These are distinctive and very desirable alpines with narrow hairy leaves and branching, pendent heads of fragrant, tubular flowers in summer. They are intolerant of winter wetness but prove reliable in rock garden crevices and walls.
Sun. Well-drained soil.

O. alborosea bears white, pink-flushed flowers in early summer that are scented of aniseed. 15cm/6in.

O. taurica has golden-yellow, honey-scented flowers in summer. 23cm/9in.

ORIGANUM

Lamiaceae

There are a number of good marjorams for the rock garden, and all have leaves with a degree of marjoram-like scent. They are especially valuable for their long-lasting flowers, which appear in high summer. Coming mainly from the Mediterranean region, they like heat and shelter and may not be reliably hardy in very cold areas.
Sun. Well-drained soil.

O. dictamnus, dittany, has rounded, grey woolly leaves and drooping heads of green bracts from which appear pink flowers. It performs best in the alpine house.
23cm/9in.

O. laevigatum makes quite a feature when grown in a generous drift, and is a perfect underplanting for *Verbena bonariensis* in the summer border. It produces a haze of small mauve flowers on wiry stems above a mat of bluish leaves. 'Hopleys' is a distinct form with more substantial flowerheads. 'Herrenhausen' is also showy.
23cm/9in.

O. rotundifolium has rounded, bluish leaves and drooping heads of bracts and pink flowers. 'Kent Beauty' is a fine hybrid that has semi-prostrate stems clad in glaucous leaves and topped with rounded bracts and purplish flowers.
23cm/9in.

OXALIS

Oxalidaceae

O. enneaphylla is a miniature alpine with fans of rounded, grey-green leaves and comparatively large white or pink-flushed flowers in spring; surprisingly (since scent is not commonly encountered in oxalis) these have an almond fragrance. There is a fine pink variety called 'Rosea'. It thrives in sheltered corners of the rock garden.
Shade. 7.5cm/3in.

LEFT *Papaver alpinum* RIGHT *Paradisea liliastrum*

PAPAVER

Papaveraceae

P. alpinum, alpine poppy. It is always a surprise to find scent in a poppy, but this species has a fair degree of musky fragrance. The flowers, which appear all summer, can be orange, yellow, pink or white and cross-fertilize freely. It pops up all over the rock garden and in paving cracks, but never becomes a weed.
Sun. Poor, well-drained soil. 10cm/4in.

PARADISEA

Asparagaceae

***P. liliastrum* (*Anthericum liliastrum*)**, St Bruno's lily, is a beautiful European alpine that has slender leaves and translucent, white, lily-like, fragrant flowers in early summer. It is easily grown in the rock garden or border.
Sun. 50cm/20in.

PATRINIA

Caprifoliaceae

P. triloba* var. *palmata is a short, erect perennial, easily grown and hardy, which produces heads of golden-yellow, scented flowers. These appear late, in high summer. It has deeply lobed leaves and reddish stems.
Sun. Well-drained, fertile soil. 20cm/8in.

PETROCALLIS

Brassicaceae

P. pyrenaica. This is a beautiful mat-forming alpine that bears a mass of white, lilac-tinged flowers in spring; these are deliciously scented of vanilla and honey. It is suitable for the alpine house or scree.
Sun. Gritty soil.

PHLOX

Polemoniaceae

P. caespitosa is an attractive scented alpine *Phlox*. It makes low mounds of long, pointed leaves and is studded, in spring and summer, with white or pale lilac flowers. These have a heady sweet fragrance. An easy plant to grow, this alpine *Phlox* dislikes hot, dry conditions.
Sun or light shade. Well-drained, fertile soil.

***P.* 'Charles Ricardo'** is one of many *Phlox* related to *P. divaricata* with a degree of scent; it has lavender-blue flowers with a purple centre.
Light shade. Moist, well-drained soil. 20cm/8in.

***P. divaricata* 'Clouds of Perfume'** produces elegant heads of pale lavender flowers in late spring above slender, airy foliage. They have a clean, lightly honeyed scent. 'May Breeze' is a lovely white version. They can be shy flowerers.
Light shade. Moist, well-drained soil. 30cm/1ft.

P. hoodii makes prostrate mats of foliage and, in summer, bears almost stemless, scented flowers in white or lilac.
Sun. Well-drained, fertile soil.

POLYGONATUM

Asparagaceae

P. hookeri is a tiny Solomon's seal with almost stemless, sweetly scented pink flowers, borne in early summer. Shade. Moist, well-drained soil.

P. odoratum is a shorter version of the common white Solomon's seal, *P.* x *hybridum*. 'Variegatum' is a little gem, with broad white edges to its leaves. The flowers have a light scent. Shade. Moist, well-drained soil. 60cm/2ft.

PRIMULA

Primulaceae

P. auricula. This heading covers an enormous band of garden and alpine house plants. All are hardy and form rosettes of fleshy leaves, topped in spring with tubular flowers, which often have gorgeous and eccentric combinations of colours. The scent is sweet, compared by many to honeysuckle, but to my nose often a delicious blend of lemon and chocolate. To discuss cultivation I shall divide them into three groups.

The first group consists of the alpine auriculas. Unlike the other auriculas, these have no floury covering on their leaves and flowers, and they may be planted outside. Among the nicest varieties are 'Argus', with dark plum, white-centred flowers; 'Bookham Firefly', with crimson, gold-centred flowers; 'Joy', with velvety crimson, white-centred flowers; and 'Mrs L. Hearn', with cream-centred, bluish-purple flowers.

Shade from midday sun. Well-drained, fertile soil.

The second group consists of the border auriculas. These do not conform to the florist's standards for the alpine and show classes, though many are of great antiquity. They usually have a floury covering on their leaves and flowers but because of their hardiness and vigour are invariably grown outside. Among the best varieties are 'Blue Velvet', a bluish-purple with a small white centre; Old Irish Blue', a frilled, rich violet-blue with a white centre; 'Old Red Dusty Miller', a rich red with a heavy covering of flour; and 'Old Yellow Dusty Miller', a heavily floured golden-yellow. Shade from midday sun. Well-drained, fertile soil.

The third group consists of the show auriculas. These are among the wonders of the plant world; the flowers are perfectly shaped, often of extraordinary colouring, and heavily coated in meal. They are grown in clay pots (long toms are the favoured type) in cold, well-ventilated greenhouses and must be shaded from strong sunshine. Among the most popular varieties are 'C.G. Haysom', a white-edged variety; 'Chloe', a green-edged variety; 'Chorister', a yellow self; 'Fanny Meerbeck', a crimson self; 'Lovebird', a grey-edged variety; 'Neat and Tidy', a deep red dark self; and 'Rajah', a bright scarlet fancy with a green edge. The scent from a collection

LEFT *Polygonatum hookeri* CENTRE *Primula auricula* 'Argus' RIGHT *Primula auricula* 'Mrs L. Hearn'

LEFT *Primula* x *pubescens* with smaller-flowered *P. marginata* RIGHT *Sedum populifolium*

under glass is intoxicating. Shade from midday sun.

***P. latifolia* (*P. viscosa*)** is a variable species with long, often rather sticky leaves. Its heads of flowers are borne on short stems in late spring. They are usually a shade of rosy-purple and sweetly scented, but there are good cream and crimson forms. Well-drained, humus-rich soil. 15cm/6in.

P. palinuri is a handsome plant for a sheltered spot in the rock garden or the alpine house. It has broad, serrated-edged, green leaves and powdery stems, topped in early spring with pure yellow, bell-shaped flowers which have a cowslip scent. Sun. Well-drained, fertile soil. 20cm/8in.

P.* x *pubescens is the name given to a range of hybrid primulas, many sweetly scented, for crevices in the rock garden. One of the earliest and easiest to grow is 'Mrs J. H. Wilson', which has lilac, white-centred flowerheads; 'Faldonside' is crimson; 'Freedom' is a rich purple; 'Rufus' is terracotta with a biscuit eye; and 'The General' is a velvet orange-red. Sun. 7.5–15cm/3–6in.

P. reidii* var. *williamsii is a beautiful Himalayan primula with green, toothed leaves and pendent, blue or white, bell-shaped flowers that are wonderfully fragrant. This form is more robust than the species itself: it succeeds in a shady trough or a pot in the alpine house. It is short-lived but comes readily from seed. Light shade. Moist soil. 15cm/6in.

RHODODENDRON
Ericaceae

Dwarf rhododendrons are not suitable for alkaline soils, but are among the finest early-flowering shrubs for rock gardens and raised beds. They will tolerate more sunshine than their larger relatives, but dislike hot, dry conditions. Scent usually comes from the foliage rather than the flowers. I continue to discover ever more aromatic varieties – *R. kongboense*, scented of balsam; *R. campylogynum* Myrtilloides Group, scented of coconut; pale pink *R. primuliflorum* 'Doker-La'; – so this list is provided only in order to whet the appetite.
Light shade. Well-drained, neutral or acid soil.

R. cephalanthum is a bushy, usually low-growing evergreen with aromatic glossy foliage. It is attractive in spring when it produces its heads of white or pink-flushed flowers. 30cm–1.2m/1–4ft. Z7

R. flavidum is a dwarf rhododendron with aromatic, evergreen leaves and clusters of primrose-yellow flowers in spring that forms an erect bushy shrub. 'Album' is a taller version with larger leaves and white flowers. 90cm/3ft. Z6

R. sargentianum has aromatic, evergreen leaves and clusters of pale yellow or cream flowers in spring. It

is an attractive, compact shrub but is often reluctant to bloom.
60cm/2ft. Z8

SEDUM
Crassulaceae
S. populifolium is an erect, woody *Sedum* with slightly fleshy leaves shaped like those of a poplar. It is an interesting plant, and its greenish-pink flowers, produced in late summer, have a scent reminiscent of hawthorn but without the fishy undertones.
Sun. Well-drained soil. 46cm/18in.

STACHYS
Lamiaceae
S. citrina is a diminutive relative of lamb's ears. Its felted grey-green leaves are fragrant of chocolate mints when rubbed. Pale yellow flowers are produced in early summer.
Sun. Well-drained soil. 15cm/6in.

THLASPI
Brassicaceae
T. cepaeifolium* subsp. *rotundifolium is a connoisseur's alpine that bears numerous heads of rosy-lilac, sometimes white, highly fragrant flowers in early summer. The stems spread underground from a fleshy rootstock and appear as rosettes of dark, round leaves. It is suitable for the alpine house or scree.
Sun. Gritty soil. 5–10cm/2–4in.

TRILLIUM
Melanthiaceae
T. luteum has lemon-yellow flowers which are pleasantly scented, unlike those of the common *T. erectum* which are rather fetid. They appear in spring, each standing upright above the characteristic three large leaves, that are attractively patterned in green and brown. It is easily grown and is an obvious candidate for a raised bed in shade.
Cool, humus-rich, retentive soil. Shade. 30cm/1ft.

Trillium luteum

RHODIOLA
Crassulaceae

***R. rosea* (*Sedum rosea*, *S. rhodiola*)** is a curious plant that always attracts attention. It forms a woody base which is studded in pink buds early in the year. These gradually expand into fleshy stems bearing glaucous blue leaves, and in early summer they are topped with yellow stars. Even curioser, the scent is in the roots, which, when broken, smell of roses. This is a lovely plant at the front of the border as well as in the rock garden.
Sun. Well-drained soil. 30cm/1ft.

Rhodiola rosea

POND & WATERSIDE PLANTS

ACORUS
Acoraceae
A. calamus, sweet flag, was used for strewing floors in the Middle Ages. The strap-like leaves are scented of cinnamon when bruised; the roots are even more fragrant. Cones of sober greenish-yellow flowers appear in summer. It is not especially ornamental, but its cream-striped version 'Argenteostriatus' is more so. Shallow water or damp ground. 90cm/3ft.

APONOGETON
Aponogetonaceae
A. distachyos, water hawthorn, is a shade-tolerant aquatic, whose tuberous roots grow in the mud while the leaves float on the surface of the water. From late spring, spikes of white flowers emerge, and in the evening they release a scent of vanilla. It is one of the stalwarts of the garden pond, though sometimes over-generous with its seedlings.

COTULA
Asteraceae
C. coronopifolia, brass buttons, is a short annual which self-sows freely at the pond edge and in shallow water. It is most often grown for its small, golden, button-like flowers, but its foliage releases an aromatic lemon fragrance when crushed. There is a cream-flowered version called 'Cream Buttons'. 15–30cm/6–12in.

CYPERUS
Cyperaceae
C. longus, galingale, is an attractive though invasive British native for the pond margin. It has shining green, grassy leaves and branching, chestnut-brown flowerheads in the summer. The stems release a sweet, mossy scent when broken; and the fragrance is also present in the roots. 60cm–1.2m/2–4ft.

FILIPENDULA
Rosaceae
F. ulmaria, meadowsweet. This familiar inhabitant of European river banks makes a splendid garden plant. It is most ornamental in its golden-leaved, and, to a lesser extent,

RIGHT *Aponogeton distachyos*
FAR RIGHT *Filipendula ulmaria*

FAR LEFT *Houttuynia cordata*
LEFT *Lysichiton camtschatcensis*
BELOW *Mentha aquatica*

golden-variegated, forms, 'Aurea' and 'Variegata'. Their plumes of creamy white flowers, borne in summer, have a heavy scent, reminiscent of hawthorn but without the fishy undertones.
Light shade. Moist soil. 60cm/2ft.

HOTTONIA
Primulaceae

H. palustris, water violet, is a European aquatic plant which bears whorls of scented lilac flowers, 23cm/9in above the water, in early summer. It grows underwater and is a good oxygenator.

HOUTTUYNIA
Saururaceae

H. cordata has become very popular in its variegated form 'Chameleon', whose heart-shaped leaves are streaked with green, yellow and red. The species itself has dark metallic green leaves, that colour well in the autumn. The foliage of both is sharply scented when bruised; British gardeners tend to think it smells of orange peel, American gardeners of rotten fish! Spikes of white flowers are produced in summer, and they are particularly ornamental in the double-flowered, green-leaved 'Flore Pleno'. It can become invasive and is easier to control when grown in a tub in very shallow water.
Sun or shade. Damp soil or shallow water. 15–46cm/6–18in.

LYSICHITON
Araceae

L. camtschatcensis is the white counterpart to the familiar and evil-smelling yellow bog arum, *L. americanus*. It is slightly smaller in all its parts, but is still a large, architectural plant. The pure white spathes appear in early spring and have none of the fetid undertones of the yellow bog arum; the scent is clean and sweet. The huge, banana-like leaves soon follow.
Sun or light shade. Damp soil or ditches. 90cm/3ft.

MENTHA
Lamiaceae

Mints are often invasive and must be treated cautiously. They will attempt to weaken your resolve with their refreshing scents, but containers and secure beds are their proper homes. Many gardeners plant them in buckets that are then inserted into the border; drainage holes have to be pierced through the bottom.
M. aquatica, water mint, is a British native and has whorls of mauve flowers and serrated, oval leaves. It is extremely vigorous in wet ground.
Up to 1.2m/4ft.
M. longifolia, horse mint, has woolly grey leaves and heads of lavender-blue flowers and excels in the bog garden.
Up to 1.2m/4ft.

LEFT *Mentha pulegium* CENTRE *Nymphaea odorata* var. *minor* RIGHT *Nymphaea* 'Laydekeri Lilacea'

M. pulegium, pennyroyal, makes attractive prostrate mats of small, shining green leaves, and is very much at home in damp soil. It is a haze of mauve when in flower in late summer and has a pungent mint scent.
15cm/6in.

NYMPHAEA
Nyphaeaceae
Waterlilies give us attractive rafts of round leaves on the water's surface, and the flower buds, which appear all summer, are fascinating to watch as they rise to the surface and unfurl their pointed petals. Many, such as white *N. odorata* and its variety *minor* have an exotic, sweet scent. They are planted in spring either directly into the soil bottom of the pond, or in baskets of soil enriched with well-rotted manure. When grown in baskets, they may need to be lifted, divided and re-planted every few years. They like still water and although they will thrive at shallower and deeper depths, most enjoy being 30–46cm/12–18in below the surface.
Among the best scented hybrids are: 'Fire Crest', a deep pink; 'Laydekeri Lilacea', a soft lilac-rose; 'Marliacea Albida', a superb white, suitable for larger ponds; 'Masaniello', a deep rose colour with a good, sweet scent; 'Odorata Sulphurea Grandiflora', a large sulphur yellow; 'W.B. Shaw', a pale pink; and 'Rose Arey', a bright rose pink.

PRIMULA
Primulaceae
P. alpicola produces white, yellow, violet and purple flowers with the scent of cowslips, particularly evident in the evening. The colour forms are fairly stable and you can produce monocolour groups from selected seed. It flowers in spring and early summer, and plants usually produce just one umbel of flowers on each stem. Light shade. Moist soil. 46cm/18in.
P. chionantha. This lovely, easily grown primula carries whorls of sweetly scented white, yellow-eyed flowers in late spring. Sun or shade. Moist soil. 60cm/2ft or more.
P. florindae, giant Himalayan cowslip, is a magnificent and robust primula which is ideal for damp borders and the pond edge. It blooms late, towards high summer, and produces large powdery heads of sulphur-yellow flowers which are powerfully lemon-scented; the fragrance of a generous group will fill the evening air. Orange and red forms are available but in my view the yellow stands supreme. The foliage is rounded and a shining green. It is very happy on lime.
Sun or light shade. 90cm/3ft.
P. ioessa produces stems topped with comparatively few flowers, but they are a good size and very fragrant. It varies in colour from

FAR LEFT *Primula alpicola* var. *violacea*
LEFT *Primula florindae*

mauve-pink to deep violet.
Light shade. Damp soil. 10–30cm/4–12in.

P. munroi produces scented flowers in white, lavender and other colours in early summer.
Sun. Moist soil. 30cm/1ft.

***P. prolifera* (*P. helodoxa*)** is a lovely candelabra primula that produces whorls of large bright yellow, lemon-scented flowers in early summer. It is easily grown but often short-lived. It thrives on lime.
Light shade. 90cm/3ft.

P. sikkimensis comes in various shades of yellow and has a fine lemon scent. The flowers appear in early summer, in one or two superimposed umbels at the end of the stems. Attractive but perhaps not in the first flight of primulas.
Light shade. Moist soil. 46cm/18in.

***P. wilsonii* var. *anisodora* (*P. anisodora*)**, a perennial, has leaves and roots that are strongly scented of aniseed. It is one of the candelabra primulas, producing tall, slender stems hung with umbels of very dark crimson, green-eyed funnels in early summer.
Light shade. Moist soil. 46cm/18in.

SAURURUS
Saururaceae

S. cernuus, American swamp lily or lizard's tail, is an aquatic plant that has lush green, heart-shaped leaves and in summer produces dense, nodding spikes of scented white flowers.
Shallow water or pond edge. 60cm/2ft.

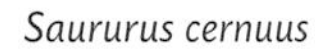

Saururus cernuus

ROSE GARDENS

Roses are the undisputed sovereigns of the scented garden. Their fragrances are sophisticated and diverse, sometimes delicate, sometimes heady. They bloom profusely, contribute exuberant splashes of colour, and often keep flowering for weeks on end. There is a wealth of varieties of different character, size and habit of growth and they tolerate a range of soils and climates. Indeed, they present the gardener with so rich a choice that it is often difficult to know how to exercise restraint and set about making a selection.

I think the best starting point is to consider the setting into which they will be put and the effect you wish to create. Different categories of rose require different treatments and evoke different moods. They are all, however, sun-lovers, and this should be borne in mind at the outset. Some roses, it is true, will accept a degree of shade – such as the Albas and climbers like 'Madame Alfred Carrière', 'Zéphirine Drouhin' and 'Albéric Barbier' – but most need several hours, at least, of full sunlight each day in order to perform well. Furthermore, they dislike cold winds and very exposed and draughty spots. Hedged and walled enclosures are ideal, and here their fragrances will be held captive.

Where the setting is very formal, Hybrid Teas, with their uniformity of growth and perfection of flower shape, may be the ideal candidates. I prefer to see them in mono-colour groups – guardsman's scarlet against emerald grass, cream against warm orange brick – but a mixture of varieties does bring life to a small front garden or a drab city street. Some Hybrid Teas are scentless or give only a faint whiff of tea. But when a rich 'rose' fragrance overlays the tea scent, some truly sumptuous concoctions result, as in 'Alec's Red', 'Fragrant Cloud', 'Prima Ballerina', 'Whisky Mac' and the old Hybrid Teas, 'Ophelia', 'Lady Sylvia' and 'Madame Butterfly'.

The Floribundas are even better bedding roses. They have never been famed for their scent and they are still likely to disappoint. I took a stroll along the rows in a nursery

Striped Rosa mundi (*Rosa gallica* 'Versicolor') blooms with *R.* 'Charles de Mills': a fleeting but beautiful vignette.

The Hybrid Musk rose 'Felicia' is combined in this raised bed with the Rugosa roses 'Roseraie de l'Hay' and 'Blanche Double de Coubert'. All three roses are repeat-flowering, and inject their scent into the air – 'Felicia' with a fruitier flavour than the sumptuously perfumed rugosas. Valerian and geranium are among the accompaniment.

field once and more than half the roses I smelled were either without scent or, even worse, downright nasty; yellow roses are most likely to offend. But rich scent is present in a number of varieties and rose breeders are pursuing it further. 'Arthur Bell', 'Chinatown' and 'Margaret Merril' (one of the best scented white bedding roses) are outstanding. Their lavish display is particularly welcome in paved gardens, where they can be combined with small-flowered Polyanthas, Miniature and Patio roses and pompon-flowered Shrub roses like 'Cécile Brünner' and myrrh-scented 'Little White Pet' (excellent as a standard). Like Hybrid Teas, they bloom all summer and autumn, entering the stage when the surge of early-flowering roses is dying away.

The idea of having bedding roses in isolation on bare soil mounded up like a grave is now luckily on the wane. Apart from looking ugly, this is a great waste of good earth. For spring, you could underplant with hyacinths, honey-scented muscari and, if you can turn a blind eye to their dying foliage later, sweet-scented daffodils. For summer, you could have snapdragons or, even better, nostalgically perfumed heliotropes. Or make a permanent edging of camomile, catmint, thymes, cottage pinks or *Geranium macrorrhizum*.

In the more relaxed setting of a country or cottage garden, or an informal suburban garden, which many of us possess in some form or other, stiff formal roses can easily look out of place. Here roses have to participate in the rough-and-tumble of the border and share ground with other shrubs and wispy perennials; they may be lapped by rough grass or a stream; and they may have a backdrop of fields and trees. Groups of Floribundas and Polyanthas often fit comfortably into such surroundings but it is the shrub roses that are most at home.

Shrub roses are simply flowering shrubs; they are not pruned to stumps each year, but instead are encouraged wherever possible to form a natural structure that, depending on variety, can be anything from 1–3m/3–10ft in height and spread. The earliest shrub roses, which start to open in spring, include many species and hybrids with single flowers and small leaves, and these are especially suited to wilder garden areas, woodland clearings, and more naturalistic plantings in border and meadow: 'Cerise Bouquet' is electrifying

among cow parsley. Most only bloom once – the little gem 'Stanwell Perpetual', with double pink flowers, is an exception – but afterwards they do not necessarily cease to contribute. Some, such as *R. rubiginosa* (*R. eglanteria*) and *R. primula,* waft scent from their leaves, while others produce a bountiful display of hips. The more striking single-flowered varieties and the early doubles (mainly forms or descendants of *R. rugosa*, *R. spinosissima* (*R. pimpinellifolia*), *R. foetida* and *R. rubiginosa*) will hold their own against the most flamboyant of companions in the summer border. The great spicy-scented saucers of 'Frühlingsgold' and 'Nevada' are, for example, stunning with fiery oriental poppies.

RUGOSA ROSES

A scented garden should not be without one of the Rugosas. Their powerful scents, well-flavoured with clove, infuse the air around them; the single white *R. rugosa* 'Alba' and the double white 'Blanche Double de Coubert' are arguably the most scented of all roses, and the sulphur yellow 'Agnes' has a lemon fragrance all of its own: so potent that when once I wore it as a buttonhole at a wedding, heads turned two pews in front of me trying to detect the perfume. There are no other roses that give a longer display of flowers than the double Rugosas, and few roses give as impressive a crop of hips. On top of all this, they are luxuriant in foliage, pest and disease free, and depart in the autumn in a burst of golden yellow.

Rosa rugosa 'Alba'

The arrival, at midsummer, of the old shrub roses, the old-fashioned, blowsy beauties that have come to us largely from the nurseries of nineteenth-century France, marks the high point of the scent-gardener's year (at least for me). Their petal-packed flowers, which come in every conceivable shade and combination of white, pink, magenta and crimson, deliver an intoxicating sweetness wafting across the garden for almost a month. Old rose perfume, rich, complex and intense, is the norm among these roses, though it varies greatly in composition and flavour. Old shrub roses fall into several classes. The Gallicas are short and bushy with a refined, full scent, strongly coloured flowers, dark leaves and a moderate amount of thorns. Because of their suckering habit they make very good low hedges, but they are easily accommodated near the front of any sunny bed. They are very happy in the drier conditions of the gravel garden or 'Mediterranean' border where the perfume will blend with the gummy aromas of *Cistus* and the scents of lavender and

Philadelphus such as 'Belle Etoile' have a strong airborne fragrance that enriches the background scent of a rose garden.

rosemary. 'Charles de Mills', 'Président de Sèze' and Rosa mundi (*R. gallica* 'Versicolor') are superb varieties that float their perfume on the air.

The Damasks and Albas, with softer-coloured flowers and grey-green leaves, are taller, as are the rather coarser Provence/Centifolia and Moss roses. Some of them, especially the Albas, will make attractive free-standing shrubs but most benefit from having their long growths wrapped around a framework of metal or wooden posts.

The Damasks are spicily scented and include one variety in their ranks, 'Ispahan', which blooms for longer than any other old shrub rose. 'Celsiana', 'La Ville de Bruxelles' and the incomparable 'Madame Hardy' are also in the first flight. Among the delicately perfumed Albas, I would single out the White Rose of York, *R.* x *alba* 'Alba Semiplena', which follows up its show of gloriously scented white flowers with a display of orange hips; 'Madame Legras de Saint Germain', 'Céleste' and 'Great Maiden's Blush' are also irresistible.

The scent of the Provence/Centifolia roses and the moss roses is usually strong and heady and carries well. Among the former I rate 'Fantin-Latour' and 'Petite de Hollande' (a short rose for the front of the border) very highly; and among the latter, 'William Lobb' and 'Nuits de Young'.

These tall roses have only one drawback. After their sumptuous midsummer display of flowers, they slip into an uneventful retirement. You can turn a blind eye if you are only growing a few but a collection of them can present a problem. For the devotees, there are really two solutions. The first is to grow them in their own enclosure where they cannot become an eyesore later. The second is to interplant with late-flowering perennials, shrubs like *Buddleja* and *Hebe*, and weave *Clematis* into them.

You can also favour repeat-flowering roses. In this category come the Hybrid Perpetuals and fabulously scented Bourbons, roses with old-fashioned flowers but which do continue to bloom intermittently after midsummer (though they do usually have some of the stiffer habit and coarser, large-leaved growth of the modern bush rose). Many have strong fruity scents, raspberry often being the dominant flavour; the Bourbons 'Honorine de Brabant' and 'Adam Messerich' possess it, as does the Hybrid Perpetual 'Ferdinand Pichard'. Few roses can rival the Bourbon 'Madame Isaac Pereire' for strength of fragrance.

But even these roses are rarely as reliable and showy in their later crops as China roses, which sit well at the front of the border and are also successful in tubs – *R.* x *odorata* 'Pallida' has such a long season that it is called the monthly rose. Also good are the Portland and Damask Perpetual roses, which are like small Damasks but with richer colouring; 'Madame Knorr' and 'Marchesa Boccella' are excellent varieties. Crimson 'De Resht' is one of my favourite of all roses. We can also look to the Hybrid Musks to prolong the season. Like the Rugosas, these roses have an intense and far-reaching perfume, but with distinctive fruity and spicy flavours of their own. They are also distinctive in appearance and carry Floribunda-like trusses of flowers in a range of creamy, yellowy and salmony shades, colours that are absent from all the classes of old shrub roses. They are also among my favourite roses and can be used as free-standing shrubs, as climbers or as hedges.

Another breed of repeat-flowering shrub rose has emerged in recent decades. From David Austin Roses of Albrighton, Wolverhampton, in England, come the 'English Roses' that combine the colours, shapes and scents of the old shrub rose with an ability to bloom intermittently all summer. Like the Bourbons and Hybrid Perpetuals, English roses sometimes inherit the stiffer habit and coarser, large-leaved growth of the China roses but they are first-rate, usually fabulously fragrant plants that have become extremely popular worldwide, replacing the older shrub roses in many people's gardens; they do very well in hot climates, too. Other modern shrub roses that repeat include 'Golden Wings', 'Nymphenburg' and 'Cerise Bouquet'; these do not have old rose flowers.

I have mentioned rose hedges several times. Informal flowering hedges can be a wonderful feature in the garden, especially where the setting is predominantly green. Rugosas are commonly used, being vigorous, bushy, floriferous and disease free; 'Scabrosa', 'Sarah van Fleet' and 'Fru Dagmar Hastrup' are particularly good choices. Hybrid Musks, especially silver-pink 'Felicia', are also well suited for hedging. For a low

Rosa 'Königin von Dänemark' hangs its highly perfumed flowers close to a gravel path, its gawky base concealed by a box hedge.

hedge, upright Floribundas like 'Chinatown', Portlands like 'De Resht', Dwarf Polyanthas and *R.* x *odorata* 'Pallida' are suitable, as well as the suckering Gallicas (there is a superb double hedge of striped Rosa mundi (*R. gallica* 'Versicolor') at Kiftsgate Court in Gloucestershire, England). In more natural settings, use *R. rubiginosa* and its Penzance hybrids, with their apple-scented leaves, and *R. canina*, and interplant with honeysuckles.

Shrub roses are so generous and varied in their production of scent that you may feel they do not need fragrant companions to enhance their flavours. But I can never resist introducing fruity *Philadelphus*, peonies, irises, *Dictamnus*, *Lilium regale* and spicy cottage pinks to supplement the scents of the midsummer roses; and *Buddleja*, *Escallonia*, hybrid lilies, *Salvia*, herbaceous *Clematis*, lavenders and bergamot to complement the late performers.

Old-fashioned roses are interplanted with perennials and more modern, repeat-flowering roses to extend the season in this handsome rose garden.

There is never enough ground space for all the roses you want to grow and it is fortunate that the family can also be grown vertically. Scented climbing roses can be trained against any sunny wall, along pergolas and fences, or up wooden tripods erected at the back of borders. On walls they can join company with wisteria and ceanothus, myrtles, passionflower, *Buddleja crispa* and *Carpenteria*; on pergolas with *Akebia*, jasmines and honeysuckles. Many richly scented varieties of bush and shrub rose have climbing counterparts ('Ena Harkness', 'Etoile de Hollande', 'Souvenir de la Malmaison', for example) and many can be turned into climbers simply by training them upwards ('Aloha', 'Madame Isaac Pereire', 'Madame Plantier'). But climbing roses vary greatly in character. Some, such as 'Aimée Vibert' and 'Noisette Carnée', have clusters of tiny, double or semi-double, button flowers; some, such as 'Guinée' and 'Paul's Lemon Pillar', have fine tea-rose flowers; others, such as 'Lawrence Johnston' and 'Cupid', have large, open, single or semi-double flowers; and some, such as 'Gloire de Dijon' and 'Madame Alfred Carrière', have large flowers congested with petals. Some bloom continuously all summer and some give one show, with perhaps a short encore in the autumn.

The range of scents is also great. The Noisette climbers, with their clusters of small flowers, have a pervasive fragrance well-flavoured with fruit and spice. 'Lady Hillingdon' is tea-scented, as is 'Gloire de Dijon', though the tea is blended with sweeter flavours. 'Constance Spry' has a scent of cold cream or calamine lotion, said to resemble myrrh; the scent of the rambler 'Félicité Perpétue' is similar. There are many others with an exceedingly rich fragrance, among them 'Madame Abel Chatenay', 'Etoile de Hollande', 'Crimson Glory', 'Madame Butterfly' and 'Madame Grégoire Staechelin'.

The once-flowering Rambler roses can be used in the same way but usually dislike being lashed back to a wall. The smaller varieties, like apple-scented *R. wichurana* and its hybrids, are at home on pergolas, ropes and wire mesh fences or wandering through fruit trees; 'Rambling Rector' is outstanding in this role. But the big ramblers like 'Bobbie James', 'Seagull' and the monstrous 'Kiftsgate', with their pervasive fruity scent flavoured with incense, need very large trees or a large expanse of shed roof, very solidly supported. A friend of mine once saw a small summerhouse with a 'Kiftsgate' rose planted on each corner and was wondering how long it would be before the structure collapsed; the original 'Kiftsgate' rose is over 15m/50ft high and 24m/80ft across.

ROSES

GALLICA ROSES

The Gallicas are the oldest garden roses. They bloom only once, at midsummer, but give a sumptuous display of crimsons, magentas and bright pinks; the fragrance is invariably the rich, true old rose perfume. They make short, compact, bushy shrubs that are prone to suckering and are useful as low hedges. Being tolerant of poorer and drier soils than other roses, they are excellent in the borders of grey-leaved shrubs and perennials. They need little pruning but respond to some thinning of shoots and the removal of weak wood, which may be carried out after flowering.
Z6

'Assemblage des Beautés' has shocking magenta-crimson, fully double flowers that age to purple.
1.2m/4ft.

'Belle de Crécy' has richly scented double flowers that begin cerise but soon assume grey and mauve tints. It forms an arching shrub and has grey-green foliage.
1.2m/4ft.

'Belle Isis' is a parent of 'Constance Spry' and has the same myrrh/calamine lotion scent. The double flowers are flesh-pink and are set off well by the grey-green leaves.
1.2m/4ft.

'Camayeux' is one of the curious striped roses, its double white flowers being splashed first with crimson-pink and then, as they age, with purple and grey.
1.2m/4ft.

'Cardinal de Richelieu' bears perfect, almost ball-shaped, double flowers of rich crimson-purple and has a delicious scent. The foliage is dark green.
1.2m/4ft.

'Charles de Mills' is one of the best Gallicas. The bright crimson-pink flowers are extremely flat when half open but expand to reveal beautifully quartered, double blooms that turn to violet and purple. The scent is powerful. It is a vigorous and generous rose.
1.5m/5ft.

'Duc de Guiche' is similar to 'Assemblage des Beautés', with perfect, cup-shaped flowers in bright magenta-crimson; they have a green eye and reflex almost into a ball-shape as they age. It is less compact in growth than other Gallicas. The scent is magnificent.
1.2m/4ft.

'Duchesse de Montebello' is a splendid Gallica with blush-pink double flowers that make an arching shrub clad in light green foliage.
1.2m/4ft.

RIGHT 'Charles de Mills'
FAR RIGHT 'Cardinal de Richelieu'

LEFT *Rosa gallica* 'Versicolor' CENTRE 'Tuscany Superb' RIGHT 'Céleste'

R. gallica var. officinalis, the apothecary's rose, is a fine bushy rose with highly scented, semi-double, light crimson flowers illuminated by bright yellow stamens. It is an ancient rose and still one of the best.
1.2m/4ft.

R. gallica 'Versicolor' (Rosa mundi) is the most popular of the striped roses. It resembles the apothecary's rose, of which it is a sport, except that the flowers are heavily streaked with white. Like its parent, it is an outstanding Gallica.
1.2m/4ft.

'Président de Sèze' is another outstanding Gallica with beautifully shaped double flowers in a blend of crimson, magenta and lilac. The scent is powerful and delicious. It makes a neat shrub and has grey-green leaves.
1.2m/4ft.

'Tricolore de Flandre' has well-scented, semi-double blush-white flowers heavily striped in magenta-purple. It is untypical of Gallicas in its profusion of thorns.
90cm/3ft.

'Tuscany Superb' is one of my favourite Gallicas, with sumptuous deep maroon-crimson flowers that are tightly bunched around golden-yellow stamens. The perfume is not as rich or strong as in some other roses.
1.2m/4ft.

ALBA ROSES

The Albas are romantic shrub roses with grey-green leaves and an abundance of pink or white flowers at midsummer. Their perfume is light and sophisticated. They make fairly large upright plants that take their place well at the back of the border. They are also useful in shadier spots where other roses would not be expected to thrive. They need only periodic thinning after flowering, though they respond well to a more severe winter pruning when their long growths may be shortened by about 90cm/3ft.

'Alba Maxima' (Great Double White, Jacobite Rose) is a tough old rose, not as elegant as some but possessing a very rich scent. The untidy double flowers are creamy white.
2m/6ft.

'Alba Semiplena' (White Rose of York) is one of the roses grown for the distillation of attar of roses. Its semi-double pure white flowers, lit by golden stamens, have a powerful scent and are followed in the autumn by striking clusters of red hips.
2m/6ft.

'Céleste' is a beautiful Alba with semi-double shell-pink flowers set against especially good grey foliage. The scent is rich and sweet and it has a sturdy upright habit.
2m/6ft.

'Félicité Parmentier' is a short Alba with flat, petal-packed flowers of flesh-pink that reflex almost into a ball shape. 1.2m/4ft.

'Madame Hardy'

'Great Maiden's Blush' (**'Cuisse de Nymphe'**) is my favourite Alba and one of the loveliest old shrub roses. It makes a fine branching shrub and the blush-pink double flowers have a delicious fragrance.
1.5m/5ft.

'Königin von Dänemark' (**'Queen of Denmark'**) is a beautiful rose with rich pink, double, highly scented flowers. It is excellent when trained to grow up posts or into an apple tree.
2m/6ft.

'Madame Legras de Saint Germain' has unusual yellow-flushed double white flowers and splendid grey foliage. It is one of the best in this group and has the added advantage of possessing very few thorns.
2m/6ft.

'Madame Plantier' bears large clusters of creamy petal-packed flowers and is a very good tall rose for training up posts and apple trees.
3.5m/12ft.

DAMASK ROSES

The Damasks are midsummer roses with greyish foliage and fine scents. The flowers are carried in generous bunches. They require only a light thinning of weak and overcrowded shoots after flowering.
Z5

'Celsiana' makes a very pleasant grey-green shrub and its semi-double, clear pink petals are folded around prominent golden anthers. The scent is rich and strong.
1.5m/5ft.

'Ispahan' has a long flowering season and lives up to its evocative name. The scent is sumptuous and the double flowers are a romantic pink.
1.5m/5ft.

'La Ville de Bruxelles' is a splendid and vigorous Damask, luxuriant in foliage and bearing clusters of very large flowers. These are pure pink and the petals are packed around a button eye. The scent is excellent.
1.5m/5ft.

'Madame Hardy' is the first shrub rose I ever grew and remains a firm favourite. The flat, double, pure white petals incurve around a green eye and are set off perfectly by fresh green foliage. The scent is deliciously fruity.
1.5m/5ft.

PORTLAND AND DAMASK PERPETUAL ROSES

These roses are closely related to the Damasks but are a little smaller and bloom throughout the summer and autumn. These are the roses for the front of the border and for small gardens. Unfortunately, there are few varieties available; the following are particularly outstanding:

'De Resht' has small magenta-pink flowers that are extremely fragrant and carried over a long period. It makes a small, compact shrub, well clad in green leaves. I think it one of the best shrub roses; it also makes a good hedge.
90cm/3ft.

'Madame Knorr' (**'Comte de Chambord'**) is one of the best shrub roses. Its large flowers are bright pink and intensely fragrant and are borne on and off for many months. It makes a bushy, erect shrub.
1.2m/4ft.

'Marchesa Boccella' (**'Jacques Cartier'**) is similar to 'Madame Knorr' but the pink flowers are less cupped. It also flowers repeatedly.
1.2m/4ft.

PROVENCE ROSES

The Provence or Centifolia roses are rather thorny, coarse in leaf and lax in habit but their flowers are large and the profusion of nodding heads at midsummer is a lovely sight. The fragrance is also intense and far-reaching. They should be pruned in the same way as Alba roses and benefit from a reduction of their long stems in winter.
Z6

R.* x *centifolia is the cabbage rose featured in Dutch paintings. The double, pink flowers are powerfully scented and nod in clusters against the grey-green leaves. It is a shrub of lax habit but a charmer.
1.5m/5ft.

***R.* x *centifolia* 'De Meaux'** is a miniature Centifolia bearing a profusion of pink flowers that are fully double.
60cm/2ft.

'Fantin-Latour' is one of the loveliest of all the pink shrub roses. The cupped, petal-packed flowers are softly coloured and clear, and the fragrance is exquisite. The foliage is dark green and smooth.
1.5m/5ft.

'Petite de Hollande' is a splendid and compact small Centifolia for the front of the border. The small double flowers are bright pink and the scent is superb.
1.2m/4ft.

'Robert le Diable' has flowers coloured with an extraordinary suffusion of greys and purples splashed with pink and red. It is a small bushy shrub that is very lax in habit and succeeds well when spilling down a sunny retaining wall.
90cm/3ft.

'Tour de Malakoff' is a large lanky plant best lashed around wooden posts or trained against a wall. But it is a show-stopper in bloom for the flowers are big and blowsy, coloured a dazzling magenta at first but later taking on violet and grey tints. The fragrance does not disappoint.
2.3m/7ft.

MOSS ROSES

The Moss roses are either direct mutations or have been developed from mutations of the Centifolias or the Damasks. They are characterized by the presence of bristles or soft mossy growth around their flower stalks and buds. With some notable exceptions, such as 'William Lobb', they are not outstanding roses and their value is principally as curiosities. They are usually coarse in growth and many are prone to mildew. Their flower scent, however, has the same sophisticated and refreshing quality as the Centifolias; the mossy covering also has its own fragrance that is often powerfully balsamic. They should be pruned in the same way as Centifolias.

'Capitaine John Ingram' is a dark crimson-velvet rose, fully double and with an especially strong scent. The

LEFT *Rosa* x *centifolia* 'Cristata' CENTRE 'Fantin-Latour' RIGHT 'William Lobb'

LEFT *Rosa* x *centifolia* 'Muscosa' CENTRE 'Boule de Neige' RIGHT 'Madame Isaac Pereire'

colouring varies according to the weather and age of the flower and the blooms take on attractive purple tints. The buds have a light covering of reddish moss. It makes a dense shrub.
1.5m/5ft.

R. x *centifolia* 'Muscosa' (Old Pink Moss, Common Moss) is the original Moss rose. It has extremely fragrant double flowers in clear pink and plenty of green moss.
1.2m/4ft.

R. x *centifolia* 'Shailer's White Moss' ('White Bath') releases a very rich scent from its double white flowers and has good dark foliage and plenty of moss.
1.2m/4ft.

'Comtesse de Murinais' has superb blush-white double flowers and the fragrance from the bright green moss is remarkable. A tall, vigorous rose, it needs some support.
2m/6ft.

'Général Kléber' has bright satin-pink flowers that open double and flat. It makes a bushy plant and has good lush foliage and green moss.
1.2m/4ft.

'Gloire des Mousseuses' has exceptionally large double blooms of clear pink with a fine scent. It has plenty of green moss.
1.2m/4ft.

'Maréchal Davoust' has double flowers in a blend of carmine and purple colours. It makes a neat shrub with grey-green leaves and dark moss.
1.2m/4ft.

'Mousseline' is an excellent compact and healthy shrub rose that blooms continuously through summer and autumn. The flowers are semi-double and blush-pink with a good scent.
1.2m/4ft.

'Nuits de Young' is an especially dark rose with double, maroon-purple flowers illuminated by golden stamens. It makes a compact but scantily clad shrub and has little moss. It is a sensation at its best.
1.2m/4ft.

'William Lobb' (Old Velvet Moss) has large, sumptuous semi-double flowers that fade from dark crimson to magenta, violet and grey. The scent is superb. It is a tall, vigorous, well-mossed rose that needs support, but is one of my favourite of all shrub roses.
2.5m/8ft.

BOURBON ROSES

The Bourbons straddle the boundary line between the old and new roses. They combine petal-packed, old-fashioned flowers with the ability to produce further flushes of blooms after midsummer. Their perfume is often very strong and fruity. They are vigorous roses, sometimes with lush and dark 'modern' foliage, and require regular pruning: a light pruning of flowered shoots after the first midsummer flush and a reduction of the long stems by a third or more in late winter.
Z6–8

LEFT 'Souvenir de la Malmaison' RIGHT 'Variegata di Bologna'

'Adam Messerich' has semi-double, rich pink flowers that possess a powerful raspberry fragrance. It makes a bushy, upright shrub and blooms throughout the season.
1.5m/5ft.

'Boule de Neige' bears small clusters of pure white globular flowers throughout the summer and autumn. They have a rich scent and show up well against the dark foliage. It makes a slender, erect shrub.
1.2m/4ft.

'Commandant Beaurepaire' blooms only at midsummer but makes a sumptuous show of large, double, pink flowers that are striped and flecked with carmine, purple and scarlet, and have a good scent. It makes a dense shrub clad in rather pale, pointed leaves.
1.5m/5ft.

'Louise Odier' is one of the best Bourbons. The bright lilac-pink flowers resemble camellias in their rounded shape and the perfume is very strong. It blooms throughout the season and makes an attractive shrub, well clad in fresh green leaves.
1.5m/5ft.

'Madame Isaac Pereire' is described by Graham Stuart Thomas, the great rosarian, as 'possibly the most powerfully fragrant of all roses'. The magenta-pink flowers are huge, rather untidy and even a little vulgar, but its perfume more than compensates for any faults. It makes a vigorous, leafy bush and blooms in bursts through the season.
2.3m/7ft.

'Madame Lauriol de Barny' breathes an exceptionally good fruity scent. It produces its large, double, silvery-pink flowers on and off through the season but its main burst is at midsummer. It is attractive when trained against a pillar.
2m/6ft.

'Madame Pierre Oger' has globular flowers in translucent creamy-pink touched with rose and a strong sweet scent. It blooms throughout the season.
1.5m/5ft.

'Reine Victoria' bears lilac-pink, silky flowers that are beautifully cupped and have an especially rich scent. It blooms throughout the season.
2m/6ft.

'Souvenir de la Malmaison' is invariably the most bewitching rose on the stands at the Chelsea Flower Show in London, with its beautifully quartered, pale pink flowers, well endowed with perfume. It blooms continuously and gives an especially fine autumn display.
60cm–2m/2–6ft.

'Variegata di Bologna' has blush-white flowers striped with crimson and is the most effective of the paler striped roses. The blooms are beautifully cupped and fully double. Its midsummer performance is followed by sporadic flushes later in the season.
1.5m/5ft.

LEFT 'Mrs John Laing' CENTRE 'Buff Beauty' RIGHT 'Cornelia'

HYBRID PERPETUAL ROSES

The Hybrid Perpetuals are very similar to the Bourbons and are often grouped together. They have old-fashioned flowers that are produced at midsummer and then usually in bursts thereafter. Pruning is as for Bourbons.

Z6–8

'Baron Girod de l'Ain' has bright crimson double flowers, pencilled at the edges with white. It has a superb scent and blooms throughout the summer.

1.5m/5ft.

'Empereur du Maroc' is a deep maroon-crimson and very richly scented. It is rather a weak grower and prone to disease but at its best is magnificent.

1.2m/4ft.

'Ferdinand Pichard' is my favourite striped rose. It has a strong scent of raspberry and the double pink flowers are heavily streaked in crimson and purple. It makes an attractive bushy plant and flowers repeatedly.

1.5m/5ft.

'Gloire de Ducher' bears huge reddish-purple flowers and is particularly notable for its extravagant autumn display. It is very fragrant. It produces tall arching branches and needs support.

2.3m/7ft.

'Mrs John Laing' is one of the best Hybrid Perpetuals, flowering repeatedly and possessing an excellent scent. The cupped lilac-pink flowers are shown off well against the grey-green foliage.

1.2m/4ft.

'Reine des Violettes' is also in the first flight of Hybrid Perpetuals. The flowers open purple and fade to soft violet and are beautifully quartered and well scented. It makes a most attractive shrub with greyish leaves and almost thornless stems.

2m/6ft.

'Souvenir d'Alphonse Lavallée' is not commonly offered but is a rose to hunt for. The double flowers are a sumptuous dark maroon-crimson and captivate all who see them. The scent is appropriately rich. It makes a tall, open shrub and is best pegged down or trained on to a support.

2.3m/7ft.

'Souvenir du Docteur Jamain' is my favourite dark rose. The flowers are an intense damson-purple and deliciously scented. Its main season is at midsummer but it produces a second flush in the autumn. It should be planted out of strong midday sun.

2m/6ft.

HYBRID MUSKS

These roses, most of which were bred by the Revd Joseph Pemberton in Essex, England, in the early part of this century, are powerfully fragrant, free-blooming and vigorous shrubs that deserve to be in every scented garden. The scent is more fruity than musky. Their main display is at midsummer, just as the old shrub roses are tiring, and they continue intermittently through the summer, with a triumphant final flush in the autumn. They carry their blooms in trusses, in the manner of a Floribunda, and the scent is usually rich and pervasive. They may be pruned back by a third or more in early spring.

'Buff Beauty' is one of the loveliest Hybrid Musks. It bears fully double flowers in apricot-yellow that have a rich tea-rose scent. The foliage is excellent, beginning bronze and maturing to dark green.
1.5m/5ft.

'Cornelia' carries large clusters of small, rosette-shaped flowers that are a blend of apricot, cream and pink. Its autumn display is especially notable. It has a powerful fragrance.
1.5m/5ft.

'Felicia' makes a fine bushy shrub, smothered in double, silvery-pink flowers at midsummer and maintaining a good display through the summer and autumn. It has a rich fragrance.
1.5m/5ft.

'Francesca' has semi-double flowers that begin apricot and fade to a warm yellow. The scent is strong, with a tea-rose flavour. It is a graceful shrub with good glossy foliage.
2m/6ft.

'Moonlight' bears trusses of almost single, creamy-white flowers that are superb against the dark leaves and reddish-brown stems. It has a strong fragrance.
2m/6ft.

'Penelope' is a popular Hybrid Musk with salmon-pink buds opening to

CHINA ROSES

These are small, dainty roses that flower repeatedly and are ideal for the front of the border. They are a little tender and perform best in warm, sheltered sites and against walls. Regular pruning is unnecessary, except for the removal of dead and weak wood.
Sun. Z7–8

'Comtesse du Cayla' has almost single flowers in bright colours – a blend of salmon, orange and pink – and possesses an exceptionally rich tea-rose scent.
90cm/3ft.

***R.* x *odorata* 'Pallida' (Old Blush China)**, the monthly rose, is valued for its continuity of flowering. Its silvery-pink flowers have an excellent sweet scent and it makes an upright, almost thornless, twiggy bush.
1–2m/3–6ft.

Rosa x *odorata* 'Pallida'

semi-double, creamy-pink flowers that have a strong scent. It gives a fine autumn display and concludes the year with coral-pink hips. 2m/6ft.

'Vanity' carries large, almost single flowers in deep pink continually through the summer and autumn. The scent is strong and sweet. 2m/6ft.

RUGOSA ROSES

Rugosa or Japanese roses and their hybrids are among the most potently scented of all garden shrubs, their spicy sweet perfume infusing the air on still, damp days. The double-flowered varieties usually continue blooming generously from early summer until autumn, while the single-flowered varieties produce crops of plump, tomato-shaped hips. The rough-textured foliage is distinctive and often luxuriant and assumes good yellow autumn colouring. Plants are quite resistant to pest and disease problems. They make excellent flowering hedges, and may be pruned over lightly in early spring. Z2

'Agnes', a hybrid between *R. rugosa* and *R. foetida* 'Persiana', is one of my favourite roses. The double flowers are an unusual amber-yellow and the scent is a potent blend of lemon and spice. It is not generous with flowers after its first early summer flush. 2m/6ft.

'Blanche Double de Coubert' is arguably the most fragrant of all roses. The dazzling white flowers are semi-double and glow against the dark green leaves; they are borne continually throughout the summer and autumn. 1.5m/5ft.

'Conrad Ferdinand Meyer' is a vigorous Rugosa hybrid, whose long stems may need to be substantially reduced in early spring. The scent from the double, silvery-pink flowers is especially rich. It is relatively prone to rust. 2.5m/8ft.

'Fru Dagmar Hastrup' has single fragrant flowers in clear pink followed by crimson hips. It is bushy and compact and makes a fine flowering hedge. 1.2m/4ft.

'Mrs Anthony Waterer' has a good crop of richly scented, double crimson flowers in early summer but few thereafter. It is more spreading than upright. 1.2m/4ft.

'Roseraie de l'Hay' is a popular and vigorous Rugosa with semi-double, crimson-purple flowers and a rich scent. It has especially lush, fresh green foliage. 1.2–1.5m/4–5ft.

R. rugosa has single flowers, variable in colour between pink and carmine-purple, and these are well scented. The clash with the bright red hips is startling. 2.3m/7ft.

***R. rugosa* 'Alba'** is worthy of a place in any garden. It bears its pure white,

ABOVE 'Roseraie de l'Hay'
FAR LEFT 'Vanity'
LEFT 'Fru Dagmar Hastrup'

FAR LEFT 'Dupontii'
LEFT *Rosa primula*

pervasively scented flowers over a long period and they are joined in autumn by large orange hips.
2.3m/7ft.

'Sarah van Fleet' has semi-double, well-scented flowers in clear pink and blooms continuously. It is a vigorous, upright, bushy shrub and makes a good hedge.
2.5m/8ft.

'Scabrosa' is a luxuriant Rugosa, lush in foliage and bountiful with its large, single, crimson-purple flowers and its crop of orange hips. The scent is rich and sweet. It makes good hedging.
1.2m/4ft.

SPECIES AND NEAR-SPECIES SHRUB ROSES

'Dupontii' has single white flowers with the delicious scent of banana. It is a beautiful rose – the crisp, pure blooms with a boss of golden stamens are offset by grey-green foliage. It flowers after midsummer, giving one splendid show but providing some orange hips later.
2.3m/7ft. Z6

'Headleyensis' is a hybrid of the golden rose of China, *R. hugonis,* and like its parent blooms in early summer. The single, creamy-yellow flowers are very fragrant and are displayed on arching brown branches well clad in ferny foliage.
2.3m/7ft. Z6

R. primula is an essential ingredient of the fragrant garden. The ferny leaves release the scent of incense, particularly strongly on humid days or after a shower of rain; this is especially marked early in the season when the foliage is young. Small, single, primrose-yellow flowers, sweetly fragrant, are produced in early summer and look particularly eyecatching against its mahogany stems.
1.5m/5ft. Z7

***R. pulverulenta* (*R. glutinosa*)** is not commonly offered but is of interest to the scent-lover for the fragrance of its foliage – a blend of orange and pine. It has small pink flowers followed by large, globular red hips. It makes a low prickly shrub and is suitable for a dry, sunny border.
90cm/3ft.

***R. rubiginosa* (*R. eglanteria*)**, the sweet briar or eglantine, is another indispensable species, cherished for the scent of green apples released by its foliage. The fragrance is strongest at the tips of the shoots. A fine hedging plant, it should be clipped in late winter. Single pink flowers, themselves sweetly scented, appear in early summer and are followed by an impressive display of red hips. Strongly scented foliage is passed on to many of its forms and hybrids, among which 'Lady Penzance', with less appealingly scented single, coppery-pink flowers, 'Lord Penzance', with sweetly scented, single, pinky buff-yellow flowers (both provide a show of hips later), and 'Manning's Blush', a more compact shrub with pleasantly scented, double, blush-white flowers, are outstanding. 2m/6ft or more. Z6

***R. spinosissima* (*R. pimpinellifolia*)**, the burnet or Scottish rose, gives some highly scented and attractive varieties including 'Double White' and 'Double Pink', both with a deliciously sweet perfume and globular flowers. The double yellow, *R.* x *harisonii* 'Harison's Yellow', is a fine buttery tone, but the scent is not so appealing; there are, however, double yellow Scottish roses with pleasant scents – I grow one, but it came as a cutting from an unnamed shrub. 'Stanwell Perpetual' is a

LEFT 'Fritz Nobis' CENTRE 'Golden Wings' RIGHT 'Frühlingsgold'

particularly fine hybrid that, unlike these others, continues to bloom all season after its main midsummer display; the double flowers are blush-pink and very fragrant and the foliage is grey-green. All these roses make thorny plants well furnished in small leaves.
1.5m/5ft. Z5

MODERN SHRUB ROSES

Under this heading come a range of roses of diverse parentage and character, which are often very different in personality from the Old Shrub Roses and are of more recent origin. They include the numerous English Roses bred by David Austin, many of which have an outstanding perfume – here I feature only a small selection from among the best. The majority need little pruning, other than the removal of dead and weak wood; but shrubs benefit from having several of their oldest stems cut to the ground periodically.

'Cerise Bouquet' is a graceful rose with small grey leaves and clusters of cerise rosette-shaped flowers borne throughout the summer. These are a vibrant cerise and have a strong raspberry scent. It may be grown as a rambler.
2.7m/9ft.

'Claire Austin' is an English Rose with lemony-white, double rosette flowers, which possess a beautiful vanilla and myrrh scent. It has good disease resistance, and grows well as a climber.
90cm–2.7m/3–9ft

'Fritz Nobis' blooms only once, in early summer, but makes a superb display. It has Hybrid Tea flowers in clear pink that have a good clove scent; these are followed by an abundance of reddish hips.
2m/6ft.

'Frühlingsgold' is a magnificent rose for early summer with long, arching branches and large, single, pale yellow flowers that are powerfully fragrant. It is splendid with oriental poppies.
2.3m/7ft.

'Frühlingsmorgen' has large, single flowers that are rose-pink with pale yellow centres. The scent is rich and sweet. It occasionally provides later crops of flowers but its main display is in early summer.
2m/6ft.

'Gertrude Jekyll' is a superb, healthy English Rose with large, rich pink, double rosette flowers possessing a powerful old rose perfume.
1.2m/4ft.

'Golden Wings' is an excellent, compact rose that blooms continuously with large, single, warm yellow flowers. It has a rich and sweet scent. 2m/6ft.

'Graham Thomas' is a splendid English Rose from David Austin carrying apricot-yellow, old-fashioned flowers intermittently all summer. Since yellow is absent from the old shrub rose palette, this is a very valuable introduction. It has a strong

tea perfume. It is a vigorous, upright rose that will grow energetically if not hard pruned in winter.
2m/6ft or more.

'Munstead Wood' is one of my favourite English Roses. It has large sumptuous rosettes of deep velvet-crimson, which have a rich and fruity perfume. 90cm/3ft.

'Nymphenburg' releases a powerful apple scent from its large, double flowers that are a blend of salmon-pink, yellow and orange. It blooms continuously through the summer and makes a big, arching shrub.
2.5m/8ft.

'Pretty Jessica' is a small English Rose with rich pink flowers of old shrub rose fullness and a very powerful old rose fragrance. It repeats well.
90cm/3ft.

'Scepter'd Isle' is a soft pink English Rose with a strong myrrh scent.
1.2m/4ft.

'The Countryman' is an English Rose with large, deep pink, old rose flowers and a powerful rose scent. It has a good arching habit and Portland rose foliage, and gives at least two flushes of flower.
90cm/3ft.

'The Generous Gardener' is an English Rose with large double cup-shaped flowers in pale pink. It has a powerful old rose perfume, and grows well as a climber.
2m–3m/6ft–10ft

'Wild Edric' is an English Rose of *rugosa* parentage, with richly fragrant semi-double flowers in purplish-pink. It makes a good hedge.
1.2m/4ft.

HYBRID TEAS

The Hybrid Teas give poise and pointed perfection in the rose flower. As bushes, they are invariably coarse and gawky, self-conscious and stiff in the border and very unattractive in winter when they present only thorny, woody stumps. Their place is in a formal setting or somewhere not too prominent that can be avoided in winter. In a vase or buttonhole they are displayed at their best. Scent has been forsaken by many breeders in pursuit of the ideal show bloom, but there are still richly fragrant varieties in abundance and in recent years there has been an increased awareness among breeders of the importance of satisfying the nose as well as the eye. Hybrid Teas should be cut down to 15–25cm/6–10in from the ground in early spring; trim lightly in late autumn to prevent cane breakage in winter winds. They may also require regular spraying with insecticides and fungicides for best results, though modern varieties are often more resistant to problems.

'Alec's Red' has a superb, sophisticated perfume and is an excellent Hybrid Tea. The cherry-red flowers are freely produced all summer and are well displayed against the dark, glossy leaves.
90cm/3ft.

'Apricot Silk' has large reddish-apricot flowers with a good scent.
90cm/3ft.

'Blessings' produces well-scented, salmon-pink blooms all summer.
90cm/3ft.

'Blue Moon' is the popular silvery-lilac Hybrid Tea, and probably the best 'blue' rose; with the creamy-browns, this shade also takes the prize for decadence. It has a strong fruity perfume.
90cm/3ft.

'Buxom Beauty' is a newer variety with good disease resistance and large magenta-pink flowers with a superb scent. 90cm/3ft.

RIGHT 'Blessings'
FAR RIGHT 'Blue Moon'

'Crimson Glory' is a strongly scented old Hybrid Tea with large velvet-crimson flowers. The necks are weak but it is a lovely rose. There is also a striking climbing version.
60cm/2ft; 4.5m/15ft as a climber.
'Dainty Bess', a parent of 'White Wings', is a single-flowered Hybrid Tea with large silvery-pink flowers. It makes a fine show and has a good sweet scent.
90cm/3ft.
'Dutch Gold' is a fine scented Hybrid Tea with pure golden-yellow flowers, freely produced all summer.
90cm/3ft.
'Eden Rose' is a robust rose with large, scented flowers in deep pink.
90cm/3ft.
'Ernest H. Morse' is a popular and reliable Hybrid Tea with very bright crimson-red flowers from shapely buds. 90cm/3ft.
'Especially for You' is a splendid, disease-resistant variety with clusters of yellow, well-scented flowers.
90cm/3ft.
'Fragrant Cloud' is a much-loved rose with an exceptionally rich perfume. It makes a vigorous bush and produces its coral-red flowers in abundance through the season; the blooms glow against the dark foliage. It is also available as a climber.
90cm/3ft.
'Ice Cream' is a disease resistant variety with bronzy leaves and white, richly scented flowers.
90cm/3ft.
'Indian Summer' has strongly fragrant, creamy-apricot flowers, and good dark glossy, disease resistant foliage. 90cm/3ft.
'Josephine Bruce' is one of those sumptuous dark velvet-crimson roses for which I always fall. The scent is very good and it is more reliable than 'Papa Meilland'. 90cm/3ft.
'Just Joey' has large, well-scented blooms in a blend of pinks and coppery-orange. 60cm/2ft.
'La France' is of interest as probably the first Hybrid Tea ever raised, in 1865. The pale pink flowers have an old rose character and a strong scent.
1.2m/4ft.
'Mama Mia!' is a newer variety with well scented, coral-orange flowers.
90cm/3ft.
'Mister Lincoln' is a popular dark red with a good fragrance.
90cm/3ft.
'Mullard Jubilee' is a vigorous and reliable Hybrid Tea with large rose-pink flowers and a good scent.
60cm/2ft.
'Ophelia' is an old variety, much loved. The blush-pink flowers are strongly scented and it makes a vigorous, upright plant. There is a climbing version and two fine sports, 'Lady Sylvia' with pale pink flowers and 'Madame Butterfly' with soft pink flowers.
90cm/3ft.
'Papa Meilland' is one of my favourite Hybrid Teas. The blooms

LEFT 'Eden Rose' CENTRE 'Fragrant Cloud' RIGHT 'Just Joey'

are the darkest damson-red and the fragrance is strong and sophisticated. Unfortunately, it is a weak and unreliable rose outside and needs a warm, sheltered position; it is superb under glass.
60cm/2ft.

'Paul Shirville' is a powerfully scented, salmon-pink rose. It is a vigorous hybrid that has become very popular.
90cm/3ft.

'Prima Ballerina' is a very reliable Hybrid Tea with richly scented, rose-pink flowers.
90cm/3ft.

'Silver Jubilee' is, according to the well-known British rose grower Peter Beales, 'one of the best roses ever raised'. It is very free-flowering with clusters of silvery-pink flowers suffused with apricot and cream. It has especially dense, glossy foliage.
90cm/3ft.

'Simply the Best' is a newer variety with strongly scented, orange-yellow flowers and good disease resistance.
90cm/3ft.

'Wendy Cussons' is a very popular rose with deep cerise blooms and a rich fragrance.
60cm/2ft.

'Whisky Mac' is a much-grown hybrid with powerfully scented, amber-yellow flowers. It needs good soil and suffers in hard winters.
90cm/3ft.

'White Wings' is a very beautiful rose with single white flowers. The petals are arranged around a boss of crimson stamens. It makes a tall upright plant.
1.2m/4ft.

FLORIBUNDA ROSES

Like Hybrid Teas, Floribundas are valued for their continuous summer display. They can also be rather stiff and self-conscious bushes but some, such as 'Margaret Merril', fit well into mixed borders. The flowers are not as perfect in shape but they appear in large clusters and make a very colourful display. They may require regular spray applications of fungicides and insecticides, but modern varieties tend to be healthier. Pruning consists of reducing the strongest stems by half in late winter and removing the weaker stems altogether. Floribundas are not generally as well endowed with scent as the Hybrid Teas, but the following are very good.

'Amber Queen' is a popular new rose with fully double, well-scented amber flowers.
60cm/2ft.

'Apricot Nectar' has apricot yellow flowers with a superb fragrance.
60cm/2ft.

'Arthur Bell' is popular and has an excellent scent. The blooms are semi-double, opening rich yellow and fading to creamy-lemon.
60cm/2ft.

'Blue for You' is a newer variety with richly scented, bluish-purple semi-double flowers and good disease resistance. 90cm/3ft.

'Chinatown' is a big, vigorous shrub with large, double flowers in clear yellow. It makes a good shrub and hedging rose and the scent is outstanding.
1.5m/5ft.

'Dearest' is a very popular Floribunda with impressive clusters of semi-double, rich salmon-pink flowers and a strong scent. The blooms do not tolerate wet weather.
60cm/2ft.

FAR LEFT 'Paul Shirville'
LEFT 'Silver Jubilee'

MINIATURE AND PATIO ROSES

Miniature and Patio roses are for pots and window boxes. They look out of place in borders and in any case you would have to raise them somehow to discover their scent. Many varieties do not possess a scent worth commenting on; the following are good.

'Flower Power' has salmon-pink flowers continuously produced over a long season. 30cm/1ft.

'Regensberg' has double light pink flowers with white edges and reverse. The scent is excellent. 30cm/1ft.

'Sweet Dream' has double, apricot-pink flowers. 46cm/18in.

'Sweet Dream'

'Dusky Maiden' is a sumptuous old variety with single flowers in velvet-crimson, lit by golden anthers. 60cm/2ft.

'Elizabeth of Glamis' is a popular rose, though it suffers in hard winters and is prone to disease. The salmon-pink flowers are beautiful and the scent is good. 60cm/2ft.

'English Miss' bears shapely, well-scented flowers in pale pink. 60cm/2ft.

'Fragrant Delight' has strongly scented double flowers in coppery-salmon. 90cm/3ft.

'Hot Chocolate' is a newer variety with well scented flowers in unusual shades of coppery-brown. 90cm/3ft

'Korresia' is a very popular Floribunda with large clear yellow flowers. It is an excellent rose with a rich perfume. 60cm/2ft.

'L'Aimant' has superbly scented, coral-pink flowers. 90cm/3ft.

'Margaret Merril' is one of the best Floribundas. The blush-white flowers are borne in small clusters and have an outstanding fragrance. 60cm/2ft.

'Princess of Wales' is a beautiful blush-pink, white rose with a light but lovely scent. 90cm/3ft.

'Sheila's Perfume' has shapely flowers bicoloured in yellow and red. 90cm/3ft

POLYANTHA-POMPON ROSES

These are excellent roses for the front of the border. They are bushy, compact plants and the bunches of little flowers are borne all summer.

LEFT 'Margaret Merril' CENTRE 'Princess of Wales' RIGHT 'Cécile Brünner'

Once popular as bedding roses, there are now few varieties in circulation, and fewer still with a good scent.

'Cécile Brünner', the sweetheart rose, is a miniature shrub with tiny Hybrid Tea rose flowers in pale pink. It blooms continuously and has a delicate, sweet scent. There is a climbing version that, unlike its parent, is vigorous and luxuriant in foliage. As a shrub, 90cm/3ft; as a climber, 7.5m/25ft.

'Katharina Zeimet' has clusters of double white flowers.
60cm/2ft.

'Little White Pet' is a dwarf sport of the rambler 'Félicité Perpétue' and has the same cold cream scent. It is a pretty rose which bears small creamy-white rosettes from pink marked buds all summer and autumn.
60cm/2ft.

'Mervrouw Nathalie Nypels' has semi-double flowers in pink.
60cm/2ft.

'Perle d'Or' is like a yellow version of 'Cécile Brünner'; it begins buff-yellow and fades to a pinky-cream and has a delicate, sweet scent.
1–2m/3–6ft.

'Yesterday' has lilac-pink flowers.
90cm/3ft.

'Yvonne Rabier' has semi-double, white flowers.
60cm/2ft.

GROUND-COVER ROSES

These roses are for sprawling down banks, around the base of pillars, and down low walls. They come from all parts of the rose kingdom and have differing characters.

'Cardinal Hume' is a low rose of spreading habit with deliciously scented, old-fashioned, double flowers in plum-purple. These are followed by hips.
90cm/3ft.

'Daisy Hill' has large, single, pink flowers followed by a good show of hips. 1.5m/5ft.

R. x *jacksonii* **'Max Graf'**, a Rugosa hybrid, has single, silvery-pink, apple-scented flowers and good glossy foliage.
60cm/2ft.

'Scintillation' produces its large clusters of semi-double blush-pink flowers over a long period. The scent is excellent.
1.2m/4ft.

CLIMBING ROSES

Climbing roses offer a variety of scents at nose height. They include plants with Tea, Hybrid Tea, Floribunda, Bourbon and China rose character, and the Noisettes. As a general rule, the Teas, Chinas and Noisettes enjoy the warmth and protection of a sunny wall; while the others may also be grown in the open on pillars, pergolas and fences, or against walls with a less favoured aspect. Most of these roses flower repeatedly. Pruning consists of tying-in the strong, long shoots each winter,

'Aloha'

bending them along horizontal wires (you need cut their ends only when they are outgrowing their allotted space) and shortening the lateral growths from these stems by two-thirds.

'Aimée Vibert' (Noisette) produces sprays of small, white, double flowers, with yellow stamens, in summer and usually flowers repeatedly. It has good glossy foliage and few thorns. 4.5m/15ft.

'Alister Stella Gray' (Noisette) bears deliciously sweet-scented flowers throughout the summer and autumn. They are both yolk-yellow in bud and open into large, quartered, ivory-white blooms. 4.5m/15ft.

'Aloha' (Floribunda) is a first-rate climber and powerfully tea-scented. The quartered, rose-pink flowers are borne continuously. 3m/10ft.

'Belle Portugaise' (Tea) is a beautiful pale pink, well-scented climber for glasshouse and mild climates. It blooms in one big early flush. 4.5m/15ft.

'Céline Forestier' (Noisette) is a fine climber with old rose character and a powerful tea scent. The large flat flowers are double, quartered and creamy-yellow and are borne continuously. 2.5m/8ft.

'Climbing Cécile Brünner' (Polyantha) is a climbing sport of the sweetheart rose. Its tiny pink flowers are softly but sweetly fragrant. It flowers once, in early summer and is a vigorous and hardy rose. 7.5m/25ft.

'Climbing Château de Clos-Vougeot' (Hybrid Tea) has sumptuous deep maroon-red flowers that have a rich perfume. It produces some later flowers after its main summer display. 4.5m/15ft.

'Climbing Columbia' (Hybrid Tea) is a superb, well-scented rose, with elegant, pink tea-rose flowers continuously produced, ideal for a glasshouse or mild climate. 4.5m/15ft.

'Climbing Devoniensis' (Tea) is a creamy-apricot rose, strongly tea-scented, for a warm wall or glasshouse. 3.5m/12ft.

'Climbing Ena Harkness' (Hybrid Tea) has weak-necked flowers that hang attractively downwards. They are deep velvet-crimson and are strongly perfumed. It has one main summer flush and some flowers later. 4.5m/15ft.

'Climbing Etoile de Hollande' (Hybrid Tea) is a superb and very popular climber with powerfully perfumed, crimson-red blooms. 4.5m/15ft.

'Climbing Lady Hillingdon' (Tea) is an outstanding rose whose apricot-yellow tea flowers contrast very effectively with the purple-suffused stems and foliage. It is reliable against a warm wall, flowering repeatedly, and has a tea scent. It is one of my favourite climbers. 4.5m/15ft.

'Climbing Lady Sylvia' (Hybrid Tea) is a fine pink rose with perfect buds and a strong scent. It flowers repeatedly. 'Climbing Ophelia' is similar but a paler pink. 3.5m/12ft.

'Climbing Madame Abel Chatenay' (Hybrid Tea) is an old Hybrid Tea, popular in Britain as a bush and a climber. The blooms are soft pink and intensely fragrant and it flowers repeatedly. 3m/10ft.

'Climbing Mrs Herbert Stevens' (Tea) is a fine old variety with shapely cream flowers and a strong

tea scent. It is a vigorous, hardy plant and flowers repeatedly. 6m/20ft.

'Constance Spry' (Modern Shrub) has exceptionally large flowers, clear pink and petal-packed, and a plant in bloom is a magnificent sight. The scent is of myrrh (like cold cream/ calamine lotion), strong but not very sweet. This is a very lovely rose. 6m/20ft.

'Desprez à Fleur Jaune' (Noisette) is a very fine climber whose clusters of creamy quartered flowers, tinged pink and yellow, are borne ceaselessly all season. The fragrance is powerful and fruity. It requires a warm wall and is good under glass. 5.5m/18ft.

'Gloire de Dijon' (Tea) is one of my favourite climbing roses. The old-fashioned, petal-packed blooms are buff-apricot and look splendid even against orange-red brickwork. It is hardy, flowers repeatedly, and has a rich tea scent. 4.5m/15ft.

'Guinée' (Hybrid Tea) is a stunning rose with sumptuous dark maroon-crimson flowers and a strong perfume. Its main display is in summer, after which it blooms sporadically. I would not want to be without it. 4.5m/15ft.

'Kathleen Harrop' (Bourbon) is completely thornless and bears its clear pink, strongly scented blooms all season. To my mind, it is lovelier than its parent, 'Zéphirine Drouhin'. 3m/10ft.

'La Follette' (*Rosa gigantea* hybrid) is a vigorous rose with lax heads of loose, petal-packed salmon-pink flowers for mild climates. A rose in full bloom in early summer is a magnificent sight. 6m/20ft.

'Lawrence Johnston' (*R. foetida* 'Persiana' hybrid), named after the maker of Hidcote garden in Gloucestershire, is a popular vigorous climber with semi-double, bright yellow flowers with a good fragrance. It blooms early and has subsequent flushes throughout the season. 7.5m/25ft.

'Leverkusen' (Kordes hybrid) has semi-double, lemon-yellow flowers and a sweet lemon scent. It flowers repeatedly after its main summer display. It may be grown as a free-standing shrub. 3m/10ft.

ABOVE 'Constance Spry' LEFT 'Guinée' RIGHT 'Kathleen Harrop'

FAR LEFT 'Maigold'
LEFT 'New Dawn'

'Madame Alfred Carrière' (Noisette) is one of the very best climbers, succeeding even on a shaded wall; it may also be grown as a shrub. The large, white, pink-tinged flowers are produced all season and are powerfully scented.
6m/20ft.

'Madame Grégoire Staechelin' (Hybrid Tea) blooms only once, in early summer, but makes a superb display. The large, semi-double flowers are flesh-pink with a deeper reverse and are followed by good orange hips. It has a strong, sweet scent, and is arguably one of the finest of all climbing roses.
6m/20ft.

'Maigold' (*R. spinosissima* hybrid) makes one impressive early summer display. The semi-double flowers are rich buff-yellow and are powerfully scented. It may be grown as a lax shrub. It is not reliably winter hardy in very cold regions.
3.5m/12ft.

'Maréchal Niel' (Noisette) is a famous glasshouse and mild climate rose with nodding tea-rose flowers in pale yellow, produced in a good early flush and sporadically later.
4.5m/15ft.

'New Dawn' is a sport of 'Dr W. Van Fleet', a shrub rose and hybrid of *R. wichurana*. It is one of the finest pink climbers (a soft, clear pink) and in the first flight of all roses. The foliage is healthy and glossy and the shapely semi-double blooms, which are fruitily fragrant, are borne continuously. 'New Dawn' is disease-free and very hardy.
3m/10ft.

'Noisette Carnée' ('Blush Noisette') is an extremely free-flowering rose that bears clusters of semi-double, lilac-pink flowers. It has a rich clove fragrance and grows well in the open, even as a free-standing bush. 4.5m/15ft.

'Paul's Lemon Pillar' (Hybrid Tea) is another favourite of mine. The blooms, perfect in bud, are very large and creamy-lemon and the fragrance is delicious.
6m/20ft.

'Sombreuil, Climbing' (Tea) is a superb white rose for a warm wall or glasshouse. The blooms are flat, fully double and tea-scented, and it flowers repeatedly.
2.5m/8ft.

'Souvenir de Claudius Denoyel' (Hybrid Tea) has bright crimson-red, old-fashioned flowers, deliciously scented, which are borne sporadically after the main early summer display.
5.5m/18ft.

'Zéphirine Drouhin' (Bourbon) is a very popular, thornless climber, succeeding even on a shady wall. The semi-double flowers are bright cerise pink (not everyone's favourite colour) and well scented, and are borne ceaselessly all season. It may be grown as a shrub.
3.5m/12ft.

RAMBLER ROSES

This is the name given to the species climbers, and to the hybrids derived from crossing the species climbers with garden roses. They bloom only once, usually just after the main shrub rose season, but can be relied upon for a magnificent show. The flowers, though generally small, are borne in great bunches. Many then produce a display of hips. The scents are often very fruity: *R. wichurana* gives its green apple scent to many hybrids. Ramblers are generally better in open positions than against walls, where they often succumb

RIGHT 'Bobbie James'
BELOW 'Albertine'

to mildew. They are at their best scrambling into trees or trained over buildings and along fences. The species need little, if any, pruning; but the hybrids benefit from having some of their older canes removed, and their lateral growths shortened, as for climbing roses; but with once-blooming Ramblers, this should be done immediately after flowering, not in winter.

'Albéric Barbier' (*R. wichurana* hybrid) is a fine Rambler with glossy, almost evergreen, foliage and clusters of double, quartered, creamy-yellow flowers with a delicious apple scent. It blooms at midsummer but produces many later flowers. 6m/20ft.

'Albertine' (*R. wichurana* hybrid) is a popular Rambler with distinctive coppery-pink flowers. It makes a memorable midsummer display and the fruity scent carries far.
4.5m/15ft.

'Alexandre Girault' (*R. wichurana* hybrid) has clusters of large, fully double, coppery rose-pink flowers. It is an excellent rose with a strong apple scent.
4.5m/15ft.

R. banksiae* var. *banksiae, the double white Banksian rose, is much better endowed with scent than its double yellow cousin. It needs the warmth of a sunny wall and succeeds well in a Mediterranean climate. The blooms are small and fully double and are borne in summer. Pruning is tricky because the best blooms are borne on two- or three-year-old wood, and thus should be limited to the removal of very old wood.
4.5m/15ft. Z8

'Bobbie James' (*R. multiflora* hybrid) is one of the best Ramblers for training into a tree. It has good glossy foliage and the semi-double, white flowers, filled with yellow stamens and borne in large clusters, are powerfully and fruitily fragrant.
9m/30ft.

R. bracteata, the Macartney rose, performs best in warm climates, though, like its offspring 'Mermaid', it often succeeds against shaded walls. Its single white flowers, with a prominent boss of golden stamens, have a fine lemon scent and are produced intermittently throughout summer and autumn. It has attractive, dark, glossy, evergreen foliage and behaves more like a wall shrub than a climber.
4.5m/15ft. Z7

***R. brunonii* 'La Mortola'** has the simple charm of a wild rose and is well clad in downy, grey-green leaves. The white flowers are single, filled with yellow anthers, and richly perfumed, and are borne in clusters after midsummer. It is not suitable for very cold gardens.
6m/20ft. Z8

'Easlea's Golden Rambler' (Hybrid Tea) has large, double, butter-yellow flowers in Hybrid Tea style, but it blooms only once. The foliage is

glossy and distinctive. It is a very fine Climber/Rambler with an intense fragrance.
4.5m/15ft.

'Emily Gray' (*R. wichurana* descendant) has well-scented, semi-double, buff-yellow flowers and good glossy foliage.
3.5m/12ft.

'Félicité Perpétue' (*R. sempervirens* descendant) bears a mass of small, pink-tinged white rosettes after midsummer and is one of the loveliest Ramblers. It has a distinctive calamine lotion or cold cream scent.
6m/20ft. Hardy to Z7

***R. filipes* 'Kiftsgate'** is a monster of a rose. The clusters of small, single, creamy flowers, filled with yellow anthers, are produced soon after midsummer and waft a rich fragrance. They are followed by a mass of orange hips.
12m/40ft or more.

'Francis E. Lester' (Hybrid Musk parentage) bears its single, white flowers, tinged with pink, in large trusses at midsummer and they waft a delicious fruity scent. A crop of orange hips follows. It may also be grown as a shrub.
4.5m/15ft.

'François Juranville' (*R. wichurana* descendant) has double, quartered flowers in rose-pink and an apple scent. It is a fine sight when giving its summer display.
7.5m/25ft.

'Goldfinch' (*R. multiflora* descendant) is a small Rambler with single, yellow flowers, fading to white in sunshine (try it facing northwest), and a rich, fruity scent.
3m/10ft.

R. helenae follows up its midsummer show of single, creamy-white flowers – borne in dense, round clusters and intensely scented – with a bountiful display of small red hips.
6m/20ft.

'Kew Rambler' (*R. soulieana* hybrid) has greyish foliage and clusters of single flowers, light pink with white centres, after midsummer. The scent is powerfully fruity.
5.5m/18ft.

R. laevigata is a Chinese species but has naturalized itself in parts of the United States where it is known as the Cherokee rose; it is also the State Flower of Georgia. The large, single, white flowers, filled with golden stamens, are powerfully and spicily scented. It is not hardy in cold climates. Its hybrid, 'Cooperi' (Cooper's Burma Rose), is more frequently seen in Britain; it makes a fine early-summer show against a warm wall.
6m/20ft. Z7

R. moschata, the true Musk rose, was rediscovered by the rosarian Graham Stuart Thomas in E. A. Bowles' garden at Enfield, Middlesex, England, in 1963 and is once again a popular Rambler. Its glory is its late flowering – throughout high summer and into early autumn – and the delicious, sweet musk scent that wafts from the large clusters of single white flowers. The filaments, rather than the petals, are the source of the perfume. It performs best against a wall.
3m/10ft. Z7

***R. mulliganii* (*R. longicuspis*)** bears large heads of single creamy flowers that waft a banana fragrance. It is a vigorous rose. Z9

R. multiflora has been an important species in the development of modern roses. It is a small Rambler or arching shrub that produces large clusters of single, creamy-white

FAR LEFT 'Félicité Perpétue'
LEFT *Rosa filipes* 'Kiftsgate'

LEFT 'Paul Transon' CENTRE 'The Garland' RIGHT 'Wedding Day'

flowers just after midsummer. These have a pervasive, fruity scent.
4.5m/15ft. Z5

'Paul's Himalayan Musk' (parentage unknown) is another outstanding giant for leading into large trees. The clusters of small double rosettes, in pale lilac-pink, are borne after midsummer and waft a fruity scent.
9m/30ft.

'Paul Transon' (*R. wichurana* descendant) is an interestingly coloured rose that looks particularly good against old brickwork (as at Sissinghurst Castle, Kent, England). The flat, double flowers are a sort of coppery-salmon colour. They are produced in abundance after midsummer and sporadically later and have a strong apple scent.
4.5m/15ft.

'Rambling Rector' (*R. multiflora* descendant) is a good white-flowered Rambler for leading into old fruit trees and over sheds. The blooms are semi-double, with yellow stamens, and have a strong fruity scent. Hips follow.
6m/20ft.

'Sanders' White Rambler' (*R. wichurana* descendant) is a fine rose bearing a mass of small, pure white, double rosettes, fruitily scented, after midsummer.
5.5m/18ft.

'Seagull' (*R. multiflora* descendant) is a spectacular and vigorous Rambler with large clusters of semi-double, white flowers that are intensely and fruitily fragrant.
7.5m/25ft.

'The Garland' (*R. moschata* × *R. multiflora*), a favourite of Gertrude Jekyll and still one of the loveliest Ramblers, is a wonderful sight at midsummer, when it bears its clusters of small, semi-double, creamy flowers. The scent is of oranges.
4.5m/15ft.

'Veilchenblau' (*R. multiflora* descendant) is one of those extraordinary crimson roses with violet and grey shadings. It is less richly coloured than 'Bleu Magenta' but much better endowed with scent. The blooms are semi-double, with yellow stamens, and are borne soon after midsummer.
4.5m/15ft.

'Wedding Day' is an excellent and vigorous Rambler with single, creamy flowers, yellow in bud, and with orange-yellow stamens, carried in very large clusters after midsummer. It is ideal for leading into trees and over buildings. The powerful fragrance is of oranges.
9m/30ft.

R. wichurana, the parent of so many good Ramblers, is itself worthy of cultivation especially as a ground-cover rose, when it makes a dense, almost evergreen, carpet. The single white flowers, powerfully apple-scented, are produced after midsummer and are followed by orange hips. 4.5m/15ft.

The Jubilee Rose Garden at RHS Garden Wisley

RHS GARDEN WISLEY

'At RHS Garden Wisley, scent has tended to play a secondary role to visual impact, but now it is receiving more emphasis, with fragrant plants such as witch hazels being found positions close to paths rather than being put in the centre of beds. Winter is a particularly rich time for scents in the woodland garden around Battleston Hill, and *Daphne bholua* 'Peter Smithers' is one of the best, together with, a little later, yellow-flowered *Corylopsis*, whose primrose fragrance was one of the late Queen Mother's favourite scents. The heady scent of Loderi rhododendrons is another feature here. We encourage visitors to hunt out scent among the plants displayed in the Alpine House, especially among the cyclamen which people do not expect to be scented, and to touch the leaves of the many different scented *Pelargonium* which are put out in the main glasshouse in early summer. The hedge of the semi-double, deep pink English Rose 'Wild Edric' by the Jubilee Rose Garden is a notable scented feature, and in autumn there are a number of *Cercidiphyllum* trees around the garden exuding a potent fragrance of toffee apple.'

Colin Crosbie, Curator at RHS Garden Wisley

HERB GARDENS

Botanically, most non-woody, non-shrubby plants are herbs. But in horticulture, we take the term to mean those plants that are useful to us, whether for medicinal, culinary or cosmetic purposes. A large number of plants come into this category, including shrub roses, peonies, primroses and balsam poplar; but in this chapter I have listed only the more obvious herbal plants and allowed those that nowadays fit more squarely into other categories to drift into other chapters. The scents of the herbs described in this chapter come mainly from leaves, roots and seeds, not flowers, and the flavours are mostly spicy or camphorous, sometimes sweetened with rose and fruit, and sometimes heightened with mint and *Eucalyptus*.

There are many ways of growing herbs in the garden. They may be given their own corner and either arranged in a formal pattern or allowed to mingle casually with each other. They may be grown in pots and window boxes. They can be used to make lawns, paths, seats and hedges. And they may be treated exactly as other garden plants and placed in mixed borders.

The earliest gardens were herb gardens, and herbs have a long and close association with garden history, literature and folklore. A collection of herbs always seems to have an air of the past about it and looks effective in traditional settings of symmetrical beds and straight paths. The other reason why this treatment works well is that many herbs are naturally wispy (even weedy), and an emphatic groundplan imposes structure and draws attention away from the worst offenders.

Low box hedging can be a useful part of the formal groundplan, enclosing the beds and even criss-crossing through the centre. Box does not mind supporting and being shaded by the foliage and flowerheads of floppy plants, providing it does not have to shoulder the burden for too long. If the herbs are herbaceous and are cut back once or twice in the season, they will give the box plenty of breathing time.

The wispy nature of many herbs is traditionally countered by setting them in a strong, formal design.

Golden marjoram and chives form part of the aromatic edging of this intimate herb garden with its narrow paths, box topiaries and sheltering walls. The different leaf colours of herbs can create attractive tapestries, though in winter lavender and other silver plants are no ornament in damp climates.

Like box, wall germander (*Teucrium fruticans*) and green and grey *Santolina* are amenable to clipping and may also serve as edging material; they are sun-lovers, however, and do not tolerate the foliage of other plants resting on them. The most ambitious use of these three shrubby plants is to weave them into interlacing and labyrinthine patterns or 'knots'. As centrepieces for herb gardens, miniature knots are of absorbing interest, though, of course, labour-intensive. The gaps may be filled with small bulbs and short perennials or with gravel.

You can take your herb garden in quite a different direction. Non-shrubby herbs are often inveterate colonizers and if you are not of a neat-and-tidy mind, you can let them get on with it. The result will be an aromatic wild garden, with self-seeding misty fennels in bronze and green, balms in green and gold, blue-flowered borage and architectural angelica. I should avoid herbs which run underground furiously, like the mints, which are very difficult to control. With the rest, selective removal of flowerheads, cutting down and poisoning will give the garden some semblance of order.

Cooks like their herbs in one place, somewhere easily accessible from the house. But in my garden the herbs are everywhere, in the company of flowering shrubs and perennials, rock plants and bulbs. Here and there they are in little groups but often there is just a solitary herb wedged between more flamboyant neighbours.

If you are happy to scatter your herbs, you can use their colours, scents and characters to help create a range of effects. Herbs from the Mediterranean hillsides and scrubland can be united with other plants from the same or similar habitats to create a scheme of muted colours and spicy, camphorous aromas, evocative of the maquis. Sun and well-drained soil is the recipe for success, and gently sloping banks are ideal. It is in the heat of the day that the scents will be at their richest.

There is no shortage of shrubby candidates with grey, grey-green and grey-blue leaves for a Mediterranean scheme. Lavenders, sages, *Santolina*, rue, blue-flowered *Caryopteris*, Jerusalem sage (*Phlomis fruticosa*) with soap-scented flowerheads, *Teucrium* and *Artemisia*

Cistus, Salvia and silver-leaved sub-shrubs bring a Mediterranean flavour to this cobbled herb garden.

can all be included. Rosemaries are essential to give some sprawling height and inject further sweetness into the bouquet garni. *Cistus*, for their gummy fragrances and papery flowers, must be here in abundance, and so must thymes, rippling along the front of the bed. Hyssop, with its rich blue flowers in summer, is also indispensable. *Calamintha*, and even *Dianthus*, may be added to provide some complementary flavours – respectively, the scent of mint and fruit, and the scent of clove. Asphodels, *Verbascum* and brooms will provide plumes of bright yellow, and marjoram some pools of gold. If the bed is backed by a wall, a myrtle could be planted to lift the scheme to nose height. And what about *Perovskia* for late-summer colour, and Gallica roses for a touch of romance? All you need now are olives and pencil-slim cypress trees in the background; sea buckthorn (*Hippophae rhamnoides*) and weeping silver pear (*Pyrus salicifolia* 'Pendula') are good substitutes for olives in cold climates, and pencil-slim forms of juniper and chamaecyparis hardy substitutes for cypresses.

Many of the Mediterranean herbs are in the first flight of traditional garden ornamentals, and look quite at home when used singly, tucked into the corners of buildings and the paving cracks of paths and patios, and when associating with the garden's lusher flora.

Rosemary is one of the best medium-sized evergreen shrubs for a sunny wall, to my mind especially attractive in narrow beds where it spills forward on to the path. Forms with rich blue flowers I prize the most. In association with creamy brooms and blue ceanothus they look stunning. The unique scent of rosemary can be enjoyed all year and is an appetizing contrast to the pineapple of Moroccan broom and the bitter lemon of lemon verbena.

Lavenders bulge over paths at a lower level. As your legs brush past them they will release their fragrances, and when they are in bloom, you can draw your fingers over their flowerheads; this is one aromatic herb whose flowers do not disappoint. A drift of hardy lavenders in mixed colours – the range runs from purple through several shades of violet-blue to pink and white – is a pastel delight that one encounters far too rarely. And, of course, lavenders are much-loved companions for a host of cottage-garden favourites like roses and mock orange, Madonna lilies and peonies.

There are a number of desirable rosemaries and lavenders on the borderlines of hardiness, and in cold climates these may be grown in pots and housed under glass for the winter. In summer they can be assembled beside garden seats and up flights of steps. Trailing rosemary and woolly and toothed lavenders come into this category and each has its own distinctive fragrance. These will provide the complementary aromas to other fragrant pot plants such as pineapple sage (*Salvia elegans*), blackcurrant-scented sages (*S. discolor*, *S. microphylla*) and peppermint, rose and fruit-scented *Pelargonium*.

BAY

Bay can be the most architectural of herbal pot plants. Pruned into topiary shapes, it adorns the entrance of many a grand house and fashionable restaurant (where I once saw it studded with lemons to make a very plausible *Citrus* tree). In the garden such self-conscious shapes may also have a place, flanking a doorway or a painted seat. Outside very cold regions it can also be grown in the ground, but if it is likely to encounter much frost, you should not expose its trunk through clipping. Honey-scented flowers are a bonus to the aromatic leaves. (See page 262 for *Laurus*.)

Low-growing herbs like thymes and marjoram can be used to make fragrant walkways. Popping out of paving cracks down the length of a sunny path, the bushy forms of *Thymus vulgaris* and *Origanum vulgare* will create a welcome obstacle course for the feet and soften the hard surface with a haze of green, silver and golden foliage. You can actually walk on the more prostrate thymes – the forms of *T. serpyllum* – and as long as the pathway does not see very heavy wear, the proportion of paving to vegetation may be reversed; stepping stones are needed over the green and grey patterned carpet only for wet-weather crossings and as platforms for weeding. These creeping thymes can also be woven into square, rectangular and circular Chinese rugs, to spread at intervals down wide terraces, or to be centrepieces for herb and rose gardens. Many patterns can be attempted, using patches of pale pink, mauve, crimson and white-flowered plants, and when in bloom, the rugs shimmer with bees. The most famous thyme lawns are at Sissinghurst Castle in Kent, England.

Two other herbs are flat enough to make lawns: camomile and Corsican mint (*Mentha requienii*). Mossy, fruit-scented camomile is always a pleasure to walk and sit on, and is a useful alternative to grass on hot, dry ground. But, like a thyme lawn, it has to be weeded by hand, so I would not plant a large expanse of it. One of the best ways to use camomile and Corsican mint is as fragrant seats, which can be created by cutting a section out of a bank or giving a raised bed arms and a backrest. Corsican mint likes different conditions from camomile – a little moisture and shade – so choose accordingly. Camomile – preferably the non-flowering form 'Treneague' – may also be tried woven into a grass lawn, as indeed may creeping thymes and pennyroyal (*Mentha pulegium*). Their scents give an additional dimension to a game of croquet.

Mention of mints leads me to the second great category of herbs. Not all herbs demand sun and good drainage; there is a merry band of them that can cope with colder, damper and shadier sites and heavier soils. As well as the mints, this includes angelica, borage, feverfew, meadowsweet, fennel, lovage, lemon balm, bergamot, sweet cicely, chives and parsley. These plants are mainly green and herbaceous rather than grey and shrubby, and the scents, still predominantly from leaves, are mainly fresh, wholesome vegetable fragrances, enhanced by fruit and spice (and occasionally spoiled with onion), rather than camphorous, medicinal and resinous aromas. They are also less inclined to infuse the air, the fragrances usually having to be coaxed by hand. They are easily accommodated in the border. Aniseed-scented fennel is outstanding in the spring, its green and bronze foliage providing a feathery companion to early shrub roses, smilacina, tulips and wallflowers.

A theatrical way of bringing herbs within easy reach, this display features parsley, lavender, variegated sage and applemint.

It can be cut down at midsummer and a second crop of leaves will appear. A similar treatment can be meted out to sweet cicely (*Myrrhis odorata*). This is another beautifully airy perennial, which gives a double dose of scent; its white flowers are fragrant as well as its leaves.

One would grow bergamot for its unique scent whatever it looked like, but it happens to be a good summer border plant. It blooms for a long time, comes in a number of good colour forms, and has an interesting mophead shape. 'Cambridge Scarlet' is especially striking; there are very few hardy perennials with proper red flowers. This form looks well in the herbaceous border with purple *Salvia* and glaucous blue foliage.

Angelica is a statuesque plant when in flower and beautiful when silhouetted against stone, grass or water. Most of the heads need to be removed before they drop seeds to avoid a profusion of seedlings; but some have to be left since plants die after flowering. Mints can also be a problem, but by running underground not by seeding. They cannot be trusted in mixed beds and are best confined by paving or grown in a bucket that has had its bottom knocked out before being sunk into the soil. The two most beautiful mints are variegated applemint, *Mentha suaveolens* 'Variegata', many of whose leaves emerge almost pure white; and buddleja mint, *M. longifolia*, with soft grey leaves and good mauve flowers in summer. The former has a fine fruity scent.

BASIL

One of the richest and warmest of spicy fragrances is provided by sweet basil, but being a tender, tropical plant it has to be given special treatment. Seed sown indoors in spring must not be planted out until all danger of frost is past. Then it can be slotted into the front row of the herbaceous border or grown in a pot by the back door to waft scent into the air. The purple-leaved form, 'Dark Opal', is particularly ornamental and aromatic. To prolong the season, you can make a second sowing outside in midsummer and pot up some of these plants in early autumn to bring on to a sunny windowsill indoors; pinching out the growing tips ensures bushy growth.

Angelica archangelica, with its distinctive 'green' scent, flowers behind *Geranium psilostemon*.

HERBS

ACINOS
Lamiaceae
Acinos alpinus, alpine basil, is a very attractive low perennial with purple, *Salvia*-like lipped flowers in summer and strongly aromatic grey-green leaves. A nice plant for a raised bed. Sun. Well-drained soil. 20cm/8in.

ALLIUM
Alliaceae
***A. cepa* Proliferum Group**, tree onion, bears clusters of small onions on top of its tubular stems, which may be used for flavouring stews and salads. The leaves have a typical pungent scent and may be chopped up and used like chives. Plant 20cm/8in apart. Sun. 60cm/2ft.
A. fistulosum, Welsh onion, has evergreen leaves and makes a good substitute for chives in the winter. 60–90cm/2–3ft.
A. sativum, garlic, has pungent flat leaves and whitish flowers in summer. It is a popular culinary herb. Cloves planted in autumn or spring will increase and be ripe for lifting in high summer or autumn respectively. Plant 15cm/6in apart and 2.5cm/1in deep. Sun. Light, well-drained soil. 30–60cm/1–2ft.
A. schoenoprasum, chives, is a very ornamental herb, especially in its giant variety, *sibiricum*. The clumps of hollow, onion-scented, grassy leaves are neat and lush and are topped with domed flowers, usually in a shade of rose-pink. Plants may be shaved to the ground in early summer and a second flush of foliage and flowers appears. It makes an attractive edging for a herb garden. Sun. Good, fertile soil. 10–38cm/4–15in. Z3

ANETHUM
Apiaceae
A. graveolens, dill, is a hardy annual with feathery foliage and flat heads of yellowish flowers in high summer. The leaves have a spicy scent and are used for flavouring vegetables and fish, while the aromatic seeds are used in vinegars and in water to ease stomach upsets. Sow *in situ* in the spring and thin to 23cm/9in apart. Sun. Well-drained soil. 60cm/2ft.

ANGELICA
Apiaceae
A. archangelica has large, hollow, juicy stems that have a distinctive cool scent when bruised. It is the herb garden's most architectural subject, with its stout branching growth and its globular, green flowerheads. Its young leaf stalks

RIGHT *Allium schoenoprasum*
FAR RIGHT *Anethum graveolens*

give their muscat flavour to stewed fruits; the sliced stems are candied to use as decorations for cakes; the fragrant roots are used as an aid to digestion; and the leaves may be chopped and used in salads. It seeds itself furiously unless the heads are removed in time.
Light shade. Retentive soil. 1.5m/5ft.

ANTHRISCUS
Apiaceae
A. cerefolium, chervil, is a hardy annual with attractive ferny leaves and umbels of white flowers in summer. The foliage has a sweet aniseed scent and is used in soups, sauces and salads; it can be shaved to the ground to produce a further crop. Sow thinly *in situ*, in spring, and it will self-sow thereafter.
Light shade. Cool, moist soil. 46cm/18in.

APIUM
Apiaceae
Apium graveolens, wild celery, is a biennial with leaves strongly celery-scented and used to flavour soups.
Sun or light shade. Most soils. 90cm/3ft.

ARTEMISIA
Asteraceae
A. abrotanum, southernwood, is a shrubby plant with filigree, grey-green leaves: the foliage is enjoyed by some for having a 'sweet and lemony' scent but to others (myself included) its pungency is rather offensive; its alternative common name is 'old man'! If it is hard pruned every spring, it makes a handsome cushion of foliage. It was used as a strewing herb, as an antiseptic and as a tonic.
Sun. Poor, well-drained soil. 60–90cm/ 2–3ft. Z6
A. absinthium, wormwood, has an even more pungent smell and can be used to repel moths and flies. But the form 'Lambrook Silver' is a fine silvery shrub with deeply cut, silky leaves and is worth a place among white, pink and blue flowers in spite of its smell. Medicinally, wormwood is used against worms and for easing indigestion. It is hardy and evergreen.
Sun. Well-drained soil. 60–90cm/2–3ft. Z5
A. dracunculus, French tarragon, has a warm spicy scent and is a popular herb for seasoning. It has dark green, lance-shaped leaves and drooping white flowers in high summer. Grow from cuttings and plant 30cm/1ft apart. It needs a sheltered position and it is sensible to give it some protection through the winter. Russian tarragon is hardier but an inferior plant. Sun. Well-drained soil. 60cm/2ft. Z5
A. pontica, old warrior, is a small version of southernwood, and makes a lovely haze of misty grey-green foliage. It is an energetic colonizer.
Sun. 60cm/2ft. Z6

ABOVE *Artemisia absinthium* 'Lambrook Silver'
FAR LEFT *Angelica archangelica*
LEFT *Anthriscus cerefolium*

LEFT *Borago officinalis* CENTRE *Chamaemelum nobile* RIGHT *Coriandrum sativum*

BORAGO
Boraginaceae

B. officinalis, borage, is a hardy annual that seeds itself freely in most soils. Its leaves and peeled stems have a delicate, cucumber scent and can be used in salads or to flavour drinks; the sky-blue, starry flowers, borne in drooping panicles all summer, were once candied and can also be added to salads.
Sun or light shade. 30–60cm/1–2ft.

CALAMINTHA
Lamiaceae

C. grandiflora is a neat bushy perennial that is useful for edging the herb garden or for the rock garden. It has small, sweetly aromatic leaves, which are used to make herbal teas, and lilac-pink, sage-like flowers that are produced over a long period in summer.
Sun. Well-drained soil. 46cm/18in.

C. menthifolia produces pale pink flowers from dark calyces in summer, and has leaves that are scented of mint.
Sun. Well-drained soil. 60cm/2ft.

C. nepeta subsp. ***nepeta*** (***C. nepetoides***) is another excellent, long-flowering, edging plant with mint-scented leaves that blooms later, during the autumn; its lavender flowers are loved by bees.
Sun. Well-drained soil. 30cm/1ft.

CARUM
Apiaceae

C. carvi, caraway, is usually treated as a hardy biennial, the seed being sown at the end of the summer to be harvested the following year. The entire plant is aromatic, from the lacy, evergreen leaves to the parsnip-like roots. The camphor-scented seeds are used in bread and cakes and, when crushed into boiling water, provide relief from flatulence. The umbels of white flowers appear in early summer.
Sun. Well-drained soil. 60–90cm/2–3ft.

CHAMAEMELUM
Asteraceae

C. nobile, camomile, is a low, creeping perennial with mossy, fruitily scented foliage and daisy-like flowers in summer; the flowers are infused into boiling water to make camomile tea. An entire camomile lawn is difficult to manage, though it does provide a cool green carpet for areas too dry for grass. The non-flowering variety, 'Treneague', is the best for lawns; otherwise choose the double-flowered 'Flore Pleno'.
Sun. Well-drained soil. 15cm/6in.

CORIANDRUM
Apiaceae

C. sativum, coriander/cilantro, has seeds that have a spicy orange scent when ripe; they are used to flavour soups and curries (to me it tastes of soap!). It is an annual, and seeds are best sown outside in spring. Mauve flowers appear in summer and as the seedheads ripen they should be

Foeniculum vulgare

cut and hung over newspaper to dry, somewhere warm and airy. The leaves have a fetid smell, as do the seeds before they are properly ripe.
Sun. 46cm/18in.

FOENICULUM
Apiaceae
F. vulgare, fennel, is one of my favourite foliage plants. The mounds of fresh green, feathery leaves are a fine, hazy complement to brightly coloured flowers and chunky leaves, and are particularly appealing when shimmering with raindrops. Shave the plants to the ground as the flowerheads are forming in early summer for a second crop of juvenile growth. There is a bronze version, 'Purpureum', which is wonderful in hot colour groups; it comes true from seed and, like green fennel, self-sows furiously if allowed. The scent from the foliage is of aniseed, and the leaves are used to flavour fish.
Sun. 2m/6ft, if allowed to flower.

GALIUM
Rubiaceae
G. odoratum, woodruff, has the scent of new-mown hay, or coumarin, when dry, and used to be hung in bunches to scent the air or placed in the linen cupboard to scent the sheets. It is a prostrate perennial with whorls of slender leaves and branching heads of white flowers in early summer. It is an attractive plant for growing around shrubs or in the woodland garden.
Shade. 15cm/6in.

GEUM
Rosaceae
G. urbanum, herb bennet, has clove-scented roots that are used to flavour drinks. There is a faint clove fragrance in the leaves too, but the golden-yellow flowers, borne in high summer, are scentless.
Light shade. 30cm/1ft.

HELICHRYSUM
Asteraceae
***H. italicum* (*H. angustifolium*)**, curry plant, is one of those neat, dumpy little shrubs that help to counter the wispy untidiness of their companions. Its evergreen mounds of silver foliage make excellent cornerposts or edging for the herb garden, though they are likely to be killed in severe winters in colder regions. In high summer it is topped with puffs of golden flowers. Its only drawback is its scent. Some people find the hot curry fragrance ambrosial, but I am afraid I don't. Plant *Santolina* instead, if you prefer subtler scents.
H. microphyllum, dwarf curry plant, grows to 30cm/1ft.
Sun. Well-drained soil. 60cm/2ft. Z8

HYSSOPUS
Lamiaceae
H. officinalis, hyssop, is an attractive evergreen perennial, especially valuable for its flush of rich blue flowers in late summer and autumn; bees love them. The slender foliage

RIGHT *Geum urbanum*
FAR RIGHT *Galium odoratum*

LAURUS
Lauraceae

L. nobilis, bay or bay laurel, in clipped pyramid or lollipop shapes, has become the symbol of the gardener with good taste. Unfortunately, its evergreen leaves are scorched by cold winds and plants are cut to the ground by hard frosts. Cautious gardeners, and gardeners in inhospitable areas, will grow it in a tub and bring it indoors for the winter. Others will grow it in the border and rely on its powers of rejuvenation after winter setbacks. Its leaves have a familiar aromatic fragrance, but the yellow tufts of flower, produced in spring, are also scented, of honey. There is a pale green, willow-leaved form called *angustifolia* and a less hardy yellow-leaved variety called 'Aurea'. Shelter from wind is important.
Sun or shade. Most soils. 4.5m/15ft. Z7

Laurus nobilis

is pleasantly aromatic. Plants should be hard pruned in spring to keep them compact and they then make neat edging plants. There is a splendid dwarf blue subspecies called *aristatus*, and less good white- and pink-flowered forms. Hyssop tea is made from the 'tops' (flowers and leaves).
Sun. 30–60cm/1–2ft.

LAVANDULA
Lamiaceae

There is a wealth of lavenders available with which to line paths and place on strategic corners. They have one of the most pleasant and nostalgic of herb scents, and on a hot summer's day it can infuse the air and transport you to dry hillsides of southern Europe. The hardier sorts associate well with rosemary and *Cistus* in an informal shrubby mix, as well as providing the material for low hedges. The less hardy sorts are best grown in pots and taken into a cold greenhouse for the winter. They should be pruned in spring. Full sun. Well-drained soil.

***L. angustifolia* (*L. officinalis*, *L. spica*)**, common lavender, the source of the true oil of lavender. It is a variable plant, found wild in the western Mediterranean region and naturalized in parts of central Europe. The grey-green foliage is exceptionally fragrant, as are the spikes of lavender-purple flowers borne in summer. The compact forms commonly grown in gardens include 'Munstead', in lavender-blue; 'Hidcote', in deep violet and with very silvery foliage; and 'Twickel Purple', in violet and with broader,

LEFT *Lavandula angustifolia* 'Hidcote' CENTRE *Levisticum officinale* RIGHT *Melissa officinalis*

richly scented leaves. 'Folgate' is a superb blue. 'Loddon Pink', in mauve-pink, and 'Nana Alba', a dwarf white, are interesting and worthwhile as colour variants but are less scented. Sun. Well-drained soil. 30–43cm/12–17in. Z6

L. dentata has toothed green leaves and stout stems bearing lavender-blue flowers. It has a distinctive medicinal fragrance when rubbed but is not one of the more scented varieties. It is not reliably hardy. 60cm/2ft. Z9

L. lanata is a very different species, with broad, woolly, silver leaves and violet flowers. It makes a very dense plant and is excellent in a pot; but it is not hardy and has little fragrance. 60cm/2ft. Z9

L. stoechas, French lavender, is my favourite. It has curious flowerheads, like inflated seed-pods, which are crowned with a tuft of purple bracts; they are always a talking point. In a mild year it is in flower more or less continually; a hard frost kills it but invariably a host of seedlings appear in the spring. There are good white forms under the name of subsp. *stoechas* f. *leucantha*, and a stunning closely related mauve species, *L. pedunculata* subsp. *pedunculata* with an even more impressive topknot; these I grow in pots and carry under glass for the winter. They all have a strong medicinal scent. 60cm/2ft. Z8–9

Hybrid Lavenders

There are many hybrid lavenders in circulation. The 'Dutch' clones are generally late-flowering. *L.* x *intermedia* 'Grappenhall' is a large, vigorous late-flowering hybrid with broad, grey-green leaves and lavender-purple flowers. 'Grosso' is also large, with splendid purple-blue spikes and grey leaves. *L.* x *intermedia* 'Alba' is a good large white.

LEVISTICUM
Apiaceae

L. officinale, lovage, is a tall herb of little beauty but it has a refreshing vegetable scent; used in stews, the dark, segmented leaves impart a strong celery taste. With its umbels of yellow flowers, borne at high summer, it resembles a slender angelica.
Sun or light shade. 1.5m/5ft.

MELISSA
Lamiaceae

M. officinalis, lemon balm, is not high on my list of desirable plants. It is dull and nettle-like to look at, seeds itself everywhere, and its scent is that of cheap lemon soap, not sharp and tangy like lemon verbena. The golden and golden-variegated forms, 'All Gold' and 'Aurea', are worthier of attention.
Sun or light shade. 90cm/3ft.

FAR LEFT *Mentha arvensis* 'Banana'
LEFT *Mentha spicata* var. *crispa* 'Moroccan'
BELOW *Monarda* 'Cambridge Scarlet'

MENTHA
Lamiaceae

The scents of mint leaves are cool and refreshing. But most varieties are rampant colonizers and are best planted in confined beds or in bottomless buckets sunk into the soil. Sun or light shade.

***M. arvensis* 'Banana'** has small leaves with minty scent containing a definite hint of bananas! A curiosity.
46cm/18in.

M.* x *gracilis, ginger mint, is usually seen in its yellow-variegated form, 'Variegata'. It has a warm, spicy mint scent and can be used in salads.
46cm/18in.

M. longifolia, buddleja mint, is an attractive mint with woolly, grey leaves and mauve flowers.
75cm/30in.

M.* x *piperita, peppermint, is usually seen in its black form, subspecies *piperita,* which has dark purplish-green leaves and a delicious peppermint scent. White peppermint, f. *officinalis*, is greener; f. *citrata*, eau-de-cologne or bergamot mint, is bronze-flushed and has the most refined of mint scents. It has produced some interesting scented variants: 'Basil' (minty basil), 'Chocolate' (mint chocolate), and 'Grapefruit', 'Lemon' and 'Lime' all with a citrus tang.
30–60cm/1–2ft.

M. requienii, Corsican mint, is minute and is excellent for troughs and paving cracks. It likes moisture and warmth.

M. spicata, spearmint, is a green and sharply toothed herb. It has a fine spearmint scent and is a good culinary plant. The variety *crispa* has curly green leaves and lilac flowers in summer.
60cm/2ft.

***M. suaveolens* 'Variegata' (*M. rotundifolia* 'Variegata')**, variegated applemint, is the most ornamental of mints, with soft green leaves heavily splashed with white. The scent is of russet apples. It is good in salads and sauces.
60cm/2ft.

M.* x *villosa* var. *alopecuroides, Bowles' mint, is tall with downy leaves. It has a fruity mint scent and many consider it the best culinary variety.
90cm–2m/3–6ft.

MONARDA
Lamiaceae

M. citriodora, lemon bergamot, is a half-hardy annual with whorls of pinkish-purple flowers in summer. The leaves are more lemony than other bergamots. Sun. 30cm/1ft.

M. didyma, bergamot or bee balm, is a herb that looks well in the herbaceous border, while in the herb garden it contributes a welcome splash of strong colour. The mopheads of hooded flowers, produced in high summer, are scarlet

and are striking. The pointed leaves have a delicious scent, a blend of lemon and mint, and can be infused into boiling water to make Oswego tea. The hybrid 'Cambridge Scarlet' is similar but superior; 'Gardenview Scarlet' is also excellent.
Sun, but it resents dry soil. 90cm/3ft. Z4
M. fistulosa is comparable but with smaller heads of lilac-purple flowers and less scent. Sun. Tolerates dry soil better than *M. didyma*. 90cm–1.2m/3–4ft. Z3

Monarda Hybrids
Monardas also come in a range of pink, purple and white hybrids, some of the best being 'Beauty of Cobham' (pale pink), 'Croftway Pink', 'Prärienacht' (magenta-purple), 'Violet Queen', 'Scorpion' (magenta) and 'Snow White'. Modern *Monarda* tend to be more resistant to mildew than older varieties.
Sun. Moist soil. 90cm/3ft.

MYRRHIS
Apiaceae

M. odorata, sweet cicely, is a graceful perennial that is related to cow parsley. The large, lacy leaves are scented of liquorice and aniseed and can be used in salads; the roots used to be boiled as a vegetable. Umbels of cream flowers appear in spring and are followed by black seeds. It is a lovely plant for shade and in the wild garden.
Light shade. Retentive soil. 60–90cm/2–3ft.

OCIMUM
Lamiaceae

O. americanum, lime basil, has bright green, citrus-scented leaves, and like all the basils is a frost-tender annual. Sun. 30cm/1ft.
O. basilicum, sweet basil, a tropical plant, is grown as a half-hardy annual and is best sown under glass in spring and planted out in summer; it also makes a good pot herb on the windowsill. Its triangular leaves are scented of clove, and are used to flavour tomatoes, soups and sauces. 'Dark Opal', a form with bronze leaves, is especially rich in scent and taste and is a sombre foil for pale flowers and silver foliage in the herb garden. Basil needs a warm, sheltered position. There are a number of named varieties, notably 'Cinnamon' with purplish, spice-scented leaves, and 'Horapha' which has maroon-tinted leaves scented of aniseed.
Sun. Light, fertile soil. 46cm/18in.
O. x citriodorum, lemon-scented basil, lives up to its name. Sun. 30cm/1ft.
O. minimum, bush basil, has smaller leaves and is a touch less aromatic but because of its compact growth makes a good pot plant. Sun. 20cm/8in.

ORIGANUM
Lamiaceae

O. majorana, oregano or knotted marjoram, is usually grown as a half-hardy annual outdoors, or as a pot perennial on the kitchen windowsill. Its small grey leaves have a warm, spicy scent.
Sun. Well-drained soil. 30cm/1ft.
O. onites, French marjoram, is a hardy perennial with fresh green, highly aromatic leaves. It has more flavour than English marjoram.
Sun. 30cm/1ft.
O. vulgare, common or English marjoram, is the most commonly grown species and makes a fine sprawler for the front of the border. The balsam scent is strong.

Myrrhis odorata

Golden-leaved 'Aureum' is especially striking and is an indispensable foliage plant for the herb garden; the mauve-pink flowers are rather a disastrous colour combination, though. There are also variegated forms. 'Compactum' is slightly shorter in growth. Subspecies *hirtum* has grey-green leaves and white flowers. Sun. 23cm/9in.

PETROSELINUM
Apiaceae

P. crispum, parsley, is a hardy biennial that needs warmth and moisture to germinate well. Soak the seed in warm water for 24 hours before sowing; sow outdoors in spring for a summer crop, and in high summer for a crop the following spring. Plants can be cut back for a new flush of foliage. There are curly and plain-leaved varieties, all of which have a refreshing vegetable scent.
Sun. Fertile, retentive, preferably alkaline soil. 30cm/1ft.

ROSMARINUS
Lamiaceae

Rosemary is a mainstay of the scented garden and its fragrance is deliciously evocative of Mediterranean holidays, Italian *tagliata*, and Sunday lunches of roast lamb. It makes an evergreen shrub of relaxed shape, that sits comfortably on house corners, bulging over paths; common rosemary may also be used as a hedge – prune after flowering. No variety will tolerate excessive frost, but some are hardier than others. All need shelter from cold winds. Full sun. Well-drained soil.
R. officinalis, common rosemary, has long been a favourite garden plant. It has grey-green leaves and in spring smothers itself in pale violet-blue flowers. 'Miss Jessopp's Upright' is a robust, erect-growing form.
1.2m/4ft. Z8
Its variants are more or less hardy, but are worth trying. It is prudent to take cuttings in the summer. Variety *albiflorus* 'Lady in White' is a good white; 'Majorca Pink' a good pink. 'Aureus' has gold-splashed foliage. 'Sissinghurst' is a good blue and has proved very tough in my garden over the years; 'Benenden Blue' is short with narrow, dark leaves and blue flowers; and 'Fota' and 'Severn Sea' are shorter growing with even brighter blue flowers. 'Green Ginger' has leaves with a distinct ginger tang. Prostratus Group is a prostrate rosemary for trailing down retaining walls, with good blue flowers, but it is not at all hardy (Z9). 46–90cm/18in–3ft. Z8

SALVIA
Lamiaceae

S. lavandulifolia, Spanish sage, has elegantly narrow grey-green leaves and good violet-blue flowers in summer.
Sun. Well-drained soil. 46cm/18in.
S. officinalis, sage, is another small evergreen shrub that is as valuable

LEFT *Petroselinum crispum* 'Moss Curled' CENTRE *Rosmarinus officinalis* RIGHT *Salvia officinalis* 'Tricolor'

RUTA
Rutaceae

R. graveolens, rue, in its metallic blue form 'Jackman's Blue', should be one of the very best small evergreen shrubs. The ferny leaves have a pungent scent, reminiscent to some of orange. But it should not be planted by anyone with sensitive skin, and certainly not touched (especially on sunny days), or blistering may occur. The variegated form is miffy. Clip back in early spring.
Sun. Well-drained soil. 90cm/3ft. Z5

Ruta graveolens 'Jackman's Blue'

in the flower border as in the herb garden. It is particularly attractive sprawling over paving. 'Berggarten' is a very fine form with rounded leaves; 'Albiflora' is a good white-flowered form. Generally, I would grow the coloured-leaved forms in preference to the dusty green; the sage scent is just as marked. 'Icterina' has yellow variegation; 'Purpurascens' is purplish; and the less vigorous and more tender 'Tricolor' is splashed white, green and purple. Violet-blue hooded flowers appear in early summer. Clip in spring. It needs a sheltered position.
Sun. Well-drained soil. 90cm/3ft.

SANGUISORBA
Rosaceae

S. minor, salad burnet, has serrated leaves that give off a refreshing scent. It is used in salads and drinks, and has a flavour reminiscent of cucumber. Purple and green flowerheads appear in summer.
Sun. Well-drained soil. 60cm/2ft.

SANTOLINA
Asteraceae

S. chamaecyparissus, cotton lavender, has a pungent scent that appeals to some and not others. But as a foliage plant it is always admired. It makes a mound of silver-grey coral, topped in summer with golden-yellow button flowers. It responds well to clipping and can be used as a low hedge or for knot gardens. There is a dwarf, compact form called *nana* for more intricate work.
Sun. Well-drained soil. 46cm/18in. Z7

S. pinnata* subsp. *neapolitana is a more upright species with lemon-yellow buttons.
30cm/1ft. Z6

***S. rosmarinifolia* subsp. *rosmarinifolia* (*S. virens*, *S. viridis*).** The green-leaved *Santolina* has its attractions too.
46cm/18in.

Santolina chamaecyparissus

SATUREJA

Lamiaceae

***S. douglasii* (*Clinopodium douglasii*)**, yerba buena, is a tender trailing evergreen with small mint-scented leaves and white flowers.
Sun. Well-drained soil. 15cm/6in.

S. hortensis, summer savory, is a half-hardy annual whose small linear leaves have a pungent thyme-like scent. They are used to flavour beans. Whorls of lilac or white flowers are borne in summer. Sow outdoors in spring or grow in pots on the windowsill.
Sun. Well-drained soil. 20cm/8in.

S. montana, winter savory, is a perennial, semi-evergreen shrub and is more commonly grown than *S. hortensis*. It is equally strongly scented and is a useful culinary herb. Lilac flowers appear in summer. Plant with thyme at the front of the border. Sun. Well-drained soil. 38cm/15in.

S. spicigera, creeping savory, has strongly scented leaves and white flowers.
Sun. Well-drained soil. 10cm/4in.

TAGETES

Asteraceae

T. lucida, winter tarragon, is a half-hardy perennial with aniseed-scented leaves.
Sun. Well-drained soil. 60cm/2ft.

TANACETUM

Asteraceae

***T. parthenium* (*Chrysanthemum parthenium*)**, feverfew, is one of the prettiest weeds when bearing its heads of white daisies, but it seeds itself everywhere. The foliage has a pungent scent and used to be used, infused in boiling water, to treat fevers; it is still popular as a treatment for migraine. The golden-leaved form, 'Aureum', and several double-flowered forms, are commonly cultivated.
Sun or light shade. 46cm/18in.

T. vulgare, tansy, has a similar camphor-like scent and is used to make tansy tea. It has elegant leaves but must be sited carefully since it is an errant colonizer. Yellow button flowers are carried in summer. The variety *crispum* has attractive curled leaves.
Sun or light shade. 90cm/3ft.

TEUCRIUM

Lamiaceae

T. chamaedrys, wall germander, is a low-growing shrub whose small oval leaves have a pungent, aromatic scent. Reddish-purple, lipped flowers are borne in late summer. It is often used in knot gardens as an accompaniment to box or as an edging to a formal bed.
Sun. 15–30cm/6–12in.

T. marum has small aromatic grey-green leaves and pink flowers in summer: a handsome edging plant.
Sun. Well-drained soil. 30cm/1ft.

LEFT *Satureja montana* CENTRE *Tagetes lucida* RIGHT *Tanacetum parthenium*

LEFT *Thymus* 'Silver Queen' RIGHT *Thymus serpyllum* 'Pink Chintz'

THYMUS
Lamiaceae

Thymes are an essential part of the scented garden. The prostrate forms can be grown in paving cracks and thyme lawns, where they can be trodden upon; the bushy forms spilling over the edges of paths, where they can be brushed against. All have a familiar thyme aroma but each is subtly different and shaded with other flavours. They can be short-lived, and a summer shearing to encourage youthful vigour and periodic renewal from cuttings may be necessary, especially with upright varieties. All need a sheltered position. Sun. Well-drained soil.

T. **'Bressingham'** has a prostrate habit, grey leaves and pink flowers.

T. caespititius **(*T. azoricus*)** makes a cushion of slender foliage resembling tufts of pine needles. The scent is also of pine, shaded with orange. Pale lilac flowers appear in high summer 2.5–7.5cm/1–3in.

T. **Coccineus Group** has dark leaves and rich purple flowers. 7.5cm/3in.

T. **'Culinary Lemon' (*T. citriodorus* hort.)**, lemon thyme, is a bushy thyme with an aromatic lemon scent. It has green leaves and lilac flowers. There are many popular varieties including 'Aureus', with gold-variegated leaves, and 'Silver Queen', with silver-variegated leaves. Shelter is important for these very desirable plants, but they are unreliable in very cold, wet areas. 23–30cm/9–12in. Z4

T. **'Fragrantissimus'** has white flowers and grey-green leaves scented of orange. 30cm/1ft.

T. herba-barona is a semi-prostrate thyme that is scented of caraway. It has shiny green leaves and rosy-purple flowers at high summer. 5–13cm/2–5in.

T. pseudolanuginosus is not one of the more fragrant thymes but is grown for its woolly grey leaves. 15cm/6in.

T. pulegioides has pink flowers and lemon-scented leaves. 'Bertram Anderson' and 'Aureus' are good golden-leaved selections. 7.5cm/3in.

T. serpyllum, wild or English thyme, provides us with a range of mat-forming thymes for lawns and paving cracks. It has green hairy leaves, with a true thyme scent, and lilac-pink flowers at high summer. Other attractive and desirable forms include var. *albus*, with white flowers; and 'Pink Chintz' with grey-green leaves that are offset by delicately coloured pale pink flowers. 2.5–7.5cm/1–3in.

T. vulgaris, common thyme, has dark green leaves and varies in colour from lilac to rosy purple. 15–20cm/6–8in.

RHS GARDEN ROSEMOOR

‘An annually staged scented feature at RHS Garden Rosemoor is the display of potted freesias and ‘Paperwhite’ narcissi under glass in the Fruit and Vegetable Garden. These are in flower in early spring before space is needed for tomatoes and cucumbers. Scented shrubs are used throughout the grounds, placed where visitors can get close to them. In the colour-themed Spiral Garden, *Philadelphus* ‘Beauclerk’ and *P.* ‘Belle Etoile’ deliver a punch of scent in early summer, while all through the summer season there is a cocktail of fragrance in the two rose gardens. One of these is devoted to old-fashioned shrub roses, accompanied by rambler roses trained along ropes; the other, the Queen Mother’s Rose Garden, is filled with more modern bush roses. In the Winter Garden there is also a good undercurrent of scents, including from *Daphne* such as *D. odora* ‘Aureomarginata’ and *D. bholua* ‘Jacqueline Postill’, which has survived very low temperatures here.’

Jonathan Webster, Curator at RHS Garden Rosemoor

The vine arch in the Potager with the Cottage Garden beyond at RHS Garden Rosemoor, Devon

PLANTING INDOORS, IN SUMMER POTS & IN MILD CLIMATES

Flower scents are especially potent in warm, moist conditions, and the flora of warm temperate and tropical climates is richly endowed. Heavy, exotic scents, fruity and spicy, sometimes cloying and heady, are to be found here in abundance, together with powerful leaf aromas.

Equally memorable are the scents of the drier climates of the Mediterranean, parts of Australia, southern Africa and California. The most typical fragrances are perhaps those of the resinous leaves of conifers and *Eucalyptus*, of the shrubs of the scrubby hillsides and maquis, the dusty heaths, rocky terrains and garigue. But, as in the tropics, there is also an abundance of flower scents. The fragrances are typically lighter or more purely fruity or aromatic than those of warm, humid climates – *Acacia*, *Carpenteria*, *Coronilla* and broom are some of the natural flavours. But gardeners in these regions can draw on plants with heavy, exotic scents from warmer, humid parts of Asia, Africa and South America – jasmines, *Hoya*, *Gardenia* and *Citrus*, for example – to enrich the bouquet.

Gardening in Mallorca over the past eight years, I have had the opportunity to test out many of the plants described in this chapter outdoors. In Britain and much of Europe and North America, most of the scented plants of milder regions have to be protected from the elements. However, some may be tried outside in sheltered spots. In Britain, a sunny wall may suit *Buddleja auriculata*, *Coronilla*, *Euphorbia mellifera*, lemon verbena, *Pittosporum* and *Prostanthera*, and maybe even *Acacia*, *Callistemon*, *Leptospermum* and

Scented *Pelargonium* make a lively summer pairing with fragrant purple heliotrope.

michelias (now grouped under *Magnolia*). An unheated greenhouse will offer an even more favourable microclimate for such plants, while an unheated porch, with a solid roof and glass sides, may provide enough protection for half-hardy rhododendrons and camellias, which can cope with lack of overhead light; I also grow *Jasminum polyanthum* like this in Wales. Other plants require winter heat. Some can be grown as house plants. A sunny windowsill suits scented-leaved *Pelargonium* and fragrant cactus. Where the light is a little less intense, you may be able to grow *Stephanotis*, *Hoya*, *Citrus* and some orchids. *Gardenia*, too, if you are green-fingered: it is one of my very favourite scents, a

Scented *Pelargonium* is grown with variegated *Felicia* and yellow *Helichrysum*, and raised up so its leaves can be rubbed. *Pelargonium* offer an astonishingly wide range of leaf scents, including peppermint, pine, apple, lemon, orange and the familiar rose fragrance, which takes many people back to their grandparents' generation, when every front porch had its geraniums.

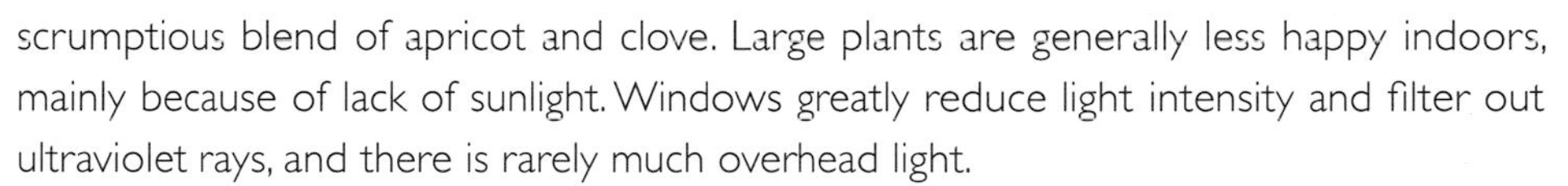

scrumptious blend of apricot and clove. Large plants are generally less happy indoors, mainly because of lack of sunlight. Windows greatly reduce light intensity and filter out ultraviolet rays, and there is rarely much overhead light.

An ideal environment is provided by a greenhouse or conservatory, where lighting, temperature and humidity are all managed for the welfare of the plants. The plants you can grow here are largely determined by the temperature you maintain. Few of us can afford to support a tropical environment throughout the year. What most people want to know is how low a temperature they can get away with and still be able to grow a wide range of plants. The majority of plants described in this list of tender plants will be happy if the temperature is kept above freezing. A minimum winter temperature of 40°F/5°C will just about keep them in growth. But these levels are rather chilly for them, and for us; many winter-flowering plants will be discouraged from blooming, you will have to watch your watering very carefully because plants that fall dormant will need to be kept almost dry, and there will be little incentive for you to linger on cold days. A minimum temperature of around 50°F/10°C is much more comfortable and gives much better results, and since this is the season when you will most appreciate an indoor garden, I would plump for this higher level, if feasible. The temperatures given in the plant portraits are the lowest optimum growing temperatures.

However, many plants can be overwintered in low temperatures under glass and taken outside in pots for the summer. Plants in flower, such as brugmansias, lilies, hedychiums and heliotropes, can be stood around to waft their fragrances, while those with scented leaves, such as lemon verbena (*Aloysia*), *Eucalyptus*, *Prostanthera* and *Salvia*, can be put beside seats for you to tweak.

Winter is the most important season in the glasshouse. Most of the shrubs and climbers inside it will be evergreen so you are assured a backdrop of greenery. Forced hyacinths and narcissi and an array of spring bulbs, such as *Muscari macrocarpum*, will provide good splashes of colour and layers of scent. But there are many other exciting

The bubblegum flavours of *Citrus* flowers combine with the zesty-scented leaves and fruits to make superlative fragrant plants; 'Meyer' lemon is one of the best choices for growing in the house. They are thin-skinned and juicy, and you get a good crop without needing to do any pollination.

flowering plants. The various *Acacia* provide a succession of fluffy yellow flowers through the season and will fill the air with their violet mimosa scent. This contrasts well with the exotic fragrances of jasmine and *Citrus* blossom.

Of all the various *Citrus* trees available, *C.* x *meyeri* 'Meyer' lemon would always be my first choice. It has good flushes of bubblegum-scented white flowers and is a reliable and continual cropper. It is the height of sophistication to be able to reach out and pluck a lemon from your own tree. The scented fruits are thin-skinned and juicy. Fruity flower scents for winter come from all quarters. The slender white panicles of *Buddleja asiatica* possess a superb soft lemon perfume. The pot primula, *P. kewensis*, is also sweet and lemony. And especially rich and strong is the orange fragrance exhaled by the reddish-purple stars of *Daphne odora*. The soapy lemon scent that is released from the leaves of *Eucalyptus citriodora* is not in the same league, but the fruity scents of *Salvia* and *Pelargonium* provide refreshingly sharp complementary flavours.

Daphne odora is not as hardy as its golden-edged form, 'Aureomarginata', and is best grown under glass. Here it will bloom in mid-winter and freely disperse its rich orange scent. The fragrance of all winter-flowering shrubs and climbers is fuller and more easily savoured indoors, and even hardier plants such as *D. bholua* and *Clematis cirrhosa* may be offered hospitality.

As spring gets under way, other fruity scents are released – peach from freesias, lemon from *Boronia megastigma*, and, later, banana from *Magnolia figo* and more peach from yellow *Coronilla*. Some of these overlap with the thick honey scent of *Euphorbia mellifera*.

The white flowers of *Pittosporum tobira* are fragrant of orange blossom, not honey, and are among the blooms you can introduce to maintain a succession of exotic scents through the spring. Bulbous *Pamianthe peruviana* is very desirable and wafts its scent richly in the evening. Tender rhododendrons provide an array of spicy lily scents throughout the season. In Wales, I have them flowering in succession from February to June, and shrubby Natal plum, *Carissa macrocarpa*, is well worth having, in spite of the hint of mothballs in its perfume.

Exotically scented climbers arrive in strength during the summer. *Stephanotis* opens early and continues throughout the season. *Hoya*, wax flower, can deliver an equally clean, sweet scent – *H. lanceolata* subsp. *bella* is particularly good.

More jasmines open during the summer, together with other scented climbers: *Beaumontia*, *Mandevilla*, *Dregea* (*Wattakaka*) and *Trachelospermum*. These are all excellent in cooler temperatures and with delicious, but not overpowering, fragrances. Also, do not overlook the more tender Tea and Noisette climbing roses which produce cascades of scented flowers – 'Belle Portugaise', 'Climbing Columbia', 'Climbing Devoniensis', 'La Folette', 'Maréchal Niel' and 'Sombreuil' chief among them (see Roses, pages 214–47).

Among summer-flowering scented shrubs, brugmansias are probably the most spectacular. Although red spider mites are a problem, a specimen in fine health and full flower is a memorable sight. The sweet scent is superb and especially strong at night.

Lilies and hedychiums are also in full stride. Beside these thick, heavy scents you need some contrasts. The leaf aromas of *Pelargonium* are a source of pleasure all year. Peppermint, apple, orange, lemon, spice and rose are all available. Acid lemon is also offered by *Aloysia citriodora* and pineapple and blackcurrant by *Salvia*.

In autumn comes the apricot scent of *Osmanthus fragrans*. Another favourite of mine for this season is acidanthera, a bulbous plant now assigned to the genus *Gladiolus*. You can flower it outside in a sunny border but a potful on the terrace or indoors is a treat for the nose. The blooms are tropically sweet and waft their fragrance in the evening. Acidantheras are produced in such quantity by the Dutch bulb firms each year that you can treat it as an annual with a clear conscience; it can be difficult to persuade to bloom after its first season.

A more unusual bulb is *Cyrtanthus mackenii*, worth growing for its banana-scented flowers. Its blooming usually coincides with the second crop of flowers on *Coronilla* and the first crop from seed-sown freesias, and this makes a pleasant 'fruit salad' of fragrance. Lemon-scented *Buddleja auriculata* is also in flower now. *Camellia sasanqua* varieties bloom in the autumn and waft a light scent. Heliotropes brought back indoors will continue to exhale their vanilla-like perfume and it is also well worth bringing sweet basil inside, for culinary as well as hedonistic reasons. The scent of a variety like 'Dark Opal' will hang in the air, contributing an undercurrent of spice to complement the sharper flavours.

Trachelospermum jasminoides does well outdoors in warmer regions, but elsewhere is an appealing candidate for growing under glass.

TENDER PLANTS

Note: The temperatures given in this chapter are the minimum required for keeping plants in growth; most will stand 10°F/5°C lower, and some will even tolerate a slight frost.

ACACIA
Mimosaceae

Acacia bloom in winter and spring, and their fluffy heads of round yellow flowers have a distinctive, often strong, violet/pea scent. They succeed as pot plants, and sometimes in sheltered spots outside, but they are vigorous growers and can quickly outgrow their allotted space. They can be hard pruned after flowering. Pots may be plunged outside in a sunny border for the summer. Sun or light shade. Min. temp. 40°F/5°C.

A. baileyana, Cootamunda wattle, is one of the most beautiful half-hardy evergreen trees and has finely-cut, glaucous blue-grey leaves on pendulous branches and bright yellow flowers in spring. 'Purpurea' is a striking purple-flushed variant.
Up to 9m/30ft.

A. dealbata, a florist's mimosa or silver wattle, is a popular species with pinnate leaves in silvery blue-green and very fragrant lemon-yellow flowers in early spring. In mild areas it will succeed outside in a sheltered border or against a sunny wall. I grow it in my garden but one was killed in a very hard winter; fortunately a seedling appeared later in the paving.
Up to 15m/50ft or more.

A. podalyriifolia, Queensland silver wattle, is a lovely shrub with rounded leaves, in silvery blue-green, and long racemes of rich yellow, scented flowers in winter and spring. It is also successful in mild areas against a sunny wall.
3m/10ft.

A. retinodes, wirilda, has a fine sweet scent and often blooms for many months, beginning in late winter. The long, slender leaves are dark green and the flowers are pale yellow. It may also be tried outside in mild areas.
Up to 9m/30ft. Z9–10

ALOYSIA
Verbenaceae

***A. citrodora* (*Lippia citriodora*)**, lemon verbena, has a sharp lemon fragrance that is released by its leaves and it is one of my favourite scents. I grow mine as a pot shrub to be stood outside beside a seat in summer and to be brought in under glass for its winter hibernation. But in mild areas, it can be trusted outside

FAR LEFT *Acacia baileyana*
LEFT *Aloysia citrodora*

LEFT and CENTRE Two colours of *Babiana stricta* RIGHT *Beaumontia grandiflora*

against a sunny wall. It is deciduous, with lance-shaped leaves and panicles of insignificant flowers in summer. Prune in spring. A scented garden should not be without it; it is very effective when grown as a standard.
Sun. Up to 3m/10ft. Min. temp. 40°F/5°C.

BABIANA
Iridaceae

B. stricta, baboon flower, looks rather like a freesia and has a violet scent. It is the most commonly grown of a number of scented *Babiana* species – others including *B. ambigua, B. fragrans* and *B. odorata*. The flowers are borne in short racemes and are accompanied by pleated, sword-shaped leaves. There are many colour forms and hybrids available in shades of purple, yellow and white. The corms, a popular food of baboons in southern Africa, should be potted up – and re-potted annually – in the autumn and kept fairly dry until shoots appear. Plants bloom in late spring.
Sun. 20cm/8in. Min. temp. 40°F/5°C.

BEAUMONTIA
Apocynaceae

B. grandiflora, Herald vine, is a desirable Indian climber for a pot or border in the cool greenhouse. The broad leaves have a glossy surface and a downy underside and the large white flowers, trumpet-shaped but prominently lobed, have an exotic scent. These appear in clusters during the summer. The plant needs to be pruned after flowering.
Sun or light shade. Up to 6m/20ft or more. Min. temp. 40°F/5°C.

BORONIA
Rutaceae

Boronias are Australian evergreen shrubs with fruitily aromatic foliage and often powerfully lemon-scented flowers, which succeed on a sunny windowsill as well as in a conservatory. They may be hard pruned after flowering and their pots plunged outdoors for the summer.
Sun. Min. temp. 40°F/5°C.

B. megastigma has small flowers, solitary and pendent, which appear in profusion among the narrow leaflets in early spring. They are unusually coloured – brown-purple on the outside and mustard yellow within – and waft an irresistible lemon scent. 60cm/2ft.

BOUVARDIA
Rubiaceae

***B. longiflora* (*B. humboldtii*)** is a small, semi-evergreen shrub from Mexico that bears a profusion of exotically scented, tubular white flowers from summer until winter. It needs a warm winter temperature but is otherwise easily grown in the house or conservatory. Plants should be cut back after flowering.
Sun or light shade. Im/3ft. Min. temp. 50°F/10°C.

FAR LEFT *Brugmansia arborea* 'Knightii'
LEFT *Buddleja auriculata*

BRUGMANSIA (DATURA)
Solanaceae

Brugmansias (angel's trumpet) are familiar pot and greenhouse deciduous shrubs which, in spite of their exotic appearance, do not need high temperatures. The huge pendent trumpets, strikingly lobed at the mouth, are often powerfully and sweetly scented, especially at night. They are also poisonous, and inhaling them deeply can have a narcotic effect. Flowers are carried freely throughout summer and early autumn and are accompanied by large leaves. They need plenty of water and feed during the growing season and may be stood outside in the warmer months. They are often grown as standards and pollarded after flowering. They can be cut back to within 15cm/6in of the ground in late winter. Red spider mites can be a serious problem.
Light shade. 3m/10ft or more. Min. temp. 40°F/5°C.
B. arborea and its double form 'Knightii' have very fragrant white flowers, as does *B. suaveolens*, which also has pink and yellow variants. *B.* x *candida* is best known in its variety 'Grand Marnier' which is less scented but has beautiful apricot flowers.

BRUNFELSIA
Solanaceae

B. americana, lady of the night, is, as its name indicates, a night-scented beauty. The large, lobed flowers open pale yellow and fade to white and breathe a spicy-sweet fragrance. Hailing from South America, this leathery-leaved shrub enjoys warmth and humidity but grows happily in a pot and flowers well during the summer. Up to 3m/10ft. Min. temp. 40°F/5°C.
B. pauciflora (B. calycina) is the most common species in cultivation. Its flowers fade from deep violet to pale violet to white over a three-day period giving it the common name of yesterday, today and tomorrow. 60cm/2ft.

BUDDLEJA
Scrophulariaceae

The two evergreen *Buddleja* included below have a fruity and sweet scent, more refined than the honey of their hardy relatives. They succeed under glass in a border or in pots which may be plunged outside for the summer, and can be pruned after flowering.
Sun. 3m/10ft or more. Min. temp. 40°F/5°C.
B. asiatica has long, tapering, grey-green leaves and slender drooping panicles of white flowers, intensely lemon-scented, in late winter and spring. No cool glasshouse should be without it.
B. auriculata is hardier and will succeed outside in many areas against a sunny wall – it grows tall and fast. Mine in Wales is occasionally cut to the ground in very hard winters but always regenerates strongly. Its panicles of creamy flowers, produced in autumn and winter, are less than half as long as those of *B. asiatica*, but broader, and its leaves are also shorter and dark green in colour. The scent is zesty lemon.

CARISSA
Apocynaceae

C. macrocarpa (C. grandiflora), Natal plum, is an attractive evergreen shrub with single, white, jasmine-like flowers. These are exotically sweet-scented but there is a definite hint

of mothballs at close range. They are borne in late spring and are followed by edible red fruits. It has leathery, dark green, oval leaves. 'Nana' is a dwarf, compact form.
Light shade. 4.5m/15ft in the wild; 2m/6ft in a pot. Min. temp. 50°F/10°C.

CEDRONELLA
Lamiaceae

C. canariensis (*C. triphylla*), the false balm of Gilead, has slender ternate leaves which, when bruised, have a pungent aroma of fruit and mint. It carries whorls of white or mauve flowers in summer.
Light shade. 1m/3ft. Min. temp. 40°F/5°C.

CESTRUM
Solanaceae

C. nocturnum, a fast-growing evergreen shrub, is one of the most potently scented plants for mild climate gardens and glasshouses. The clusters of pale green tubular flowers appear in summer and in the evening release a richly honeyed, complex floral fragrance that travels far. It can be hard pruned in spring.
Light shade. 3.5m/12ft. Min temp. 40°F/5°C.

CITRUS
Rutaceae

Citrus give us a treble dose of fragrance. The fruit and leaves are sharply fruity when bruised; the former, of course, being softer and sweeter in flavour when nosed or savoured in the air and when cut open. The white flowers, star-shaped and fleshy, are exotically sweet, with a definite hint of bubblegum. They grow well in pots in the cool conservatory and will fruit if the temperature is sufficiently high; they benefit from being stood outside in a sunny position during the warmest summer months. Plants may be lightly pruned in spring, if necessary. Scale insects can be a problem.
Sun. Min. temp. 40°F/5°C (higher if possible).

C. x *aurantium*, Seville orange, is one of the hardier and more reliable *Citrus* and a handsome foliage plant. It is also exceedingly fragrant in fruit and flower. The rind from its small bitter fruits yields an essential oil, and its large flowers are the source of the perfume, oil of neroli. In addition, its oranges make the best marmalade. 'Bouquet de Fleurs' is a highly fragrant dwarf variety.
Up to 9m/30ft.

C. x *limon*, lemon, has good-sized white flowers opening from purplish buds and makes a handsome shrub. The compact hybrid *C.* x *meyeri* 'Meyer' is the most popular of all *Citrus* for the house or conservatory, being robust, and flowering and fruiting freely. In fact, I rate it as one of the best of all house plants, and have grown it for years; the fruits are thin-skinned and juicy. Among

LEFT *Citrus* x *aurantium* (Sweet Orange Group) 'Valencia Late' RIGHT *Citrus* x *limon* 'Villa Franca'

COSMOS
Asteraceae

C. atrosanguineus has sumptuous, velvet-red flowers, almost black on opening. They are produced in late summer and have the mouthwatering scent of bitter chocolate. Outside the warmer regions, it is best protected with a mulch; alternatively, it may be lifted and stored like a dahlia. Growth begins very late, in spring, and it is easy to presume too soon that your plants have perished.
Sun. 60cm/2ft.

Cosmos atrosanguineus

other lemon varieties, 'Variegata', with cream-variegated leaves and green-streaked lemons and 'Villa Franca', a reliable cropper with large fruits, are also desirable.
3m/10ft.

CLERODENDRUM
Lamiaceae

C. chinense var. *chinense* (*C. fragrans* var. *pleniflorum*) is a deciduous shrub from the Far East with heart-shaped leaves and rounded heads of double white, deliciously sweet shop-scented flowers in summer and autumn. It succeeds as a house plant or in the warm greenhouse and should be cut back hard after flowering. Unfortunately, it is very attractive to red spider mite.
Sun. Up to 2m/6ft. Min. temp. 40°F/5°C.

CLETHRA
Clethraceae

C. arborea, lily of the valley tree, is a small evergreen tree from Madeira that is very handsome when it is carrying its panicles of dangling, bell-shaped flowers, white and piercingly fragrant, in late summer and autumn. The leaves are broadly lanceolate and deep green. It may be pruned after flowering but will need to be renewed occasionally from cuttings.
Light shade. 9m/30ft in the wild. Min. temp. 40°F/5°C.

CORONILLA
Papilionaceae

C. valentina subsp. *glauca* is a popular and first-rate shrub which blooms abundantly in spring and early summer and usually again in the autumn. The pea flowers are golden-yellow, carried in rounded clusters, and have a fruity scent. The evergreen leaves consist of five to seven glaucous blue-green leaflets and are a perfect foil for the flowers. It succeeds outside in milder areas, in sheltered borders or against sunny walls. There is a lovely lemon-yellow form, 'Citrina', and a form with cream-variegated leaves, 'Variegata'.
Sun. 60cm–1.5m/2–5ft. Min. temp. 40°F/5°C.

CRINUM
Amaryllidaceae

C. amoenum has heads of slender white, well-scented flowers with protruding purplish filaments in summer.
Sun or light shade. 46cm/18in.
Min. temp. 40°F/5°C.
C. asiaticum is a large and imposing bulbous plant, with huge bulbs, broad strap-like leaves and clusters

of spidery white flowers in summer. These have a clean sweet scent. It does well for me in moist, fertile soil in Mallorca.
Sun or light shade. 90cm/3ft.
Min. temp. 40°F/5°C.

C. moorei produces heads of large and beautiful, scented pale pink trumpet flowers from the bold foliage in late summer. There is a good white form, *album*.
Sun or light shade. 90cm/3ft.
Min. temp. 40°F/5°C.

CYCLAMEN
Primulaceae

C. persicum is well-known as an autumn-flowering bedding and pot plant, but it can be hard to find strongly scented plants among the hundreds on display in the garden centres. In mild climate gardens or home-grown under glass, it flowers in early spring. In the best forms, the small flowers, with their erect, twisted petals, have an intensely sweet fragrance. They are white, pink or rose-purple and can be stained carmine at the mouth, and are accompanied by patterned foliage. Pot plants should be dried off in late spring and put in a sunny cold frame, which is airy but dry. Only when new growth is observed should they be watered again and, if necessary, re-potted. The large florist's hybrids are scentless.
Sun or shade. 20cm/8in. Min. temp. 40°F/5°C; dislikes very warm conditions.

CYMBOPOGON
Poaceae

These tropical oil grasses are intensely aromatic and the basis of several perfumery oils. *C. citratus* provides lemon-grass oil and is used in Asian cuisine; *C. nardus* gives citronella oil; and *C. martini* is scented of rose and is the source of palmarosa oil.
Sun. 30cm/1ft. Min. temp. 50°F/10°C.

CYRTANTHUS
Amaryllidaceae

C. mackenii is a bulbous plant from southern Africa whose tubular white flowers have a banana-like scent. These are borne in umbels, predominantly in spring or autumn, and are accompanied by strap-shaped leaves. A marsh plant, it needs plenty of water when growing but enjoys some shade and a drier spell during the summer. Cream, red and pink varieties and other sweetly scented *Cyrtanthus* species are also available. 30cm/1ft. Min. temp. 40°F/5°C.

DAPHNE
Thymelaeaceae

D. odora, winter daphne, is less hardy than its more common form 'Aureomarginata', with yellow-edged leaves and, in cold areas, needs the protection of a cool conservatory. Here it is a good evergreen producing its heads of reddish-purple

LEFT *Coronilla valentina* subsp. *glauca* CENTRE *Cyclamen persicum* 'Halios Violet' RIGHT *Cymbogon citratus*

starry flowers in late winter and early spring, and filling the room with its sophisticated orange perfume. It should be put outside for the summer, somewhere that is shaded for the hottest part of the day. There is a white form, *alba*. Sun. 1.5m/5ft. Min. temp. 40°F/5°C. Z7

DATURA
Solanaceae
D. inoxia (*D. meteloides*) is a tuberous-rooted perennial usually grown as a half-hardy annual; it comes easily from seed. It makes an excellent summer container plant. Its large white, pink or lavender trumpets are intensely and sweetly fragrant in the evening, and they are set off by grey, fetid-smelling leaves. The double form, bicoloured in white and rich purple, is arresting. Sun. 60cm/2ft. Min. temp. 40°F/5°C.

DIANTHUS
Caryophyllaceae
D. caryophyllus, carnation. The florist's carnations are very popular specialist greenhouse plants. Many of the more colourful, streaked and striped varieties are deficient in scent but others, notably white 'Fragrant Ann', are well endowed with clove perfume and are worthy of any buttonhole. Flowering time is determined by the pinching out of the sub-lateral shoots; plants whose young growths are pinched out in summer will have their flowering delayed until winter. The summer-flowering border carnations, though hardy, also succeed in pots indoors; see Alpines.
Sun. 1–1.5m/3–5ft. Min. temp. 45°F/7°C.

DIOSMA
Rutaceae
D. ericoides, breath of heaven, is an evergreen shrub from southern Africa whose needle-like foliage is pungently aromatic and whose small white flowers, borne in late winter, are honey-scented.
Sun. Neutral or acid soil. 60cm/2ft. Min. temp. 40°F/5°C.

Dianthus caryophyllus 'Coquette'

DREGEA
Apocynaceae
D. sinensis (*Wattakaka sinensis*) is a desirable evergreen climber for the conservatory, bearing pendent umbels of white starry flowers during the summer. These are delicately streaked with pink and have a honey-sweet scent. Interesting seed-pods sometimes follow. In mild areas, it may be tried outdoors, against a sunny wall. Sun. 3m/10ft. Min. temp. 40°F/5°C.

ECHINOPSIS
Cactaceae
E. candicans is one of several commonly grown species of torch cactus which have scented nocturnal flowers. The flowers are white and borne in summer, and the perfume

FAR LEFT *Datura inoxia* 'Evening Fragrance'
LEFT *Dregea sinensis*

LEFT *Diosma ericoides* RIGHT *Elettaria cardamomum*

is intense and exotic. It is an easily grown plant, columnar in shape.
Sun. 1m/3ft. Min. temp. 50°F/10°C.

E. oxygona, Easter lily cactus, is a South American spiny cactus of spherical shape, which has large, blush pink, white, petal-packed flowers. These last only a short time but they have a light sweet scent and are very beautiful. *E. ancistrophora* is also white and scented, and there are a number of scented *Echinopsis* hybrids mostly in shades of pink, red and mauve.
Sun. 10cm/4in. Well-drained soil. Min. temp. 40°F/5°C but very cold hardy if dry.

E. spachiana is a taller columnar torch cactus, with blush-pink, white nocturnal flowers with a sweet scent.
Sun. 90cm/3ft or more. Min. temp. 40°F/5°C.

ELETTARIA

Zingiberaceae

E. cardamomum, cardamom, is a perennial member of the ginger family, and its broad spear-shaped evergreen leaves have a warm spicy scent. The dried seeds are used in Asian cuisine. It needs hot humid conditions to do well, and is not often encountered in the UK.
Sun or light shade. Up to 3.5m/12ft. Min. temp. 50°F/10°C.

EPIPHYLLUM

Cactaceae

E. anguliger, fishbone cactus. This sweetly scented bushy epiphytic cactus with slender, indented, leaf-like stems is a reliable bloomer and quite stunning when carrying its huge creamy flowers in late summer. It must not be over-watered but is not as adapted to drought as other cacti. It will succeed in the house on a windowsill.
Sun or light shade. Up to 1m/3ft. Min. temp. 50°F/10°C.

E. oxypetalum, Dutchman's pipe cactus, is an easily grown epiphytic cactus of tall scandent habit, which has scented and striking white, nocturnal flowers in succession during the summer.
Sun or light shade. 3m/10ft or more. Min. temp. 40°F/5°C.

EUCALYPTUS

Myrtaceae

E. citriodora, lemon-scented gum, is a very tender *Eucalyptus* and, although it may be stood outside for the summer, it requires frost protection in winter. The long leaves, hairy in the juvenile stage and becoming smooth in the adult, are scented of lemon; the fragrance is too soapy for me, but others love it. It makes a good evergreen conservatory shrub and may be pollarded in spring to keep it short.
Sun. 2m/6ft or more; 45m/150ft in the wild. Min. temp. 40°F/5°C

EUCHARIS

Amaryllidaceae

E. amazonica, Amazon lily, is a

GARDENIA
Rubiaceae

G. jasminoides, Cape jasmine. *Gardenia* is one of the best known house and greenhouse plants and has one of the best-loved fragrances – spicily clove-like with the flavour of sun-ripened apricots. It sells on sight and on smell in garden centres, but needs ample warmth and humidity to perform well and often proves unreliable. It does much better in hot climates, thriving outdoors as a summer pot plant in the Mediterranean and United States. It makes an attractive glossy-leaved evergreen shrub which may be cut back after flowering. The double white blooms are borne in summer and autumn. 'Kleim's Hardy' is a dwarf single-flowered form.
Light shade. Acid or neutral soil. Up to 1.5m/5ft. Min. temp. 50°F/10°C.

Gardenia jasminoides

bulbous plant that requires warmth and humidity to give of its best but makes a good pot subject for the house or warm conservatory. The white flowers, which are carried in umbels on stout stems and resemble nodding daffodils, are exotically scented and are accompanied by broad, strap-like, evergreen leaves. It likes humus-rich soil and plenty of water both during and after flowering. Light shade. 60cm/2ft. Min. temp. 60°F/15°C.

FREESIA
Iridaceae

Freesias are most familiar as cut flowers but because it is the modern hybrids, with their bright and varied colour range, that are usually offered, their fragrance is often disappointing. By growing your own corms in pots, you can choose from among the small-flowered species and larger-flowered varieties to ensure that you get a good dose of that rich fruity peppery scent, and the flowers last much longer than those on cut stems. *F. alba,* which is white with yellow and purple markings, and *F. caryophyllacea*, which has cream and yellow flowers, are particularly well-scented and do well in pots. Among the named hybrids, 'White Swan', in creamy white, 'Yellow River', in canary yellow, and 'Romany', a mauve double, have a good fragrance. Corms should be planted in autumn and will bloom in winter or spring; they should be dried off after the leaves have faded. They are easily grown bulbs in Mediterranean gardens. Sun. 30cm/1ft. Min. temp. 50°F/10°C.

LEFT *Eucharis amazonica* RIGHT *Freesia fergusoniae*

GELSEMIUM

Gelsemiaceae

G. sempervirens, Carolina jessamine, is a popular climber in Carolina, where I have seen it used to cover porches and telegraph poles, but I have never encountered it in Britain outside a conservatory. It is an attractive plant with clusters of golden-yellow, funnel-shaped flowers in spring and early summer. These are sweetly violet-scented but not as rich in fragrance as jasmine. There is a double form, 'Flore Pleno'.

Sun or light shade. 4.5m/15ft. Min. temp. 40°F/5°C. Z8

GENISTA

Papilionaceae

G. x spachiana (Cytisus x spachiana) has sweetly scented yellow pea-flowers borne in slender racemes during winter and spring, and is a cheerful pot plant for the house or conservatory. It makes a large evergreen shrub but may be trimmed after flowering. It is susceptible to red spider mite.

Sun. Up to 3m/10ft. Min. temp. 40°F/5°C.

GLADIOLUS

Iridaceae

G. murielae (G. callianthus). This gladiolus is produced by Dutch bulb growers by the thousand each year and is offered by nearly every garden centre. Corms should be planted in spring, 10cm/4in apart and 10cm/4in deep, in pots. These may be placed outside during the summer and as the flowers begin to open in the autumn, some may be brought back indoors. They may also succeed in sunny borders. The white blooms are striking with their pointed petals and maroon blotch, and the scent from them is exotically sweet and especially powerful in the evening. Corms should be dried off after the foliage has faded; those growing in outside borders should be lifted and stored in a warm place. They can be difficult to persuade to flower again This is an indispensable plant for the scent-conscious gardener.

Sun. Im/3ft. Min. temp. 40°F/5°C.

Other highly scented but less commonly grown gladiolus species include violet *G. carinatus* and coppery *G. liliaceus*.

G. tristis is a far cry from the blowsy florist's gladioli and can be tried outside in the warmer regions; otherwise, it should be grown in a pot in a cold greenhouse. The large cream flowers, marked in green and maroon, are borne in spring among the slender leaves and have a glorious sweet, spicy, honeyed scent, which is particularly strong at night. 'Christabel', in deeper yellow, is a fine hybrid.

Full sun. Fertile, well-drained soil. 46cm/18in.

LEFT *Hoya carnosa* RIGHT *Hoya lanceolata* subsp. *bella*

HEDYCHIUM
Zingiberaceae

Ginger lilies are spectacular rhizomatous perennials that may be tried in sheltered, sunny borders outside in the mildest areas, but are usually grown in pots in the greenhouse or for standing on terraces in the summer. The scent from their flowerheads is appropriately exotic and heady. The blooms are borne on stout stems and accompanied by paddle-shaped leaves. They enjoy rich, moist soil and their rhizomes should be only lightly covered with soil.

H. coronarium, white ginger lily, bears heads of large, powerfully and fruitily fragrant (apricot to my nose), white flowers with yellow blotches in late summer. It requires warmer conditions than other species.
Sun. 2m/6ft. Min. temp. 50°F/10°C.

H. densiflorum has long spikes of coral-coloured flowers, with protruding red filaments, in late summer. 'Stephen' is a superior selection.
Sun. 2m/6ft or more. Min. temp. 40°F/5°C.

H. gardnerianum, Kahili ginger, is the most common and, in my view, loveliest ginger lily. The flowers, produced in late summer, are lemon-yellow with protruding red filaments and are beautifully partnered with blue-green leaves. The scent is spicily sweet, reminiscent of *Viburnum*, with a mothball-scented undertone.
Sun. 2m/6ft. Min. temp. 40°F/5°C.

H. villosum* var. *tenuifolium is an attractive short ginger for a pot, producing sweetly scented white flowers from purplish buds in late summer.
Sun. 60cm/2ft. Min. temp. 40°F/5°C.

H. yunnanense is a handsome ginger with very fragrant white flowers and protruding orange stamens.
Sun. 90cm/3ft. Min. temp 40°F/5°C.

HELIOTROPIUM
Boraginaceae

H. arborescens, heliotrope or cherry pie. The shrubby and standard purple heliotropes of the Victorian garden, which have to be propagated by cuttings and overwintered in warmth, have been largely replaced today by seed-raised annuals like 'Marine'. But for strength of perfume, you have to go back to the old cultivars, like 'Mrs J.W. Lowther', 'Chatsworth', and dark purple 'Princess Marina'. These waft their vanilla fragrance freely, and make fine conservatory pot plants which can be stood outside for the summer or planted in borders to be lifted and repotted (or propagated) in the autumn. In warmth, they will bloom all year.
Sun. 1m/3ft or more. Min. temp. 40°F/5°C.

HOYA
Apocynaceae

Hoya, wax flower, give us a range of scented evergreen climbers and shrubs for the warm conservatory. They do well as house plants. They have fleshy leaves and pendent umbels of thick-petalled, waxy flowers in summer, which can have a sweet or less sweet fragrance. They may be cut back after flowering if necessary. They like a humus-rich, acid soil and a moist atmosphere, and the climbers grow best in a conservatory border against a wall. Among the more obscure species with a very good scent are *H. lacunosa*, a cascading plant with small white flowers, and *H. nummularioides*, whose flowers have a prominent pink centre.

H. australis is a climber with exotically fragrant white or blush-pink flowers with reddish markings. Light shade. 4.5m/15ft. Min. temp. 60°F/15°C.

H. carnosa, common wax flower, is an elegant climber with white, pink-centred flowers. It has a pleasant but rather meaty scent, particularly pronounced in the evening. There are several variants available. Light shade. 6m/20ft. Min. temp. 50°F/10°C.

H. lanceolata* subsp. *bella is an epiphytic shrub which succeeds best cascading from a hanging basket. I have it in the house hanging down a hi-fi speaker. The sweetly honey-scented flowers are white with pinkish centres, and produced in small clusters. Light shade. 46cm/18in. Min. temp. 60°F/15°C.

HYMENOCALLIS
Amaryllidaceae

Spider lilies are bulbous South American plants, closely related to pancratiums, with flowers that resemble spidery daffodils or small tentacled jellyfish. These are honey-scented, mainly nocturnally and sometimes spicily, and appear in umbels above the strap-like leaves in summer. Grow the deciduous varieties in a light soil and keep them dry in winter. Sun. 60cm/2ft. Min. temp. 50°F/10°C; 60°F/15°C for evergreen varieties.

***H.* x *festalis* (*Ismene* x *festalis*)** is deciduous with fragrant white flowers.

H.* x *macrostephana is a fine white-flowered hybrid between two highly scented species, *H. narcissiflora* and *H. speciosa*. Being almost evergreen, it appreciates some extra warmth and moisture in the winter.

***H. narcissiflora* (*Ismene calathina*)**, the Peruvian daffodil, is a deciduous species with very fragrant white flowers.

H. speciosa is evergreen with greenish-white flowers and needs extra warmth and moisture in winter.

HYMENOSPORUM
Pittosporaceae

H. flavum, Australian frangipani, is an evergreen shrub or tree with shiny oval leaves and panicles of exotically

LEFT *Hedychium densiflorum* 'Stephen' CENTRE *Heliotropium arborescens* 'Lord Roberts' RIGHT *Hymenocallis* x *macrostephana*

scented tubular flowers in late spring. These open cream-coloured and turn a rich yellow. It does well for me in Mallorca in the part shade of a wild olive tree.
Sun. 3m/10ft or more. Min. temp. 40°F/5°C.

JASMINUM
Oleaceae

No conservatory or greenhouse should be without the scents of a jasmine. If the heady fragrances of royal, common or pot jasmine are too much for you in an enclosed space, then you could try the sweeter, bubblegum-flavoured *J. azoricum* and *J. sambac,* or the finely perfumed Australian *J. suavissimum;* these are all less vigorous than *J. officinale* and *J. polyanthum*. The conservatory jasmines are mainly evergreen climbers, excellent for clothing pillars and rafters. By careful selection of varieties, you can have flowers in every season. They should be pruned and thinned lightly after flowering, as flowers are borne on new growths. They succeed best when their roots are slightly restricted, so transfer them into bigger sizes of pot only very gradually. All the species below do well for me in Mallorca. Sun or light shade.

J. angulare is a species from southern Africa with fairly large, fragrant white flowers. 3m/10ft. Min. temp. 40°F/5°C.

J. azoricum has white flowers with a clean, citrus-flavoured jasmine scent. It is in bloom almost continually in summer and autumn.
3m/10ft. Min. temp. 40°F/5°C.

***J. grandiflorum* 'De Grasse'** has large, strongly scented white flowers and is the famous jasmine of the perfume industry. It is a good pot jasmine for the greenhouse, flowering in autumn and winter.
3m/10ft. Min. temp. 40°F/5°C.

J. laurifolium* f. *nitidum, windmill jasmine, has spidery white flowers from purplish buds and blooms mainly in summer.
3m/10ft. Min. temp. 40°F/5°C.

J. polyanthum, Chinese or pot jasmine, is the familiar garden centre jasmine with heavily scented white flowers, from reddish buds, in winter and spring. It can be grown outside in mild areas, and will do well indoors in a cool, shady spot with minimal frost protection.
3m/10ft. Min. temp. 40°F/5°C.

J. sambac, Arabian jasmine, is the species used for scenting tea. It has distinctively broad leaves, and bears its large white flowers almost continuously, even through the winter if the temperature is high enough. 'Grand Duke of Tuscany' is a curious double-flowered form.
3m/10ft. Min. temp. 50°F/10°C.

LEPTOSPERMUM
Myrtaceae

L. scoparium, manuka or New Zealand tea tree, is a small evergreen

LEFT *Jasminum azoricum* CENTRE *Leptospermum scoparium* 'Red Damask' RIGHT *Lilium speciosum*

RIGHT *Luculia gratissima* 'Rosea'
FAR RIGHT *Magnolia doltsopa*

shrub with slender, pointed leaves that are aromatic when bruised. It has become popular with gardeners in the milder areas where it may be grown outside. It gives an attractive show of white flowers in late spring; there are many colour variants in shades of pink and red. They make compact plants, and the dwarf forms will succeed on a sunny windowsill. Sun. 2m/6ft or more. Min. temp. 40°F/5°C.

LILIUM
Liliaceae
Most lilies do well in pots and many of the scented hardy species, like *L. regale* and *L. auratum*, are a pleasure to have indoors and will bloom earlier than those outside. But here I have listed only those lilies that grow particularly well in pot culture. Sun or light shade. Well-drained, humus-rich soil. Min. temp. 40°F/5°C.
L. formosanum is an exquisite white lily. The large trumpet flowers, purple-flushed on the outside, have a sweet scent. It is short-lived and prone to virus but is easily raised from seed, flowering in its first year. 1.2m/4ft.
L. longiflorum is the florist's Easter lily. The long, pure white, fragrant trumpets open during the summer, but may be forced for spring. It is also easily raised from seed, usually flowering in its second year. Lime-tolerant. 1m/3ft.
L. speciosum is an intoxicatingly scented lily with recurved flowers, almost like the turk's cap lily which is so popular with florists. The thick white flowers are usually shaded and spotted with carmine or crimson and there are numerous colour forms. The variety *rubrum* is a rich carmine and exceptionally beautiful. It blooms in late summer but is easily forced.
1.2–2m/4–6ft.

LUCULIA
Rubiaceae
Luculias are evergreen shrubs with powerfully fragrant tubular flowers and are extremely attractive shrubs for the warm conservatory. They enjoy plenty of water when in growth and may be cut back after flowering.
Sun or light shade. Min. temp. 50°F/10°C.
L. grandifolia is a very handsome shrub or tree with oval, red-veined leaves and large clusters of white flowers in summer. 2m/6ft or more.
L. gratissima carries its large clusters of exotically sweet, light rose pink flowers in late autumn and winter. 1–2m/3–6ft or more.

MAGNOLIA (MICHELIA)
Magnoliaceae
M. doltsopa, an evergreen tree with long leathery leaves, has cream flowers in spring which are strongly and fruitily scented. It is a highly desirable plant for milder gardens, including in the UK where it will take light frost. It needs an acid or neutral soil.
Sun or light shade. 9m/30ft or more. Min. temp. 40°F/5°C.
M. figo is described in W. J. Bean's *Trees and Shrubs* as one of the most scented of all shrubs. The flowers exhale the fruity fragrance of bananas or pear-drops and a few flowers will scent an entire room. It will succeed outside in the mildest areas, but makes a good pot plant for a glasshouse. It is a slow-growing bushy evergreen with glossy leaves, and the small creamy yellow flowers, flushed with purple,

LEFT *Mandevilla laxa* RIGHT *Nymphaea capensis*

appear in succession during spring and early summer. It needs an acid or neutral soil.
Sun or light shade. 3m/10ft or more. Min. temp. 40°F/5°C.

MANDEVILLA
Apocynaceae
M. laxa (*M. suaveolens*), Chilean jasmine, is a popular and highly desirable deciduous climber for growing under glass. The white flowers are jasmine-like but very large and possess a clean sweet scent like *Gladiolus murielae*. They are produced in clusters among the heart-shaped leaves during the summer. The plant prefers a border or large tub to a pot and may be lightly pruned in spring. The popular bright pink *Mandevilla* × *amabilis* 'Alice du Pont' is unscented. Light shade. 3m/10ft or more. Min. temp. 40°F/5°C.

MILLETTIA
Papilionaceae
M. reticulata (*M. satsuma*) is an attractive evergreen climber in the pea family. Its grape-like clusters of rich reddish-purple flowers appear over a long period in summer and have a good honeyed scent.
Sun or light shade. 4.5m/15ft or more. Min. temp. 40°F/5°C.

NYMPHAEA
Nymphaeaceae
Many tropical waterlilies have rich fruity scents. They need warmth – a water temperature of 70°F/20°C – but are otherwise easy to grow in baskets in a conservatory pool or in water-filled tubs. In early autumn the baskets are lifted out of the water and the tubers stored in moist sand at 55°F/12°C. Blue waterlily (*N. capensis*), pink-flowered 'General Pershing' and blue-flowered *N. stellata* are scented day-blooming waterlilies; *N. caerulea* is fragrant at night.

ORCHIDS
A visit to an orchid house can be an intoxicating experience. Fruity, flowery, spicy and heady – all the exotic scents are here. But this is, in the main, a specialist's world, in which temperature, humidity and ventilation must be carefully controlled. There is no space here to go into the intricacies of cultivation or to sample more than a fraction of the many thousands of species and hybrids in existence but I am at least able to provide a glimpse through the misted glass; I should warn, however, that the scents seem to vary within species as much as flower colour, and my descriptions may not tally with plants you are sniffing.
The majority of cultivated orchids are epiphytic, that is to say, they grow naturally on branches and rocks, storing moisture in swollen stems known as pseudobulbs. Under glass they require special soil-free compost which is fibrous and free-draining.

LEFT Orchid *Vanda tricolor* CENTRE *Osmanthus fragrans* RIGHT *Pamianthe peruviana*

Pendent varieties are best grown in hanging baskets or suspended rafts or in mossy nests attached to cut tree and shrub branches (rhododendron and hawthorn wood is particularly good). Erect-growing epiphytic varieties and terrestrial orchids can be cultivated in clay pots. In summer they need shade from strong sunshine, plenty of water and a daily misting; in winter they need less water, unless still in growth, and some appreciate a fairly dry rest period. A minimum winter night temperature of 60°F/15°C and a maximum summer day temperature of 80°F/25°C suit most. There are a great many powerfully and sweetly scented species and hybrids among the *Cattleya* orchids – *C. velutina*, hyacinth-scented *C. labiata* and gardenia-scented *C. loddigesii* are notable – and among the *Coelogyne* orchids, including *C. cristata*, *C. nitida* and *C. pandurata*. Many of the cymbidiums smell deliciously fruity, often of apricots – *C. eburneum* and *C. tracyanum* are particularly good. Spicy scents are often encountered among the *Lycaste* orchids, such as *L. aromatica* and *L. cruenta*, and among the *Epidendrum* orchids, including *E. anisatum* and *E. nocturnum*.

Sweet and spicy scents are found in the *Encyclia* orchids (*E. alata*, *E. citrina* and *E. fragrans*); *Dendrobium* and *Bulbophyllum* orchids are also likely to be either spicy or sweet – *Dendrobium heterocarpum*, *D. nobile*, *D. moschatum* and *Bulbophyllum lobbii* are notable – but many are very nasty indeed. *B. caryanum*, for example, smells of rotting fish.

There are also a host of scented varieties among the *Angraecum* (*A. eburneum*, *A. sesquipedale*), *Maxillaria* (*M. picta*, *M. venusta*), *Odontoglossum* (*O. pulchellum*), *Oncidium* (*O. ornithorrhynchum*), *Vanda* (*V. parishii* – now correctly *Vandopsis parishii* – *V. tricolor*) and *Stanhopea* orchids (*S. tigrina* smells of vanilla).

OSMANTHUS
Oleaceae

O. fragrans is an Asian shrub with evergreen leaves and bearing clusters of tiny, pale yellow flowers. These have a delicious apricot scent. I have seen it growing outside in gardens in southern and western USA, but in the UK it is not considered very hardy. I have it in the greenhouse where it is a trouble-free pot plant, flowering in the autumn. I also grow the form *aurantiacus*, whose flowers are soft orange in colour.

Sun or light shade. 3m/10ft. 40°F/5°C.

PAMIANTHE
Amaryllidaceae

P. peruviana is an evergreen bulbous plant much prized for its large, exotically scented white flowers. These have spreading petals and green stripes and the fragrance is especially powerful in the evening. Although it requires less water in winter than in summer, bulbs

LEFT *Passiflora alata* CENTRE *Pelargonium* 'Rose' RIGHT *Pittosporum tobira*

should not be allowed to dry out completely. It blooms in late winter or early spring.
Part shade. Rich, well-drained soil. 60cm/2ft. Min. temp. 55°F/12°C

PANCRATIUM
Amaryllidaceae
The two Mediterranean bulbous plants described below, both powerfully sweet-scented and with fairly erect, slightly glaucous leaves, can be tried outside at the base of a sunny wall in the mildest areas. But they do well in pots under glass, appreciating a dry, summer baking; they should be fed and watered regularly through the winter. Plant 15cm/6in deep in well-drained soil. Sun. Min. temp. 40°F/5°C.
P. illyricum is the more reliable species. It bears its umbels of starry white flowers in early summer. 46cm/18in.
P. maritimum, sea lily, bears its wispier white flowers in late summer and has narrow, evergreen leaves. 30cm/1ft.

PASSIFLORA
Passifloraceae
P. alata is one of the glasshouse passionflower species with a good sweet scent. A vigorous climber, flowering over a long summer period, it has crimson-red flowers with a jellyfish-like centre of wavy purple, red and white filaments. *P* x *belotii* is a richly scented hybrid with pink flowers and violet filaments. Sun or light shade. 4.5m/15ft. 40°F/5°C.
P. incarnata is a wonderful well-scented passionflower with lavender-purple jellyfish-like flowers. Native to North America, it is a herbaceous climber, dying back each winter, and therefore worth trying outside in milder areas of the UK. Its rich purple hybrid 'Incense', also fragrant and quite hardy, is taller and very free-flowering. Sun or light shade. 2m/6ft. Min. temp. 40°F/5°C.

PELARGONIUM
Geraniaceae
The familiar pot geraniums of windowsills, balconies, terraces and bedded summer borders all have some degree of scent. The distinctive 'rose-geranium' fragrance is, however, usually much more evident in soft-leaved zonal *Pelargonium* than in the smooth and leathery-leaved regal and ivy-leaved hybrids. There are dozens of varieties available, far too many to list here, and selection has to be by the colour and pattern of flowers and leaves. But there are *Pelargonium* hybrids and species with strong scents and with scents that vary greatly from the rosy norm. Indeed, the group provides a wider range of leaf scents than any other I know, including *Salvia*. They are usually less showy in flower, but you cannot have everything. All are easy to grow, if they are given well-drained soil and they are not over-watered, and they are usually very tolerant of neglect.

POLIANTHES
Agavaceae

P. tuberosa, tuberose, is a tender perennial with a legendary scent. The white funnel-shaped flowers are intensely and exotically fragrant, laced with coconut, and are carried in erect racemes in summer and autumn. It needs plenty of water when in growth; it should be dried off and stored in sand, like a dahlia, in winter and started into growth again in late winter. The double-flowered form, 'The Pearl', is grown more often and is even more strongly scented.
Sun. Well-drained soil. 60cm/2ft. 60°F/15°C.

Polianthes tuberosa

Keep them fairly dry in winter.
Sun. 30–90cm/1–3ft or more. Min. temp. 40°F/5°C.
Among the downy-leaved *Pelargonium*, *P. tomentosum* and the brown-blotched *P.* 'Chocolate Peppermint' smell of peppermint; the dwarf Fragrans Group smells of nutmeg or pine, and *P. odoratissimum* of apple. *P. abrotanifolium*, with finely-cut leaves, has a fragrance reminiscent of southernwood, *Artemisia abrotanum*. Silver-variegated 'Lady Plymouth' smells of mint.
P. crispum 'Major' (Prince Rupert geranium), *P.* 'Citronella', and *P.* 'Mabel Grey' have leaves scented of lemon; *P.* 'Prince of Orange', of orange.
P. graveolens and *P.* 'Attar of Roses' smell of roses; *P. denticulatum* of balsam and lilac; 'Clorinda' smells of cedar; and *P. quercifolium* is pungently spice-scented.
P. triste and *P. gibbosum* have flowers that are sweetly scented in the evening; these tuberous and gouty species must be kept completely dry in winter.

PITTOSPORUM
Pittosporaceae

Pittosporums can be badly knocked in hard winters. They are excellent tub plants, with attractive evergreen foliage, and the fragrance from their flowers is especially heavy under glass.
Sun. Min. temp. 40°F/5°C.
P. tobira, Japanese pittosporum, blooms in spring. The flowers are large and creamy white and carried in conspicuous umbels; and the scent is the sweet bubblegum scent of orange blossom. The foliage is

quite broad and round and there is a lovely form with white margins to the leaves called 'Variegatum'.
Up to 3m/10ft or more. Z8

PLECTRANTHUS
Lamiaceae
***P. madagascariensis* 'Variegated Mintleaf'** is a trailing evergreen sub-shrub used as an ornamental colonizing groundcover in mild climates. The white-edged, nettle-like leaves have a minty scent. The flowers are white.
Sun or light shade. 15cm/6in. Min. temp. 40°F/5°C.

PLUMERIA
Apocynaceae
P. rubra, frangipani, is one of the trees which scents the evening breeze in the tropics. It is an exotic, fruity scent which comes from the clusters of funnel-shaped flowers. These can be any colour, from white and yellow to orange and pink, and are borne throughout the summer. They are accompanied by large, paddle-shaped leaves. The tree hails from Central America – where I was amazed to see it roasted, dry and wind-battered growing wild on coastal rocks – but has been widely planted wherever it will thrive, and given moisture it becomes luxuriant. In cold climates it needs a warm conservatory and should be kept almost dry in winter when it is without leaves. The form *acutifolia* has large white flowers with a prominent yellow eye.
Sun. 3m/10ft or more. Min. temp. 50°F/10°C.

PRIMULA
Primulaceae
P. kewensis used to be a popular golden yellow primula for brightening up glasshouses in winter and spring. The scent from the whorls of flowers is very sweetly flavoured with lemon. It is easily grown and comes readily from seed sown in spring or summer.
Light shade. 30cm/1ft. Min. temp. 50°F/10°C.

PROSTANTHERA
Lamiaceae
These evergreen shrubs, known as mint bush, have small, strongly aromatic leaves and showy flowers, also scented, in late spring or early summer. Their common name is deceptive since the foliage of some species does not smell of mint. They are worth trying outside in very mild areas, against a sunny wall, but they make good pot shrubs in the conservatory.
Sun. Min. temp. 40°F/5°C.
P. cuneata is a small spreading shrub whose dark leaves are powerfully scented of wintergreen or plasticine. The lipped flowers are mauve-white with purple markings. It is moderately hardy outside.
60cm/2ft.
P. melissifolia is strongly mint-scented and the clusters of violet flowers are eyecatching. Up to 3m/10ft.
P. ovalifolia has leaves scented of wintergreen or plasticine and has short racemes of mauve-purple flowers. Up to 3m/10ft.
P. rotundifolia has mint-scented oval leaves and short racemes of violet-blue flowers. Up to 3m/10ft.

QUISQUALIS
Combretaceae
Q. indica, Rangoon creeper, is a fast-growing creeper for the glasshouse rafters. It bears small fragrant flowers all summer that are white when they open in the evening and turn to pink, red or orange.

FAR LEFT *Plumeria rubra*
LEFT *Primula kewensis*

LEFT *Prostanthera cuneata* RIGHT *Rhododendron* 'Fragrantissimum'

Sun or part shade. 4.5m/15ft or more. Min. temp. 50°F/10°C

RHODODENDRON

Ericaceae

Many of the most powerfully scented rhododendrons are from warmer temperate climates and need some winter protection in colder areas; they can be grown outside in the milder regions of the United Kingdom. They make excellent container plants for the shadier parts of the cool conservatory and for porches that may have no overhead light and little heating. Many of these rhododendrons are epiphytic and of gawky habit, but they can be pruned and shaped after flowering. Rhododendrons can also be grown against walls or posts. They need acid soil. The flowers are usually white and spicily lily-scented and mostly produced in spring. They are all very beautiful, and I cannot resist collecting them.

Light shade. 2m/6ft or more. Min. temp. 40°F/5°C.

R. edgworthii is a distinctive species with thick, felted, grey-green, deeply veined leaves and large white flowers, flushed pink. It has a superb lily fragrance. Hybrids crossed with *R. ciliatum* are sometimes available, and should be seized upon, as they produce scented plants that flower indoors in late winter.

R. formosum* var. *inaequale has large white, yellow-blotched flowers on a short plant.

R. lindleyi has distinctive, large white trumpet flowers and, to my nose, a lighter scent than others.

R. maddenii* subsp. *crassum flowers later than its cousins, at midsummer, and makes a larger, more robust shrub. My form is not well scented but other clones of it are better. *R. m.* subsp. *maddenii* Polyandrum Group has flowers with pink buds, yellow throats and a cream flush.

Scented Hybrids

'Countess of Haddington' frequently has a pink flush to its white trumpet flowers and a note of liquorice in its scent. 'Lady Alice Fitzwilliam' and 'Fragrantissimum' are the best known scented tender rhododendrons, both with white flowers and an outstanding lily fragrance; the former is more compact in habit with better mid-green foliage, the latter has perhaps the stronger scent. 'Sesterianum' is similar to 'Fragrantissimum' but produces pinker buds – it is a superb plant. 'Logan Early' is rare but a wonderful April shrub with big white, gloriously scented flowers. 'Jim Russell' has frilly edges to its white, pink-flushed flowers.

Vireya Rhododendrons

These need frost-free conditions. In this tribe are numerous species and hybrids in an array of colours including vibrant reds

LEFT *Salvia confertiflora* CENTRE *Salvia discolor* RIGHT *Salvia elegans* 'Scarlet Pineapple'

and oranges. Many of them are scented. *R. jasminiflorum*, with long tubular white flowers, is one of the best. *R. polyanthemum* is a scented orange-flowered species. Among the hybrids, cream 'Moonwood' is very handsome.

SALVIA
Lamiaceae

Many of the shrubby *Salvia* have scented leaves and among them *S. discolor* and *S. elegans* are my favourite; indeed, they are among my favourite of all leaf scents. They also have striking flowers. Both make sub-shrubby pot plants of manageable size that can be stood outside, beside seats, for the summer or even planted in the border. Propagation is by cuttings, but *S. elegans* is the more amenable and will even root in a glass of water.
Sun. Min. temp. 40°F/5°C.

S. clevelandii **'Winnifred Gilman'** is a good form of shrubby Jim sage, with strongly aromatic grey-green leaves and whorls of violet-blue flowers in summer.
60cm/2ft.

S. confertiflora is an eyecatching plant that flowers in early autumn. It has thin, orange-brown, velvety flower spikes and large, pointed leaves scented of roast lamb and mint sauce when crushed. It benefits from the warmth of a wall to bloom before the frosts, and is only hardy in milder areas.
Full sun. 1.5m/5ft.

S. discolor smells strongly of blackcurrant. The scent comes from the long sticky flower stems and from the green leaves, that have surprising grey-white undersides. The flowers, which appear all summer, are small, hooded and purple-black and protrude from grey-green calyces. It is a lax grower, sparsely clad in foliage but its fragrance excuses it these faults.
Up to 1m/3ft.

S. elegans **'Scarlet Pineapple' (*S. rutilans*)** has soft, fresh green leaves with a rich smell of pineapple. It makes a bushy shrub and is topped with scarlet flowers all summer. The variety 'Tangerine' has a citrus scent.
Up to 1m/3ft.

SELENICEREUS
Cactaceae

S. grandiflorus, queen of the night, is a slender climbing cactus from the West Indies. It opens its large white flowers, which resemble those of epiphyllum, on summer nights and exhales a powerful and exotic perfume. An easy conservatory plant, it succeeds in pots or in the border.
Sun. Up to 4.5m/15ft. Min. temp. 50°F/10°C.

SOLANDRA
Solanaceae

S. maxima, capa de oro. This showy evergreen climber from Mexico

FAR LEFT *Stauntonia hexaphylla*
LEFT *Stephanotis floribunda*
BELOW *Vigna caracalla*

has large, powerfully fragrant, trumpet flowers in golden-yellow with maroon markings. The scent is strongest in the evening, and is exotically sweet, laced with coconut. It is a vigorous plant, clad in glossy leaves, and may be pruned after flowering; the flowers are produced throughout the summer. It should be kept fairly dry in winter and early spring until the flower buds appear. *S. grandiflora* is similar and equally potent.
Sun. 9m/30ft. Min. temp. 40°F/5°C.

STAUNTONIA
Lardizabalaceae
S. hexaphylla is a handsome evergreen climber that may be tried against a warm wall in mild areas. The rich fragrance comes from the white, pink-tinged starry flowers which are carried in small racemes in spring.
Sun or light shade. 9m/30ft. Min. temp. 40°F/5°C.

STEPHANOTIS
Asclepiadaceae
S. floribunda, Madagascar jasmine. *Stephanotis* flowers have a well-known and well-loved perfume. It is clean and exotically sweet, particularly potent in the evening. The waxy white blooms are produced among the fleshy, glossy leaves in clusters any time from spring until autumn. The main stems and lateral growths may be pruned back in late winter. It makes a very good house plant – I have it in my bedroom – where it can be trained over a hooped framework in a pot; in a conservatory it can be grown as a climber. The compost should not be allowed to become too dry.
Light shade. 60cm–4.5m/2–15ft or more. Min. temp. 50°F/10°C.

VIGNA
Papilionaceae
V. caracalla (Phasiolus caracalla), snail or corkscrew vine, is a climber with curious curled flowers in summer. These are lilac and white and have a good honeyed, swee-pea scent.
Sun or light shade. 4.5m/15ft or more. Min. temp. 40°F/5°C.

CALENDAR OF SCENT: PRINCIPAL PLANTS

SPRING

Trees
Magnolia x *loebneri* 'Merrill', *M. salicifolia*
Nothofagus antarctica
Populus balsamifera, *P. trichocarpa*

Shrubs
Cytisus x *praecox*
Daphne odora 'Aureomarginata'
Magnolia vars
Mahonia aquifolium
Oemleria cerasiformis
Osmanthus x *burkwoodii*, *O. delavayi*
Pieris spp.
Rhododendron Loderi Group, *R. luteum* (and most azaleas)
Skimmia spp.
Ulex europaeus
Viburnum x *burkwoodii*, *V.* x *carlcephalum*, *V. carlesii*, *V.* x *juddii*

Wall Shrubs
Azara microphylla
Eriobotrya japonica
Euphorbia mellifera
Pittosporum tenuifolium

Climbers
Clematis armandii, *C. montana*
Wisteria sinensis

Bulbs
Hyacinthoides non-scripta
Hyacinthus vars
Muscari armenicacum 'Valerie Finnis'
Narcissus vars
Scilla mischtschenkoana

Annuals & Biennials
Erysimum cheiri

Alpines
Androsace spp.
Daphne spp.
Primula spp.

Tender Plants
Acacia spp.
Boronia megastigma
Buddleja asiatica
Coronilla valentina subsp. *glauca*
Freesia spp.
Gladiolus tristis
Jasminum polyanthum
Muscari macrocarpum
Rhododendron spp.
Viola odorata

EARLY SUMMER–MIDSUMMER

Shrubs
Daphne x *burkwoodii* 'Somerset'
Elaeagnus commutata, *E.* 'Quicksilver'
Erica arborea, *E. erigena*, *E.* x *veitchii*
Magnolia maudiae, *M. sieboldii*, *M.* x *wieseneri*, *M. wilsonii*, *M. yunnanensis*
Ozothamnus ledifolius
Philadelphus spp.
Rhododendron spp.
Syringa spp.

Wall Shrubs
Choisya ternata
Cytisus battandieri

Climbers
Holboellia latifolia
Lonicera spp.

Roses
Climbing Roses
Rambler Roses
Species and Near-Species Shrub Roses
Modern Shrub Roses
Old Roses: Gallica, Alba, Damask, Portland, Provence, Moss
Repeat-flowering Shrub Roses: Bourbon, Hybrid Perpetual, Hybrid Musk, China, Rugosa

Perennials
Convallaria majalis
Crambe cordifolia
Iris graminea, *Iris* hybrids
Maianthemum racemosa
Paeonia vars
Tellima grandiflora
Valeriana officinalis

Annuals & Biennials
Hesperis matronalis
Matthiola incana
Oenothera stricta

Alpines
Dianthus spp.
Dianthus vars

Tender Plants
Citrus spp.
Hoya spp.
Stephanotis floribunda

MIDSUMMER–LATE SUMMER

Trees
Catalpa × *erubescens*
Juglans regia
Magnolia obovata
Ptelea trifoliata
Tilia spp.

Shrubs
Buddleja davidii vars
Clethra alnifolia,
C. barbinervis
Genista aetnensis

Wall Shrubs
Abelia triflora
Itea ilicifolia
Magnolia grandiflora vars
Myrtus communis

Climbers
Clematis rehderiana
Jasminum officinale
Lonicera periclymenum 'Serotina'
Trachelospermum asiaticum,
T. jasminoides

Roses
Hybrid Tea Roses
Floribunda Roses
Polyantha-Pompom Roses
Miniature and Patio Roses
Climbing Roses
Rambler Roses
Modern Shrub Roses
Repeat-flowering Shrub Roses: Bourbon, Hybrid Perpetual, Hybrid Musk, China, Rugosa

Perennials
Clematis heracleifolia
Echinacea vars
Phlox paniculata vars
Saponaria officinalis 'Alba Plena'

Bulbs
Cardiocrinum giganteum
Lilium spp.

Annuals & Biennials
Iberis amara
Ipomoea alba
Lathyrus odoratus
Lobularia maritima
Matthiola incana
Mirabilis jalapa
Nicotiana spp.

Water & Bog Plants
Primula florindae

Herbs
Lavandula spp.
Monarda didyma

Tender Plants
Cestrum nocturnum
Cosmos atrosanguineus
Datura vars
Gardenia jasminoides
Heliotropium arborescens
Plumeria rubra
Polianthes tuberosa

AUTUMN

Trees
Cercidiphyllum japonicum
Cydonia oblonga

Shrubs
Clerodendrum bungei
Clerodendrum trichotomum var. *fargesii*
Elaeagnus × *ebbingei*
Viburnum × *bodnantense* vars

Climbers & Wall Shrubs
Buddleja auriculata
Clematis rehderiana

Roses
Repeat-flowering Shrub Roses: Bourbon, Hybrid Perpetual, Hybrid Musk, China, Rugosa

Perennials
Actaea matsumurae 'Elstead Variety', *A. simplex* Atropurpurea Group and 'Brunette'

Bulbs
Amaryllis belladonna

Tender Plants
Cyclamen persicum
Gladiolus murielae
Hedychium coronarium,
H. gardnerianum
Osmanthus fragrans

WINTER

Shrubs
Daphne bholua, *D. mezereum*
Hamamelis spp.
Lonicera fragrantissima,
L. × *purpusii*, *L. standishii*
Mahonia japonica
Sarcococca spp.
Viburnum × *bodnantense*,
V. farreri

Wall Shrubs
Chimonanthus praecox
Prunus mume

Perennials
Iris unguicularis

Bulbs
Crocus spp.
Galanthus vars
Iris reticulata

Tender Plants
Hyacinthus (forced)
Narcissus (forced)

SCENTED PLANTS BY HABITAT

SUN / WELL-DRAINED SOIL

Shrubs
Cistus
Colletia
Cordyline
Cytisus
Daphne
Elaeagnus
Erica
Escallonia
Genista
Hebe
Ozothamnus
Ulex

Wall Shrubs
Carpenteria
Cestrum
Cytisus
Eriobotrya
Itea
Myrtus
Pittosporum

Perennials
Dictamnus
Iris
Nepeta
Salvia
Verbena

Bulbs
Amaryllis
Crocus
Eucomis
Hermodactylus
Hyacinthus
Iris
Lilium
Muscari
Narcissus
Scilla
Tulipa

Annuals & Biennials
Abronia
Dianthus
Erysimum
Exacum
Gilia
Lobularia
Matthiola
Nemesia
Oenothera
Papaver
Petunia
Reseda

Alpines
Daphne
Dianthus
Origanum

Herbs
Calamintha
Chamaemelum
Foeniculum
Helichrysum
Laurus
Lavandula
Origanum
Rosmarinus
Salvia
Thymus

SUN / MOIST SOIL

Shrubs
Buddleja
Calycanthus
Chionanthus
Clerodendrum
Clethra
Cornus
Daphne
Elaeagnus
Magnolia
Osmanthus
Paeonia
Philadelphus
Phillyrea
Rosa
Syringa
Viburnum

Wall Shrubs
Abelia
Azara
Buddleja
Chimonanthus
Edgeworthia
Euphorbia mellifera
Magnolia grandiflora
Prunus mume

Climbers
Clematis
Holboellia
Jasminum
Rosa
Stauntonia
Trachelospermum
Wisteria

Perennials
Agastache
Campanula
Clematis
Echinacea
Hemerocallis
Iris
Nepeta
Paeonia
Phlox
Saponaria
Valeriana
Viola

Bulbs
Crinum
Lilium
Narcissus
Tulipa

Annuals & Biennials
Centaurea
Dianthus
Heliotropium
Lathyrus
Nicotiana
Oenothera
Scabiosa
Verbena

Water & Bog Plants
Filipendula
Primula

Herbs
Mentha
Monarda

SHADE

Shrubs
Corylopsis
Daphne
Hamamelis
Illicium
Lonicera
Magnolia
Mahonia
Oemleria
Osmanthus
Pieris
Rhododendron
Sarcococca
Skimmia
Viburnum

Wall Shrubs
Camellia
Choisya

Climbers
Actinidia
Clematis
Lonicera
Pileostegia

Perennials
Actaea
Convallaria
Geranium
Hosta
Lunaria
Maianthemum
Meehania
Phlox
Primula
Tellima

Bulbs
Cardiocrinum
Cyclamen
Galanthus
Hyacinthoides
Lilium
Scilla

Annuals & Biennials
Hesperis

Alpines
Phlox
Rhododendron

Water & Bog Plants
Filipendula
Primula

Herbs
Angelica
Myrrhis

Creamy santolina, lavender and aniseed-scented bronze fennel merge their scents in this dry habitat planting, speared by *Verbascum* 'Helen Johnson'.

INDEX

Page numbers in *italics* indicate an illustration; those in **bold** indicate a boxed entry.

ZONE RATINGS

The hardiness zone ratings given for each plant – indicated in the text by the letter Z and the relevant number – suggest the approximate minimum temperature a plant will tolerate in winter. However, this can only be a rough guide. The hardiness of a plant depends on a great many factors, including the depth of its roots, its water content at the onset of frost, the duration of the cold weather, the force of the wind, and the length and heat of the preceding summer.

Approximate range of average annual minimum temperatures

Z1	below –50°F/–45°C
Z2	–50°F/–45°C to –40°F/–40°C
Z3	–40°F/–40°C to –30°F/–34°C
Z4	–30°F/–34°C to –20°F/–29°C
Z5	–20°F/–29°C to –10°F/–23°C
Z6	–10°F/–23°C to 0°F/–18°C
Z7	0°F/–18°C to 10°F/–12°C
Z8	10°F/–12°C to 20°F/–7°C
Z9	20°F/–7°C to 30°F/–1°C
Z10	30°F/–1°C to 40°F/4°C

BIBLIOGRAPHY & SELECTED READING

SCENT AND SCENTED PLANTS

Brownlow, Margaret *Herbs and the Fragrant Garden* Darton, Longman and Todd, London, 1963

Genders, Roy *Scented Flora of the World* Robert Hale, London, 1977

Hampton, F. A. *The Scent of Flowers and Leaves* Dulau & Co., London, 1925

Proctor, Michael and Yeo, Peter *The Pollination of Flowers* Collins, London, 1973

Sanecki, Kay N. *The Fragrant Garden* Batsford, London, 1981

Thomas, Graham Stuart *The Art of Planting* Dent, London, 1984; Godine, Boston, 1984

Verey, Rosemary *The Scented Garden* Michael Joseph, London, 1982; Van Nostrand Reinhold, New York, 1981

Wilder, Louise Beebe *The Fragrant Garden* Dover, New York, 1974

GENERAL PLANT REFERENCE

Austin, David *The English Rose* Conran Octopus, London, 2011

Beales, Peter *Classic Roses* Collins Harvill, London and Glasgow, 1985; Henry Holt & Co., New York, 1985

—— *Twentieth Century Roses* Collins Harvill, London, 1988; Harper & Row, New York, 1989

Bean, W. J. *Trees and Shrubs Hardy in the British Isles* (4 volumes) John Murray, London, (8th edition) 1980

Beckett, Kenneth A. (ed.) *The RHS Encyclopaedia of House Plants* Century, London, 1987

Chatto, Beth *The Damp Garden* Dent, London, 1982

Cox, Peter *The Smaller Rhododendrons* Batsford, London, 1985

—— *The Larger Species of Rhododendrons* RHS/Batsford, London, 1979

Cubey, Janet, Edwards, Dawn and Lancaster, Neil (eds.) *RHS Plant Finder 2014* Royal Horticultural Society, 2013

Evans, A[illegible]d *The Peat Garden and its Plants* Dent, London, 1974

Fox, [illegible]ek *Growing Lilies* Croom Helm, Kent, 1985

Gr[illegible]Wilson, Christopher and Matthews, Victoria *Gardening on Walls* Collins, London, 1983

[illegible]per, Pamela and McGourty, Frederick *Perennials* HP Books, Los Angeles, 1985

[illegible]gwersen, Will *Manual of Alpine Plants* Ingwersen & Dunnsprint, Sussex, 1978

Lloyd, Christopher and Bennett, Tom *Clematis* Viking, London, 1989; Capability's Books, Deer Park, Wisconsin, 1989

Matthew, Brian *Dwarf Bulbs* Batsford, London, 1973

—— *The Larger Bulbs* Batsford, London, 1978

Paterson, Allen *Herbs in the Garden* Dent, London, 1985

Perry, Frances *Water Gardening* Country Life, London, 1985

Rogers Clausan, Ruth and Ekstrom, Nicolas *Perennials for American Gardens* Random House, New York, 1989

Royal Horticultural Society *Dictionary of Gardening* Oxford University Press, 1951

Thomas, Graham Stuart *Climbing Roses* Dent, London, 1965

—— *Perennial Garden Plants* Dent, London, 1976; McKay, New York, 1977

—— *Shrub Roses of Today* Dent, London, 1974

—— *The Old Shrub Roses* Dent, London, 1979; Branford Newton Centre, MA, 1979

—— *The Rock Garden and its Plants* Dent, London, 1989; Timber Press, Portland, OR, 1989

Wyman, Donald *Wyman's Gardening Encyclopedia* Macmillan, New York, 1986

ACKNOWLEDGEMENTS

The author would like to thank Helen Griffin and Nicki Davis of Frances Lincoln for their great care in managing this project to fruition, and Andrew Lawson for contributing such sumptuous photographs. Huge thanks also to Matteo la Civita, who drew and helped to design the planting plans, and to Kathryn Pinker for painting them so beautifully.

PICTURE CREDITS

L = left, R = right, C = centre, T = top, B = bottom

26 Pyrkeep, 27 knın, 40 V.J. Matthew, 71R Ilko Iliev, 73L Paul J Martin, 73R clearimages, 75 Bernd Schmidt, 77L Jorge S[illegible]do, 78R Galushko Sergey, 81 Georg Slickers, 83L Aleksander Bolbot, 84L LianeM, 85R P.Tummavijit, 88R Kostyantyn Ivanyshen, 89 Magnus Mansk[illegible]3R Phil Robinson, 94R B747, 96C MRTfotografie, 99L Eugene Berman, 101L almgren, 101C Alena Brozova, 101R Steve Bower, 104L KULISH [illegible]ORIIA, 106 Mykhaylo Palinchak, 111 A_Lein, 112L mitzy, 113L Kathy Burns-Millyard, 115R MIMOHE, 127 Laura Bartlett, 130 Bildagentur Zoon[illegible]mbH, 131R Megan R. Hoover, 133 Elena Elisseeva, 134L Repina Valeriya, 34C Bildagentur Zoonar GmbH, 134R Emily Goodwin, 135L hjschneic[illegible]39L Debu55y, 140R Serge Vero, 141R Colette3, 143L Martin Fowler, 145R sarra22, 146C Ying Geng, 147 hanmon, 148T Kuttelvaserova Stuche[illegible], 148B Sementer, 153T ekawatchaow, 156L mikeledray, 157L V. J. Matthew, 157R Mark III Photonics, 158L Vladimir Arndt, 158R LianeM, 161R [illegible] Gruendemann, 162C Becky Sheridan, 175TR Inomoto, 182R Lijuan Guo, 185R giulianax, 187 pjhpix, 189R khds, 199 Hiyoman, 200L kukuru[illegible]06L Bos11, 209T Jeff Kinsey, 209B Sever180, 210R dabjola, 211BR PhotoWeges, 231 A. Barra, 235R Kathryn Willmott, 236L M.Choco, 258L Bil[illegible]ntur Zoonar GmbH, 258R Krzysztof Slusarczyk, 260L fotomaton, 260C babetka, 261TL PhotoWeges, 276 Matt Howard, 281R kajornyot, 2[illegible] Cillas, 287R Chhe, 288 Cindy Underwood, 289L Junlapatchara, 290L roroto12p, 291R Philip Bird, 295C Forest & Kim Starr

Royal Horticultural Society: 70L, 74L, 76L, 82L, 92R, 102L, 115R, 122, 142, 145L, 177L, 181T, 185L, 206R, 212C, 227L, 242L, 267B[illegible]5C, 294R, 300R; RHS/Lee Beel 124–5, 155–6; RHS/Mark Bolton 31, 211TR; RHS/Claire Campbell 184R; RHS/Janet Cubey 200R; RHS/Paul [illegible]bleton 289R; RHS/Ali Cundy 162R; RHS/Sue Drew 286R; RHS/Adam Duckworth 190–1; RHS/Philippa Gibson 78L, 188C, 188R, 207C, 207R, 2[illegible]85L; RHS/Wilf Halliday 227R; RHS/Jerry Harpur 6-7, 270–1; RHS/Neil Hepworth 178T, 284; RHS/Leigh Hunt 172R, 230C, 266C, 300C; RHS/Jason Ingram 150R; RHS/Cecile Moisan 85L, 227C; RHS/David Nunn 212R; RHS/Barry Phillips 166, 261BL, 264TL, 268C; RHS/Katy Prentice 163; RHS/Zebrina Rendall 137L, 181B, 282R; RHS/Rebecca Ross 146L, 246–7, 283L; RHS/Tim Sandall 79L, 138, 139R, 140L, 151R, 161L, 173TR, 179L, 184L, 184C, 205L, 210L, 225L, 260R, 262, 264TR, 285R, 286L, 292L, 293R, 194L, 296L, 300L, 301BR; RHS/Carol Sheppard 64, 71L, 97, 99C, 99R, 103, 108R, 117, 132C, 135R, 137C, 149L, 156R, 175TL, 176R, 186L, 189L, 202R, 224L, 224R, 230R, 232BL, 259BL, 263L, 266L, 266R, 268R, 291C, 292R, 296C, 296R, 299L; RHS/Niki Simpson 178R; RHS/Mike Sleigh 149R, 150L, 178L, 180C, 205R, 236R, 237R, 241BR, 245R, 293L, 301TC; RHS/Graham Titchmarsh 72, 74R, 83R, 102R, 131L, 146R, 162L, 179C, 180L, 201R, 211TL, 213TR, 213B, 218, 228R, 228C, 229R, 234L, 235L, 237L, 238, 239C, 239R, 239C, 239R, 240, 242R, 243BL, 243TR, 244L, 244R, 245L, 245C, 259BR, 259TR, 261BR, 263C, 263R, 265, 267T, 268L, 269L, 269R, 281L, 282L, 292C, 299R; RHS/Wendy Wesley 208R; RHS/Christopher Whitehouse 212L

All other photographs copyright Andrew Lawson, with thanks to the garden owners, including: 12 Barnsley House, Gloucestershire, designer Rosemary Verey; 15, 60–1 Gowers Close, Sibford Gower, Oxfordshire; 20–1 Exbury Gardens, Southampton; 36–7 Manor House, Blewbury, Oxon; 43 Sticky Wicket, Dorset; 66–7 Mr & Mrs Gunn, Ramster; 126 Olympic Park, London, plantings by Sarah Price, James Hitchmough & Nigel Dunnett; 129 Penelope Hobhouse, Bettiscombe, Dorset; 144R Evenley Wood, Northants; 171, 221 Haseley Court, Oxfordhire; 192; Mr & Mrs Farquar, Old Cottage Inn, Piddington; 196 designer Kathy Brown; 214 designer Sir Hardy Amies; 216–17 Old Manor House, Charlbury, Oxfordshire, designer Sue Grant; 222–3 Seend Manor, Wiltshire, designers Julian & Isabel Bannerman; 250–1 designers Tessa Traeger & Patrick Kinmouth; 252 Chilcombe House, Dorset; 272 Pettifers, Oxfordshire; 305 *You* magazine, RHS Hampton Court Show 2000, designers Isabelle van Groeningen, Gabriella Pape

To Jill

Frances Lincoln Limited
74–77 White Lion Street
London N1 9PF
www.franceslincoln.com

RHS Companion to Scented Plants

Planting plans on pages 46, 48, 50, 52 illustrated by Kathryn Pinker

First Frances Lincoln edition 2014

Published in association with the Royal Horticultural Society.

A catalogue record for this book is available from the British Library.

978-0-7112-3574-8

Printed and bound in China.
1 2 3 4 5 6 7 8 9

The Royal Horticultural Society is the UK's leading gardening charity dedicated to advancing horticulture and promoting good gardening. Its charitable work includes providing expert advice and information, training the next generation of gardeners, creating hands-on opportunities for children to grow plants, and conducting research into plants, pests and environmental issues affecting gardeners.
For more information, visit: www.rhs.org.uk or call 0845 130 4646.